Reaganomics

Reaganomics

An Insider's Account of the Policies and the People

William A. Niskanen

Published for the Cato Institute

New York   Oxford
OXFORD UNIVERSITY PRESS
1988

Oxford University Press

Oxford   New York   Toronto
Delhi   Bombay   Calcutta   Madras   Karachi
Petaling Jaya   Singapore   Hong Kong   Tokyo
Nairobi   Dar es Salaam   Cape Town
Melbourne   Auckland

and associated companies in
Berlin   Ibadan

Published by Oxford University Press, Inc.,
200 Madison Avenue, New York, New York 10016

Oxford is a registered trademark of Oxford University Press

Library of Congress Cataloging-in-Publication Data

Niskanen, William A., 1933–
Reaganomics : an insider's acount of the politics and the people / by William A. Niskanen.
p. cm.
"Published for the Cato Institute."
Bibliography: p.
Includes index.
ISBN 0-19-505394-X
1. United States—Economic policy—1981–   2. Tax and expenditure
limitations—United States.   I. Cato Institute.   II. Title.
HC106.8.N57   1988
338.973—dc19   87-30291

2 4 6 8 9 7 5 3 1

Printed in the United States of America
on acid-free paper

Contents

About This Book

My primary objectives in this book are to explain the origin of Reaganomics, what policy changes were proposed and implemented during the Reagan administration, the relation between changes in policy and changes in the economy, and the probable future of Reaganomics.

The Reagan years were a challenging, exciting, and turbulent period in the history of American economic policy. Reagan's initial economic program was more ambitious and comprehensive than that of any president since Franklin Roosevelt. Many of the supporters of the Reagan program, I believe, promised more than could be delivered and then blamed the problems that developed on the surviving officials, whom they did not regard as "true believers." Many of the critics and, surprisingly, some of the supporters do not yet understand the rationale for the initial economic program. A misunderstanding of the Reagan program unfortunately has led to divisiveness on economic policy and threatens to undermine some of the program's major accomplishments. My hope is that we can learn the right lessons from the Reagan record and, on the basis of these lessons, resolve the major problems that remain.

This book is not a personal memoir. My role in the Reagan administration was not sufficient to warrant such a book. Most of the source material for this book is available from public records. My interpretation of these events, however, is strongly shaped by my personal experience as both supporter and internal critic—as a participant in and witness to these events.

Most of this book was written in 1986, and the book was completed in the summer of 1987. I do not pretend to have anticipated the sharp drop in the stock market on "Black Monday" (October 19, 1987), nor am I confident about its effects on future economic policies and conditions. In retrospect, the primary condition that led to Black Monday was a severe tightening of U.S. monetary policy from February thorough September, a policy that both reduced expected future earnings and increased current bond yields. The tight monetary policy, in turn, appears to have been part of the U.S. commitment to maintain the support level for the dollar exchange rate resulting from the Louvre agreement in February.

One immediate effect of Black Monday was to reduce or eliminate the support level for the dollar, freeing the Federal Reserve to restore money growth. Other effects included an agreement between the administration and Congress to meet the deficit reduction target for fiscal year 1988 and a delay and probable weakening of the proposed trade legislation. The combination of monetary restraint, the decline in stock prices, and the fall of the dollar will probably lead to lower growth in 1988 but not, I believe, to a recession. The text of this book has not been changed to reflect these developments. For the moment, I am comfortable with my conclusions (in Chapter 5) that the Louvre agreement would not prove to be stable and (in Chapter 10) that economic conditions in 1988 would be moderately satisfactory but weaker than expected.

In writing this book my most awkward task has been the evaluation of the role of the key people who formulated and implemented the Reagan program. I am reminded of Lytton Strachey's comment that "it is perhaps as difficult to write a good life as to live one." This problem is compounded by the fact that I worked with these people in pursuit of a common goal. Although I occasionally disagreed with each of them I found most of these individuals to be able, energetic, thoughtful, and likeable. In general, it is misleading to attribute the failures and missed opportunities of an administration to the personal weaknesses of its key officials, even if doing so makes good copy for a brief period. Good people are not sufficient for good government. My prior experience in the federal government led me to recognize that "the best and the brightest" have been responsible for some of the major domestic and foreign policy failures of the postwar years. My experience in the Reagan administration leads me to praise some officials and to criticize others—in both cases, I hope, with an understanding of the incentives and constraints that each individual faced.

A Personal Note

In late 1972, Governor Ronald Reagan convened a small group at the Century Plaza Hotel in Los Angeles. He introduced his remarks by observing that conventional political processes, including the recent reelection of a Republican president by a huge margin, would probably not be sufficient to restrain the growth of government spending. He may also have reflected that real state spending was growing at a record rate during his tenure as governor of California.

He then asked us to address an unconventional measure—a constitutional amendment to limit the spending and tax authority of the state. That meeting was the birth of the modern tax limitation movement. This group later drafted and promoted an initiative amendment, appropriately called Proposition 1, to limit the spending and tax authority of the state of California. Although this initiative was defeated in November 1973, a similar amendment was later approved in California and in a number of other states and was the model for the proposed balanced budget/tax limitation amendment to the federal constitution.

That meeting was also my first personal contact with Ronald Reagan. For some years since his role as a spokesman for Barry Goldwater during the 1964 presidential campaign, I had been vaguely intrigued by Reagan's sharp criticisms of many of the activities of contemporary government. And my prior experience in two mid-level federal positions (as a defense analyst under Robert McNamera and later as a budget analyst under George Shultz and Caspar Weinberger) led to my own transformation from a young technocrat to an advocate of smaller government. Like many academics I was also flattered by the attention of a major politician. I was most impressed, however, that Reagan seemed to be the only leading politician who had any prospect for braking the momentum of the modern state. From my perspective his convictions on economic policy were surprisingly good, and he had a record of seeking out new ideas and new advisors. So I became an enthusiastic early supporter of Reagan's economic policy agenda. I later served on the 1974 Local Government Reform Task Force in California and as part of an economic advisory group to Reagan's 1976 primary campaign for the Republican presidential nomination. For personal reasons I had no role in the 1980 campaign, but I later prepared two papers for the post-election transition teams.

From April 1981 through March 1985, I served as a member of the Council of Economic Advisers in the Executive Office of the President. For most of that period, I had CEA responsibility for "microeconomic" issues—budget and tax policies that affect specific sectors of the economy, regulations, and international trade. During my last nine months in that position, following the resignation of Martin Feldstein, I also served as acting chairman of the CEA, although without formal designation in that role. In that capacity I participated in the senior economic councils, such as the "troika" and the "core group," which shaped the major budget and economic policies for Reagan's second term. Although I was not present at the birth of Reaganomics or during its necessary transformation into a more sustainable program, I was a minor participant in and witness to many of the actions that implemented the Reagan economic program.

A final note of both caution and optimism: there is ample reason to believe that conventional political processes will not resolve the major perceived problems of government. Those who support a more limited federal government are prone to pessimism, fearing that no one can brake the growth of government as President Reagan did not. At the same time, there is reason to share Reagan's visceral optimism that somehow these problems will be resolved. Some day we will learn not to expect too much of government. Liberals may learn to distinguish between a virtue and a requirement, whether this involves caring for one's neighbors or wearing a seat belt. Conservatives may learn to distinguish between a sin and a crime, where this involves a wide range of personal and consensual activities. One or more constitutional amendments may be necessary as a mutual restraint on the use of the powers of government by either group to achieve their respective goals. One can only hope that the day has not yet passed when the powers of the modern state are beyond control by the consent of the governed.

November 1987   W.A.N.
Washington, D.C.

Reaganomics

CHAPTER ONE

Promises and Precedents

"Reaganomics" represents the most serious attempt to change the course of U.S. economic policy since the New Deal. This book describes and evaluates the Reagan economic program, its intellectual and political roots, its successes and failures, the role of the key participants, and how the program will shape the future. The record to date, in summary, is mixed. Although the administration failed to meet most of its initial policy objectives, the change in policy was sufficient to lead to a gradual improvement in general economic conditions.

As this book was completed, the Reagan record was not complete. The second term agenda was not yet fully implemented. There is often some lag between changes in policies and economic conditions. And, most important, ideas cast an even longer shadow. The future of Reaganomics, however, will depend in part on an understanding of the basis for the policies and their effects on economic conditions. What was proposed? What happened, and why? What critical choices remain to be addressed?

For this book the record of each of the four key elements of the Reagan economic program is judged by two standards—the record of the Carter administration and the initial objective of the Reagan administration. A comparison of the Reagan record with what the Carter administration might have done is, I believe, too subjective, and a comparison with some concept of optimal policy abstracts too much from the political environment. In many dimensions the Reagan economic record is superior to the Carter record, and that is the basis for the continued popular support for the general program. In most dimensions the Reagan record has not met the president's own initial objectives, and that is the basis for the continued disappointment of his strongest supporters. An evaluation of the Reagan record is thus very dependent on the standard by which it is judged.

PROMISES

A Program for Economic Recovery

On February 18, 1981, four weeks after his first inauguration, President Reagan presented Congress with *A Program for Economic Recovery*. The four "key elements" of this program were as follows:

- A budget reform plan to cut the rate of growth in federal spending.
- A series of proposals to reduce personal income tax rates by 10 percent a year over three years and to create jobs by accelerating depreciation for business investment in plant and equipment.
- A far-reaching program of regulatory relief.
- In cooperation with the Federal Reserve Board, a new commitment to a monetary policy that would restore a stable currency and healthy financial markets.

This program was based on a longstanding Reagan conviction that "the most important cause of our economic problems has been the government itself." The unifying and distinctive theme of the Reagan program was that "only by reducing the growth of government can we increase the growth of the economy." The general direction was to diminish the role of the federal government in the American economy—reduce the growth of spending, reduce tax rates, reduce regulation, and reduce the growth of the money supply.

The Reagan economic program, like the Reagan constituency, reflected a range of views on economic policies. For the traditional Republicans a lower growth in federal spending was a necessary complement of any reduction in taxes. This view was shared by most officials in prior Republican administrations and by the senior Republicans in the Senate. For the new "supply-siders" a reduction in tax rates was necessary to induce the economic growth that would permit a lower growth in federal spending. This view was shared by most of the younger Republicans in the House. This difference in fiscal priorities, reflecting prior controversy among congressional Republicans and in the 1980 Republican presidential primaries, surfaced early in the preparation of the initial Reagan program and was never fully resolved.

At one time there seemed to be the basis for an agreement between these groups. Following the 1980 election a number of transition teams were formed to prepare the initial agenda for the new administration. This process, however, floundered for lack of direction and clear priorities. To focus and energize the process, two young Republican congressmen, David Stockman and Jack Kemp, coauthored a long memorandum describing an "economic Dunkirk" for the Republicans unless the proposed tax cuts were matched by a large reduction in spending for discretionary domestic programs, and this memo was leaked to the press in early December. Kemp supported Stockman for appointment as director of the Office of Management and Budget (OMB), and Stockman later acknowledged that he supported the tax cuts primarily to bring pressure for reduced spending. This initial coalition of traditional Republicans and supply-siders, however, proved to be tenuous.

In early January 1981 a small group was formed to develop the initial economic and budget projections under the leadership of Stockman, already named as director of OMB. Stockman, Murray Weidenbaum (later nominated as chairman of the Council of Economic Advisers), and Alan Greenspan (the CEA chairman under President Gerald Ford) represented the traditional view that reduced spending growth was the first priority. Norman Ture, Craig Roberts, and Steve Entin—economists who had worked with various congressional staffs and who were appointed to senior positions in the Treasury—represented the supply-side view that a reduction in tax rates was the first priority. The immediate issue was this question of fiscal priorities and, in turn, who best represented Reagan's own views. Some wordsmith temporarily papered over this issue by describing a reduced growth of federal spending as "the leading edge of our program" and a reduction of tax rates as "equally important and urgent"; in other words, both elements of the proposed fiscal policy were given equal priority. There is every reason to believe that Reagan shared both views and was singularly unconcerned about this controversy among his advisers. Yet this controversy continued to divide both presidential advisers and congressional Republicans. Supply-siders were quick to characterize the traditional view as "the politics of austerity." As a candidate in the 1980 primaries, George Bush had described the supply-side position as "voodoo economics," and Senator Howard Baker (the Senate majority leader during the first term and White House chief of staff beginning in 1987) later described it as "a riverboat gamble." The proposed positions on regulation and monetary policy reflected a broader consensus but a somewhat weaker commitment.

The most distinctive characteristics of the initial Reagan program were the positions on the deficit and on monetary policy. The program did *not* establish a balanced budget as a goal of fiscal policy, nor did the program reflect the Keynesian perspective that the deficit was the primary instrument by which fiscal policy affects the economy. The very brief discussion of the deficit was limited to a conditional forecast that the combination of the proposed fiscal policies and the expected economic conditions would lead to a balanced budget by fiscal year 1984. Changes in the deficit were considered one of the outcomes, rather than the primary goal or instrument, of fiscal policy; to this extent, the Reagan program represented a break from the position of both prior Republican and Democratic administrations.

The Reagan program was also the first to recognize monetary policy as the primary instrument that affects total demand in the economy. This position also reflected a break from the Keynesian perspective that had been dominant for thirty years and forced recognition of the potentially awkward problem that the Federal Reserve, the primary agent of monetary policy, was stubbornly protective of its independence.

Several characteristics that might have been expected of a program for economic recovery were conspicuously missing. Most important, there was no explicit rationale for the set of proposed policies, although several had been prepared. George Gilder, the author of the popular book *Wealth and Poverty,* had been commissioned to write an introduction to the report. The Treasury prepared a supply-side explanation of the proposed reduction in tax rates. The hold-over CEA staff contributed a Keynesian explanation of the tax cuts as a means to increase demand. A failure to agree on any of these explanations led to the rejection of all of them, and the opportunity to explain the intellectual and empirical basis for the proposed changes in economic policy was forgone.

In addition, the initial program barely acknowledged the international dimensions of economic policy. One paragraph described how the proposed policies were expected to improve the international economic environment, but there was no mention of the principles that would guide our economic relations with other nations. The implicit assumption was that international conditions were not an important consideration affecting the proposed policies.

The scope and direction of the new Reagan program has sometimes been described as the mirror image of the New Deal, but that comparison is somewhat misleading. Franklin Roosevelt, facing much more severe economic problems, had only a vague initial program other than a campaign commitment to balance the budget. The Reagan program was the most explicit initial program for changing the direction of economic policy of any president. Moreover, the Reagan program fully accepted the major surviving elements of the New Deal. A rapid defense buildup was considered necessary to support the worldwide U.S. military role and presence that first developed during World War II. The major income security programs enacted during the 1930s were described in the initial program as "essential commitments [that] now transcend differences in ideology, partisanship, and fiscal priorities." Reagan's targets were the accumulation of programs and policies enacted beginning with President Lyndon Johnson—not those enacted under Franklin Roosevelt, whom he frequently praised. There remains only a mirror image in perceptions: Roosevelt became convinced that an expanded role of the government was necessary to solve the major economic problems of 1933; Reagan believed that the growth of government was the major source of the economic problems of 1981. Each of these perspectives appears to have been supported by the current electorate.

The 1981 Economic Forecasts

Economic conditions in early 1981 were generally unsatisfactory. Output was increasing markedly from the short, sharp recession of 1980, but the outlook was not encouraging. The consumer inflation rate was about 12 percent and the prime rate peaked at 21.5 percent, both peacetime highs. Productivity growth had been very low since 1973. Market forecasters expected continued low growth and high inflation. The Carter administration had refused to acknowledge any responsibility for these "stagflation" conditions and blamed them on structural problems in the U.S. economy and on external conditions such as the second oil shock.

The change in policies proposed by the Reagan administration, of course, was expected to contribute to an improvement in economic conditions, and this was reflected in the administration's initial forecasts. Table 1.1 summarizes the then current estimates of general economic conditions in 1980, the last Carter forecasts for 1981 through 1984, and the initial Reagan forecasts for these years. As the table indicates, the early 1981 Carter and Reagan forecasts were quite similar. Both administrations predicted an increase in the growth of total demand (as measured by the current-dollar gross national product) through 1982, followed by a gradual subsequent decline in this rate. The Carter forecasts projected a typical recovery of real (inflation-adjusted) GNP from the 1980 recession; the Reagan forecasts projected a somewhat stronger recovery. Both forecasts projected a gradual decline in inflation and interest rates, starting in 1981 or 1982. In terms of the usual optimism of administration forecasts, the information available in early 1981, and the proposed changes in policy, the initial Reagan forecasts were reasonable; they appeared unusually optimistic only in comparison with the Carter forecasts. At that time, it is important to remember, almost all major economic forecasters projected that economic conditions would lead to a substantial federal surplus by 1983 or 1984 without a change in fiscal policy. The Congressional Budget Office forecasted that the

Table 1.1   U.S. Economic Conditions and Forecasts

	Calendar Year				
	1980	1981	1982	1983	1984
Gross national product[a]					
Carter	9.8	12.3	12.6	12.2	11.5
Reagan		11.0	13.3	11.8	10.1
Real gross national product[a]					
Carter	0.0	1.7	3.5	3.7	3.7
Reagan		1.4	5.2	4.9	4.2
Consumer price index[a]					
Carter	12.6	12.6	9.6	8.2	7.5
Reagan		10.5	7.2	6.0	5.1
Unemployment rate[b]					
Carter	7.2	7.8	7.5	7.1	6.7
Reagan		7.8	7.2	6.6	6.4
Treasury bill rate[b]					
Carter	11.5	13.5	11.0	9.4	8.5
Reagan		11.1	8.9	7.8	7.0

[a] Percentage change from fourth quarter to fourth quarter.
[b] Annual average (%).

Reagan fiscal policies would lead to only a small increase in the deficit. The initial Reagan forecasts did not deserve the later characterization as a "rosy scenario," however optimistic they appeared in retrospect.

The early 1981 Reagan forecasts, however, reflected one major technical problem and one major risk. The major technical problem was that the forecast growth of current-dollar GNP was higher than that consistent with the stated monetary-policy assumption that "the growth rates of money and credit are steadily reduced from the 1980 levels to one-half those levels by 1986." In other words, the assumed growth in "money velocity" (total spending for final production per dollar of the money supply) was higher than that consistent with historical experience. Beryl Sprinkel (named Treasury undersecretary for monetary affairs in 1981 and chairman of the CEA in 1985) made this point to Stockman when the forecasts were first prepared. The forecast GNP path, however, was essential to maintain a plausible basis for a balanced budget by 1984, so the higher numbers were retained without changing the monetary-policy assumption. This was neither the first nor the last time that an administration's economic forecasts were influenced by desired budget outcomes; the consequence, of course, was the diminished credibility of both the economic and budget forecasts.

The major risk was whether it was possible to reduce gradually both the inflation rate and the unemployment rate. For many years economic policy had been based on the assumption of a "Phillips curve" trade-off between the inflation rate and the unemployment rate. Although the Phillips curve had not proved to be stable for periods of more than a few years, there was good theory and substantial evidence backing the view that an *unexpected* reduction in the growth of demand would increase the unemployment rate temporarily. The new administration assumed that an *announced* gradual reduction in the growth of the money supply, combined with the supply-side tax incentives, would permit a gradual reduction of both the inflation rate and the unemployment rate. As expressed in the initial program, "central to the new policy is the view that expectations play an important role in determining economic activity, inflation, and interest rates." There was a plausible basis for the initial Reagan forecasts *if* people changed their expectations about inflation on the basis of the proposed policy changes. The contrast of public pronouncements on inflation and the actual inflation record during the prior fifteen years, however, undermined the credibility of the commitment by the new administration and the Federal Reserve. As a rule, inflation expectations change only slowly. In the past that provided an incentive for the government to increase the fiscal or monetary stimulus in order to reduce the near-term unemployment rate. In 1981 the stability of inflation expectations presented a risk that the proposed reduction in the growth of federal spending and the money supply would lead to a temporary increase in unemployment.

The March 1981 Budget

On March 10, 1981, President Reagan submitted a comprehensive revision to the fiscal year (FY) 1982 budget that had been submitted by outgoing President Carter in mid-January. The scope of this revision was unprecedented, reflecting both the major changes in fiscal policy and the energy of the new budget director. The major changes in the budget included a large increase in defense spending, reduced spending for nearly 300 other programs, and a major reduction in tax rates, plus a re-estimate of the budget on the basis of the new economic forecasts. Table 1.2 summarizes the last Carter budget and the changes proposed in the initial Reagan budget by major category of budget outlays and receipts.

The general changes in priorities reflected in the initial Reagan budget were similar in direction but greater in magnitude than in the last Carter budget. (The difference in current-dollar budget pro-

Table 1.2   The Federal Budget for FY 1982

	Fiscal Year[a]				
	1981	1982	1983	1984	1985
Outlays					
Defense and international					
Carter budget	172.4	196.6	223.3	251.4	282.3
Change	1.0	3.3	14.5	16.4	33.8
Transfers and services					
Carter budget	352.0	388.6	431.2	471.2	515.2
Change	−2.6	−24.4	−39.9	−53.7	−69.2
General government					
Carter budget	85.7	94.2	99.5	102.7	104.7
Change	−1.2	−15.4	−20.7	−27.0	−30.9
Other					
Carter budget	75.8	78.2	78.6	79.8	81.0
Change	−4.3	−9.2	−14.0	−16.8	−21.8
Total outlays					
Carter budget	685.9	757.6	832.6	905.0	983.2
Reagan budget	678.8	712.0	772.5	823.9	895.1
Additional savings to be proposed	—	—	−29.8	−44.2	−43.7
Target outlays	678.8	712.0	742.7	779.7	851.4
Receipts					
Carter budget	607.5	711.8	809.2	922.3	1,052.6
Individual rate reductions	−6.4	−44.2	−81.4	−118.1	−141.5
Investment incentives	−2.5	−9.7	−18.6	−30.0	−44.2
Other	1.7	−7.6	−0.1	−3.5	−17.0
Reagan budget	600.3	650.3	709.1	770.7	849.9
Surplus or deficit (−)					
Carter budget	−78.4	−45.8	−23.4	17.3	69.4
Reagan budget					
Projected	−78.5	−61.7	−63.4	−53.2	−45.2
Target	−78.5	−61.7	−33.6	−9.0	−1.5

[a] In billions of dollars.

jections, however, somewhat understates real increases and over-states real decreases because the Reagan budget was based on a lower inflation forecast.)

A general concern about the state of the U.S. armed forces, rein-forced by the Soviet invasion of Afghanistan, led Carter to propose a 4.4 percent real (inflation-adjusted) annual increase in outlays for defense and international affairs from FY 1981 through 1985; the

Reagan budget proposed a 8.6 percent real annual increase over this period. The major programs providing income transfers and social services (education and labor services, health, social security and other income transfers, and veterans' benefits and services) had grown rapidly during the prior fifteen years to become the largest component of the federal budget. The Carter budget for these transfers and services proposed a 1.5 percent real annual increase through FY 1985; the Reagan budget proposed a slight decrease, with proposed cuts in a variety of small programs offsetting a continued increase in the major income-transfer programs. Carter proposed to reduce spending for the hundreds of general government programs, ranging from science to revenue sharing, at a 3.0 percent real annual rate; the Reagan budget proposed to reduce these programs at a 9.6 percent real annual rate. Changes in the other components of the budget (interest payments, cross-program allowances, offsetting receipts, and off-budget outlays) did not reflect a significant policy change, with the exception that the new budget proposed a substantial reduction in off-budget federal credit programs.

The last Carter budget proposed only a 1 percent annual increase in total real outlays through FY 1985. The first Reagan effort to reduce the growth of government spending proposed a 0.2 percent annual increase in total real outlays. In summary, the initial Reagan budget is best described as a major reallocation, providing a strong increase in defense spending and a substantial reduction in spending for several hundred discretionary domestic programs but only a small reduction, relative to the last Carter budget, in the growth of total real government spending—a major change, but not a fiscal revolution.

The proposed changes in federal taxes were more substantial. The last Carter budget projected that "receipts would reach peak proportions of GNP each year, rising to 24.0 percent of GNP by 1986," but suggested that "future tax reductions will be required to lower tax burdens and as incentives to business investment and innovation that would help revive productivity and reduce inflation." The new administration moved quickly to avoid the projected increase in the relative tax burden, proposing a phased reduction of individual income tax rates and the depreciation periods on business investment. Each of the two major tax proposals was projected to reduce receipts by a substantial amount relative to the Carter projections (contrary to the charge that the Reagan program was based on the "Laffer curve" concept, according to which a reduction in tax rates would increase tax receipts), and the relative tax burden was projected to decline to 19.3 percent of GNP by FY 1984.

Changes in the surplus or deficit, of course, reflect the difference

in the growth of outlays and receipts. The last Carter budget projected a budget surplus in FY 1984 on the basis of a slow growth of
outlays and a rapid growth of receipts. The revised FY 1982 budget
submitted by the new administration projected a continued deficit
through the budget horizon on the basis of a slower growth of both
outlays and receipts. A deceptive and controversial feature of the
revised budget, however, concealed the continued deficit. In addition to the many outlay savings proposed in the revised budget, the
projected "target" outlays were reduced by unspecified "additional
savings to be proposed," Stockman's "magic asterisk," beginning in
the FY 1983 budget. The only deficit projection presented in the
revised budget was based on these target outlays and showed a small
surplus beginning in FY 1984, but the specific proposals included in
this budget were not sufficient to achieve this result. The traditional
Republican concern about a balanced budget continued to be subordinated to other goals, in this case the defense buildup and the
tax rate reductions. The language of the revised budget, however,
would suggest otherwise. In addition to the four key elements of the
initial program, the revised budget added a fifth objective: that "we
must move, surely and predictably, toward a balanced budget." One
could also discern the increasing influence of David Stockman in the
statement that "restraining the growth of federal spending lies at the
center of the program for economic recovery."

The 1980 Campaign

There was no reason for anyone to be surprised by the main features of the Reagan economic program—at least, no one other than
the cynics who doubted Reagan's commitment to his campaign rhetoric or the skeptics who doubted that his promises could be translated into a specific program. The main features of this program
were summarized in the first internal policy memorandum of the
Reagan campaign in August 1979. They were fully described in a
major campaign speech on September 9, 1980, before the International Business Council in Chicago. This speech was the outgrowth
of a meeting with a group of businessmen and economists who had
served in the Nixon and Ford administrations: George Shultz, Caspar Weinberger, William Simon, Paul McCracken, Alan Greenspan,
Murray Weidenbaum, Charls Walker, Walter Wriston, and James
Lynn—and Martin Anderson, a younger Hoover Institute economist
who had long been a Reagan adviser. (Anderson was later named
domestic policy adviser to the president, Weidenbaum was appointed chairman of the CEA, Weinberger was named Secretary of
Defense, Shultz was appointed Secretary of State in mid-1982, and

the others in this group served on the President's Economic Policy Advisory Board.) In this speech Reagan summarized the four objectives of his future economic program and promised to initiate this program in the first ninety days.

This speech anticipated the initial program and the revised FY 1982 budget in considerable detail, with only a few exceptions. Control of government spending was to be achieved by restraining the growth of old programs, avoiding new programs, and eliminating "waste, fraud, extravagance, and abuse." The first exception was that there was no mention in this speech, or at any other time during the 1980 campaign, that the services or benefits provided by any existing federal program would be reduced. However characteristic of the avoidance of hard choices in American campaigns, this position was grossly misleading, as was recognized by the Reagan advisers who were knowledgeable about the federal budget. There is a great deal of waste in the federal budget, but much of this waste has the same political source as the programs; it occurs because some member of Congress does not want a military base or an office to be closed, some contract to be reduced, or federal employment to be reduced in his or her district. Moreover, most of the waste consists of programs for which the benefits of the last dollar of spending are not worth the additional costs to the economy, even if the programs are efficiently managed. Any realistic attempt to control the growth of federal spending must include a reduction in the services and benefits provided by some programs—especially if spending for other programs, defense in this case, is projected to increase. (One prospective irony was that Caspar Weinberger, who had gained the reputation of "Cap the Knife" as a former director of OMB and who led the Spending Control Task Force, was later to be a primary agent of spending growth as Secretary of Defense.)

A second exception was the projected level of defense spending. In supplementary tables distributed with the September speech, defense outlays in FY 1985 were projected to be $280 billion. After the Carter administration raised its own projections of defense spending, the revised FY 1982 budget proposed defense outlays of $304 billion for FY 1985. A third exception involved the tax proposal. The September speech proposed indexing the individual income tax after the proposed rate reductions; this proposal was not included in the initial proposal by the new administration but was later added by Congress. On balance, even with these exceptions, the September speech proved to be a remarkably accurate guide to the initial Reagan economic program.

Any campaign generates commitments to specific economic groups, and the 1980 Reagan campaign was not unusual in this respect. A candidate has a strong temptation to make commitments to some groups of swing voters, whether or not these commitments are consistent with his or her general economic agenda. Republican candidates in particular had long attempted to broaden their support from labor and the South. Speaking at a Chrysler plant in Detroit, Reagan suggested that he would ask Japan to reduce its auto exports to the United States. In a speech to the National Maritime Union, he promised support of the maritime industry. A letter to Senator Strom Thurmond of South Carolina promised to relate imports of textiles and apparel to the size of the U.S. market. Other commitments were made privately to the Teamsters, the construction unions, and the tobacco farmers. Candidate Reagan did not make many such commitments, but those identified also provided a guide to future policies affecting these and other groups.

Vintage Reagan

More than any other person in current American politics, Ronald Reagan had seen the mountain come to Mahomet. Since his entrance into the political arena as a spokesman for Barry Goldwater in the 1964 campaign, he had conveyed one consistent theme: government is more likely to be the source than the solution to the perceived problems of the time. In a national television address in October 1964, he criticized a wide range of federal programs, including some that were considered to be politically invulnerable—farm subsidies, TVA, urban renewal, social security, the proposed job corps, foreign aid, a variety of government regulations, and the progressive income tax. This speech probably did not help Goldwater, but it greatly increased the visibility of Reagan as a spokesman for the conservative cause.

Over the years in other speeches, he was critical of federal aid to education, the effects of welfare on the family, the Interstate Commerce Commission, the provision of medical care to veterans with no service-connected disability, and the regulation of energy, in addition to the traditional Republican criticism of deficit financing. As the governor of California, he started the tax limitation movement by promoting a constitutional amendment to limit the total taxing authority of the state. In his 1976 campaign for the Republican nomination, he proposed a major transfer of federal programs and tax resources to the states. One intriguing dimension of Ronald Reagan and an indicator of his probable behavior as president is that he maintained his general theme about government as the problem even when serving as governor of the nation's largest state, a period during which real state government spending increased at a record rate.

For the most part these speeches proved to be an accurate guide to his positions as a presidential candidate and president, with three major exceptions. As he approached the 1980 campaign, he dropped his criticisms of social security, endorsed a proportional reduction of tax rates, and muted his criticism of deficit financing. Reagan's earlier speeches, however, may be a more accurate guide to his personal views than his later positions as a candidate and president. With few expressed changes in his own position, Reagan witnessed a massive shift in the position of the electorate in his direction. Views that were once regarded as those of right-wing extremists became the views that would elect a president.

THE ORIGINS OF REAGANOMICS

Any comprehensive change in government policy has multiple roots in objective conditions as well as in both popular perceptions and intellectual positions. The initial Reagan economic program was a response to an accumulation of economic problems during the prior fifteen years and was shaped by a major change in the perspectives of economists.

Changes in the Economy

A comparison of economic and fiscal conditions in 1965 and 1980 conveys only part of the developments that led to the changes in economic policy. In 1965, economic growth was 6 percent, the inflation rate was about 2 percent, and the unemployment rate was 4.5 percent. Economic growth slowed sharply after 1973 and was negative in 1980. Average real hourly earnings increased very slowly after 1973. The consumer inflation rate, temporarily braked by monetary restraint that led to three recessions, increased to about 12 percent in 1980, and the unemployment rate increased to over 7 percent. From 1965 to 1980 the real value of corporate equity declined over 40 percent. The dollar came under increasing pressure in foreign exchange markets and declined substantially until the summer of 1980. Federal spending increased from 17.9 percent of GNP in FY 1965 to 22.2 percent in FY 1980 despite a decline in the relative spending for defense. Inflation and the rising cost of social security raised the weighted-average marginal federal tax rate from 23 percent in 1965 to 36 percent in 1980. A broader concern about these general economic conditions, which affected most of the population, reduced the relative concern about the distribution of these conditions among various groups in the population.

Changes in Popular Perceptions

A series of other developments reduced public confidence in the government. When President John Kennedy challenged the American people to "Ask not what your country can do for you. Ask what you can do for your country," few people reflected on whether the implied relation between the citizen and the state was consistent with democratic values. When President Johnson embarked on the Great Society, few people questioned whether the massive expansion in federal functions was consistent with the Constitution. This perspective on the government as the expression of our national will and the solution to perceived problems of almost any kind began to erode, however, in the late 1960s. An unsuccessful war in Vietnam became an unpopular war. A wave of urban riots and campus demonstrations reflected the reduced consensus on both domestic and foreign policy. Revelations of the Watergate burglary and cover-up led to the resignation of President Nixon and restraints on both the budgetary authority and war powers of the president. From 1969 through 1980 the United States experienced three recessions, two oil shocks, and the transformation of fourteen Third World countries into Soviet-proxy states. A mad mullah in Iran held fifty-two Americans hostage for over a year. Both domestic and international conditions appeared to be progressively out of control. President Carter, reflecting the confusion in his administration, misinterpreted this perception of governmental impotence as a "malaise" of the American spirit.

Changes in Economic Theory

The stage was set for a major change in policy by the new Reagan administration. The character of the change in economic policy, moreover, was shaped by a number of major developments in economics. For the first three decades after World War II, conventional wisdom among economists supported an activist role of the federal government. A Keynesian perspective dominated the approach to "macroeconomic" issues, such as the level of total output and real income, the unemployment rate, the inflation rate, and interest rates. Changes in government spending, tax receipts, and the deficit were believed to be sufficient to smooth economic fluctuations and maintain the economy on a high-growth path. Output and the price level were thought to be linked by the Phillips-curve trade-off of the unemployment rate and the inflation rate. Monetary policy was thought to have a secondary role, operating only through its effects on interest rates.

Another activist perspective, called "welfare economics," dominated the approach to "microeconomic" issues such as the composition of government spending, the structure of taxes, and the nature of government regulation. Welfare economics provided a theory of what functions governments should perform, based on the provision of services that the private sector would not supply in adequate amounts and on the correction of market failures. These two perspectives contributed to a confidence that governments could achieve all their economic policy goals if they had enough policy instruments. The age of the economist witnessed such implausible events as Walter Heller (the chairman of the Council of Economic Advisers) discussing taxes with Lyndon Johnson while bouncing around Johnson's ranch on a hunting trip and systems analysts from the Pentagon helping to design the war on poverty.

The consensus among economists, as in the general population, began to unravel in the late 1960s. Milton Friedman provided the first effective challenge to the Keynesian perspective in his presidential address to the American Economic Association in 1967, an address that summarized the logic of the monetarist perspective. The developing evidence suggested that changes in total demand were primarily dependent on changes in the money supply, not on changes in the fiscal variables. This was an especially awkward recognition for economists in the executive branch, because the Federal Reserve, formally an agent of Congress, was (and is) stubbornly independent. A later development of the Chicago school, called "rational expectations theory," reoriented macroeconomics to focus on the effects of expected future conditions on individual economic decisions. One important implication of this theory is that only *unexpected* changes in monetary policy have an effect on real economic conditions. Among other findings, this theory explained why the Phillips curve had not proved to be stable, and it provided some basis for optimism that inflation could be reduced without a severe effect on unemployment. There remained a residual commitment to Keynesian economics, particularly among older economists. The influence of the Keynesian perspective, however, had already peaked when President Nixon declared that "now I am a Keynesian."

A new field of economics, now called "public choice," also developed in the 1960s. This new field, applying economic theory and game theory to the behavior of government, demonstrated that the processes and institutions of government are also subject to numerous types of failure. The primary effect of this new field was to balance but not replace the theory of what government should do, which was based on welfare economics. The primary potential contribution of this field, the effects of which are yet to be realized, is an understanding of how the explicit and implicit constitutional rules by which government operates can be changed to improve its responsiveness to the interests of the general population.

A third development involved more of a shift of focus rather than a new theory. An increasing proportion of economists were specializing in the application of microeconomic theory to a wide range of government programs, regulations, and taxes. Since the mid-1960s the number and influence of microeconomists in staff positions has increased across the government. The first microeconomist was appointed as a member of the Council of Economic Advisers in 1968. In recent years ten federal departments and several agencies reporting to Congress each employed more than one hundred economists. Economists at universities and research institutes provided a rapidly developing literature of empirical studies demonstrating the adverse effects of a wide range of federal economic policies.

One application of microeconomics, what is now called "supply-side economics," deserves special attention because of the popular identification of the Reagan program with this term. It is important to understand what this term means and does not mean. First, supply-side economics is most accurately described as the application of microeconomic theory to the effects of fiscal policy on the incentives to work, save, and invest and on the allocation of resources in the economy. In other words, this term implies a focus on the "micro" effects of the *details* of the budget and the tax code, rather than on the "macro" effects of *total* government spending, tax revenues, and the deficit. (Herb Stein, a chairman of the CEA under President Nixon and a conventional "demand-side fiscalist," may have invented this term at a 1976 conference in Charlottesville, Virginia, when he described the public finance economists who focused on these micro effects as "supply-side fiscalists.") The primary conclusion of this body of analysis is that the economic effects of government spending and taxes depend importantly but not exclusively on the details of the budget and the tax code. Few economists would now argue with this conclusion.

The difference between the conventional demand-side approach to fiscal policy and the new supply-side approach is best illustrated by a debate in Congress in early 1977. Following the Carter election, House Democrats introduced an unprecedented third budget resolution to the FY 1977 budget, proposing a one-time $50 tax rebate and an increase in federal spending in order to increase demand. The appropriateness of this measure was questionable, even in conventional terms, because economic growth was strong in 1976. Instead of merely opposing this measure, House Republicans offered a substitute proposal for an across-the-board reduction of tax rates.

Congressman John Rousellot argued that "the purpose of a permanent tax reduction is to reduce the tax bias against work, saving, and
investment" and that the proposed tax rebate would not have this
effect. For any given increase in the expected deficit, the House Republicans argued correctly that a reduction in tax rates is superior
to a tax rebate because of the difference in incentive effects. The
debate on the Rousellot proposal became mired in controversy about
whether it would have a sufficient effect on demand and whether
the proposed tax cuts were "fair." The House Republicans, although
defeated on this measure, had made a point and found an issue on
which to claim to be the party of new ideas.

Supply-side economics, however, was *not* a new economic theory.
As of 1981 there were no distinctive supply-side texts, no courses,
no distinguished scholar, and no school of supply-side economists.
This body of analysis does not conclude that a general reduction in
tax rates would increase tax revenues, nor did any government economist or budget projection by the Reagan administration ever make
that claim. Arthur Laffer, a bright and energetic economist who had
served in the budget office under Nixon, once drew a curve on a
paper napkin to demonstrate that a reduction of some high tax rates
could increase revenue; the existence of a "Laffer curve," however,
was neither new (except by that name) nor controversial. Jude Wanniski of the *Wall Street Journal* and other journalists who promoted
the Laffer curve as a symbol of supply-side economics unfortunately
trivialized the substantive contribution of the focus on the micro effects of fiscal policy. Supply-side economics does not address the effects of government borrowing; specifically, it does not provide a
basis for concluding that deficits do not matter. Moreover, monetarism and supply-side economics are more complementary than competitive; monetary theory provides an explanation of total demand
in the economy, and supply-side economics focuses on the effects of
fiscal policy on the output or supply-side of the economy. Some supply-side economists also have controversial views about monetary
policy, but these views do not derive from a microeconomic analysis
of public finance. In summary, there was no "supply-side revolution" in economic theory.

The major effect of these several developments among economists
was to reduce their optimism that a few simple changes in economic
policies would be sufficient to resolve the major perceived economic
problems. Economic policy, like military power, came to be recognized as a very blunt instrument. Conditions in both the economy
and the government do not permit a fine-tuning of economic policy
to meet temporary conditions or very discriminating policy objectives. The major effect of these developments on the new adminis-

tration was the opportunity to shape an economic policy based on the use of monetary policy to restrain total demand and changes in the budget, taxes, and regulation to increase supply. The most important general principles guiding the initial Reagan program were its long-run orientation and its reliance on markets as the primary process for organizing economic activity.

Changes in Economic Policy

Most of the economic policies of the new administration, moreover, represented an acceleration rather than a reversal of policy trends initiated during the late 1970s. There was substantial precedent for each of the four key elements of the initial Reagan program in the prior decade.

The defense buildup, for example, started late in the Carter administration with substantial support in Congress. Real defense spending had declined 36 percent from FY 1968 through FY 1978 but increased 11 percent by FY 1981. The Ford and Carter administrations neither initiated nor reduced many domestic spending programs, but the momentum of programs initiated in the Johnson and Nixon administrations continued to increase the federal spending share of GNP, especially in recession years. The major budget challenge of the new Reagan administration was that spending for many domestic programs would have to be reduced or terminated if the proposed acceleration of defense spending was to be financed without a continued increase in the federal budget share of GNP.

The tax revolt also started in the late 1970s, initially in the states and later in Congress. The first attempts to limit taxes, however, were not encouraging. An amendment to limit the total taxing authority of the state, although promoted by Governor Reagan, was defeated in California in 1973, and a similar amendment was defeated in Michigan in 1976. The measure introduced by Representative John Rousellot for a proportional reduction in federal income tax rates, offered as a Republican substitute for a Democratic proposal for increased spending and a temporary tax rebate, was defeated in Congress in early 1977.

The watershed year proved to be 1978. Tennessee and Michigan approved general limits on the taxing power of the state, and California approved a reduction in local property taxes. Support in Congress for a reduction in federal tax rates increased rapidly in both parties. A reduction of the capital-gains tax rate was approved against the opposition of the Carter administration. In October 1978 the Senate approved an amendment by Democratic Sen. Sam Nunn to the FY 1979 budget resolution, combining a 30 percent reduction in

federal income tax rates, proposed earlier by Republicans Rep. Jack
Kemp and Sen. William Roth, and a general limit on federal spending. Although the House had earlier defeated a similar proposal by
Rep. Marjorie Holt by a narrow margin, the House Democrats voted
to instruct their conferees to support the Nunn amendment. This
proposal was defeated in conference only by the threat of a veto by
President Carter.

Support for the new supply-side approach to fiscal policy, however, continued to gain momentum in both parties. The annual reports of the Joint Economic Committee, under the leadership of
Democratic Sen. Lloyd Bentsen, supported the combination of
spending restraint and a reduction in tax rates in both 1979 and
1980. In August 1980 the Senate Finance Committee approved a tax
measure very similar to that endorsed by candidate Reagan. A bipartisan consensus for the major provisions of the tax measures proposed by President Reagan was in place before he was inaugurated.

The precedents to the Reagan policy of deregulation were more
mixed. The Carter administration supported continued regulation
of energy prices and usage, the stringent 1977 amendments to the
Clean Air Act, a system of voluntary price and wage guidelines, and
the very damaging credit controls in the spring of 1980. At the same
time there was considerable support for reducing the older forms of
economic regulation. The initial measures to deregulate domestic air
travel originated in the Civil Aeronautics Board in 1976, suggesting
that the regulatory agencies were not all "captured" by the regulated
industries; these measures were endorsed and extended by Congress
in 1978 with bipartisan support. Measures that authorized a partial
or phased deregulation of trucking, railroads, and banks were approved by Congress in 1980. And in September 1980 Congress established a one-year deadline on the price controls on oil. The record of the late 1970s suggested that the new administration would
have substantial support for reducing the traditional forms of economic regulation but very little support for reducing the newer types
of regulation of health, safety, and the environment.

The increased role of monetary policy also had important roots in
the 1970s. The Federal Reserve first established internal targets for
the growth of the money supply in January 1970. Increased public
concern about monetary policy led Congress in 1975 to approve a
resolution requiring the Federal Reserve to announce one-year growth
targets for several measures of money and credit. A 1978 law required both the administration and the Federal Reserve to make an
annual report on the progress in achieving specified goals involving
inflation, unemployment, and investment. In October 1979, following the appointment of Paul Volcker as chairman of the Board of

Governors and in response to a continued decline in the dollar and pressure from other central banks, the Federal Reserve adopted a new operating policy with the objective of achieving closer control of the money supply. The issues that led to an increased attention on money growth, rather than on interest rates, were not broadly understood, but the institutions, procedures, and people were in place to support the monetary policy objectives of the new administration.

A PROSPECTIVE EVALUATION

Any new administration is in part a captive of history. Several parallel developments during the fifteen years prior to 1981, however, set the stage for a substantial potential change in economic policy. Lower economic growth, rising inflation, and increasing tax rates led to a popular demand for some change in economic policy. The several conditions that led to a reduced popular confidence in the government increased the appeal of policy changes that would reduce the role of government in the American economy. Several complementary changes in the perspectives of economists and an increasing number of empirical studies shaped the choice of policies to meet these concerns. And there was broad bipartisan agreement in Congress by the late 1970s for the direction of change in each of the major dimensions of federal economic policy.

All that was missing was a president who could shape a coherent economic program and articulate the rationale for this program to Congress, the press, and the American public. For most voters Ronald Reagan was the logical candidate and the logical president for the time. For over fifteen years he had articulated a quite consistent set of views that appealed to an increasing share of the American electorate. His experience as governor of California established his credentials as an effective politician and administrator. And he was the best public speaker of any national politician since Franklin Roosevelt and John Kennedy. There are few periods in American history for which a president so closely matched the current demands on this role. Few presidents have had a greater opportunity to guide and shape federal economic policy.

How Coherent Was the Initial Reagan Program?

Any political coalition large enough to elect a president includes many people who may not agree on many issues other than the choice of president. The Reagan coalition was no different. The coalition of traditional Republicans, supply-siders, neoconservatives, social conservatives, the business community, and selected unions who supported Reagan reflected a wide range of views of economic issues. No coherent economic program could serve all their interests. The initial Reagan economic program reflected some of the tensions within the coalition. On balance, however, this program was reasonably coherent in that there was a reasoned basis for believing that the proposed changes in policy would be sufficient to achieve most of the announced policy objectives.

Two major risks to the Reagan program, however, were recognized from the beginning. First, a large reduction in domestic spending would be necessary to reduce the growth of the total federal spending and to balance the budget, given the proposed increase in defense spending and the proposed reduction of tax rates. Moreover, an even larger proportional reduction in spending for the hundreds of discretionary domestic programs would be necessary, as the major income-security programs were to be maintained. Although this condition was recognized by budget experts, candidate Reagan did not mention it during the 1980 campaign, and there was no mandate or apparent consensus for such large reductions in domestic programs. Unless President Reagan could make an effective case for such reductions, the proposed defense buildup and tax rate reductions could be financed only by an increase in government borrowing. The traditional Republican objective of a balanced budget apparently might again be deferred indefinitely in favor of other policy objectives.

A second risk, discussed earlier, was whether inflation could be reduced without a recession and an increase in unemployment. A recession in turn would increase government spending and reduce tax revenues relative to the initial budget projections. The prospect for reducing inflation without adverse temporary consequences was based on a slow, steady reduction in money growth and a rapid adjustment of inflation expectations to this announced policy. A record of unstable money growth and administration policies, however, reduced the prospects for success of this policy. There was less reason for concern about a contrary risk, expressed by a number of leading economists, that the proposed tax cuts would themselves be inflationary. Inflation expectations, as revealed in interest rates and exchange rates, generally declined after announcement of the policies of the new administration.

The coherence of a prospective policy, of course, is a matter of perception. Economic advisers to the Reagan administration expected that a reduction in money growth would reduce the growth of demand while the reduction in tax rates and regulation would increase the supply of output, both effects contributing to a reduction in inflation. Economic advisers to prior administrations of both parties regarded the Reagan program as incoherent because they expected monetary restraint and a reduction in tax revenues to have conflicting economic effects on total demand and the inflation rate. The Reagan program promised to provide an important test of these competing perspectives.

How Revolutionary Was the Initial Reagan Program?

A revolution implies a comprehensive change in policies. In this respect the initial Reagan economic program was a revolution. Few prior administrations had proposed to reduce the growth of government spending and make a general reduction in tax rates except following a war. The Reagan administration was the first to recognize monetary policy as the primary instrument to control total demand and the inflation rate. A revolution is based on broad popular unrest, shaped by changes in intellectual perspectives, and tested by prior attempts to implement similar policies. The Reagan program reflected each of these conditions.

A revolution, however, also implies a substantial change in policies. In this respect the Reagan economic program is best described as an evolution. The March 1981 budget proposed only a small reduction in the growth of real federal spending relative to the last Carter budget, not a reduction in the level of spending. The proposed reduction in tax rates was not sustainable without a further reduction in spending. The "far-reaching program of regulatory relief" had little initial substantive content. And the program proposed a slow, steady reduction in the growth of the money supply, not a fundamental change in the targets or procedures of monetary policy.

In summary, the initial Reagan economic program was a "conservative" program primarily in the sense that it represented a rather cautious evolution of a number of policy changes initiated in the late 1970s. The opportunity for a more substantial change in economic policies would depend on the success of this initial program.

CHAPTER TWO

Spending

A budget reform plan to cut the rate of growth
of federal spending.

The new Reagan administration recognized that "the President's
overall economic plan cannot succeed without a sharp reduction in
the spending growth trend built into current law and policy." The
task of reducing the growth of total federal spending, however, was
compounded by the president's commitments to strengthen the defense program and to protect the major income security programs,
total spending for which was about 60 percent of the FY 1981 budget. In addition, interest payments on prior debt were about 10 percent of the FY 1981 budget. A reduction in the growth of total
spending thus would require a substantial reduction in the level of
spending for the hundreds of other programs financed by only 30
percent of the FY 1981 budget.

The budget task was further compounded by the absence of any
apparent mandate or consensus to reduce these other programs. As
a candidate Reagan had promised to reduce "waste, fraud, extravagance, and abuse" across the government, but he had not mentioned
that a substantial reduction of these other programs was necessary
to make his budget plan coherent. The success of the Reagan economic program would thus depend on building a consensus to reverse the expanded role of the federal government that had developed since 1965. There should have been no mystery about the
Reagan budget arithmetic. (I made these same points in a paper to
the transition team and in lectures and news columns in November
1980 and February 1981, on the basis only of Reagan's Chicago speech
and published budget data.)

THE REAGAN BUDGET RECORD

Total Outlays

Figure 2.1 illustrates the level of real federal outlays during the Carter administration and the proposed and actual real outlays during the first term of the Reagan administration. As this figure shows, the growth of real federal spending during Reagan's first term was somewhat lower than during the Carter administration but much higher than the initial forecast. Real federal spending increased at a 3.7 percent annual rate during the first term, lower than the 5 percent annual rate during the Carter administration. The growth of real federal spending during the first term was still substantially higher than the 2.4 percent annual growth of real GNP. By FY 1985, moreover, real federal spending was 15 percent higher than the initial forecast, about $120 billion in 1985 dollars, and this difference between actual and forecast real spending was almost identical to the increase in the real deficit. In other words, had Reagan achieved his initial budget objectives, the real deficit would not have increased. Total federal spending in FY 1982 through 1985 is almost perfectly explained by the same conditions that determined federal spending in the prior postwar years. The most conservative president since the 1920s, a Republican Senate, and the energies of a remarkable budget director were not sufficient to change this pattern.

Why was it so difficult to reduce the growth of real federal spending? Some of the reasons are inherent in the general conditions that determine federal spending, and some were the result of specific conditions faced by the Reagan administration. First, the share of federal outlays that were relatively uncontrollable under current law increased from about 25 percent in the mid-1960s to about 70 percent in FY 1981. Most of these relatively uncontrollable outlays were for the many formula-payment programs, such as social security and Medicare, that can be reduced only by changing the basic authorizing legislation. In addition, there were substantial outlays for interest payments and for other prior-year contracts and obligations. Second, nearly half of the relatively controllable outlays were for national defense, a program that the Reagan administration proposed to increase rapidly. Third, the monetary restraint that led to the extended 1981–1982 recession and the unexpectedly rapid decline in inflation temporarily increased real spending for both the uncontrollable and controllable programs. Fourth, our political system seems to be willing to address a "housecleaning" budget only in the first year of each presidential term. Only the proposed FY 1982 and FY 1986 budgets represented a thorough attempt to scrub the budget

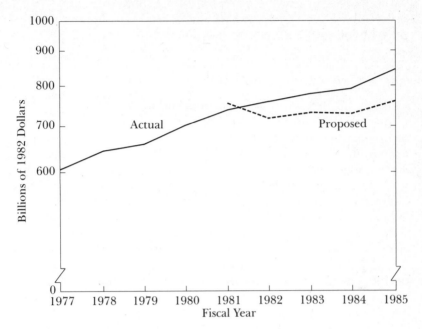

Figure 2.1 Total Real Federal Outlays

of less-important spending. The FY 1983 through 1985 budgets were best described as "housekeeping" budgets.

Most important, there turned out to be relatively few consistent fiscal conservatives in the administration or in either party in Congress. Many of the smaller programs that constitute the American welfare state were created under Republican presidents and continued to be defended by Republicans in Congress. All too often, the conservatives in both parties were more protective of programs that served their own states and favored constituencies than of their commitment to a responsible fiscal policy. Both the administration and the congressional supply-siders must share the blame for the final reason why spending was so difficult to control—the failure to make some part of the tax reductions proposed in 1981 contingent on a corresponding reduction in spending. After the 1981 tax bill was approved, all that the administration had to offer those who would lose benefits or services from spending restraint was the vague general benefit of lower future deficits. Politicians of both parties found that the bird in hand was worth more than the two in the bush.

The continued growth of real federal spending, at a rate higher than the growth of the economy, was the major failure of Reagan's first term and the major cause of the deficits that threaten the sustainability of other elements of his economic program.

Defense and International Affairs

Spending for defense and international affairs was about 25 percent of total federal outlays in FY 1981. The defense program was the one major federal program that Reagan proposed to increase. As it turned out, the defense budget was also the only major component of the budget that did not increase as rapidly as first proposed. Figure 2.2 illustrates the level of real spending for defense and international affairs during the Carter administration and the proposed and actual real outlays during the first term of the Reagan administration. As the figure shows, the rapid increase in real defense spending began in the last two years of the Carter administration and continued at about the same rate through FY 1985. Real spending for defense and international affairs increased at a 4.8 percent annual rate during the Carter administration and at a 6.9 percent annual rate during the first term of the Reagan administration. By FY 1985, annual real spending was about 30 percent higher than in FY 1981 and about 50 percent higher than in FY 1979. From the

Figure 2.2   Real Outlays for Defense and International Affairs

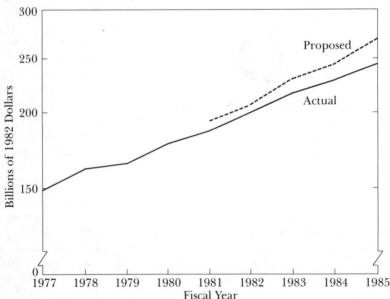

first year, however, real spending was lower than proposed in the
first Reagan budget.

Defense

As with many elements in the Reagan program, the defense buildup
represented an acceleration of changes initiated late in the Carter
administration. A number of conditions led to broad bipartisan support for the defense buildup beginning in FY 1980. The Soviets continued to increase their strategic nuclear forces, despite several arms
control agreements and a period of U.S. restraint. A series of communist coups in Third World countries was followed by the revolu-
tions in Nicaragua and Iran and the Soviet invasion of Afghanistan.

Although these conditions provided the political impetus for the
defense buildup, the character of the buildup was determined primarily by the longer-term objectives of the military services, and the
rate of growth of real spending became the primary political issue.
At no time during this record peacetime increase in defense spending was there any substantial review of U.S. foreign policy objectives
and military commitments. The defense buildup under both Carter
and Reagan accepted, without serious question, the strategy of global
containment, extended deterrence, and collective security that had
guided U.S. foreign and defense policy from Truman through
Johnson. In terms of these objectives, the defense program was (and
is) clearly underfunded. The continuing problem of U.S. defense
budgeting, however, is that the government has not limited its objectives and commitments to the defense program the nation is willing
to support. As a consequence, the defense program has generally
appeared to be unbalanced and inadequate, a piece of a larger program that the nation is not prepared to support, rather than a balanced program to meet limited objectives.

Again, it is important to recognize that the defense buildup was
designed to support traditional postwar U.S. objectives, not an expansion of these objectives. The primary contribution of the one major new program, the strategic defense initiative (SDI), would be to
reduce the vulnerability of the land-based missile force, a force that
is uniquely valuable only to maintain the potential for extended deterrence. The one new dimension of U.S. foreign policy under Reagan—the selective support of local forces to challenge communist
government in Afghanistan, Angola, and Nicaragua—had little direct budget cost. The primary effect on the budget of the most controversial foreign policy and defense proposals—such as the sale of
weapons to Saudi Arabia, additional funding for the IMF, the initial
MX deployment, and support for the Nicaraguan *contras*—was an
increase in spending for other programs, which was the price of ap-

proval of Reagan's initiatives. In each of these initiatives, the president got most of what he proposed but at the cost of a loss of influence on other components of the budget. Effective control of the federal budget may require a president who has no other agenda that requires the approval of Congress.

The defense buildup from FY 1981 through 1985 proceeded on two tracks. Real spending for procurement increased at a 13.5 percent annual rate, and real spending for research and development (including spending by the Department of Energy for the development and testing of nuclear weapons) increased at an 11 percent annual rate. In contrast, real spending for military personnel increased at a 4.1 percent annual rate, the combination of a 1 percent annual increase in personnel and a 3 percent annual increase in real compensation per member of the armed forces. And real spending for operations and maintenance increased at a 3.7 percent annual rate. The focus of the defense buildup thus was on weapons modernization rather than an increase in the size or readiness of the military forces.

The rapid increase in real defense spending through FY 1985, however, was not matched by corresponding increases in the measurable dimensions of military capability. This is best reflected in the force structure. From FY 1981 through 1985, as indicated by Table 2.1, most elements of the force structure increased much less than the 30 percent increase in real defense spending. Although candidate Reagan, like John Kennedy, had charged that the United States faced a "window of vulnerability", the vulnerability of the land-based strategic missiles continued to increase.

Other measures of military capability, as compiled in a 1985 study by the Congressional Budget Office (CBO), tell a similar story. The number of weapons purchased increased much less than real procurement spending. The Department of Defense described its overall readiness rates as "steady or slightly increasing." Stocks of munitions increased as a percentage of war reserve requirements, but stocks of other critical items declined as a percentage of requirements. The most substantial increase in capability was the quality and experience of military personnel, a combined effect of higher relative compensation and a restored pride in military service. For example, the percentage of Army recruits who were high school graduates increased from 54 percent in 1980 to 90 percent in 1984, and reenlistment rates also increased substantially. The CBO study concluded that "despite widespread improvements, most of these aggregate indicators have not increased markedly, with a few exceptions like personnel quality."

The broad consensus that sustained the defense buildup for six

Table 2.1 U.S. Defense Manpower and Forces

	FY 1981	FY 1985	Change (%)
Average strength[a]			
Military	2,064	2,146	4.0
Civilian	947	1,037	9.5
Strategic forces			
Missiles	1,573	1,651	5.0
Bomber squadrons	25	20	−20.0
General-purpose forces			
Land force division	19	20	5.3
Tactical air wings	41	40	−2.4
Naval forces			
Carriers	12	13	8.3
Submarines	81	96	19.0
Other warships	196	213	8.7
Amphibious ships	59	60	1.7
Airlift and sealift			
Airlift squadrons	17	17	0
Sealift ships	60	59	−1.7

[a] In thousands.

years ended in 1985, when Congress reduced the budget authority of the Department of Defense for FY 1986. Several conditions contributed to the erosion of this consensus. As the foregoing information suggests, it became increasingly unclear whether the increase in military capability was worth the higher cost. A growing perception of mismanagement was only reenforced by revelations of $600 toilet covers and $7,000 coffee machines. Secretaries of State Alexander Haig and George Shultz both chafed at the reluctance of the military to commit forces in support of current foreign policy objectives, and the defense buildup did not seem responsive to the conditions that provided its initial impetus. In several cases, such as the MX missile and aid to the *contras,* an unusually weak administration case reduced its credibility on other defense issues. Most important, it became clear that a continued defense buildup would require either a substantial reduction in domestic spending or a substantial tax increase, conditions that either Congress or the president would not accept.

The administration's initial guidance on the defense budget was rather casual. During the campaign of 1980, Reagan proposed a 5 percent annual increase in real defense outlays. After Carter's FY 1982 budget also proposed a 5 percent real increase, the new administration decided that a higher real increase was necessary to demonstrate a stronger commitment to defense. The March 1981 revision of the FY 1982 budget proposed a 9.4 percent increase in real defense outlays through FY 1985. At that time, however, the Department of Defense had not developed a program plan consistent with the proposed budget, and David Stockman regarded the proposed defense budget as only tentative guidance, pending further review.

As it turned out, there was no regular substantive review of the defense program and budget by the White House. On two occasions, however, Stockman tried to initiate such a review. On August 3, 1981, shortly after approval of the 1981 budget and tax legislation, Stockman informed the president that the projected deficit had increased and proposed an unusual fall initiative on the budget. Congress had approved only $35 billion of the $41 billion of proposed budget cuts, and the weakening economy was reducing the growth of tax receipts. A revised defense budget was expected to be a major part of this fall initiative. A meeting with the president on August 18 in Los Angeles failed to produce the desired budget guidance. Stockman made a number of specific proposals that would reduce the growth of defense spending by $20 billion or more over three years. The Department of Defense, however, had recently completed its Five-Year Defense Plan (FYDP) based on the March budget, and Weinberger would not address any reduction from this plan. The president was characteristically reluctant to make a hard choice between his advisers, and he instructed Stockman and Weinberger to develop options with an agreement on their budget effects. A meeting chaired by Edwin Meese on August 26 in Santa Barbara was no more successful. Weinberger again did not present any options and argued at length against any changes. Meese instructed Weinberger to prepare promptly an analysis of two options. The Defense response on September 3 was a set of simple charts, including one illustrating the different budget proposals using cartoon soldiers of different sizes. A meeting with the president on September 9 back in Washington addressed six options but did not lead to a resolution. Because the president's speech on the fall initiative was initially scheduled for September 14, time was running out. Jim Baker and Ed Meese finally elicited a decision from the president, which they understood to involve a reduction of $20 billion over three years but, on examination, turned out to involve about $15 billion in outlay savings. In any case, the entire fall initiative, announced on September 24, proved to be ill fated. So soon after the extended debate on the 1981 budget and tax legislation, Congress was not prepared to reopen the budget, and it rejected the entire package.

Several lessons were learned from this episode. Weinberger would not permit any OMB review of the defense budget. A concern about the rapid defense buildup was broadly shared by the White House staff and the cabinet. The president would not listen to argument about the content of the defense program and would accede to only small reductions in the initial defense budget guidance. Over time, it also became apparent that there was little effective review of the defense budget in the Office of the Secretary of Defense (OSD). The administration's defense budget was little more than a stapled package of the budget requests from each service.

After the 1984 election Stockman made one other effort to scrub the defense budget as part of the "core group" review of the FY 1986 budget and the second-term agenda. This group, chaired by Ed Meese, also included Jim Baker, Don Regan, Malcolm Baldrige, Dave Stockman, Dick Darman, Jack Svahn, and myself. The initial inclination of the core group was to "finesse" another dispute with Weinberger by applying a general freeze on real outlays for defense and other programs. Stockman quickly educated the group that a consistent freeze concept could not be applied across the whole budget. He then presented to the group several optional defense budgets designed to minimize the effects of a lower spending path on the defense program. This was (and is) a moderately simple task for an informed person; so much of the defense budget is procurement that major savings can be achieved, without changing the force structure, by stretching procurement schedules. The basic Stockman proposal would have led to constant real outlays in FY 1986 and a 3 percent real growth in later years. This proposal was strongly supported by every member of the core group. Weinberger was asked to contribute to these preliminary deliberations but declined.

A meeting in early December in the Cabinet Room provided the first opportunity to review these options with the president and Weinberger. The discussion at this meeting was less substantive than the similar meetings in 1981. Weinberger took the initiative to make a tenuous case that the U.S. defense budget should be determined only by the Soviet threat and was independent of domestic economic conditions and priorities, a case that the president later repeated in defending the proposed budget. The discussion was entirely about the conditions affecting the total defense budget. At no time during this two-hour meeting was there any discussion of the Stockman proposals or of the content of the defense program and budget. It was again clear that the president would not consider defense options from anyone other than Weinberger. It also became clear that Don Regan, who had strongly supported a lower defense budget in the core group, was a tower of jelly on this issue in front of the president. This meeting produced no agreement or guidance. A second meeting, delayed by a Weinberger trip to NATO headquarters, had the same effect. Weinberger was finally asked to come up with some defense saving. In response, he proposed a "cut" of $8 billion in his FY 1986 proposal, most of which involved pulling forward some spending into FY 1985 and reestimates. The president's FY 1987 budget proposed a $30 billion increase in budget authority for defense, a proposal that had almost no support in either the administration or in Congress. A measure of this misjudgment is that Congress reduced the FY 1986 defense budget authority by more than $8 billion, ending the largest peacetime defense buildup.

Over this period Congress was the only effective check on defense spending but was also part of the problem. The growth of real defense spending slowed sharply after FY 1983, and Congress, for the first time in many years, reduced the new budget authority for defense in FY 1986. At the same time, however, Congress regularly resisted the closing of bases or the termination of contracts to meet the lower budget targets. Congress has an important constitutional role in defense policy that it has yet to sort out, paying too little attention to the basic defense missions and too much attention to minor management issues. One of the few times Congress considered basic defense strategy was in July 1984, when the Senate narrowly defeated a proposal by Sen. Sam Nunn to withdraw 90,000 troops from Europe. There is some prospect for improving the congressional review, however, probably led by younger Democrats such as Sen. Nunn and Rep. Les Aspin. In February 1986 the first report of the President's Blue Ribbon Commission on Defense Management, chaired by David Packard, had plenty of blame to go around: "Today, there is no rational system whereby the Executive Branch and Congress reach coherent and enduring agreement on national military strategy, the forces to carry it out, and the funding that should be provided."

International Affairs

Spending for international programs (foreign economic and military aid, international agencies, and the conduct of foreign affairs) was about 2 percent of total outlays in FY 1981 and increased at a real annual rate of only 0.6 percent during the first term. There was little controversy about these programs within the administration. Stockman approved most of Shultz's budget requests with little review, in exchange for Shultz's support on other issues in the cabinet. The major change in these programs was the concentration of foreign aid on Israel and Egypt, two countries that have now become dependent on receiving about half of all U.S. economic aid. Few interna-

tional programs other than aid to Israel and export subsidies, however, have much congressional support, and approval of the most
controversial proposals has usually required a side deal with Congress on other issues. For this reason the total cost of these international programs has been somewhat more than their direct budget
outlays.

Transfer Payments and Social Services

Spending for transfer payments and social services was about 55
percent of total federal outlays in FY 1981. About two-thirds of these
outlays and about 35 percent of total outlays were for the "core social safety net programs" that the administration promised to preserve and maintain. These core programs included the basic retirement program of social security, unemployment benefits, cash benefits
to dependent families and the elderly poor, and the full veterans
program. Almost all transfers by these core programs (except the
small amount of cash benefits to dependent families and the elderly
poor) are not income tested; that is, they are available to all people
in a specific group, regardless of income.

The March 1981 revision of the FY 1982 budget proposed a continued moderate growth of these core programs and a substantial

Figure 2.3   Real Outlays for Transfers and Social Services

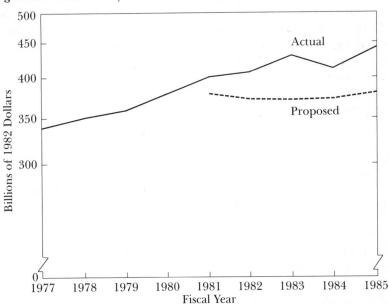

reduction of real spending for the many peripheral welfare programs initiated since 1965. The largest proportionate reductions were proposed for education and employment services, housing assistance, and food assistance to those with incomes above the poverty line. The initial Reagan budget proposed no significant changes in the rapidly growing budget for medical services.

Figure 2.3 illustrates the level of real spending for transfers and social services during the Carter administration and the proposed and actual real outlays during the first term of the Reagan administration. The Reagan administration was moderately successful in reducing the growth of real spending for these programs. The rate was reduced from an annual growth of 4.6 percent during the Carter administration to an annual growth of 2.5 percent during Reagan's first term. As will be seen, real spending for every major transfer and social service program increased more (or declined less) than first proposed. The three primary reasons for the continued growth of real spending for these programs were the explosion of payments for farm income supports, the failure to win congressional approval for all the proposed program reductions, and a rate of economic growth that was lower than the initial forecast.

Social Security

Spending for social security was about 21 percent of total federal outlays in FY 1981 and increased at a 2.9 percent real annual rate during the first term. From the beginning of the administration, most social security benefits were considered "entitlements" and were off limits to budget cuts. The March 1981 budget proposed only small changes in social security—eliminating or reducing the minimum benefit, student benefits, disability benefits, and death benefits where there is no survivor—most of which were later approved.

A more thorough review of social security, however, could not be deferred indefinitely. The basic old age, survivors, and disability insurance (OASDI) program was projected to run out of money within a few years, despite the substantial tax increases approved in 1977 and a continued rapid growth of employment. A part of the problem was that social security benefits to current retirees were indexed to the consumer price index, an index that substantially overstated the inflation rate through 1981. The new administration formed an interagency working group on social security in February. This group was chaired by Health and Human Services (HHS) undersecretary David Swoap and included representatives of the Treasury, Labor, the White House Office of Policy Development, OMB, and CEA. I joined this group in April as the CEA representative. In parallel with the work of this group, Rep. Jake Pickle and Sen. William Armstrong were developing a congressional response to the social security funding problem. The first meetings of the working group were addressed to a proposal that had been prepared by HHS and the Social Security Administration (SSA). This proposal addressed the near-term funding problem by eliminating or reducing many of the "welfare" elements of the social security program, some of which were proposed in the March budget. These proposed cuts were more than enough to resolve the short-run funding problem, but they did not address the rapidly growing unfunded liabilities of the basic benefit programs.

Steve Entin (a Treasury economist) and I made a case for an alternative proposal. The near-term benefit cuts would be restricted to those sufficient to maintain the trust fund balance and to avoid the expected charge of "balancing the budget on the backs of the poor and the elderly." In addition, our proposal addressed the long-term problem by changing the formula for indexing future benefits and by gradually increasing the age for full retirement benefits. The proposed change to base the benefits of future retirees on the level of prices rather than wages had previously been endorsed by the Hsiao report in 1976, and Rep. Pickle had tentatively endorsed an increase in the age for full retirement benefits. Although our proposal was supported by the Labor and OMB representatives, it was strongly opposed by Robert Myer, the deputy commissioner and former chief actuary of SSA. Myer was a vigorous defender of the concept that social security should continue to be the nation's primary pension system rather than a floor on real retirement income. He also defended the long-term funding status of social security, based on SSA's arcane concept of a rolling seventy-five-year actuarial balance, despite a recognition that substantial future tax increases will be necessary to fund the projected benefits. Myer's tactics were much like those of Weinberger; he refused to address any alternative to the SSA proposal. His tactics were successful because none of his superiors—SSA commissioner Jack Svahn, David Swoap, or HHS secretary Richard Schweiker—were sufficiently knowledgeable about social security or concerned about its long-run problems to challenge Myer. The proposal that was forwarded to the cabinet council on human resources was only a slight modification of the initial HHS–SSA proposal.

The cabinet council meeting in late April transformed an unsatisfactory proposal into a political disaster, primarily because Stockman wanted additional near-term budget savings. The major issue concerned a proposed reduction of early retirement benefits from 80 percent of full benefits to either 75 percent or 70 percent, effective in January 1982. Stockman insisted that the early retirement benefits be reduced to 55 percent of full benefits, with the same short notice. The council rejected the Treasury-CEA proposal to change the indexing formula in favor of a Stockman proposal to reduce the annual adjustments by half for a seven-year period. This proposal was supported by Schweiker and by White House domestic policy adviser Martin Anderson and was opposed by the Treasury, Labor, and CEA representatives. The package that emerged from this meeting served the interests of three groups: SSA protected the basic social security benefits, HHS and Martin Anderson supported a reduction in the welfare elements of the system, and Stockman won tentative approval of a $110 billion multi-year budget saving. This package also turned out to be the major domestic policy mistake of the Reagan administration—an extraordinary political misjudgment by Stockman and Schweiker, both of whom had served in Congress through 1980.

The rest of this episode was almost an anticlimax. The cabinet council proposal was sent to the White House on May 9, without the promised study of the number of people affected by the various proposed changes. A one-hour presentation to the president on May 11 left him with his eyes glazed by technical detail and no alternative but to accept or reject the package. At a meeting with Jim Baker later that afternoon, Schweiker, Stockman, and Anderson assured Baker that the proposal was technically sound and politically feasible. After having lost their case at the working group and cabinet council level, the Treasury and CEA representatives did not speak up at the meetings with the president and with Baker, a mistake for which I deserve some responsibility. Baker was skeptical about forwarding this package to Congress, but the major victory on the budget resolution on May 7 provided a basis for optimism, and he authorized Schweiker to announce the package on May 12. On release of this package, the administration experienced its first major reversal. Democrats took the lead in blaming the administration for proposing more cuts than necessary to resolve the near-term funding problem. House Speaker Tip O'Neill stopped any further review of social security by Jake Pickle. On May 20 the Senate approved a resolution critical of the administration's package by a vote of 92–0.

There were a number of legacies of this unfortunate episode. The Democrats had found an issue that would carry them through the 1982 elections at the cost of deferring any action on social security until 1983. The administration would never again propose or support a change in the basic social security program without a guarantee of bipartisan support. (In 1985, for example, the administration did not support a proposal by the Senate Republicans to eliminate the cost-of-living adjustment for social security for one year.) Another lesson that it should have learned is that short-term budget concerns and program reform are often inconsistent. Unfortunately, both Congress and the White House have very short horizons, reducing the prospects for reform. The administration also should have learned that it did not have to take the lead on all issues; in this case, there was reason to believe that the congressional review initiated by Rep. Pickle and Sen. Armstrong would have led to a good bill. A final effect of this episode was on the White House review process. Jim Baker learned not to trust either the substantive or political judgment arising from the cabinet council process. In this case the president was presented with only one complex package and a short deadline. Baker would later ensure that more options were presented and that there was more time for a political evaluation after the cabinet-level review.

Social security had become a minefield for the administration, but the funding problem would not go away. The solution was to establish the National Commission on Social Security Reform in December 1981. The White House, the Senate, and the House each selected five members of the commission, with the White House choosing the chairman. The commission was charged to develop a recommendation by December 31, 1982. The outcome of the process was substantially determined by the initial personnel choices. The White House selected Alan Greenspan as chairman, apparently without knowledge or concern that as an adviser to President Ford, Greenspan had endorsed the very expensive wage-indexing formula for social security benefits, a decision that was the primary cause of the funding problem. Greenspan, in turn, selected Robert Myer as the staff director of the commission, thus ensuring that the commission would not address any significant reform of the social security benefits structure. Apparently by instruction, the commission made no decisions prior to the November 1982 election. After agreeing on the magnitude of the funding problem, the commission deadlocked on the solution to this problem, with the expected division between those who proposed to increase taxes and those who proposed to reduce the growth of benefits. After an extension of the deadline to January 15, this deadlock was broken only by a compromise arranged by Jim Baker and his aide Dick Darman. At no time were the social security specialists in the administration informed or consulted about these deliberations. Among those excluded from this process was Martin Feldstein, who had recently replaced Weidenbaum as CEA chairman and was a recognized expert on social security.

The outcomes of this process of drafting legislation by a commission served the political interests of the administration but were wholly inconsistent with the president's expressed policy objectives. Congress approved the commission recommendation with only a few changes, reducing the tax on retirement benefits and reducing the earnings penalty. This was sufficient to diffuse the political threat of social security to the administration and to defer any further consideration of the basic social security program until the next administration. The substance of the final legislation, however, was contrary to the president's objectives in a number of ways. Coverage was extended to new federal workers and employees of nonprofit organizations, and state and local government employees were no longer allowed to withdraw from the system. General revenues were committed to the basic social security fund for the first time. Most important, about 78 percent of the social security deficit was reduced by tax increases. The only significant change in the benefits structure was to increase the age for full retirement benefits from 65 to 67 early in the next century.

The major problems of the social security system have not yet been resolved. Social security is effectively an intergenerational Ponzi game. The first generation of retirees have received a very high return, but the bills are now coming due. Current social security taxes are now higher than federal income taxes for a majority of workers. Today's new workers will earn a very low or negative real return on their "contributions" to social security, even if the promised benefits are realized. Social security tax rates may increase to 25 percent or more early in the next century. Although the evidence is not clear, the social security system probably reduces private saving and earnings by the elderly. The administration botched an opportunity to sort out these problems and indefinitely deferred their resolution. Stockman deserves the blame for seeking too much near-term budget savings in 1981, Baker for being willing to accept almost any package in 1983. The Democrats' exploitation of the issue only compounded the problem. Only a Democratic administration, however, may have the political freedom to sort out the fundamental problems of social security—if we can wait that long.

Health

Spending for health programs (excluding those for the military and veterans) was about 10 percent of total federal outlays in FY 1981 and increased at a 5.7 percent real annual rate during the first term. These programs include Medicare, Medicaid, and a variety of other services. Although these programs were not considered part of the core social safety net, the initial Reagan budget proposed only small changes in these programs. The growth of Medicaid grants would be reduced in exchange for greater state flexibility in administering this program. Several dozen categorical grants would be consolidated into two block grants. Growth of spending for the discretionary medical services and training programs would be reduced. Although many of these initial proposals were approved, spending for health services continued to grow at a rapid rate.

The later proposals for changing the health programs had a mixed record. As part of the federalism initiative in 1982, the administration proposed to assume the states' costs of the Medicaid program in exchange for state assumption of the federal costs of aid to families of dependent children (AFDC) and the food stamp program. Congress did not approve any part of this federalism initiative. This program of health insurance for the poor is working quite well, however, and there is not a compelling case for substantial reform of the federal role in this program. The administration was more successful in changing Medicare, the health insurance system for the elderly and disabled. The social security amendments of 1983 authorized the substitution of a "prospective payment system" for the prior cost-based system of reimbursing hospitals for services to Medicare patients. This system, first implemented in October 1983, pays hospitals a fixed amount per patient for each of about 470 diagnosis-related groups (DRGs). Although this system has been quite successful in reducing the costs per hospital stay, it is probably not a satisfactory solution to controlling hospital costs in the long run. As with any complex system of price controls, it will lead to too much supply of some services and too little (or a reduced quality) of others, and the hospitals have quickly learned to game this system. A more fundamental reform of Medicare, such as a voucher system for both hospital and physician services, is both appropriate and necessary, as the hospital insurance trust fund is expected to be exhausted in the 1990s.

For the most part the health programs were reviewed by substantive specialists, with little involvement of the political officials in the Reagan administration. The next administration will not have this luxury.

Low-Income Assistance

Spending for direct assistance of low-income families and individuals (exclusive of Medicaid) was about 6 percent of total federal outlays in FY 1981 and increased at a 0.9 percent real annual rate during the first term. (This growth rate does not include the large one-time direct loans to public housing authorities in FY 1985.) These programs include cash transfers to dependent families and the elderly poor, the earned income tax credit, and transfers-in-kind of food, housing, and energy assistance. Among these programs, only the cash

transfers to dependent families and the elderly poor were considered to be core social safety net programs. The administration's
initial objectives for these programs were to reduce the cash and
food assistance to those with incomes above the poverty line, to simplify administration, and to reduce the growth of subsidized housing.

Most of the 1981 proposals were approved, leading to small budget savings with little direct effect on the poor. Congress also allowed
the states to require work as a condition for AFDC and food stamps
(workfare), but only a few recipients were affected. As of 1983 only
six states had implemented workfare on a statewide basis, and only
a small percentage of AFDC recipients were engaged in training or
work. Congress was less receptive to the later administration proposals affecting these programs. As mentioned earlier, the 1982 proposal to assume full federal funding of Medicaid in exchange for
full state funding of AFDC and food stamps was not approved. Congress also rejected the administration proposals in each year from
1983 on to require participation of AFDC and food stamp recipients
in a national workfare program. A later proposal to exclude from
AFDC unmarried minor mothers and those whose youngest child is
sixteen or older was also rejected.

The administration's welfare policy—shaped primarily by Robert
Carleson, who had been Reagan's welfare director in California—
was a strange contrast with its supply-side approach to tax policy.
The welfare policy tried to reduce the effect of welfare on work
behavior by tightening the work requirements. At the same time, the
reduction in benefits for those with incomes above the poverty line
increased the effective marginal tax rates on the working poor, rates
that vary from 50 to 250 percent, thus reducing the incentive to
work. The net effect of increased (but ineffective) work requirements and higher marginal tax rates was probably to reduce the work
effort of the poor. The administration's welfare policy preserved the
safety net but weakened the ladder out of poverty. A major review
of federal welfare programs was conducted by the administration in
1986 but did not sort out these issues.

Education, Training, Employment, and Social Services
Spending for education, training, employment, and social services
was 5 percent of the FY 1981 budget. These welfare support services, most of which had been created in the prior fifteen years, were
a primary target of the efforts to reduce spending. Many of the proposed changes in these programs were approved, and total real
spending for these programs declined at a 7.8 percent annual rate;

welfare support services thus became one of the two major groups of programs for which real spending was reduced.

The initial proposals to change federal education programs were to consolidate a large number of categorical grants for primary and secondary education into two block grants and to tighten the income tests for college-student grants and loans. These proposals were largely approved and proved to be the last significant change in federal education policy during the Reagan administration. The 1982 proposal to abolish the Department of Education received no support, even though the creation of the department had been only narrowly approved a few years earlier. In 1983, proposals for a small tuition tax credit for primary and secondary education and a tax-free savings account for higher education were also rejected. The report of a presidential commission permitted the president to glide through the 1984 election talking about excellence in education without mentioning educational policy. The 1985 proposal to substitute a tuition voucher for direct support of the Headstart program for educationally disadvantaged children has yet to be approved. The several Reagan education proposals were quite creative, but the administration never quite sorted out whether it wanted to reduce or reform the federal government's role in education, and it accomplished little of either.

The major change in training and employment services was the replacement of the public service employment program (CETA) with a private employment assistance program (JTPA). CETA had a very poor record of placing young people in viable jobs and was one of the few programs the administration was able to terminate. The JTPA has a better record of job placement, but the results are difficult to evaluate because a broader population is eligible for this program. The later proposals to eliminate the work incentive program (WIN) for welfare recipients and the Job Corps were not approved.

In early 1983, after the economic recovery was underway, Congress passed the Emergency Jobs Act of 1983 over the opposition of the administration. During the first year of this program, federal spending of $3.1 billion created about 35,000 new jobs, about $87,500 per job created. As of June 1985 only about half of the money authorized for this emergency program had been spent, and the number of jobs supported declined to 10,000. The dismal record of this program was characteristic of most such "countercyclical" jobs programs. The cost per job was very high, and most of the money was spent long after the recession was over.

The only substantial change in social service programs was the consolidation of a number of categorical grants into a block grant, which reduced the total funding. The administration expected that the states would use the increased flexibility to focus assistance on the most needy, but a later study suggests that this may not have been the result.

The general effect of the changes in these programs was to reduce the level of both federal funding and federal control. The basic structure of these programs, however, was maintained. For better or for worse, these changes represented only a minor rollback of the many welfare support services financed by the federal government.

Farm Income Support

Spending for farm income and price supports was only about 1.5 percent of the FY 1981 budget but increased at a 19 percent real rate during the first term, thus becoming the most rapidly growing component of the budget. This increase in budget outlays does not include nearly $10 billion of commodities distributed to farmers in FY 1983 and FY 1984 as part of the payment-in-kind (PIK) program. Federal income and price supports were higher than total farm income in FY 1983 and almost as high in FY 1985, although most farmers did not receive such supports. One can hardly imagine a more disastrous policy outcome. Budget outlays for farm supports were about $60 billion during the first term. Although the cost of farm supports escalated rapidly, real farm income declined to its lowest level in the postwar years, and the average real price of farm land declined nearly 20 percent from 1981 to 1985. As of 1985 the annual cost of these programs to consumers and taxpayers was about $21 billion for benefits worth about $4 billion to the farm community. The primary effect of these supports was to maintain roughly the same total amount of resources in American farming, despite declining farm prices and exports—thus only deferring the day of reckoning.

How did this happen? The March 1981 budget proposed only a few small changes in farm programs, including the elimination of the dairy price increase scheduled for April 1, most of which were approved. Although the administration later made a more comprehensive proposal, the major farm legislation in 1981 was largely designed by the agricultural committees of Congress. This act increased the target prices and loan rates for the major supported crops without changing the basic structure of farm supports. (The target prices are the primary instrument for supporting farm income. Participating farmers are paid an amount equal to their output multiplied by the difference between the target price and the loan rate or market price, whichever is higher; these "deficiency payments" are limited to $50,000 per farm for most crops and $250,000 per farm for a few crops. As a rule, farmers must set aside about 10 percent of their acreage to participate in this program. The loan rates set a floor on prices. Farmers borrow on their crops at the loan rate; if the market price falls below the loan rate, farmers repay their loan by forfeiting their crop to the government rather than selling to the market. In turn, any forfeited crops are held in government storage until the market price is higher than the loan rate, or the crops are contributed to domestic or foreign food assistance programs.) The revised sugar program was designed to maintain the domestic sugar price, at no budget cost, by imposing quotas on imports. David Stockman agreed to this program, which would cost American consumers about $700 million a year, in exchange for a few "boll weevil" votes on the second 1981 budget resolution.

The only element of reform in the 1981 legislation was to grant the secretary of agriculture somewhat more flexibility in setting loan rates. The administration acquiesced to this legislation because it grossly underestimated its costs and because it needed the support of the farm-state Democrats on other issues. A few months later, for example, FY 1983 outlays for farm income and price supports were projected to be $2.9 billion; actual outlays turned out to be $22.9 billion plus nearly $10 billion of commodities distributed by the PIK program.

The 1981 farm legislation would not have created any major new problems if U.S. inflation had continued to be high and the dollar had continued to be weak. Although the administration had forecast the general direction of inflation and the dollar, no one anticipated how much these conditions would change. The combination of the increasing loan rates and the rapid increase in the foreign exchange value of the dollar led to a sharp reduction in U.S. farm exports in 1982, despite the 1981 termination of the U.S. embargo on grain exports to the Soviet Union. The administration faced a dilemma— a reduction in the loan rates was necessary to increase the quantity of farm products sold, especially in the export markets, but would increase the spread between the target price and the loan rate, and thus the budget outlays for deficiency payments.

The response to this dilemma was a program to restrict supply rather than increase demand. Farmers of supported crops were offered nearly $10 billion in commodities in 1983 and 1984 in exchange for commitments to reduce the acreage planted in these crops. About 55 million acres were temporarily retired in response to these PIK subsidies. One wag remarked that PIK was so attractive that God signed up, complementing the acreage reduction with a severe drought in 1983. The combined effect of PIK and the drought substantially reduced U.S. farm output in 1983 and budget outlays for farm supports in FY 1984. A special program to pay dairy farmers to reduce their production was implemented in 1984; there was no dollar ceiling on this temporary program's payments, and many dairies received payments of over $100,000. These measures, however, only deferred the problem of excess supply until after the 1984 election. Farm exports and real farm income declined sharply again in 1985.

The administration recognized that the basic structure of the farm program was seriously flawed. The rapid increase in farm supports was not enough to prevent a substantial decline in real farm income and land prices. The media focused attention on the increase in farm foreclosures without mentioning that the bankruptcy rate among farmers was not much different from other businesses of the same size. A part of the problem was that only one-quarter of direct support payments were made to financially distressed farms. Most of the benefits of these programs accrue indirectly to owners of farm land, many of whom are not farmers.

An interagency working group was formed in early 1984 to prepare an administration proposal for the renewal of farm legislation in 1985; deputy secretary of agriculture (and later secretary) Richard Lyng was chairman of this group. Several research institutes also conducted a major review of agriculture policy in tandem with the administration review. The general consensus of these groups was that farm supports should be phased out by the end of the decade, even at the expense of continued high near-term budget outlays to ease the transition to a market-oriented agriculture. The Lyng group developed a proposal with three major provisions. Loan rates would be reduced immediately, and the loans would be changed to standard recourse loans. The ceiling on deficiency payments per farm would be gradually reduced. A paid land diversion program would be substituted for the unpaid diversion that was a condition for receiving the deficiency payments. This proposal, I believed, represented a reasonable compromise of economics and politics, providing a basis for feasible reform.

In late 1984, shortly before this proposal was scheduled for cabinet review, Stockman substituted his own proposal. The proposal was prepared by Stockman and his agricultural aide Fred Khedouri and, as with Stockman's social security proposal of 1981, was designed for near-term budget savings rather than feasible reform. The key features of this proposal were to reduce sharply the ceiling on the deficiency payments per farm in the first year and to maintain the mandatory acreage reductions. This proposal was neither good economics nor good politics. After months of effort, Lyng was not allowed to report the recommendations of his group to the cabinet, and he soon left the government. The final administration proposal was based on the Stockman proposal, with a few minor concessions to agriculture secretary Jack Block. This was only one of many cases where Stockman ran roughshod over the domestic cabinet members. My participation in both the Lyng group and the budget review group led me to understand why loyal members of the cabinet were sometimes less than enthusiastic about supporting a budget or legislative proposal designed by OMB.

As should have been expected, Congress proceeded to draft its own farm bill, ignoring the administration's proposal. The Food Security Act of 1985 maintained the basic structure of most farm programs and a continued high level of budget outlays. The most beneficial change was a reduction of the loan rates on several major commodities, which will reduce prices and increase exports. Target prices are now frozen through 1988, after which they are scheduled to decline slowly. Outlays for farm supports were expected to be about $60 billion over the first three years, two and one-half times the amount proposed in the administration's FY 1986 budget. Actual outlays proved to be about $26 billion during the first year. Several provisions of the 1985 legislation are even worse than the 1981 law. The law provides $2 billion of export subsidies, most of the benefits of which will accrue to the Soviet Union and other grain importers. The sugar program requires progressively tighter quotas on sugar imports and imposes a special burden on such fragile economies as the Philippines. The dairy program pays farmers to slaughter their entire herd; the government purchases the meat under another program.

The president expressed particular concern about these three provisions, but he signed this bill in late December 1985. Another opportunity for reform was passed up so that a few Republican seats in the Senate could be preserved in the 1986 election. The U.S. farm program is still a scandal—raising the price of food to the hungry of the world, increasing the burden to U.S. taxpayers, and restricting the output of the world's most productive farmers.

Other Transfers and Services

Spending for other transfer and service programs was about 12 percent of the FY 1981 budget. These programs include the federal employee retirement and disability programs, special retirement and disability programs for railroad workers and coal miners, unemployment insurance, veterans' benefits, and a few other small programs. Most of these programs are either obligations from prior employment or were considered part of the core social safety net. These transfers and services are available only to specific groups and, in general, are independent of other income. Total real spending for these programs increased at a 1.2 percent rate during the first term.

The administration made a few proposals to change these programs, most of which were not approved. Several proposals were made to increase the employee contributions, reduce the income base, and change the cost-of-living adjustments for the civil service and military pensions, but Congress consistently rejected these proposals. Shortly before leaving government, Stockman strongly criticized the military pension system, a charge that was unjust only to the extent that he was not careful in distinguishing between the obligations to current retirees and employees and the case for changing this system for new entrants. A proposal to return the railroad pension system to the industry was rejected. A change to tighten the disability standards for the "black lung" program was approved. The 1981 proposal to limit extended-term unemployment benefits to states where the insured unemployment rate is high was approved, but the innovative 1983 proposal to allow those who receive federal supplemental compensation the option of an earnings voucher was rejected. The administration made no proposals for substantial change in the veterans' programs during the first term; the second-term proposal to limit medical care to those with service-connected disabilities or low incomes has not yet been approved.

The programs in this group receive little budget scrutiny because most of the budget for these programs is fixed in the short run. A budget director or member of Congress has little incentive to invest political capital in reforming these programs for budget savings that may not be realized for more than a decade. Total spending for these programs, however, is now about equal to interest payments and must be addressed at some time. These programs, like interest payments, are fixed costs in the short run and can be reduced only by long-term reform. The prospects are not encouraging.

General Government

Spending for the hundreds of other activities of the federal government, from space to revenue sharing (from the sublime to the ridiculous?), was about 14 percent of total outlays in FY 1981. The March 1981 budget of the new administration proposed to reduce the level of real spending for most of these programs. For the most part, that goal was achieved.

Figure 2.4 summarizes the level of real spending for these programs during the Carter administration and the proposed and actual outlays during the first term of the Reagan administration. As

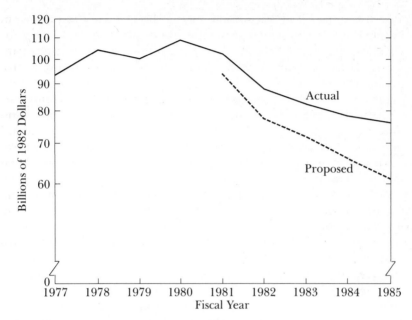

Figure 2.4   Real Outlays for General Government

the figure indicates, total real spending for these programs declined at a 7.2 percent annual rate during the first term after increasing slowly during the Carter administration. As will be seen, real spending for these programs was higher than first proposed primarily because of increases proposed by the Reagan administration. In some cases Congress reduced these programs more than the administration proposed. The substantial reductions in real spending for these programs was achieved with relatively little public notice or political controversy. Most of these reductions were achieved by squeezing personnel and reducing the number of new activities; few programs were terminated. Only the major changes in these programs deserve attention.

Science and Space
Science and space programs received progressively increased support from the Reagan administration. The initial position on these programs, however, was quite different. The March 1981 budget proposed to reduce or eliminate funding for science and engineering education, social science research, and most new science and space projects. Although Congress approved most of these cuts, the attitude of the administration changed quickly. The next administration

budget described "advances in science and technology [as] essential to the security of our nation; to the health, welfare, and safety of our citizens; and to the long-term growth and vitality of our economy" and proposed "a vigorous program of space activities." This new attitude prevailed, and real spending for science and space programs increased at a 2.5 percent annual rate during the first term.

The basis for this change in attitude, however, was probably more show business than substance. Every president (or his stage manager) since Kennedy has been enamored by the manned space program, which provides media events combining technology and heroism; it serves the same political purpose as war but at less cost. This was especially apparent in late 1984, when the White House was looking for some 1985 initiative to distract attention from the budget problem. A program to develop a space station was the result. A working group chaired by Craig Fuller, a young Meese aide, developed the proposal. In December this proposal was presented to the president at a cabinet meeting with little prior substantive review. The presentation was the crudest form of sales pitch, complete with models of the space station but without serious discussion of its missions or its cost. Some probing revealed that the scientific, industrial, and military communities each expressed little interest in the space station. Such comments were dismissed by several cabinet members as equivalent to the arguments made by those who rejected funding of the first voyage by Columbus. After a series of such sagacities, Stockman did not question the merits of the proposal but expressed the view that any major new program was inappropriate under the current budget conditions. The space station may prove to be worth its costs. I doubt it, but I do not know. The point is that the space station proposal served a political purpose that was independent of its substantive merits. (A similar consideration led to the 1986 proposal for a hypersonic transglobal aircraft and the 1987 proposal for a superconducting supercollider.) One wonders whether the political appeal of the space program will survive the 1986 explosion of the shuttle and the subsequent investigation. If not, what else might take its place?

Energy

The administration had a strangely mixed record on energy programs. The March 1981 budget proposed substantial reductions in these programs, and the next budget proposed abolishing the Department of Energy. Yet the administration first supported development of a breeder reactor and a commercial synthetic fuels industry, programs that were strongly supported by several key Senate Republicans. The congressional record was also mixed, protecting the older electric power subsidies but finally terminating the breeder reactor and the Synthetic Fuels Corporation. The strategic petroleum reserve was increased from 100 million barrels in 1980 to 500 million barrels in 1986, the only energy program to be substantially increased. The net result of these actions was to reverse the rapid increase in energy programs during the Carter administration and to reduce real spending at a 25 percent annual rate—a reduction that was much greater than that first proposed.

Transportation

The administration first proposed a substantial reduction of federal transportation programs. The March 1981 budget proposed a slower rate of highway spending, the elimination of financing for new urban rail transit systems, and an increase in user fees for airway and waterway services. The next budget proposed the elimination of federal highway aid, except for the interstate system, as part of the "new federalism" initiative. These proposals reflected the president's clear preferences and, except for the new federalism proposals, were repeated each year.

Drew Lewis, the first secretary of transportation, had other ideas, however. In 1981 and early 1982 he twice proposed an increase in highway spending and taxes, only to be rejected. As the recession dragged on into late 1982, Congress pressed for a major public works program as a "jobs bill." Although Reagan was very critical of such programs in a press conference on November 11, Lewis recognized an opportunity and made his move. He proposed to increase the federal gasoline tax from four to nine cents a gallon and to restructure some other taxes, increasing annual highway spending by $4 billion and urban transit spending by $1 billion, and he packaged this proposal with some phony estimates about job creation. (An increase in taxes to pay high-wage construction workers probably reduces total employment in the short run. In any case, as with most such "jobs" bills, the spending and employment effects would be realized only long after the recession was over.)

This proposal moved very quickly. Lewis and White House officials convinced Reagan that the highway proposal would probably head off a congressional jobs bill but could be presented as an "infrastructure" bill. (As it turned out, Congress also passed a separate emergency jobs act in early 1983). The president endorsed the highway proposal in a radio address on November 27 and submitted the proposal to Congress on November 30. With little review, this bill was approved by the House on December 7 and by the Senate on December 20. Drew Lewis resigned on December 27. In a few months it became clear that November was the trough of the recession and a strong recovery was underway. The president would not have approved this proposal had it been submitted three months before or after November 1982. In this case the president did not follow his own advice to "stay the course." As a consequence of this temporary lapse of budget discipline, federal spending for transportation at the end of the first term was almost exactly $5 billion more than first proposed. For reasons that I fail to understand, Lewis was one of those reported to be considered for the post of director of OMB after Stockman left in the summer of 1985, maybe because he knew how to manipulate the budget for political purposes.

Justice

The administration also reversed course on one other general government program, the administration of justice. The March 1981 budget proposed to fold the Legal Services Corporation and the Office of Juvenile Justice and Delinquency Prevention into a social services block grant—proposals that Congress would not approve—and to reduce other spending by a small amount. A rising concern about drugs, immigration, and terrorism, however, led to a general increase in federal enforcement activities with little controversy. Real spending for these programs increased at a 2.2 percent annual rate during the first term.

General-Purpose Fiscal Assistance

One of the more bizarre federal activities was the $5 billion general revenue-sharing program. This program, enacted in 1972, provided payments to state and local governments with no strings attached. State governments were eliminated from this program in 1981. One initial rationalization for this program was to redistribute what was expected to be a consistent federal surplus in order to prevent "fiscal drag." In every year after this program was enacted, however, the federal budget had a deficit, and the total budget of state and local governments had a surplus; in effect, the federal government borrowed money to give to governments with a surplus, without any condition that would lead this money to be used for a national purpose. The continuing support for this program was primarily from the mayors, who valued some discretionary funds for which they were not accountable to either the federal government or their own voters. President Reagan, as a former governor, was sympathetic to the view of state and local officials and resisted the first Stockman proposals to terminate this program. The administration's FY 1986 budget, however, proposed to terminate this program in 1986, one year before the authorization expired. Congress responded, with little controversy, by agreeing to terminate this program in 1987. A last-minute attempt to save this program in 1986 was not successful. This proved to be the only major federal program that was completely terminated in response to a Reagan proposal. One small step!

Other General Government Programs

The real spending for each of the other general government programs was reduced with little controversy. The budget for natural resource programs was reduced at a 5 percent real annual rate, primarily by reducing the grants for sewer construction, reducing new water projects and land acquisition, and increasing user fees. Western senators, most of them Republican, were the major opponents of larger cuts in these programs. Real spending for commerce and housing credits was reduced at a 19 percent annual rate in the first term. The administration's persistent proposals to reduce or terminate the small business credit programs, however, were not approved. Real spending for community and regional development programs was reduced at a 12 percent annual rate, but the second-term proposals to terminate some of these programs were not approved. The general response of Congress to the administration's proposals for budget reduction was to approve most of the reductions short of terminating the programs. The basic structure of most of the programs and the agencies that were the focus of the budget cuts is still intact. The "Great Society," a state of mind that spanned the Johnson and Nixon administrations, is down but not out.

Other Spending

The rest of the federal budget is the net of interest payments and undistributed offsetting receipts, an amount equal to 6 percent of total spending in FY 1981. Figure 2.5 illustrates the level of real net spending for this component during the Carter administration and the proposed and actual outlays during the first term of the Reagan administration.

Interest Payments

As a consequence of the huge increase in the deficit, interest payments became the most rapidly growing major component of the budget. The deficit was thus both the result and a major cause of the growth of total spending. Interest payments increased about $15 billion a year during the first term despite a substantial decline in interest rates, an amount that dwarfs the annual savings from program reductions. A substantial reduction in program spending every year, with all the consequent political problems, has become necessary to prevent an increase in the deficit. In the absence of either

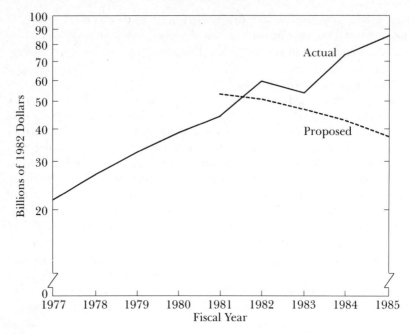

Figure 2.5   Real Interest Payments Minus Offsetting Receipts

continued budget restraint or strong economic growth, the deficit will build on itself. One should not be surprised that David Stockman became an advocate of tax increases, once Congress began to resist the proposals to reduce program spending. (Chapter 3 explores this issue in greater detail.)

Offsetting Receipts

The final category of undistributed offsetting receipts includes the government agency share of employee retirement outlays, interest receipts from the trust funds, rents and royalties from the outer continental shelf, and receipts from the sale of government property. The administration expected a substantial increase in these offsetting receipts from a proposed expansion of offshore oil leasing and property sales. In fact, the real level of these offsetting receipts declined. Congress did not approve the proposed expansion of offshore leases, and the decline in oil prices reduced the receipts from the existing leases. The property sales program, like a similar program in the Nixon administration, floundered for lack of any change in agency incentives and was later terminated. The decision to terminate this program was made by Ed Meese after reviewing a staff paper that recommended sale of eight valuable parcels in California. A similar fate probably awaits the second-term proposals to sell the naval petroleum reserves and the power marketing administrations. There is a good case for selling or even giving away a substantial amount of federal real estate and other assets, primarily because these assets are more valuable in other uses. The Reagan property initiatives, however, failed for lack of continued high-level support or a creative sales strategy. During this same period, for comparison, Prime Minister Thatcher's government in Britain successfully "privatized" a substantial part of Britain's nationalized industries and public housing.

CROSS-PROGRAM THEMES

As candidate and president, Reagan said very little about reducing spending for specific government programs, and most of the program content of the administration's spending policy was developed by Stockman. Several cross-program themes, however, were vintage Reagan.

The War on Waste

A reduction of "waste, fraud, extravagance, and abuse" was the 1980 solution to financing the combination of a defense buildup and a major tax cut. An increase in economic growth was the 1984 solution. These campaign themes were sufficient to diffuse or defer attention to the budget, but both proved to be illusory solutions to the central fiscal problem of the Reagan administration.

There is plenty of waste in the federal budget, maybe as much as the huge deficit. Some of this waste is additional spending beyond that necessary to provide the current level of a government service. Some of this waste is due to a service level that is higher than would be supported by the majority of an informed electorate. A small part of this waste is a consequence of fraud and, possibly, of extravagance and abuse, although the intended meanings of these latter two terms were never quite clear. Most waste in the federal budget, however, is there for the same reason the programs are there—because someone benefits from it. Most waste is due to behavior that is neither illegal nor venal but rather the result of the incentives faced by bureaucrats and politicians. Bureaucrats learn quickly that "whistle blowers" are more likely to be reassigned than promoted. Members of Congress are often more concerned about maintaining federal offices, installations, and contracts in their districts than in reducing waste. (I learned this lesson the hard way. A few months into my first federal position, my boss was summoned to a congressional hearing because I had tried to close thirty radar stations that the Air Force had identified as redundant.) Moreover, waste is often more difficult to reduce than the program level, because those who benefit from waste are sometimes more concentrated and vocal than those who benefit from the program. In the language of economics, efficiency in government is a "public good," a condition that all value but few have any private incentive to achieve.

Republicans are especially prone to believe that applying business methods to government will reduce waste, even without changing the basic system of incentives and constraints in government. The Reagan war on waste was more comprehensive but not much more effective than similar prior efforts. A Council on Integrity and Efficiency was formed in March 1981 to coordinate the investigations of fraud. Directives were issued in April 1981 to reduce spending on publications, travel, and consulting and to institute new debt collection procedures. Targets were later established to reduce federal employment in the civilian agencies by 75,000 and to reduce the amount of office space per employee. In September 1982 a cabinet council on management and administration, chaired by Ed Meese, was formed to provide general policy guidance, and a long-term project called Reform 88, led by OMB deputy director Joe Wright, was launched to implement and monitor the management improvement program.

In parallel with the internal management review, the President's Private Sector Survey on Cost Control, popularly called the "Grace Commission" after its chairman, J. Peter Grace, was created in June 1982. The extensive survey of wasteful federal programs and practices involved the participation of a large number of volunteer business executives and led to more than forty reports and nearly 2,500 recommendations.

It is easy to be skeptical about this entire exercise, but one should not be cynical. The primary promoter of the management improvement program was presidential counsellor Ed Meese, who could not set priorities or manage his own in-box. Meese was convinced that the president was very interested in this program and scheduled a progress report with the cabinet and president several times a year. A favorite activity was a reading of the list of federal publications most recently terminated. These meetings were like the reports of a savings bond campaign, in which the president was expected to comment favorably on the progress to date and to encourage other agencies to meet their goals. I never observed the president to sleep during a cabinet meeting, but it was a close call at these meetings; others were less careful in maintaining the appearance of attention.

The primary problem of this exercise was that its success was dependent on information and exhortation; there were no changes in the
incentives and constraints faced by individual managers. Agencies
that met their targets were not rewarded, and those (such as Defense) which ignored the exercise were not sanctioned.

The reports of the Grace Commission were also subject to some
criticism. Some of the savings estimates were larger than could be
verified. The estimate of total potential savings added large savings
sometime in the next century to small near-term savings. Many of
the recommendations involved issues in which it is difficult to distinguish waste from the objectives of Congress. The primary benefits
of the Grace Commission were the listing of many federal activities
for which the value is probably lower than the cost to most voters
and the education of many able businessmen in the grubby details
of the federal budget.

The achievements of this program should be recognized but put
in context. During the first term about $46 billion was "put to better
use," to use the careful language of the government's management
report (the net saving from these activities has not been estimated);
federal employment in civilian agencies was reduced by 78,000; the
number of federal publications was reduced by 25 percent; annual
travel costs were reduced by about $500 million; and the govern-
ment's cash management accounting systems were substantially improved. The administration claims to have adopted 70 percent of
the recommendations of the Grace Commission. This was no mean
achievement, and the many conscientious people responsible for these
improvements deserve credit. For context, however, one should recognize the following: the $46 billion "put to better use" was about
1.4 percent of total outlays during this period. The reduction in employment in the civilian agencies was more than offset by the increase of civilian employment in the Department of Defense. In
summary, the management improvements initiated by the Reagan
administration deserve to be continued and expanded. At the same
time one should not expect such improvements to have much effect
on total federal spending.

A "New Federalism"

The federal budget includes about $100 billion of grants-in-aid to
state and local governments. The Reagan administration made two
quite different proposals to change the fiscal relations between the
federal government and these other levels of government.

The March 1981 budget proposed to consolidate a larger number
of categorical grants for community development, education, health

services, job training, and social services into a smaller number of
block grants. The direct effect of these proposals was to reduce total
real federal grants by about 10 percent and to increase substantially
the authority of state and local officials to allocate these funds as
they choose. These proposals seemed to serve the interests of both
federal taxpayers and state and local officials, and most were approved in 1981 or 1982. A total of sixty-two categorical grants were
consolidated into ten block grants.

There is reason to question, however, whether federal grants without (many) federal strings serve any national purpose. The available
studies indicate that such block grants increase expenditure by the
receiving government by about forty-three cents per dollar of the
grant, and as much as eighty-five cents for education grants. The
remainder of the grant appears to be used to reduce state and local
taxes or borrowing. In contrast, expenditure by state and local governments increases by about ten cents for each additional dollar of
personal income in the state. The additional state and local spending
induced by federal grants, however, is a waste unless such additional
spending provides services that are valued outside the receiving ju-
risdiction. For federal grants to serve a national purpose, some continuing federal control is probably necessary to induce state and local officials to serve this purpose. Any federal grant for which no
controls are believed necessary should be considered a candidate for
elimination. Robert Carleson and the other White House officials
who designed the block grant proposals recognized this point but
defended the block grants as temporary measures, pending a more
thorough sorting-out of government roles in our federal system.

As it turned out, a temporary measure is all they got. In early
1982 President Reagan proposed a comprehensive transfer of programs and funding sources between the federal government and the
states. This proposal was hurriedly designed by an ad hoc group
headed by Rich Williamson, a young White House aide, but the proposal reflected long-held Reagan convictions. First, the federal government would assume full responsibility for the Medicaid program
in exchange for state assumption of the AFDC and food stamp programs. Second, the federal government would transfer more than
forty programs providing local services to the states. For a four-year
period the states would continue to receive funding from a $28 bil-
lion transition fund financed by federal excise taxes, whether or not
they chose to continue these programs. Over the next four-year period the federal taxes dedicated to this fund would be phased out,
and the states would have full fiscal responsibility for whichever of
these programs they chose to maintain.

This proposal was somewhat crudely designed and was prepared too late to be incorporated in the proposed FY 1983 budget. It was the one truly revolutionary proposal in the Reagan economic program, but it proved to have a constituency of one—the president. This proposal received no support from state and local officials because they preferred federal money, especially in the form of block grants, to raising additional funds from their own voters. The proposal also received no support in Congress, which preferred the illusion of doing good with federal money to confronting colleagues and potential opponents in the state capitals. For these reasons the proposal died as quickly as it was formulated and was not renewed.

Privatization

The primary case for selling some federal assets and activities is that they are likely to be better managed by the private sector. The federal government, for example, is a poor manager of its large loan portfolio, now over $250 billion at par value. A large part of the 770 million acres of federal land is underutilized. There is no obvious reason to maintain such a huge gold reserve or the naval petroleum reserve, both of which generate no returns. Major federal activities such as the Postal Service, the air traffic control system, Conrail and Amtrack, and the power marketing administrations are likely to be better managed by the private sector.

During the first term, however, the administration's privatization effort was very limited and generally unsuccessful. The land sales program floundered for lack of agency incentives and was terminated by Ed Meese for political reasons. The initial effort to sell Conrail to another rail company was opposed by the Conrail management and employees and was stopped by Congress.

Approval of the Gramm-Rudman act in late 1985, however, created a somewhat artificial incentive for both the administration and Congress to sell federal assets in order to meet the annual deficit targets. Such sales, however, should not be justified primarily for budgetary purposes. The sale of income-producing assets, in contrast with a spending reduction or tax increase, reduces the deficit only in the year of sale and does not increase national saving. The pressure to meet the annual deficit targets, however, strengthened the political incentive for some asset sales.

Congress approved the sale of Conrail in 1986 but only after the administration acquiesced to a public offering of the Conrail stock rather than the sale to another rail company. Although Congress was not receptive to several other proposed asset sales, the administration broadened its privatization program in 1987. The major initiatives in the proposed FY 1988 budget included the sale of Amtrack, the naval petroleum reserves, the power marketing administrations, the unassigned portion of the frequency spectrum, the helium operations, a small amount of real estate, and a small proportion of the loan portfolio. At the same time, however, the administration proposed a substantial increase in funding for the air traffic control system, without considering several private proposals to sell this system. My judgment is that most of these privatization proposals will be rejected by Congress, despite the pressure to meet the deficit targets. The case for selling such assets and activities is efficiency, not budget control, and will be accepted only if Congress is somehow motivated to be more concerned about efficiency issues.

User Fees and Cost Sharing

Each year the president's budget proposed higher user fees for federal services provided to specific groups. The March 1981 budget proposed new or higher fees for users of airways, ports, and inland waterways; Coast Guard emergency services; federal recreation areas; and nuclear waste disposal sites. By 1985 the list of proposed fees had expanded to include fees for the origination of loans and loan guarantees, custom services, meat inspection, and special services provided by the IRS. The sum of these fees would have yielded $3 to 4 billion a year, but the additional revenue was not the primary issue. Stockman pressed for these fees primarily to demonstrate a balanced sense of fairness—by reducing the subsidies to higher income groups and business users of federal services—and to reduce the growth in the demand for these services. None of these proposals have yet been approved. Few lobbies proved more effective in protecting their subsidies than the owners of private planes and boats—other, perhaps, than the users of subsidized electric power.

Late in the summer of 1982 I was asked to chair an interagency group to address the pricing policies of the federal power marketing administrations. This group met once and prepared one set of papers limited to summarizing current policies. After Congress was informed of this activity by a public-power lobbyist, I was summoned by a group of congressmen to the Rayburn House Office Building for what turned out to be a star chamber proceeding staged for their local television in the Tennessee Valley and the Northwest. Democratic Congressman (now Senator) Al Gore was the chief inquisitor. The general thrust of their tirade was that the residents of these regions had a property right to continued federal power subsidies and, among other charges, that my proposal (which had yet to be formulated) would take bread from the tables of widows. Some of the more temperate members took me aside after this proceeding and counseled me not to be angered by this display of preelection posturing. As it turned out, this was more than posturing. Republican Senators James McClure and Mark Hatfield introduced amendments to the FY 1984 appropriations for the executive office to prohibit any expenditure of federal funds to study this issue. For some time I was not allowed to think on the job about this issue. The administration decided not to raise the power pricing issue again. In 1986 and 1987, however, the administration proposed to sell the power marketing administrations—a proposal that will probably meet a similar fate.

Similarly, the administration regularly proposed concurrent cost sharing for the construction of federal water resource projects. Although local governments and private sponsors of these projects have long demonstrated a willingness to pay a higher share of these costs, approval of general cost-sharing rules was delayed until 1986. At one stage, Interior Secretary James Watts scuttled an agreement worked out by the Corps of Engineers because projects proposed by the Bureau of Reclamation would have been threatened. In the meantime the federal government continues to subsidize the provision of water to grow subsidized crops for a population that is trying to diet.

Off-Budget Instruments

The bottom line for the director of OMB is total federal outlays. Any director is tempted to seek ways to respond to political pressure by means that do not increase total outlays, even if these other means impose a larger cost on the economy. Stockman used this technique on several occasions, despite his general commitment to presenting the cost of all federal activities in the budget. The most damaging example was his 1981 commitment to maintaining the domestic price of sugar by import restraints to avoid any government purchase of sugar. Another example was his 1985 proposal to replace direct loans by the Export-Import Bank with loan guarantees. In general, however, Stockman deserves credit for reducing the amount of off-budget credit programs.

Most administrations learn to appoint presidential commissions to register concern about some current issue without making a commitment. The Reagan administration was unusually successful with this technique. Commissions on education and housing provided effective cover for a substantial reduction in real federal spending for these programs. A commission on international competitiveness was effective in deferring pressure for some form of industrial policy. In this sense these commissions were very valuable, although most of the final reports are not worth reading. The report of the housing commission, however, was unusually good. The administration conducted an organized review of the reports of each of these commissions, but these reviews had no identifiable effect on policies. The political purpose of these commissions—to buy time, not information—had already been served.

THE BUDGET PROCESS

Congressional Action

There was growing dissatisfaction with the congressional budget process during the Carter administration, and there was considerable doubt as to whether it could accommodate the Reagan budget proposals. As prescribed by the Congressional Budget Act of 1974, Congress was scheduled to approve a first budget resolution by May 15, setting targets for total receipts and for budget authority and outlays, in total and by nineteen functional categories, over three years. The various committees would then approve the tax and budget legislation, with initial action in the House, without being bound by the first resolution. A second budget resolution, scheduled to be approved by September 15, would then set a floor on total receipts and a ceiling on budget authority and outlays. This process worked moderately well only when spending for most programs was increasing, because the number of hard choices was reduced. The combination of a defense buildup and an effort to restrain other spending beginning in 1979, however, challenged this process. These fiscal strains caused increasing tension between the new budget committees and the established authorizing and appropriation committees. Approval of the budget measures was seldom on schedule, and actual outlays were substantially higher than the target outlays in the first resolution. This presented an unpromising prospect for the more ambitious budget proposals of the new Reagan administration.

Stockman's path through this maze was an obscure provision of the budget act that permitted the budget resolution to direct the various committees to report changes in legislation necessary to meet the budget targets. These changes would then be compiled in an omnibus "reconciliation" bill. (This process had also been used in 1980, but only after Carter was forced to submit a second budget for FY 1981.) The administration's tactics for gaining approval of most of its March 1981 budget proposal involved a fascinating political drama. As a rule the House and Senate budget committees independently develop a first budget resolution and then compromise on a concurrent resolution. This might have led to a satisfactory outcome, because the resolution drafted by House budget chairman Jim Jones incorporated 75 percent or so of the administration's proposals. The White House, however, was in no mood to compromise. Stockman orchestrated the submission of a substitute House budget resolution offered by Phil Gramm of Texas and Delbert Latta of Ohio. Gramm, an economist and prior collaborator with Stockman, was the youngest Democrat on the House budget committee. Latta was the senior Republican on this committee. After intensive lobbying by the administration, the Gramm-Latta version of the budget resolution was approved on May 7 by a large margin, and the Senate approved a nearly identical resolution on May 12.

A second unusual tactic, however, was necessary to sustain this victory. The House committees were developing legislation that departed substantially from the ceilings set by the first budget resolution. House Republicans could have blocked these bills one at a time by a point of order, but this risked an indefinite delay on the budget and a threat to the tax bill. The White House decided to challenge the Democratic leadership again by offering a substitute omnibus reconciliation bill, called Gramm-Latta II. Somewhat more compromise with conservative Democrats was necessary to retain their support, but this bill passed by a comfortable margin on June 26. After approval of the tax bill on July 29, the second budget resolution endorsed the totals set by the first resolution and was approved without controversy.

The administration never again had the votes to challenge the House Democratic leadership on a major budget issue as it did on the two Gramm-Latta bills in 1981. In subsequent years the initial bargaining over the budget was between the administration and the Senate Republicans, with the House waiting until it saw the shape of the Senate resolution. Other features of the 1981 process, however, set a pattern for some years. For the entire first term the first budget resolution led to a reconciliation directive. The second resolution became a dead letter. Since 1982 the first resolution has included a provision that maintains the targets set in that resolution unless a second resolution is adopted by October 1.

An increasing concern that the budget process permitted spending decisions to be independent of expected tax receipts led to several interesting congressional proposals. In 1983 the Senate considered a proposal by William Armstrong, a Republican from Colorado, and Russell Long, the veteran Democrat from Louisiana, to authorize the president to reduce outlays if the debt limit would otherwise be exceeded; this proposal was only narrowly defeated. In 1984 the House approved the concept, but not the procedures, of a "pay-as-you-go" policy that would require an increase in expected receipts if any spending measure led total outlays to exceed target outlays. The common element of these proposals was that additional spending should not be financed by increased borrowing; that is, the deficit should not be open-ended. The Senate would have limited the deficit by reducing spending, the House by increasing taxes. The stage was set for a substantial change in the budget process.

In 1985 the Reagan administration submitted its second "house-cleaning" budget, proposing to eliminate more than a dozen domestic programs and to substantially reduce other domestic programs. The budget, however, proposed another large increase in defense spending. The congressional consensus that had approved the first housecleaning budget and defense increase in 1981 had clearly disappeared. Senate Republicans offered a compromise budget, including a one-year freeze in the social security cost-of-living allowance and some small tax increases. The White House first expressed interest in this proposal. In July, however, any prospect of a grand compromise was ended when Don Regan made a deal with House Democrats that there would be no changes in social security or taxes, thereby blindsiding the Senate Republican leadership. For the first time in six years, there was no reconciliation directive. Congress terminated only one domestic program (general revenue sharing), made minor reductions in other domestic programs, and, for the first time in many years, reduced the budget authority for defense. The result was a total outlay level that was slightly higher in the first year but slightly lower in later years than that proposed by the administration. Unless the administration's optimistic economic forecasts (which, for various reasons, I had not challenged) were realized, however, the deficit would decline only slowly. Stockman resigned in July, and there was no sense of direction about future budgets.

Phil Gramm, after switching parties and being elected to the Senate in 1984, recognized an opportunity. In August and early September, when most of Washington was on vacation, Gramm worked with the OMB staff, apparently without knowledge of the White House, to develop a procedure to force action that would progressively reduce the deficit. Gramm's proposal was co-sponsored by Warren Rudman, a young Republican senator from New Hampshire, and Fritz Hollings, the respected Democratic senator from South Carolina, and quickly gained momentum. The White House endorsed the proposal early without a clear sense of its potential effects. The general features of this proposal were the following:

- The target deficit will be reduced in equal increments until it is eliminated in FY 1991.
- In August of each year OMB and CBO will estimate the projected deficit for the next fiscal year on the basis of revised forecasts and the congressional action to date. If the projected deficit is more than $10 billion above the target, the entire amount of the excess must be cut.
- In September Congress will have a final opportunity to reduce spending or increase taxes to eliminate the excess deficit.

And, most important:

- In October, if the projected deficit is still more than $10 billion higher than the target, spending for other than excluded programs will be reduced proportionately by the full amount of the excess deficit.

The primary controversy about this proposal concerned the list of programs that would be excluded from the proportionate cuts. As it worked out, about 48 percent of the budget, from social security through the wool subsidies, would be exempt from the automatic cuts, about 24 percent of the budget would be subject to only small cuts, and only about 28 percent of the budget would be subject to the full proportionate cuts. The administration would have been less enthusiastic about this process had it realized that about half of any automatic cuts would be borne by defense. After these exclusions were resolved, this proposal moved quickly, and the Balanced Budget and Emergency Deficit Control Act was attached to the debt ceiling bill and signed into law on December 12. This act is popularly known as the Gramm-Rudman-Hollings Act or, more frequently (to the consternation of Fritz Hollings), as the Gramm-Rudman Act.

This act had not yet been approved before people began to look for ways to evade it. The most obvious, a constitutional challenge, was anticipated by the authors. The act provided both an expedited procedure for court review and a fallback procedure if the automatic cuts were prohibited. A federal appeals court, with support from the Justice Department, ruled that the minor role of the Controller General was unconstitutional on the basis of the technical condition that he cannot be removed by the president. The Supreme Court affirmed this position in July 1986. The primary effect of this ruling was to substitute a congressional vote for a finding by the Controller General to trigger the proportionate cuts. The other provisions of the act survived this challenge.

There was reason to be cynical about Gramm-Rudman, because

Congress was binding itself to take actions in 1986 and beyond that it refused to take in 1985. There was also reason to be skeptical about whether the act would improve congressional incentives; the defenders of threatened programs, in particular, may have an incentive to force the broader proportionate cuts to avoid a larger selective reduction of these programs. The early record under Gramm-Rudman was mixed. The special schedule and provisions for FY 1986 worked without any significant problems. The one exception was a clever "Washington Monument" game by the Library of Congress, which, by reducing its public hours by a disproportionate amount, induced the usual cries about fiscal philistines. Congress, however, was more than two months late in approving the first resolution for the FY 1987 budget. Following optimistic revenue forecasts by both OMB and CBO, Congress was required to reduce the projected FY 1987 deficit by only $10 billion or so to avoid the automatic cuts. To its credit, Congress did not count the temporary revenue increase in the 1986 tax bill to meet this target. The measures approved to meet the FY 1987 target, however, were somewhat fraudulent. These measures included a combination of asset sales, pulling forward the final general revenue-sharing payments into FY 1986, and estimating increased revenues from tighter IRS enforcement—but no significant budget cuts. The measures made no substantial contribution to meeting the deficit targets in later years. The primary effect of the Gramm-Rudman process was to reduce the growth of real federal spending from FY 1986 through FY 1988. The actual deficit in FY 1989 and later, however, is likely to be up to $100 billion higher than the deficit targets.

My judgment of this act was first expressed by Senator Rudman: "Gramm-Rudman is a bad idea whose time has come." For those of us who maintain a residual civics-textbook perspective on our representatives, who are meant to be debating the great issues of the day, this act is presumably not the way the budget process should operate. The current budget process, however, does not work well either; most importantly, it has failed to make congressional preferences on individual programs consistent with preferences on the budget totals. Norman Ornstein, a Washington political scientist, may have made the best case for Gramm-Rudman by saying that "it takes all the fun out of being a legislator." So be it! Congress will no longer be able to increase spending for one program without reducing spending for other programs or increasing taxes, as long as this law is in place. My guess is that Gramm-Rudman will have a substantial effect on the deficit for a year or two. However, I expect that Congress will repeal, substantially change, or evade the deficit targets before approving the FY 1988 budget. Gramm-Rudman was not a

bad start, however, in reversing the major adverse legacy of Reaganomics.

Executive Action

David Stockman was the major change in the executive budget process. Stockman swarmed over the domestic budget, mastering the
details, badgering the agencies, and making his own deals with Congress. The government probably cannot sustain such a centralization
of the budget process for very long, because cabinet members and
agency heads have little incentive to defend a budget to which they
make no significant contribution. Jim Miller, Stockman's successor,
appears to share most of Stockman's objectives, but his laid-back
Georgia style is more sustainable than Stockman's frenetic activity. It
is not obvious which style is more effective.

Despite the administration's ambitious budget agenda, the president used the veto only rarely on spending bills. He vetoed several
supplementary appropriation bills and one continuing resolution
during the first term, but his first veto of a regular appropriation
bill was in the fall of 1985. My understanding was that Reagan's rare
use of the veto was to protect deals that Stockman had already made,
but only someone much closer to the president could confirm this.
Stockman, however, later revealed that he had recommended a veto
on several bills that the president signed. Reagan, borrowing a line
from Clint Eastwood, often challenged Congress to "make my day"
concerning increased taxes but not increased spending.

The executive branch lost one budget power in the first term. The
Impoundment Control Act of 1974 permitted the president to defer
specific expenditures unless overridden by a majority vote of either
house. Since court decisions in 1983 and 1986, which ruled that any
form of legislative veto is unconstitutional, both spending deferrals
and rescissions must be approved by a new bill subject to the normal
process. In effect, appropriations are both a ceiling and a floor on
allowed expenditures. The current law severely restricts the president's authority to reduce expenditures for any purpose, including
obvious waste and changed conditions.

Proposed Changes

Partly because of his experience as governor of California, President
Reagan regularly pressed for several changes in the federal budget
process. In 1982 two taxpayer groups joined to promote a federal
constitutional limit on both borrowing and taxation. One of these
groups had encouraged state legislatures to call for a constitutional

convention to draft a federal balanced budget amendment. The other group, of which I was a founder, had promoted state constitutional tax limits, beginning with that proposed by Governor Reagan in California in 1973. The proposed amendment to the federal constitution promoted by these groups in 1982 would have required a special majority of Congress to approve a budget with an expected deficit or an increase in the federal tax share of national income. This proposed amendment was strongly supported by the president, was approved by more than two-thirds of the Senate, and received the votes of a majority, but less than the required two-thirds, of the House. After thirty-two of the required thirty-four states had approved resolutions calling for a constitutional convention for this purpose, a similar amendment was reintroduced in the Senate in 1986. This version of the amendment, with a stronger balanced budget provision and a weaker tax limit provision, was defeated in the Senate by one vote in late March. These proposed amendments were consistently opposed by the Democratic leadership and the establishment press. In 1986, in addition, several senators expressed the view that a statutory approach such as Gramm-Rudman should be tried before approving a constitutional amendment for ratification by the states. This amendment is likely to be considered again only after support from additional state legislatures and the apparent failure of Gramm-Rudman.

The president also requested authority, beginning in 1984, for a line-item veto. Such authority, now granted to the governors of forty-three states, would permit the president to veto individual items in an appropriation bill rather than face an all-or-nothing choice on these bills. The available evidence suggests that a line-item veto would not significantly reduce total spending but would strengthen the power of the president over the composition of spending. That effect, of course, is just why Congress is reluctant to grant the president such authority, even though it has approved this budget management tool for the governors of the trust territories and Puerto Rico and for the mayor of the District of Columbia. The congressional power to package appropriation bills is Congress' primary instrument for protecting regional and sectoral programs and activities and will not be relinquished lightly. A limited proposal by Sen. Mack Mattingly, Republican of Georgia, to grant the president statutory authority for a line-item veto for a trial period was defeated in 1985 by a broad bipartisan coalition.

In 1986 Reagan also urged Congress to consider three other measures. He proposed that the budget resolution in future years be changed to a joint resolution subject to presidential approval, with binding expenditure categories within the budget totals. He also urged that Congress consider proposals for multi-year appropriations and a capital budget. During the State of the Union Address, he turned to ask Speaker O'Neill, in his final year in Congress, to cooperate in reforming the creaky federal budget process. O'Neill may have preferred the complexities or the outcomes of this process, however, as no action has been taken on these proposals to date.

Surely we can do better. On balance, however, one should probably not expect too much from changes in the budget process. After many years of observing this process, Alice Rivlin, the first director of the Congressional Budget Office, concluded:

> Our current problems are not primarily procedural. The budgeting process is complex and time consuming primarily because the federal government does so many different kinds of things, and because Congress is so reluctant to concentrate on major directions of policy while leaving the details to executive departments or state and local governments. We can simplify the budget process only by simplifying the government itself and changing the role of Congress. We can make the budget process less time consuming only if we are willing to make decisions less often, or to give up some checks and balances. Moreover, the world is an unpredictable place, and while we could perhaps handle predictability better than we do, no procedural change can eliminate it. Nor does the failure to make the hard decisions necessary to bring budget deficits down reflect biases built into our budget making procedures. It is simply a failure of political will and national leadership which an alternative set of procedures will not remedy.

Rivlin's observations are a counsel of despair only for those who believe that a complex government can be run by simple political processes. For the rest of us these observations are a cautionary warning that we must learn either to live with complexity, waste, arbitrariness, and the other characteristics of big government or to reduce the scale and scope of government to fit our political institutions.

CHAPTER THREE

Taxes and the Deficit

A series of proposals to reduce personal income tax rates by 10 percent a year over three years and to create jobs by accelerating depreciation for business investment in plant and equipment.

The reduction in tax rates on personal income was the most substantial change and the major achievement of the initial Reagan economic program. The main features of the initial proposal were approved by Congress in 1981 and survived subsequent changes in federal tax law in each of the next three years. The tax reform approved in 1986 further reduced individual income tax rates, with the top rate now less than half that in 1980. For the most part the *structure* of the federal tax code is now simpler, fairer, and of lower cost to the economy than in 1981. Moreover, for all these changes, total federal tax receipts as a share of GNP are now only slightly lower than during the Carter administration or than the initial Reagan projections. These changes were designed to increase after-tax rewards for work, saving, and investment. As will be explained in Chapter 7, however, they have also had some substantial unanticipated effects on the U.S. and world economy.

THE LEVEL AND COMPOSITION OF FEDERAL TAX RECEIPTS

For two decades prior to the Reagan administration, federal tax receipts averaged about 19 percent of GNP with little variation. During the Carter administration, however, the combination of rising inflation and increasing social security taxes increased the federal tax share of GNP from 19.1 percent to 20.8 percent, and the last Carter budget projected that this share would increase to 24 percent in fiscal year 1986 without a tax reduction. (For comparison, the record federal tax share of GNP was 21.7 percent in FY 1944, the year of peak war spending.) The combined effect of the several Reagan tax measures was to maintain the federal tax share of GNP at about 19

71

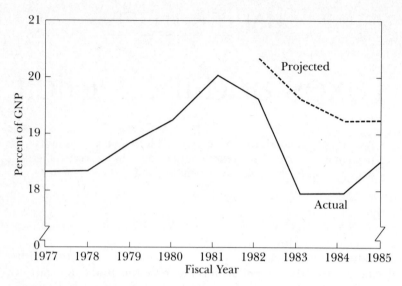

Figure 3.1 Total Federal Tax Receipts as Share of GNP

Figure 3.2 Federal Tax Receipts by Type as Share of GNP

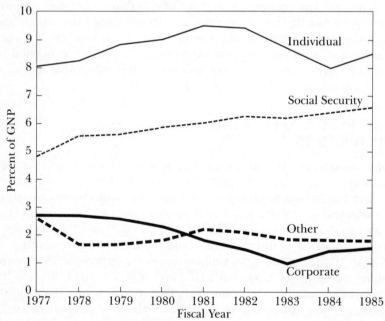

percent. Figure 3.1 illustrates the pattern of total tax receipts as a share of GNP during the Carter administration and the projected and actual receipts share during the Reagan administration through FY 1985.

As the supply-siders correctly remind us, however, total tax receipts do not provide much useful information about the effects of taxes on the economy. More information is provided by the receipts' share of GNP from the major types of federal taxes. Receipts from the individual and corporate income tax were reduced by the 1981 legislation. Subsequent changes reversed part of the 1981 changes affecting corporations and increased the receipts from the social insurance taxes and from excises. Figure 3.2 illustrates these patterns. An understanding of whether these patterns reflect a desirable change must be based, however, on a more detailed understanding of the specific changes in the tax code.

TAX PROPOSALS AND CHANGES DURING THE FIRST TERM

Tax Legislation in 1981

The initial Reagan tax proposal was quite simple. The proposed changes in the individual income tax were identical to those first proposed by Rep. Jack Kemp and Sen. William Roth, changes that had previously been endorsed by Congress in 1978 and by the Senate Finance Committee in 1980. Individual income tax rates would be reduced by 10 percent a year beginning on July 1, 1981. This would have reduced tax rates from the then-current range of between 14 and 70 percent to between 10 and 50 percent by July 1, 1984—a nearly uniform 27 percent reduction across income groups. The new administration considered two other changes to the individual income tax, but neither was included in the initial proposal. An immediate reduction in the top bracket on the income from property was rejected on grounds that it would be perceived as unfair. Indexing the individual tax code for changes in the general price level, although endorsed by Reagan during the compaign, was rejected because of a concern about the effect on tax receipts. As it turned out these decisions represented unnecessary caution about the congressional response to these measures.

The proposed changes in the depreciation allowances on business investment were necessarily more complex but represented a substantial simplification of the then-current system. The general character of this proposal had been developed by Charls Walker, a respected economist and business lobbyist, and had been endorsed by the Senate Finance Committee in 1980. The general objective of this proposal was to reduce the effective tax rates on the income from business investment and to simplify the tax treatment of this income. The nature of this proposal was very different from the proposed reduction in individual rates, but the implications were not broadly recognized. For a given level of tax receipts, the most effective way to induce additional output is to maintain the tax rate on the current level of income and to reduce the rate on additional income. For the individual income tax this approach cannot be used because it would lead to different tax rates among families with the same income. An increase in depreciation allowances or investment tax credits, however, reduces the effective tax rate on the income from new investment without reducing the tax rate on income from the existing capital stock. One effect of such measures is to reduce the value of the existing capital stock, an effect that is likely to be reflected immediately in the stock market. Over time, in addition, as new investment gradually replaces the existing capital stock, such investment incentives gradually reduce tax receipts on the income from capital. If the investment incentives are effective, they increase the capital stock per unit of labor and increase real wage rates and the tax receipts from labor. On the surface such investment incentives appear to be a shift of the tax burden from capital to labor, a perception that is the source of much political mischief. In fact such measures have the effect of redistributing wealth from the owners of the existing capital stock to labor.

The new proposal, described as the Accelerated Cost Recovery System (ACRS), substituted depreciation periods of three, five, ten, fifteen, and eighteen years for different classes of business equipment and structures for the much more complex Asset Depreciation Range (ADR) system with depreciation periods of up to sixty years. Annual depreciation within each class was accelerated to permit more substantial deductions in the early years. For the three-year class, in addition, the investment tax credit was increased from 3.3 percent to 6 percent. The five-, ten-, and fifteen-year classes were to be phased in over a five-year period, but the other changes were to be immediate. The ACRS would be effective for all investments made beginning on January 1, 1981.

For the most part the Economic Recovery Tax Act of 1981 (ERTA) was better tax legislation than the president had requested, but approval was not a sure thing. The first debate developed in the congressional budget committees in the critical month after Reagan was shot on March 30. The House Budget Committee developed a budget proposal with both higher spending and a lower deficit, including only a one-year tax cut focused on the low-and middle-income brackets. On April 10 the Senate Budget Committee voted down the president's budget because of concern about the prospective deficit. On April 22 a newspaper column reported that the Senate Budget Committee staff had "proclaimed, with unconcealed delight, that Kemp-Roth was dead." The prospect of an early major defeat of the Reagan program was reversed only by a forceful Reagan speech to a joint session of Congress on April 28. Shortly after, both houses of Congress approved the first budget resolution by a large margin, providing for the full Reagan tax proposal.

The controversy over the tax bill was not over, however. A continued concern about the prospective deficit led the White House, through Secretary Regan and Senator Dole, to float a proposed compromise to reduce the first year tax cut to 5 percent, a position that Reagan endorsed on June 4. Although the Senate Finance Committee approved an expanded version of the president's proposal on June 25, the House Ways and Means Committee continued to develop its own bill. The House bill differed from the President's proposal in two major ways. The individual rate cuts would be limited to 5 percent in 1981 and 10 percent in 1982. And the bill proposed a gradual transition to full expensing of business investment and a gradual reduction of the corporate income tax rate from 46 percent to 34 percent. Both bills included a number of other provisions. The logjam blocking a consensus on a single bill was finally broken when the Senate approved an amendment by Sen. William Armstrong on July 16 to index the individual income tax. A televised address by the president on July 27 emphasized the advantage of the Senate bill in future years, and the House approved the revised Senate bill on July 29.

The Economic Recovery Tax Act of 1981 gave the President more than he had requested but proved to be his last major victory of the first term. The only major compromise was the reduction of the first-year tax cut to 5 percent and the delay of this cut to October 1; the cumulative tax cuts by 1984 thus were reduced from 27 percent to 23 percent. (After inflation, however, the cumulative reduction in marginal individual income tax rates turned out to be only a few percent.) Most of the other provisions of ERTA, however, were also important. The individual income tax would be indexed to the general price level beginning in 1985. An amendment by a House Democrat reduced the top rate on investment income from 70 percent to 50 percent on January 1, 1982. The penalty on two-earner families was reduced. The allowable deductions for IRA and Keogh pension plans were substantially increased. Estate and gift taxes were reduced. The proposed changes in business taxation survived largely intact. Congress dropped the eighteen-year depreciation class, added a "safe-harbor" leasing provision to permit the transfer of unused tax credits and depreciation allowances to profitable firms, added a tax credit on incremental R&D spending, reduced the windfall profits tax on small oil producers, and reduced corporate income tax rates on small corporations. Although a few of these additional provisions were the result of special-interest bargaining, the administration welcomed most of these provisions as desirable changes in the tax code. The projected effect of ERTA on federal tax receipts was roughly the same as the initial proposal. In March 1981 the president's proposal was estimated to reduce receipts by $186 billion in FY 1985. In February 1982, on the basis of slightly lower economic projections, ERTA was estimated to reduce receipts by $177 billion in FY 1985.

Over time ERTA became the centerpiece of Reaganomics, both for its supporters and its critics. The administration, with some merit, attributed the unusually strong economic recovery of 1983 and 1984 to ERTA. Critics, with less apparent logic, blamed ERTA for the unusually long recession that began in August 1981 and later for the rapidly escalating deficit. As will be developed in Chapter 7, ERTA had major effects on the economy, but many of these effects were not anticipated at the time the act was approved.

Tax Legislation in 1982

The ink was barely dry on the 1981 budget and tax legislation when Stockman initiated a new proposal for additional FY 1982 budget reductions and some tax increases. The tax component of this extraordinary proposal was an increase in federal excise taxes on alcohol, tobacco, and gasoline, which was projected to increase tax receipts by $22 billion by FY 1984. After Congress rejected this fall 1981 initiative and after considerable continuing controversy within the administration, the administration proposed a set of new tax measures in the FY 1983 budget that were projected to increase tax receipts by $22.5 billion in FY 1985. These measures included a number of minor changes in business taxation, tax collection and enforcement, and the taxes dedicated to several trust funds.

The proposed FY 1983 budget also included two innovative proposals. Special tax incentives and regulatory relief would be granted to individuals and businesses in up to seventy-five designated "enterprise zones" as a means to stimulate redevelopment of depressed areas. This proposal reflected some tension in the administration between the characteristic Treasury position favoring a more neutral tax code and the activists in the White House, who wanted to use the tax code for programmatic objectives. The Treasury, OMB, and CEA had supported only an experiment with a much smaller number of enterprise zones. A much more ambitious proposal was to dedicate about $28 billion of federal excise tax receipts to a special transition fund to be used, at the option of the states, to finance more than forty federal programs that the president's New Federalism initiative proposed be turned back to the states. After FY 1988 the federal excises dedicated to this fund would be reduced by 25 percent a year. None of these distinctive Reagan proposals, however, were enacted.

The road that led to the Tax Equity and Fiscal Responsibility Act of 1982 (TEFRA) was indirect and rocky. The proposed FY 1982 budget was the first of several successive budgets that were effectively dead on arrival. After only a faint-hearted defense of the budget, Stockman began working with the Senate Republican leaders to shape an alternative budget. By late February Senator Domenici had developed a budget plan that would increase taxes by $122 billion over three years, and soon after Senator Dole developed a list of tax increases that included repeal of the 1983 individual income tax reduction. On March 24, in order to recapture the initiative on the budget and taxes, the president authorized the "Gang of 17" negotiations involving the senior budget and tax officials from the administration, the House, and the Senate. After a month of closed discussions, these negotiations broke down, primarily because House Speaker O'Neill would not support the proposed budget cuts and wanted the Republicans to accept responsibility for any tax increase. Senator Domenici quickly reintroduced his earlier budget plan and, after hurried negotiations, on May 5 the president agreed to support a tax increase of $95 billion over three years as long as it did not revise the individual income tax cuts approved in 1981. On June 10 the House approved the Senate budget proposal. President Reagan believed that he had an agreement for spending cuts that were three times the tax increases, but this turned out to be either a mistake or a bad bargain.

Several conditions affected the magnitude and characteristics of the 1982 tax legislation. Congress had approved only $35 billion of the $41 billion of budget cuts proposed for FY 1982 and was resistant to many further cuts. Each successive projection of the deficit was higher, a consequence primarily of the deepening recession. There was also one major problem with the investment incentives in ERTA. At low inflation rates the combination of the depreciation allowances and the investment tax credit on business equipment led to substantial *negative* tax rates on income from these investments, a problem that the administration first acknowledged in the 1982 *Economic Report*. A controversy also developed over the safe-harbor leasing provisions of ERTA, as a consequence of press reports that incorrectly

attributed the benefits of such tax leases to the profitable companies
that reduced their tax liabilities by such leases. The objective of this
provision was to maintain the same tax incentives for investment by
firms experiencing temporary losses as for profitable firms. The administration, however, failed to explain the economic reason for this
provision, and consequently the provision became a vulnerable target for the new tax bill.

The content of TEFRA was shaped entirely by the administration
and the Senate Finance Committee. A number of provisions had been
proposed by the administration in the FY 1983 budget—including
withholding on interest and dividends, acceleration of corporate income tax payments, modification of the completed contract method
of tax accounting, changes in the taxation of life insurance companies, increase in airport and airways excise taxes, and extension of
the social security hospital insurance taxes to federal employees. The
only major changes to ERTA were the repeal of the additional depreciation allowances scheduled for 1985 and 1986, a reduction in
the cost basis for the investment tax credit, and the repeal of the
safe-harbor leasing provisions. The first two of these measures
changed the effective tax rate on investment in business equipment
from about −50 percent to about −5 percent and should be regarded as a technical improvement to ERTA. For the most part,
however, despite an earlier threat to the third year of the individual
income tax cut, ERTA survived intact. The other major provisions
of TEFRA included strengthening the individual minimum tax, increasing the floor for casualty and medical expense deductions, increasing the cigarette and telephone excise taxes, and increasing the
rate and base of the unemployment tax.

All this was added to a minor revenue bill initiated in the House
and was approved by the Senate on July 23 without the support of
a single Democrat. Shortly after, without any hearings or markup by
the Ways and Means Committee, the House sent the bill to conference, which made only minor changes to the Senate bill. On August
19, following a televised appeal by the president, the House approved the conference bill by a close bipartisan vote. Over the next
three years TEFRA was projected to increase tax receipts by about
$100 billion.

On balance TEFRA proved to be good tax legislation. Although
the repeal of safe-harbor leasing was unfortunate and the withholding on interest and dividends was later reversed, most of the TEFRA
changes in the structure of federal taxes are likely to survive. TEFRA
proved to be a watershed, however, separating those who opposed
any tax increases and those who supported a well-crafted tax increase in the presence of a huge deficit. Some of the true believers

had already fallen by the wayside. Treasury Undersecretary Norman Ture and Assistant Secretary Craig Roberts left the administration early in 1982 in anticipation of what Roberts later described as "the unraveling of Reaganomics." Some of the earliest House supporters of the Kemp-Roth plan, such as Marjorie Holt and Clarence "Bud" Brown, however, voted for TEFRA and with the president. TEFRA proved that Reagan had a broader agenda than cutting taxes under any circumstances. Years later, however, the recriminations over the TEFRA vote continue to divide Republicans; they will be an issue affecting the selection of the Republican nominee for president in 1988.

The origin of the Highway Revenue Act of 1982 was quite different, arising from a recession-induced demand for some "jobs" bill. The major revenue provision of this act increased the federal excise on gasoline from four cents to nine cents per gallon. A number of excises on tires, oil, and light trucks were eliminated, but fees on heavy trucks and trailers were increased. These measures were projected to increase receipts by about $5 billion by FY 1985. This measure, of course, was wholly inconsistent with the New Federalism proposals of early 1982, and the additional spending was authorized only after the recovery was well underway. This substantial increase in spending and taxes for highways and mass transit was more contrary to Reaganomics but less controversial than was TEFRA.

Tax Legislation in 1983

In January 1983 the mood in the White House was as foul as the weather. The November 1982 election had increased the number of Democrats in the House by twenty-six seats. Although November 1982 was also the trough of the long recession, the newly appointed CEA chairman, Martin Feldstein, in order to establish his credibility, had forecast an unusually weak recovery in 1983 and 1984. On the basis of this forecast the baseline deficit was projected to increase about $20 billion a year for the next four years. The administration and the new Congress had no stomach for a new round of budget cutting, and the administration seemed to have run out of new ideas. The president's budget message on January 31 reflected this mood:

Today the federal budget itself has become a major victim of the economic transition:

- The inflationary revenue windfall has dried up.
- Our staggering nation debt until recently was being financed at the highest interest rates in peacetime history.
- The undelayable process of restoring our inflation eroded military

budgets and our decayed military strength has further strained our
resources.

• Despite our great strides in reducing the spending growth over the
  last two years, the vast edifice of domestic programs remains in place.

The administration was close to having run out of options that were
consistent with its initial agenda.

That was the background for the most bizarre tax proposal of the
Reagan administration. Shortly before the proposed FY 1984 budget
had to go to the printers, the White House was still looking for some
way to reduce the projected deficits. At the suggestion of Stockman
and Darman, the White House decided to propose a contingency tax
plan, including a surcharge on individual and corporation income
taxes equal to about one percent of taxable income and an excise tax
on oil of $5 dollars a barrel. These taxes would become effective in
FY 1986 for a three-year period only if (1) Congress approved the
administration's proposed FY 1984 budget, (2) the projected FY 1986
deficit on July 1, 1985, was above 2.5 percent of GNP, and (3) the
economy was growing at that time. The contingent taxes were projected to increase receipts by $46 billion in FY 1986 if they were
triggered by these conditions.

There were a number of serious problems with this proposal. A
delayed contingent tax involves the same type of constitutional issue
as the later Gramm-Rudman legislation. The surcharge would have
offset much of the reduction in individual income tax rates scheduled for July 1, 1983. The excise tax on oil would have seriously
penalized domestic oil-dependent industries, such as the petrochem-
ical industry. None of these effects were subject to any analysis or
review. Moreover, the nature of the proposed bargain was very
strange. The president in effect was telling Congress that if it reduced spending, he would authorize a tax increase. The incentives
of Congress to reduce spending would have been much stronger
had spending control been a necessary condition for avoiding a tax
increase. In any case the administration could not find a congressional sponsor for the proposal, and it became one of a series of
poorly prepared initiatives that were dead on arrival. One legacy of
this proposal is that it provided the foundation on which Martin
Feldstein based his claim that his persistent appeal for higher taxes
was consistent with administration policy.

The administration also proposed a number of smaller changes in
the tax system. The enterprise zone proposal was renewed. A small
tuition tax credit was proposed for parents of children in private
elementary and secondary schools. A tax-free savings account for
higher education was also proposed, with annual contributions limited to $1,000 per child. Both of these education tax-incentives were

limited to families with incomes below $60,000. A temporary tax credit for employers who hire the long-term unemployed was proposed. And the administration proposed several small changes in the tax code to support its Caribbean Basin Initiative. These several proposals were projected to reduce tax receipts by about $2 billion in FY 1986. One other proposal would have broadened the income and social security tax bases by the amount of employer-paid health insurance premiums in excess of $70 per month for a single plan; this proposal was part of a more general plan to limit the inflation of medical services and was projected to increase tax receipts by $6 billion in FY 1986. Although each of these smaller proposals had considerable merit, only the Caribbean Basin provisions were enacted.

The major tax proposal of 1983 was drafted by the Greenspan commission on social security, with little input from the administration. Contrary to the president's objectives, almost all the proposed changes to restore the social security reserves consisted of increased taxes, including the first dedication of general revenues to the basic social security fund. The White House, however, was so concerned about avoiding continued political controversy over social security that it endorsed the recommendations of the Greenspan commission without change. The major tax provisions of this plan were the following: coverage would be extended to all new employees of the federal government and of nonprofit organizations, and employees of state and local governments would no longer be allowed to withdraw from the system. The tax rate increase already scheduled for 1985 would be accelerated to 1984, and the rate would be increased again in 1988. The tax on self-employment earnings would be increased from 75 percent to 100 percent of the combined tax rate on employee earnings, but one-half of the rate would be deductible on the income tax. And 50 percent of social security benefits would be added to the taxable income of families with other income over $25,000 or individuals with other income over $20,000. This fourth provision was intended to make the taxation of social security benefits more nearly equivalent to that of private pensions, but it was very badly designed; the effect of this provision would have made the marginal tax rate on other income at these levels far more than 100 percent. This provision also represented the first dedication of general revenues to the basic social security fund. These changes were projected to increase receipts by about $9 billion in FY 1986.

Congress also wanted to avoid continued controversy over social security and approved the tax provisions of the Greenspan proposals with only three minor changes. A small credit against the payroll tax was substituted for the deduction of 50 percent of the self-employment tax on the income tax. Congress changed the formula

for taxing social security benefits and increased the income thresh-
olds to $32,000 for families and $25,000 for individuals. The new
formula represented an improvement over the Greenspan proposal
but still increased the marginal federal tax rates on retirement income above these levels to between 50 percent and 77 percent. The
only controversy that developed concerned the earnings penalty; the
law then current reduced social security benefits by $1 for each $2
of earnings by those under age seventy, a provision of the original
social security law that was specifically designed to discourage work
by the elderly. The Senate approved an amendment by Senator
Armstrong to repeal the earnings penalty, a change long supported
by Reagan, but the House voted to maintain the earnings penalty.
The final law reduced the earnings penalty by reducing social security benefits by $1 for each $3 of earnings. The combined federal,
state, and payroll tax rates on elderly workers, however, can still be
as high as from 83 percent to 98 percent, rates that are now matched
or exceeded only by those faced by the welfare population. Our government has yet to explain why it is appropriate to penalize private
retirement savings and earnings by the elderly and poor by such
high marginal rates.

Congress also approved two other tax bills in 1983. After a blizzard of mail organized by the bankers, Congress repealed the TEFRA
measure providing for withholding on interest and dividends. This
change was projected to reduce receipts by about $2 billion. Con-
gress also increased the tax rates for the railroad retirement plan by
39 percent, rejecting the administration's 1982 proposal to return
this plan to the industry. This change was projected to increase receipts by about $1 billion.

On balance, 1983 was not a good year for administration tax proposals. The contingency tax became an embarrassment. The special
tax proposals for enterprise zones, education, employment of the
long-term unemployed, and health insurance provisions were all rejected. Both the administration and Congress in effect delegated the
design of the social security plan to a presidential commission. And
the other tax changes reversed proposals that the administration had
earlier proposed or endorsed.

Tax Legislation in 1984

The administration's budget and tax proposals in 1984 were prepared under very different conditions than in the prior year. Real
GNP had increased 6.5 percent during 1983, and both inflation and
unemployment had declined. For the first time the prior fiscal-year
deficit was lower than projected, although it had reached a peak

peacetime rate of 6.4 percent of GNP. For several years the White House had been divided between the pragmatists who forgot that there was an election in 1980 and the ideologues who forgot that there would be an election in 1984. In 1984 the forthcoming election dominated most administration policy. In his budget message on February 1, the president cautioned "to those who say we must raise taxes, I say wait."

But he did not say no to all additional taxes. The administration proposed a dozen or so small changes in the tax system. The prior proposals for enterprise zones, tuition tax credits, tax-free savings accounts for higher education, and the taxation of health insurance premiums were renewed. As part of a more general "women's initiative," the administration proposed to expand the IRA limit for families with one earner to $4,000 and to increase the tax credit for dependent care. A number of technical changes in business taxation were also proposed, the most important of which included limits on tax-exempt leasing and industrial development bonds. The combination of these proposed changes were projected to increase receipts by about $8 billion in FY 1985 and $14 billion in FY 1987.

The finance committees in Congress were not used to addressing new tax measures every year and were not comfortable with approving tax increases in an election year. The Deficit Reduction Act of 1984 (DEFRA), however, was approved without much controversy. Congress again rejected all of the administration proposals that would have reduced receipts, but it approved the proposed restrictions on tax-exempt leasing and industrial development bonds. The rest of DEFRA was of Congress' own making. The net interest exclusion, which would have been effective in 1985, was repealed. The distilled spirits tax was increased, and the telephone excise tax was extended. The TEFRA finance leasing rules, which replaced the ERTA safe-harbor leases, were deferred until 1988. The depreciation period on structures, established at fifteen years by ERTA, was increased to eighteen years. The rules for income averaging were restricted. The holding period for capital gains was reduced from one year to six months. And there were a number of other provisions affecting the tax treatment of life insurance companies, partnerships, and certain accounting techniques. The combination of these provisions was projected to increase receipts by about $9 billion in FY 1985 and $22 billion in FY 1987. Congress managed to approve a complex tax measure in an election year with a significant increase in receipts, without increasing any tax that was visible to most voters. One provision of DEFRA, however, has ominous potential implications: to reduce fraud by recipients of federal transfer programs, Congress substantially broadened the authority for matching information from separate federal files, for the first time including IRS files. The full implications for our civil liberties of creating an effective national data bank are not yet broadly recognized.

A Summary Evaluation of the 1981–1984 Tax Measures

The net effect of the series of complex tax measures from 1981 through 1984 was to improve the structure of the federal tax system while maintaining the federal tax receipts share of GNP at about the average of the Carter administration—a substantial achievement for which both the administration and Congress deserve credit. The primary effect of these changes was to reduce the marginal tax rates on both labor earnings and income from business investment.

Table 3.1 summarizes the marginal federal income and social security tax rates for a four-person family with one earner in 1980 and 1984. With no change in tax law, marginal tax rates on earnings would have increased substantially from 1980 to 1984 for all income groups because of inflation and the scheduled increase in the social security tax. The combined effect of ERTA and the social security amendments of 1983 reduced the marginal tax on earnings, relative to the 1980 law, for all income groups. A comparison of the marginal tax rates in 1984 with those in 1980 indicates that the marginal tax rates were reduced about 5 percent for low-income families, were increased about 6 percent for the median income family, and were

Table 3.1 Marginal Federal Tax Rates on Earnings (%)

	One-Half Median Income	Median Income	Twice Median Income
Prior Law:			
1980			
Income tax	18	24	43
Social security	6.1	6.1	0
Total	24.1	30.1	43
1984			
Income tax	21	32	49
Social security	6.7	6.7	0
Total	27.7	38.7	49
ERTA:			
1984			
Income tax	16	25	38
Social security	7	7	0
Total	23	32	38

Table 3.2 Combined Marginal Tax Rates on Investment Income

	1980 Rates (%)	1982 Rates (%)
Corporations		
Equipment	5.4	−4.0
Structures	49.6	37.7
Public utilities	33.2	32.6
Inventories	35.6	35.6
Land	39.9	39.9
Total	34.5	30.0
Noncorporate business	35.8	32.7
Owner-occupied houses	18.6	18.6
Total tax rate	28.8	26.4
Total cost of capital	7.0	6.8
Standard deviation	1.7	1.7

reduced about 12 percent for higher-income families. Indexation of the individual income tax, which began in 1985 will limit further increases in the marginal income tax rate for all groups, but the scheduled increases in the social security tax will increase the combined federal tax rates on low- and middle-income families.

The major contribution of ERTA was to avoid the substantial increase in tax rates that would have occurred under the prior law. The actual change in marginal tax rates on earnings between 1980 and 1984, except for individuals with high incomes, was quite small. A more substantial tax reform or a stringent limit on federal spending sufficient to permit a reduction in total tax receipts would prove necessary to achieve a further reduction in marginal tax rates.

Table 3.2 summarizes the combined marginal tax rates on investment income in 1980 and 1982. These rates reflect the combined effect of federal, state, and local taxes on individual income, corporate income, and property. The combined effect of ERTA and TEFRA reduced the effective marginal tax rates on the income from all investments other than inventories, land, and owner-occupied houses. The weighted-average marginal tax rates were reduced about 13 percent on corporate investment, about 9 percent on noncorporate investment, and about 8 percent on all investments (including owner-occupied housing). The changes in tax law did not change the variance of the cost of capital by type of investment, but the substantial decline in inflation (not reflected in these estimates) reduced these differences.

A number of major problems affecting the taxation of investment income remained. There were still considerable differences in the effective tax rates on the income from different types of investment, differences that may not reflect the objectives of public policy, and these differences increased with the rate of inflation. The tax code still provided a strong bias in favor of debt financing, and for many investors the effective tax rates on business investment were higher than on earnings. A resolution of these problems would require a more substantial reform.

One other pattern of this period is that Congress was consistently resistant to Reagan's proposals to change the tax code for programmatic objectives. The administration and Congress each attempted to use the tax code for programmatic purposes but disagreed on the specific objectives meriting differential tax treatment. During the Reagan years Congress made it clear that any differential tax treatment would be of its own making.

THE ROAD TO TAX REFORM

Many years ago, in his October 1964 speech in support of Barry Goldwater, Ronald Reagan asked, "Have we the courage to face up to the immorality of the discrimination of the progressive surtax and demand a return to traditional proportionate taxation?" He concluded that "we need true tax reform that will at least make a start toward restoring for our children the American dream that wealth is denied to no one, that each individual has the right to fly as high as his ability and strength will take him." An idea that was regarded as that of a right-wing extremist in 1964 would become the conventional wisdom of the 1980s.

President Reagan first suggested a plan "to simplify the tax code and make it more fair for all Americans" in his 1983 State of the Union address, a low-key appeal that almost escaped public notice. At that time there were several motives for tax reform. Stockman and Feldstein considered it an opportunity to increase revenues. After Sen. Bill Bradley and Rep. Richard Gephardt, both Democrats, introduced a major tax reform proposal in 1982 with a top individual income tax rate of 30 percent, White House political officials were concerned that the Democrats would take the lead on tax reform and make it a major issue in the 1984 campaign. And the Treasury's Office of Tax Analysis had long had an agenda to broaden the tax base.

The Treasury Plan of 1984

The relative weight of political considerations increased in 1984. Strong economic conditions in 1983 reinforced the wishful thinking that economic growth might be sufficient to reduce the deficit to a tolerable level without substantial spending cuts or tax increases. Growth would be the 1984 solution to reducing the deficit. In his 1984 State of the Union address, the president called for "an historic [tax] reform for fairness, simplicity and incentives for growth. I am asking Secretary Don Regan for a plan for action to simplify the entire tax code so all taxpayers, big and small, are treated more fairly. . . . I have asked that specific recommendations, consistent with these objectives, be presented to me by December 1984." The president committed himself to a major tax reform but without revealing any of the details until after the election. Congressional Republicans, however, did not wait. Rep. Jack Kemp and Sen. Robert Kasten introduced a major reform proposal in April, with top rates on both individual and corporate income below those in the Bradley-Gephardt plan.

Responsibility for developing the Treasury plan was assigned to the Office of Tax Analysis (OTA), but the work developed very slowly, in part because of the workload of analyzing the DEFRA proposals and an attempt to resolve the dispute about the "unitary" business tax systems in several major states. Only the barest outlines of the plan were ready by midsummer. The issue of whether the plan would increase tax revenues ironically was resolved in July by Walter Mondale. Surprising almost everyone, Mondale did not endorse tax reform, called for a major tax increase, and charged that the administration was preparing a secret tax-increase plan of its own. At that time the administration's plan was secret only in that it did not exist. After DEFRA was approved and a new assistant secretary for tax policy, Ron Pearlman, was appointed, the Treasury plan developed rapidly. The developing plan was reviewed by Secretary Regan and a few other senior Treasury officials but by no officials outside of the Treasury. After I assumed the duties of acting chairman of the CEA in mid-July, I asked Regan to allow me to participate in these reviews; I was told bluntly that no one outside Treasury would be informed about the developing plan until after the election. An understandable concern about leaks during the campaign only reinforced the Treasury's effective monopoly within the administration over the formulation of tax policy. My responsibility, however, was to protect the president from facing an all-or-nothing plan developed by an agency that might have a different agenda—the characteristic and important role of the several White House policy review staffs.

Shortly after the election, I met with Charles McClure, an economist who was the deputy assistant secretary for tax policy and a primary architect of the Treasury plan, and with a few other Treasury officials to learn of the general features of the nearly completed plan. Again, I was told almost nothing that had not already been in the press. The president had given only the most general guidance to the Treasury. The combined effect of changes to individual and corporate taxes should be revenue neutral, and the top rates should be as low as possible. The Treasury, in addition, had established a guideline that the changes in individual income tax liabilities would be distributionally neutral across income groups. One other constraint developed from a minor flap during the campaign. In response to a question, the president had suggested that elimination of the deduction for home mortgage interest should be considered as part of a general tax reform. As was too characteristic, White House political officials quickly denied that the president was speaking for the administration, and he later made a commitment to maintaining the home mortgage deduction in a prepared speech before a homebuilders' association. Again, no surprises and no new information.

During the next several weeks details of the plan began to leak, and Regan persuaded the president to release the plan to the public on November 27. On the afternoon of November 26, Regan and Pearlman summarized the plan to the president and the core group at a two-hour meeting in the cabinet room, distributing copies of the plan for the first time at the meeting. The individual income part of the plan was well received and provoked little discussion. The president questioned whether the deduction for country club dues should be eliminated, forgetting his own appeal for fairness. I asked why the credit for dependent care was replaced by a deduction. As indicated, most of the discussion about the proposed changes in the individual income tax was about trivial issues. There was a general recognition that the proposed elimination of the deduction for state and local taxes would be politically controversial but was probably necessary to achieve the lower statutory tax rates. At that time, having had no opportunity for a prior review, I failed to recognize that the combined effect of the increase in the tax base and the reduction in statutory rates on taxable income would only slightly reduce *effective* marginal tax rates on family income, an effect the administration still does not understand.

The business part of the Treasury plan was a shock and provoked substantial discussion. The magnitude of the change was revealed by a table on the projected receipts. In 1990, individual income tax receipts would be reduced 7 percent, and corporate tax receipts would be increased 36.5 percent. This was an extraordinary proposal to a president who had regularly questioned whether there should be any corporate income tax. It was also an extraordinary proposal from the department that had promoted the ACRS in 1981 and from

Charles McClure, who had written a book in 1979 questioning why corporate income should be taxed twice. Although an understanding of the detailed effects of the proposed taxation of business investment developed only slowly, my first impression that the proposed plan increased tax rates on business investment to a higher level than in 1980 proved to be correct. When the president asked my evaluation of the business tax plan, I responded, "Walter Mondale would have been proud." Although I apologized to Don Regan about this remark at the "troika" breakfast the next morning, I probably lost any opportunity to be named chairman of the CEA with that one remark.

After the Treasury plan was published, it picked up some strange supporters, including George McGovern, Ralph Nader, the liberal Democrat Rep. Charles Rangel, and the Brookings Institution public finance economist Joseph Pechman. Secretary Regan's feeble defense of this part of the plan was that there is a general feeling that corporations were not paying enough taxes.

The general provisions of the Treasury plan were quite simple.. Individual income tax rates would be reduced from the current range of 11 to 50 percent over fourteen brackets (fifteen on single returns) to three rates of 15, 25 and 35 percent. The personal exemption would be increased to $2,000, and the zero bracket amounts would be increased, eliminating any federal income tax for a family of four with an income below about $12,000. The IRA limits were increased from $2,000 to $2,500 for each worker and from $2,250 to $5,000 for a one-earner family. The individual income tax base was broadened by the following:

- Eliminating the deductions for second homes, state and local taxes, entertainment expenses, and specified employer-provided fringe benefits.
- Limiting the deductions for other interest, business meal and travel expenses, and health insurance premiums.
- Allowing only those charitable deductions above 2 percent of income.
- Adding all unemployment and worker's compensation benefits to taxable income.

The net effect of these provisions (and some minor changes not listed) was a projected reduction of individual income tax receipts by 7 percent in 1990. Several minor changes in estate and gift taxation and in excise taxes were also projected to reduce receipts from these sources.

The major provisions of the taxation of business income were the following:

- The corporate income tax rate would be changed from a graduated rate of up to 46 percent to a 33 percent flat rate.
- A deduction for 50 percent of dividends paid would be allowed.
- Depreciation would be based on estimated economic depreciation, and the investment tax credit would be repealed.
- Capital gains would be taxed as ordinary income.
- Several special tax provisions specific to the oil industry, financial institutions, and private-purpose municipal bonds would be repealed.
- For the first time all depreciation, interest, inventories, and capital gains would be indexed for changes in the general price level.

The combined effects of the proposed changes in individual and business taxation would have been a 27 percent increase in the average effective tax rate on investment income and a substantial reduction in the variance in effective tax rates among different types of investment. The net effect of these provisions specific to corporations was projected to increase corporate tax receipts by 36.5 percent in 1990.

What were the origins of this plan? What led Don Regan, a successful Wall Street executive, to endorse a plan that substantially increased corporate taxes? The most direct answer is that the plan was developed by the career staff of the Office of Tax Analysis on the basis of the principles of a comprehensive income tax, with little consideration of either its economic or political effects. Many of the proposals date from those prepared under the direction of Stanley Surrey, Treasury assistant secretary for tax policy in the Johnson administration. The most substantial change in business taxes derivative from these principles was to tax the income from prior investment at the same rate as on new investment. Relative to the current tax code, this would lead to a windfall reduction in the tax on prior investment and a substantial increase in the tax on new investment. Manuel Johnson, the Treasury assistant secretary for economic policy, made this point forcefully in the internal Treasury review, but Regan ruled in favor of the OTA position—a complete reversal of the measure, initiated in the Kennedy administration and strengthened in ERTA, to reduce the effective tax rates on the income from new investment. Another consideration that also affected this change is that the proposed changes in the individual income tax reduced receipts, requiring some larger proportionate increase in corporate tax receipts to maintain total revenues.

Two other considerations affected the details of the individual income tax plan. As part of a general "family initiative," the personal exemption was increased to $2,000. Although this provision would eliminate federal income taxes for poor families, it would reduce taxes by a higher absolute amount for high-income families, and it involved a large revenue loss. The substitution of a $300 tax credit for the exemption would have equalized the value of this provision among income groups and reduced the revenue loss, but OTA maintained a consistent position against tax credits. (A tax credit reduces the tax liabilities of all qualifying taxpayers by an equal amount. The personal exemption reduces taxable income by an equal amount and thus is worth more to those facing higher marginal tax rates.) A second consideration was to reduce the tax bias against personal saving. Although the broadened IRA provision approved in 1981 had proved popular and may have increased net saving, the personal saving rate had continued to decline. The proposed increase in the IRA limits, moreover, would equalize the limits for one-earner and two-earner families.

Finally, the best explanation of Don Regan's approval of this plan is that the OTA staff, under the pressure of time and without an outside review, was in a position to present him with an all-or-nothing choice. The White House review process is often time-consuming and frustrating to a proposing agency. In this case, however, a technical review by tax specialists in OMB and the CEA and the judgment of other cabinet members would have protected both Regan and the president from a Treasury staff proposal that reversed a major feature of the initial Reagan program.

The first White House comments on the Treasury tax plan were distinctly cool, pointedly describing it as the Treasury's plan. In order to gain support for the plan, Regan scheduled a series of meetings of the cabinet council of economic affairs (CCEA) in January 1985 to discuss the plan. The major result of these meetings was to reveal the serious concern of other members of the cabinet about the business provisions of the plan, especially the concern of Commerce Secretary Malcolm Baldrige, Trade Representative William Brock, and Energy Secretary Don Hodel. In the meantime the CEA had commissioned a study, summarized in the 1985 *Economic Report*, which indicated that the plan would substantially increase the cost of capital on producers' equipment and slightly reduce the cost of capital on nonresidential structures. A concern that the plan had not been subjected to an adequate technical review led Roger Porter, the secretary of the CCEA, to form a small subcabinet group for this purpose, but this group was quashed by Regan. The next issue arose concerning the nature of the president's commitment to the plan in the 1985 State of the Union address. The Treasury wanted a rather specific commitment to the plan and an early deadline for submitting the administration's formal proposal; others wanted a more general commitment and a delayed deadline, a position that prevailed.

The Treasury plan included many desirable provisions and, from my perspective, one major flaw. The most important changes were the reduction in the statutory tax rates on individual income, changes that would substantially reduce the effect of the tax system on economic activity. The proposed indexing of depreciation, interest, inventories, and capital gains was also an attractive feature of this plan. The major flaw was the substantial increase in corporate taxes. It is an illusion to believe that one can reduce the effective tax on individuals by increasing corporate taxes. In a closed economy the corporate income tax reduces proportionately the after-tax rate of return on all types of capital. In a world of international capital mobility the U.S. corporate income tax is born primarily by American labor because the tax reduces the capital stock that complements their labor services. The corporate income tax is also a political deception because it reduces the visibility of taxes to voters, a deception that probably increases their demand for government services. The Treasury contended that the increase in corporate taxes was not an objective but was merely a result of other changes that it believed were desirable, most importantly the reduction in individual tax rates. In retrospect the president should also have specified that the Treasury plan involve no significant change in the distribution of tax liabilities between individuals and corporations, an oversight for which I bear some responsibility.

"In summary," as I wrote in the 1985 *Economic Report,* "the Treasury Department tax proposal represents a serious attempt to reduce the efficiency losses attributable to the current tax system. It directly addresses the major structural problems of the income tax system. On closer examination, some changes in the proposal may be desirable, but the Treasury Department proposal should be the starting point for serious considerations of tax reform." For better or for worse, each of the subsequent tax reform proposals adopted the general structure of the Treasury plan, an illustration of the influence of the first comprehensive proposal.

The President's Proposal of 1985

The surprising exchange of positions by James Baker and Don Regan in mid-February 1985 increased the opportunity for a more substantial change in the Treasury plan and led to a further delay. Baker and Richard Darman, the new Treasury deputy secretary, had no personal commitment to the Treasury plan and were more responsive to political considerations, but they had no background on tax issues. Although they accepted the Treasury plan as a starting point, they were especially receptive to changes that would reduce political controversy and the developing concerns of the business community. Manuel Johnson, who had opposed the depreciation provisions of the Treasury plan, was asked to develop alternative depreciation schedules that would reduce the effect of the new plan on the cost of capital. The final details of the new plan were worked out in several meetings with the president in late May. To offset the near-term reduction of corporate tax receipts from the revised depreciation schedules, Baker requested approval to phase in the increase in the personal exemption on the individual income tax. The president rejected this proposal in order to maintain the family benefits of the plan. This required the Treasury to develop an awkward temporary provision to recapture some of the "excess" depreciation on investments made under the ACRS. With this provision in place, the president's long-promised tax reform plan, sometimes called Treasury II, was released on May 29.

The individual income tax part of the president's plan differed only slightly from the Treasury plan, the changes primarily reflecting political and revenue considerations. A full deduction for charitable contributions would be maintained. At the insistence of Sen. Robert Packwood, chairman of the Senate Finance Committee, reportedly at the urging of AFL-CIO chief Lane Kirkland, health insurance premiums (over a threshold amount) and other employer-provided fringe benefits would not be taxed. The IRA limits would be increased to $4,000 per family. Income averaging would be eliminated, and the zero bracket amount would be increased to eliminate any federal tax for a family of four with an income below about $13,000. On balance, the president's plan was projected to reduce individual income tax receipts by about 5 percent, a smaller reduction than in the Treasury plan.

The business tax provisions of the president's plan differed more substantially from the Treasury plan. The most important change was the Capital Cost Recovery System (CCRS), which would provide depreciation allowances between those of ACRS and the Treasury plan. Lower tax rates for small corporations would be maintained. The dividend deduction was limited to 10 percent. The capital gains exclusion and several provisions benefitting the oil industry were maintained. Interest expenses and income were not indexed. The minimum tax was retained and tightened. And 40 percent of the "excess" depreciation on investments made under ACRS would be added to taxable income between 1986 and 1988. The combined effect of the proposed changes in individual and business taxation would have been a 12 percent increase in the average effective tax rate on investment income and a large reduction in the variance of effective tax rates among different types of investment. Corporate tax receipts were projected to be 23 percent higher in 1990, a smaller increase than in the Treasury plan.

The House Tax Bill of 1985

The president, Don Regan, and later James Baker made a major investment in tax reform as the major economic policy initiative of Reagan's second term. For several reasons, however, their support did not seem sufficient to carry tax reform and appeared to be counterproductive to the general economic program. First, the administration did not appear to understand the effects of the president's plan, and it promised more than the plan could deliver. Second, revenue-neutral tax reform seemed to be contrary to the incentives of Congress. The normal practice of Congress is to take a little money from a lot of people and concentrate the benefits on a favored constituency. A revenue-neutral tax reform, in contrast, requires a substantial increase in taxes on some groups in order to reduce taxes by a small amount for most taxpayers. The relative power of concentrated interests will usually prevent any significant tax reform unless budget conditions require a general increase in taxes or permit a general reduction in taxes. And third, both the president and Congress had other important concerns. The president's investment in tax reform diverted attention from the budget, forced a compromise on a number of other issues, and increased the leverage of the congressional finance committees over the structure of any change in the tax system.

The initial support for the president's tax proposal was broad but not deep. Most of the business support disappeared after businesses made their own calculations about the effects of the plan on their own firm or industry. A minor concession to the oil industry in the president's plan provided an opening for others to protect their own tax preferences. Governor Mario Cuomo of New York launched a campaign to protect the deduction of state and local taxes. The House Ways and Means Committee conducted an extensive set of hearings on tax reform during the spring and summer, at least assuring that the Democrats could not be charged with blocking tax reform. Treasury Deputy Secretary Richard Darman was the primary agent of the administration in shaping the committee proposal, working almost exclusively with the committee's Democratic majority. On returning from its August recess, Congress reported almost no popular interest in tax reform and turned to trade issues. As the developing consensus of the Ways and Means Committee was revealed, much of the remaining support for tax reform disappeared.

The final proposal, approved by the committee on December 3, reflected the basic structure of the president's proposal, but the changes were important. Although the personal exemption was increased to $2,000 for those taxpayers who do not itemize, it was increased to only $1,500 for those who itemize. In addition to the statutory rates of 15, 25 and 35 percent proposed by the president, the committee added a fourth rate of 38 percent on high taxable incomes. The major current deductions on the individual income tax, including the full deduction of state and local taxes, were retained. About seventy new special tax preferences, on everything from gravestones to football stadiums, were added. The committee achieved the reduction of statutory rates primarily by reducing the income levels at which each rate applies and by shifting an even larger burden to the corporate tax. For example, for a married couple filing a joint return, taxable incomes of $29,000 to $70,000 would be subject to a 25 percent rate under the president's proposal; the committee lowered this bracket to taxable incomes of $22,500 to $43,000. The combined effect of the individual tax provisions was rather strange. The effective marginal rates on total income were reduced most for the lowest and highest income groups but was not changed for those with incomes of $20,000 to $30,000. One wonders who the Democrats consider to be their constituency. Total receipts from the individual income tax would be reduced about 9 percent.

The proposed changes in the corporate income tax were more substantial. A graduated tax rate up to 36 percent was established. Depreciation allowances were substantially reduced and only partially indexed, and the investment tax credit was repealed. Total receipts from the corporate income tax would be increased about 40 percent, even more than that proposed in the initial Treasury plan. Rather than eliminating many current tax preferences, the committee increased the minimum tax on both individuals and corporations. The combined effect of the proposed changes in the individual and corporate income tax would have increased the average effective tax rates on new investment by about 16 percent, the primary reason for the strong business opposition and the basis for several estimates that the committee bill would reduce economic growth.

For the White House the committee bill presented a problem like that of a beached whale; although it smelled foul, somehow it had to be moved. House Republicans cobbled together a substitute bill in a few days to give the president something to endorse. In his weekly radio address on December 7, the president made an appeal to the House to approve some tax bill so that the Senate could address tax reform in 1986. Beryl Sprinkel, then chairman of the CEA, and Manuel Johnson, both of whom had strong reservations about the committee bill, were induced to sign a public statement that approval of either bill would be "a significant and essential step toward real tax reform." House Republicans, who had been largely excluded from the preparation of both the president's plan and the committee bill, initially refused to cooperate. On December 11 all but fourteen Republicans voted against a rule to permit a vote on the tax bill, and the rule was narrowly defeated. For several days Baker and Regan worked the Hill to save the tax bill, but without much success. On December 16, however, on returning from a trip, the president coptered to the Hill to meet with the House Republicans and saved his major second-term domestic initiative, primarily by promising to veto any final tax bill that did not include six key provisions of his May proposal. The vote on December 17 was anticlimatic; after another vote on the rule, this time supported by seventy Republicans, the Ways and Means bill was finally approved by a voice vote. Only one amendment was accepted, to provide a $100 tax credit for contributions to your local member of Congress. A seriously flawed tax bill moved to the Senate for consideration in 1986. The president again demonstrated his considerable political skills and a somewhat inconsistent commitment to the policies for which he was twice elected.

The Senate Tax Bill of 1986

The prospects for tax reform were bleak during the winter of 1986. The House tax bill had been approved only after a last-minute intervention by the president. Senate Finance Committee chairman Robert Packwood had a record of supporting tax deductions for employee fringe benefits and tax preferences for the timber industry and had expressed his view that "I rather like the tax code as it is." Most other members of the Finance Committee supported a tax preference for some industry or group.

Packwood's initial approach to develop a bill consistent with the president's guidelines reinforced these parochial concerns. Prior to the first drafting sessions, he met privately with each member of the committee for a total of about seventy hours to determine the preferences that would be the price of their support of a tax bill. The first Packwood proposal to the Finance Committee in March included his own favored preferences and many of those supported by the other members. At that point Packwood was indifferent to the approval of a tax bill, remarking that "if I get no bill, then those [tax preferences] are protected. If I get a bill and they're protected, I still win. . . . I win either way."

This proposal, however, did not generate enough revenue to meet the president's guidelines, and the next step bordered on the absurd. John Colvin, Packwood's chief tax aide, proposed to raise the necessary revenue by eliminating the business deductions for all excise taxes and tariffs. This would have had the effect of increasing the effective excise tax and tariff rates by about 50 percent, although it would be directly reflected as an increase in corporate taxes; among other problems, this proposal was strongly inconsistent with our international trade agreements. Packwood was initially skeptical of this proposal, but it served his purpose of protecting the growing list of tax preferences that he and others in the committee wished to protect. Packwood's own efforts to organize a coalition in the committee to protect a variety of tax preferences for the natural-resource industries induced other members, including the strongest advocates of tax reform, to protect their own favored preferences. The prospect for tax reform was disappearing in a black hole of accumulating preferences. On April 18 Packwood's staff informed him that this process risked losing any support for the necessary measures to broaden the tax base, and Packwood withdrew his plan.

The next stage of this process was as close to a religious conversion as most politicians are likely to experience. At a lunch with his top personal aide William Diefendorfer at a Capitol Hill pub, and after two pitchers of beer, Packwood decided to start all over. On April 24 he submitted a new plan with a top individual rate of 25 percent and a broad tax base. The new strategy was to accept only those tax preferences necessary for committee approval. Packwood was also in a hurry because he had to return to Oregon in early May to campaign in a contested primary. The new strategy was remarkably successful. Working with a bipartisan core group of six senators, Packwood gained agreement on a plan that was very close to his proposal of April 24. The major concession was, to increase the top statutory rate to 27 percent in order to maintain the deduction for interest on home mortgages. Packwood led this effort by agreeing to eliminate several preferences favored by his Oregon supporters. This process gained momentum and saved the prospect for tax reform. Shortly after midnight on May 7, the Finance Committee approved the new bill by a 20–0 vote before a cheering audience.

The plan approved by the Finance Committee included the following major changes to the individual income tax:

- The personal exemption would be increased to $2,000 (in 1988), and the standard deduction for a married couple would be increased to $5,000. The earned income credit was increased and phased out over a higher income range. These provisions would continue to be adjusted for inflation. For a family of four these provisions plus the earned income credit would eliminate federal income taxation for families with incomes below about $15,380.

- The plan formally established only two statutory rates, 15 percent and 27 percent. The actual rate structure, however, was somewhat more complicated. For a married couple the tax rate would be 15 percent on taxable incomes up to $29,300; 27 percent on taxable incomes up to $75,000; about 32 percent on total incomes up to $185,320; and 27 percent on higher incomes. The higher effective rate in the $75,000 to $185,320 range would result from a gradual phaseout of the benefits of the 15 percent rate and the personal exemption over this income range. The tax brackets would continue to be adjusted for inflation. The reduction in rates would be effective on July 1, 1987.

- The individual income tax base was broadened by eliminating deductions for state and local sales taxes in most states, nonmortgage interest and any interest payments higher than investment income, and a variety of miscellaneous work-related expenses; by increasing the threshold on medical deductions; by limiting IRA deductions to those who do not have an employer pension plan; and by eliminating the capital gains exclusion. These measures to broaden the tax base would be effective on January 1, 1987.

Total revenues from the individual income tax were projected to be reduced by about 4 percent in 1990, a smaller reduction than in any of the prior plans.

The major changes in the taxation of business income approved by the Finance Committee included a reduction of the corporate tax rate to 33 percent, elimination of the investment tax credit and the deduction of net losses on "passive" investments in real estate, a small increase in depreciation allowances (except on real estate), a reduction of the deduction for business meals and entertainment, limits on tax-exempt bonds for business purposes, and a variety of complicated transition rules affecting the phaseout of prior tax preferences. As in the current code and the House bill, depreciation allowances, interest payments, inventories, and capital gains would not be indexed for inflation. The minimum tax on corporations would also be increased and tightened. The average effective tax rate on corporate investment would be increased about 9 percent, with substantially larger increases on structures and on any debt-financed investment. Total revenues from the corporate income tax were projected to increase by about 17 percent in 1990, a smaller increase than in any prior plan.

The final vote on the Senate floor was an anticlimax. After thirteen days of debate, the forty or so proposed amendments to the Finance Committee plan were withdrawn or not offered. Only one major amendment was approved, a nonbinding resolution that Congress should not change the tax code again for five years. On June 24 the Senate tax bill was approved by a vote of 97 to 3. Sen. Pat Moynihan described the approval of this bill as "the most ethical event I've ever seen in this place." The Senate had completed a remarkable task. The power of an idea, for a brief period, overwhelmed the most parochial interests. The Senate bill achieved lower individual tax rates than any prior plan with the smallest increase in the taxes on corporate income. For a time my wavering faith in our political processes was restored. One might hope that a similar courage would be applied to resolving the serious remaining problems of federal spending and the deficit.

The Tax Reform Act of 1986

The next stage of this process proved to be more difficult than expected. A conference committee chaired by Rep. Dan Rostenkowski, including eleven members of each house, began meeting in early July to sort out the differences between the House and Senate bills. Although the House members quickly accepted the basic structure of the Senate bill, House Democrats wanted a larger tax cut for low- and middle-income individuals and a larger tax increase on corporations. Maintaining the popular IRA deductions received broad bipartisan support. Revised estimates also indicated that the Senate bill would not generate sufficient revenues to be revenue neutral. Most of the disputes, however, were about the hundreds of special preferences supported by one or more members of the conference committee.

The outcome of this process was not certain. As the compromise bill developed, Packwood was not confident that it would be approved by a majority of the Senate conferees. This process dragged on until late on Saturday, August 16, after most of Congress had already left Washington for the August recess. Senator John Danforth made a lengthy last appeal to delay the conference committee vote until after the recess, expressing impassioned concern about the limitation of two preferences that were important to his Missouri supporters. In the late evening of August 16, however, the conference bill was approved, with only two Republican senators, Danforth and Malcolm Wallop of Wyoming, dissenting.

As expected, the conference committee increased the tax cuts to individuals and increased the tax increases to corporations. As in the Senate bill, the personal exemption was increased to $2,000, but the full increase was delayed until 1989. The standard deduction for joint filers was also increased to $5,000 but delayed until 1988. The committee approved a rate structure effective in 1988 of 15 percent on taxable incomes up to $29,750, 28 percent on incomes (for joint filers) up to $71,900, an effective rate of 33 percent (for a family of four) on incomes up to $192,930, and a 28 percent rate on higher incomes. For 1987 only, the tax rates would be a blend of the current and new rates, with five rates from 11 percent to 38.5 percent. Compared with the Senate bill, therefore, the two highest rates are each one percentage point higher, and the income range for the top rate is somewhat broader. A deduction for IRA contributions would be maintained for all families with a total income of less than $50,000. The deduction for state and local sales taxes would be completely eliminated. Medical deductions would be limited to those above 7.5 percent of total income, and the deductions for miscellaneous work-related expenses would be limited to those above 2 percent of total income. In most other respects the conference bill was identical to the Senate bill. Total revenues from the individual income tax were projected to decline by about 6 percent.

The increase in business taxes was roughly midway between the House and Senate bills. The tax rate on corporate income would be graduated to a top rate of 34 percent. Depreciation allowances would be somewhat reduced, and the credit for incremental R&D expenses was reduced to 20 percent. New restrictions would be established on the completed contract method of accounting (important to the defense and construction industries) and on the private use of tax-exempt bonds. In most other respects the conference bill was identical to the Senate bill. Total revenues from the corporate income tax were projected to increase by about 25 percent in 1990, about the same as in the president's 1985 proposal.

The president quickly praised the conference committee bill for reducing tax rates by "eliminating unnecessary loopholes." But a lot of loopholes remained. The strongest supporters of tax reform were effective in establishing or preserving some special tax preference. Rostenkowski preserved the tax credit for restoring old buildings. Packwood maintained several small preferences for owners of private forests. Senator Bradley preserved the use of tax-exempt bonds for waste disposal facilities. Senator Chafee preserved a deduction for small gifts to employees and a special preference for tax-exempt bonds in Rhode Island. Senator Roth increased the depreciation allowances for chicken coops and pig pens. Other members of the conference committee were similarly creative. Senator Danforth, an Episcopal minister, protected several small preferences for ministers. Senator Dole, considering the next presidential campaign, preserved a full deduction for business-sponsored banquets with speakers through 1988 and the egregious exemption of ethanol from the federal gasoline tax. Other preferences that were established or maintained included those for reindeer hunters, military personnel, oil and gas investors, low-income housing, steel manufacturers, tuxedo-rental firms, and companies operating in Puerto Rico. Congress deserves credit for reducing or eliminating some of the major types of tax preferences, but the resulting conference committee tax bill was still far from being either simple or fair.

A number of details in the conference committee bill were deferred until Congress returned in September. These included the complicated transition rules, changes in the completed contract method of accounting, and a number of other technical details. Many members of Congress expressed concern about the conference bill, including House majority leader Jim Wright and minority leader Bob Michel. Senator Danforth became the most vocal opponent of the bill, expressing primary concern about the effects on business investment. As in September 1985, members of Congress returned to Washington reporting that popular attitudes toward tax reform ranged from indifference to hostility. The momentum of this process, however, carried the day. On September 25 the House approved the conference bill by a vote of 292 to 136. On September 27 the Senate approved this bill by a vote of 74 to 23. The vote in each House represented a roughly proportionate support and opposition within each party. In the end House Democratic majority leader Jim Wright was the only congressional leader of either party to vote against the bill. The president signed the bill on October 22, completing a process that would probably prove to be the last major economic policy initiative of the Reagan administration.

A Summary Evaluation of the Tax Reform Act

The president described the objectives of tax reform as "fairness, growth, and simplicity." Fairness would be increased by eliminating federal income taxation for poor families and by reducing the variance of taxes among families and businesses in the same income class. The tax code would be simplified by reducing or eliminating some types of deductions, although the 925-page final bill was still too complicated to meet the president's objective of return-free filing by most taxpayers. The potential effects of the tax reform act on economic growth, however, were much less than meets the eye.

First, the changes in the individual income tax would only slightly reduce effective marginal rates on family income. How could this be? The act would substitute statutory rates of 15, 28, 33, and 28 percent on taxable income for the current fourteen rates (fifteen on single returns) ranging from 11 to 50 percent. The act would reduce average individual income tax rates by 6.1 percent.

The difference between effective and statutory marginal tax rates may sound like a tax lawyer's quibble, but it has important economic consequences. The effective rate is the change in tax liabilities divided by the change in *family* income. The statutory rate is the change in tax liabilities divided by the change in *taxable* income. The effective marginal rate is the relevant rate on which to base decisions to work, seek a higher paying job, save, and invest. For a given effective rate the statutory rate primarily affects how family income is spent. A slight change in effective tax rates would have little effect on the growth of total output and income. The substantial reduction in statutory rates, however, would have important effects on the allocation of this income among different activities.

Each of the major tax plans considered involved a trade-off of higher taxable income for lower statutory rates, and the change in effective marginal tax rates was the result of that trade-off. The effects of the final tax reform act on the effective marginal rates by income class are summarized in Table 3.3. As this table shows, the changes in effective marginal tax rates range from −2.1 to 2.0 percentage points, with the average effective marginal rate declining only 0.4 of one percentage point. The effective marginal rate will increase in the $50,000 to $75,000 income class, an increasingly important group of two-worker families. Similarly, the changes in the effective marginal after-tax rate (the private return to additional income) range from −2.5 to 2.3 percentage points, with the average effective after-tax rate increasing only 0.4 of one percentage point. The effect of this small increase in economic incentives on total output is probably too small to measure.

Moreover, no tax plan that is both revenue neutral and distributionally neutral can change effective marginal tax rates. The tax reform act will achieve a small reduction in effective marginal rates only by shifting about 6 percent of individual income tax liabilities to corporations. The 1981 tax act, in contrast, significantly reduced effective marginal rates, but only at the cost of a substantial reduction in revenues and, for a given spending path, an increase in future tax rates. Measured by the percentage change in after-tax income, the tax reform act will be roughly neutral among income classes. For any given revenue from the individual income class, however, the only way to reduce effective marginal rates is to lower tax liabilities by a higher proportion as a function of income. The proper measure of tax reform is whether it reduces effective marginal rates more than average rates. The 1986 tax reform reduced effective marginal rates much less than the reduction in the average tax rate.

Table 3.3 Effective Marginal Tax Rates by Income Class

	Effective Marginal Rate (%)		
Income Class[a]	1986	1989	Change
Less than 10	1.6	0.5	−1.1
10–20	7.0	5.6	−1.4
20–30	11.9	11.7	−0.2
30–40	12.4	12.2	−0.2
40–50	16.5	14.6	−2.1
50–75	19.9	21.9	2.0
75–100	21.2	21.1	−0.1
100–200	25.6	24.8	−0.8
Over 200	23.9	23.3	−0.6
Income-Weighted Average	15.4	15.0	−0.4

[a] In thousands of 1986 dollars.

Current conditions unfortunately do not appear to permit a substantial reduction in effective marginal tax rates. We cannot afford to reduce total tax revenues until there is much more serious spending restraint than has been exercised to date. In addition, our political system does not appear ready to accept a reduction in the progressivity of effective tax rates unless some great communicator makes a case for it. Until one or more of these conditions change, there will be no opportunity for a tax reform that would substantially increase the growth of total output and income.

The combination of the reduction in statutory tax rates and the reduction or elimination of some deductions, however, will have a substantial effect on the composition of family spending. For those who previously faced a statutory rate of 50 percent, the reduction in the top statutory rate will increase the price of home mortgages and charitable deductions from fifty cents to sixty-seven cents per dollar. Similarly, for this group the repeal of the deduction for state and local sales taxes will double the price of government services financed by these taxes. The proportionate effect of these changes will be much larger than the rather small changes in the effective marginal tax rates.

In summary, the changes in the individual income tax will have very little effect on the incentives to increase income. The primary effect of these changes will be to change the source of family income and the composition of spending, reducing the adverse effects of the tax system on these decisions.

Second, the changes in business taxation will substantially increase the effective tax rates on the income from new investment in the corporate sector. For some types of investment these changes will

Table 3.4 Effective Marginal Tax Rates on New
Corporate Investment

Asset Type	Effective Marginal Rate (%)		
	1980	1985	1989
Equipment	11.4	4.5	37.3
Structures	50.2	41.7	44.2
Public Utilities	34.0	32.7	43.8
Inventories	48.5	47.7	43.4
Land	50.3	49.6	45.6
Total	40.2	37.2	42.1

lead to higher tax rates than in 1980, substantially reversing the effects of a major feature of the 1981 tax legislation. Table 3.4 summarizes the combined (federal, state, and local) effective marginal tax rates on new corporate investment for the same inflation rate and after-tax real interest rate, prior to ERTA, prior to the Tax Reform Act of 1986, and after the provisions of the new act are fully phased in.

One effect of this act, as the table indicates, is to increase the effective marginal tax rate on new investment in the corporate sector from 37.2 percent to 42.1 percent. This will increase the necessary pre-tax rate of return in the corporate sector by about 0.5 of 1 percent and will reduce the equilibrium corporate capital stock by about 8 percent.

The effective tax rates on noncorporate investment and owner-occupied housing (not shown) were not changed much by the 1986 act. For noncorporate business the elimination of the investment tax credit and the reduction in depreciation allowances are roughly offset by the reduced individual income tax rates. The 1986 act thus will lead to a lower level of domestic investment in the corporate sector, a higher level of investment in noncorporate business and owner-occupied housing, and an increase in net U.S. investment abroad. Another effect of this act, also indicated by the table, is that it will substantially reduce the variance in effective marginal tax rates among asset types and, indirectly, among industries within the corporate sector. It is not clear whether the improved allocation of investments within the corporate sector will more than offset the output effects of a lower level of corporate investment, but one 1986 study suggests that this may be the case.

On balance, the Tax Reform Act of 1986 is likely to have a small positive effect on long-run output and income. The reduction in the statutory tax rates on individual income and the reduction in the variance in effective marginal tax rates on corporate investment will improve the allocation of economic activity. The increase in the effective marginal tax rate on corporate investment will reduce the level of corporate investment. Personal consumption expenditures, in response to the increase in after-tax income, are likely to increase about 0.9 percent. Total investment by Americans is likely to decline about 3 percent; domestic investment will decline somewhat more and U.S. investment abroad will increase; and domestic investment by corporations may decline by as much as 8 percent. For 1987, however, the effects of the 1986 act were clearly adverse. The phased reduction of individual tax rates provided an incentive to defer income until 1988, and the elimination of the deduction on state and local sales tax provided an incentive to pull forward the purchase of consumer durables to 1986.

Other effects of the 1986 act should also be recognized. The anticipated effects of this act reduced corporate investment, real interest rates, and real exchange rates before the act was approved. This act will lead to a reduction of the trade and current-account deficit primarily by reducing domestic investment, the opposite effect of the 1981 tax legislation. The reduction in the statutory corporate tax rate and the real interest rate led to a substantial capital gain for the owners of existing capital stock, as revealed by the continued increase in stock and bond prices. Many of these effects, however, as with the 1981 tax legislation, were neither intended nor anticipated by the supporters of the 1986 legislation.

The Tax Reform Act of 1986 represented two steps forward toward improved tax legislation—and one step backward. Neither the administration nor Congress will want to open up the tax code during the remainder of the Reagan administration, but a new administration will probably be more receptive. In that case several features of the 1986 act should be reconsidered. The substitution of a $300 tax credit for the $2,000 personal exemption would increase revenues without increasing marginal tax rates. A reduction of the capital gains tax rate to about 20 percent would probably increase revenues by increasing realized capital gains more than the reduction in the tax rate. Including one-half of social security benefits in the taxable income of all recipients would both increase revenues and reduce the very high marginal rates on the middle-income elderly. Indexing capital gains, depreciation allowances, interest, and inventories would reduce the effective marginal tax rates on business investment, reduce the government's incentive to inflate, and reduce the vulnerability of investors to inflation. There is no substantive reason for the continued deduction of state and local income and property taxes. These and other measures to broaden the tax base should be considered before any increase in tax rates to reduce the continued large federal deficit. The Tax Reform Act of 1986 was a substantial achievement, for which the administration and key members of both parties in Congress deserve credit, but it was only the first step toward effective tax reform.

LEVELS OF THE DEFICIT AND THE DEBT

A huge deficit and the rapid increase in the federal debt will prove to be the major adverse legacy of the Reagan economic program. Most of the increase in the deficit has been due to the continued rapid growth of federal outlays, because the federal receipts' share of GNP (see Figure 3.1) was only slightly lower than the initial projections. Moreover, the resulting deficit was not part of a secret plan to bring pressure on domestic spending, contrary to a later assertion by Sen. Pat Moynihan. The administration and the congressional supply-siders were sometimes ambivalent about whether it was important to reduce the deficit, but the record clearly indicates that the increased deficit was an unintended result of the failure to reduce the growth of total spending. The administration did not have a deficit policy. It had a spending policy and a tax policy, and the deficit was an outcome rather than a target of these policies.

Figure 3.3 illustrates the pattern of the total (budget plus off-budget) federal deficit as a share of GNP during the Carter administration, and the projected and actual deficit share during the Reagan administration through FY 1985. The federal deficit, of course, reflects the combined effect of fiscal policies and economic conditions. The rapid increases in the deficits in fiscal years 1980 and 1982 were primarily due to the recessions in those years. After three years of recovery, however, the FY 1985 deficit share of GNP was roughly twice as large as in the comparable fiscal year of 1978.

For a variety of reasons the federal deficit in a specific year is not a good indicator of the federal fiscal condition. There is less reason to be concerned about an increase in the deficit resulting from a temporary increase in spending, as in wartime, or a temporary reduction in receipts, as in a recession. There is also less reason to be concerned about an increase in the deficit when inflation is high, because inflation reduces the real value of the existing debt. None of these conditions provides a rationale for the current huge deficit. The level of defense spending was not expected to be temporarily high. As of 1986, tax receipts had recovered to 19.6 percent of GNP, about equal to both the long-term average and the 1981 projection. And inflation has been stable for five years at less than one-third the rate in 1980.

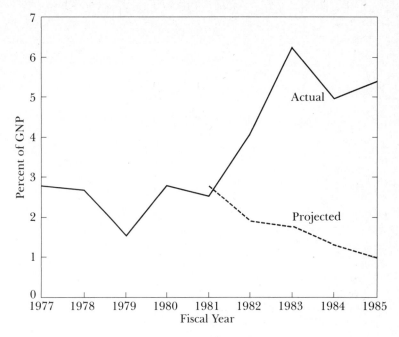

Figure 3.3   Federal Budget Deficit as Share of GNP

A more accurate indicator of the federal fiscal condition is the ratio of the federal debt (held by the public) to GNP, a measure that corrects for the overstatement of the effective deficit resulting from inflation. Figure 3.4 illustrates the pattern of this ratio during the Carter administration and during the Reagan administration through FY 1985. This comparison is even less favorable to the Reagan administration. The outstanding federal debt as a ratio to GNP declined slightly during the Carter administration, primarily because of the increase in inflation; in that sense the Carter deficits were sustainable even though they may not have been desirable. This ratio, however, increased sharply in each of the first four Reagan budgets and was projected to increase for several more years. The Reagan deficits were unsustainable in large part because of the sharp decline in inflation. Because this ratio cannot increase indefinitely, something must give. Stabilizing or reducing this ratio will require either reducing the growth of noninterest spending relative to GNP, increasing tax rates, or increasing the inflation rate (in effect, a tax on the holders of the outstanding debt). The likely prospect seems to be some combination of each of these three measures—an unfor-

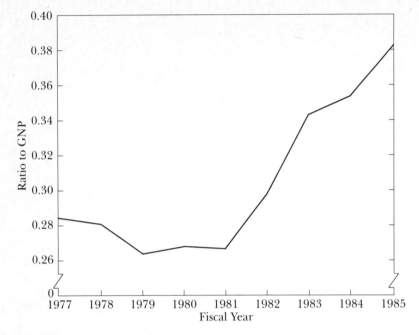

Figure 3.4   Federal Debt Held by Public (ratio to GNP)

tunate consequence of the failure to control the growth of federal spending during the first term.

ATTITUDES TOWARD THE DEFICIT

There are three reasons to be concerned about the federal deficit—fiscal, economic, and moral. Most of the controversy has been about the economic effects of the deficit, but most of the conjectures about these effects have turned out to be wrong in the short run. The necessary actions to reduce the deficit, however, are more likely to be based on the fiscal and moral concerns.

Fiscal Effects of the Deficit

The most direct fiscal effect of the deficit is the increase in interest payments. From FY 1981 through FY 1985 federal interest payments increased about $15 billion a year despite a sharp decline in interest rates. Continued deficits and interest rates at the 1985 level would increase interest payments by nearly $20 billion a year. The annual increase in interest payments is now almost as large as total spending for such programs as foreign aid, agriculture, and food stamps. The deficit itself has become one of the major sources of the growth of federal spending. As a matter of budget arithmetic, this annual increase in interest payments must at some time be offset by some combination of a progressive reduction in the growth of non-interest spending, an increase in tax rates, or an increase in the inflation rate. These fiscal effects became apparent before any of the several expected economic effects, and a concern about these effects was the primary motivation that finally led the administration and Congress to address the deficit.

There remains a serious controversy about one other potential fiscal effect of the deficit—the effect on federal spending. For many years economist Milton Friedman promoted a view that tax rates should be reduced at every opportunity, believing that the resulting increase in the deficit would increase pressure to reduce federal spending. President Reagan occasionally expressed a similar view that tax increases would not reduce the deficit, believing that Congress would increase spending by the same amount. James Buchanan (the leading public-choice economist) and Herb Stein have expressed a directly contrary view that a tax increase would reduce spending by increasing the perceived price of government services to the current voters. Some early research of mine was consistent with the Buchanan and Stein conjecture, a view I am still inclined to believe. The recent evidence, however, is not consistent with either position. A careful 1985 study indicates that in the short run, changes in federal spending appear to be independent of changes in tax receipts. Spending restraint must apparently be addressed directly. Changes in tax receipts, however, appear to be dependent on changes in spending. This study suggests that the traditional Republicans may be correct: a tax reduction is sustainable only if accompanied (or preceded) by spending restraint. The results of several later studies of this issue, however, are more consistent with the position of Friedman and Reagan. Economists and politicians unfortunately do not yet share a clear understanding of these relations.

Economic Effects of the Deficit

Most of the controversy about the deficit during the first Reagan term concerned the possible economic effects. For many years most economists and politicians of both parties shared a view that an increase in the federal deficit would increase inflation and interest rates. In early 1981, for example, Alan Greenspan, Walter Heller, and Herb Stein each expressed concerns that the proposed tax reduction would be inflationary. Stockman first used this argument to gain the president's approval for his ill-fated September 1981 initiative.

Although the view that an increase in the deficit would increase inflation and interest rates was widely shared, there was surprisingly little empirical evidence on this issue. Keynesians believed that an increase in the deficit would directly increase total demand. Many monetarists assumed that an increase in the deficit would lead the Federal Reserve to increase the money supply. Both groups assumed that an increase in the deficit share of GNP would increase real interest rates. And these views were broadly shared by politicians of both parties. Even the supply-siders accepted this perspective, but they believed that the reduction in tax rates would increase output and saving by enough to offset these effects.

My first and potentially last public controversy as a member of the CEA was the result of public remarks to the effect that the deficit does not appear to have much effect on either inflation or interest rates. I had first made some simple tests of the deficit-inflation relation in 1976 and found that the deficit did not appear to have any significant effect on inflation, either directly or through its effects on the money supply. In the fall of 1981 I made some additional tests of the effects on both inflation and interests rates and reviewed the few other available studies. At a public meeting at the American Enterprise Institute in early December, I summarized the results of these few studies. At that time I suggested that the opportunity to import capital may be one reason for the apparent absence of a relation between deficits and interest rates, but the audience rejected the plausibility of net capital inflows of any substantial magnitude. (In fact, net capital inflows increased rapidly to a level of about $144 billion in 1986). Although the transcript of my informal remarks reveals that I stated three times that these preliminary results did not indicate that deficits were of no concern, the next morning's headlines generally reported that "CEA Member Reports That Deficits Do Not Matter." Within a day the vice-president, the White House press secretary, and my colleague Murray Weidenbaum divorced themselves from my remarks, and three conservative senators called for my immediate resignation. After I made peace with the White House and the senators and refused calls from the press, the controversy died away quickly. My first exposure to Washington controversy, however, led me to be extraordinarily careful with the press and to recognize that for the White House, loyalty was a one-way street.

As the deficits increased to $100 billion and then to $200 billion, a large number of empirical studies were conducted on the effects of deficits on inflation and interest rates. In general these studies

indicate that an increase in the deficit has no direct effect on inflation and has no effect on the monetary base except in wartime. These
studies suggest that fiscal and monetary policy in the developed
countries are substantially independent in the short run. Moreover,
these studies are more consistent with a conclusion that inflation leads
to deficits—that is, that inflation increases the willingness to borrow
because it reduces the real value of the existing debt.

After inflation dropped sharply in early 1982, Stockman shifted
his argument to the effects of deficits on interest rates. This provoked the Treasury to conduct a study of this relation. This study,
released in 1984, found no effect of current deficits on interest rates
but did not provide an explanation of why real interest rates had
increased substantially in the 1980s. Martin Feldstein, modifying the
conventional wisdom, offered the explanation that real interest rates
are a function of expected *future* deficits, but a 1987 study of this
relation also rejects this hypothesis. The Congressional Budget Office reviewed about two dozen studies of the effect of deficits on
interest rates, most of which found little or no relation. There remains a strong theoretical reason why deficits have some effect on
interest rates. The general results of these studies, however, suggest
that this effect is overwhelmed by other conditions that also affect
interest rates. The best explanation why the rapid increase in the
deficit through FY 1986 did not have much effect on interest rates,
as I suggested in 1981, may have been the rapid increase in the flow
of capital from abroad.

After interest rates also dropped sharply in late 1982, Stockman
again shifted his argument. Adopting the strange reverse-Keynesian
position of Wall Street analysts, Stockman then argued that the deficit would prevent the recovery. In the spring of 1983, after the recovery was underway, he argued that the deficit would abort the
recovery. After the early recovery proved to be unusually strong,
Stockman's arsenal of apocalyptic visions about the economic effects
of the deficit was exhausted, and he went into internal hibernation
until the administration was again willing to address the budget after
the 1984 election.

One can be sympathetic with Stockman's sometimes lonely crusade
against the deficit without agreeing with his arguments. Stockman
tried to create a perception of a pending economic crisis in order to
energize the administration and Congress to address the developing
budget crisis, and he used almost any argument for which there was
outside support toward this end. And there was plenty of support
for one or more of his arguments from former chairmen of the CEA,
from Paul Volcker, and from Wall Street. After the fact, of course,
the economic apocalypse did not arrive. Since 1980 inflation has

declined by about three-fourths. Short-term interest rates have declined by about two-thirds. The economic recovery was unusually strong for the first two years, and the continued strength of the stock market suggests that the recovery may be unusually long. The political problem of the deficit was a consequence of the developing recognition that there was no "cliff" ahead—that the deficit does not have serious adverse effects on the economy in the short run. In that sense it is unfortunate that the several apocalyptic conjectures about the deficit are no longer credible. The extraordinary Gramm-Rudman procedure approved in 1985 is best interpreted as an attempt to create an artificial crisis to force a reduction in the deficit, as a substitute for the economic crisis that never arrived.

In early 1983 Martin Feldstein provided a new basis for a potential consensus by arguing that the deficit would distort the composition of the recovery. His first argument was that the budget deficits increase real interest rates and reduce investment. After it became clear that real domestic-business fixed investment was increasing rapidly, he shifted his position to an argument that the deficits increase the real exchange rate and the current account deficit on the trade accounts. Although this argument was plausible and addressed an issue of increasing political concern, there is surprisingly little evidence of this relation in either the longer U.S. experience or in the international comparisons. There is evidence that government deficits have substantial "crowding-out" effects somewhere in the world, but the allocation of these effects among sectors and countries has not been stable. Although the economic effects of government borrowing have been the subject of professional research for many years, the economics community has probably never been more confused about this issue.

The Deficit as a Moral and Constitutional Issue

There is a much broader consensus, both among the public and the politicians, that a sustained high level of government borrowing is wrong than there is any potential agreement on its economic effects. The basis for that consensus, I suggest, is moral. The current generation of voters should not have the right to finance current government services and benefits by means that require a reduction in future government spending or an increase in future tax rates. An especially sharp Oliphant cartoon makes this point; the cartoon shows President Reagan, Speaker O'Neill, an overstuffed general, and an old couple finishing a lavish meal, with a waiter handing the bill to a nearby baby.

There is less reason to be concerned about a deficit that is the result of temporarily high spending, such as for a war or a major capital-acquisition program, or of temporarily low tax receipts, such as during a recession. All of these excuses for the deficit, however, ran out in 1985, when Congress ended the rapid increase in defense procurement and the economic recovery had reached its third anniversary. The immediate problem is that our political system now reflects inconsistent preferences—for federal services and benefits that cost about 23 percent of GNP and for federal taxes that are about 19 percent of GNP. The near-term task is to resolve these inconsistent preferences. The longer-term task is to restore the historical consensus that the federal budget (excluding unusual capital spending) should be roughly balanced in peacetime over the period of an economic cycle. Something like the Gramm-Rudman procedure is probably necessary to address the near-term task. A formal amendment to the Constitution is probably necessary to address the longer-term task. As stated earlier, the huge deficits are the major adverse legacy of Reaganomics. The means by which the deficit is reduced will determine how much of Reaganomics survives.

In his first inaugural address, President Reagan observed that "you and I as individuals can, by borrowing, live beyond our means, but only for a limited period of time. Why should we think that collectively, as a nation, we are not bound by that same limitation?" Indeed! Reagan's initial conviction on this issue, as on many other economic issues, was sound. We must now pay the price of a lower future growth of either private consumption or government services as the consequence of the subordination of this conviction to other elements of the Reagan program.

CHAPTER FOUR

Regulation, Antitrust, and Trade

A far-reaching program of regulatory relief.

The Reagan program of regulatory relief promised more than it delivered. The failure to achieve a substantial reduction in or reform of federal regulations, building on the considerable momentum established during the Carter administration, was the major missed opportunity of the initial Reagan program.

REGULATION

Background

Federal regulation of the American economy grew rapidly beginning in the late 1960s. More than twenty new regulatory agencies were established by 1980, primarily to administer the developing "social" regulation of health, safety, and the environment and the expanded regulation of energy. Among the more important of these new agencies were the Consumer Product Safety Commission (CPSC), the Environmental Protection Agency (EPA), the National Highway Traffic Safety Administration (NHTSA), and the Occupational Safety and Health Administration (OSHA). During the Nixon and Ford administrations real spending by the federal regulatory agencies increased at a 17 percent annual rate. A study by Murray Weidenbaum estimated that the gross annual cost to the economy of federal regulations may have been as high as $66 billion in 1976. Other studies suggested that about one-tenth of the decline in the growth of productivity may have been attributable to the increase in regulation. Another study estimated that Americans were spending about 1.5 billion hours a year filling out federal forms.

Although the objectives of these new regulations were broadly supported, a developing concern that the increased regulation may have contributed to increasing inflation and slower productivity growth led President Ford in 1975 to direct the executive branch regulatory agencies to prepare "inflation impact statements" and authorized the newly created Council on Wage and Price Stability (COWPS) to review these statements. President Carter modified this approach to require more general "regulatory analyses" but stressed that proposed regulations need not meet a formal benefit-cost test.

The Carter record was a strange combination of substantial new regulation and substantial deregulation. Carter maintained the controls on energy prices and expanded the controls on energy uses. The 1977 amendments to the Clean Air Act substantially tightened emissions controls, in some cases by grossly inefficient means. A federal program to regulate and clean up toxic dump sites was established. A "voluntary" system of wage and price guidelines, administered by COWPS, was established. And in the spring of 1980, very stringent credit controls were imposed, contributing to a short, sharp recession in the election year.

During the Carter years, however, a movement developed to reduce the older forms of economic regulation, initiated primarily by economists in the independent agencies and supported by COWPS. In 1978, following a partial deregulation by the Civil Aeronautics Board beginning in 1976, Congress authorized the complete deregulation of domestic air travel. In 1980 Congress also approved a partial or phased deregulation of trucking, railroads, and banks. And in September 1980, following the imposition of a "windfall profits" tax on oil, Congress set a one-year deadline on the remaining price controls on oil. On balance, the growth of federal regulations slowed substantially during the Carter administration. From FY 1977 through FY 1981, real spending by the federal regulatory agencies increased by 4.5 percent a year, peaking in FY 1980. The broad support for these measures provided a basis for expecting considerable further deregulation by the new Reagan administration.

The Initial Reagan Agenda

The initial and continuing focus of the Reagan regulatory program was relief, not reform. In his December 1980 "economic Dunkirk" memo, Stockman summarized the rationale for this approach:

> A dramatic, substantial *rescission* of the regulatory burden is needed for the short term cash flow it will provide to business firms and [for] the long term signal that it will provide to corporate investment planners. A major "regulatory ventilation" will do as much to boost business confidence as tax or fiscal measures.

The new administration moved quickly to implement this approach during its first month in office. On January 22 a Task Force on Regulatory Relief, chaired by Vice-President George Bush, was established to provide general policy guidance. On January 28 a large number of pending regulations were suspended for sixty days to permit review by the new administration, and the remaining price controls on oil were terminated. On January 29 Carter's voluntary wage and price guidelines were terminated, COWPS was abolished, and the regulatory review was centralized in the OMB Office of Information and Regulatory Affairs (OIRA). Shortly after, two economists who had designed the initial regulatory agenda were appointed to key positions—Murray Weidenbaum as chairman of the CEA and James Miller as head of OIRA.

The most important of the initial measures was Executive Order 12291, issued on February 17. This order instructed the executive agencies, to the extent permitted by law, to use a maximum net benefit criterion for new regulations, the review of existing regulations, and the development of new regulatory legislation. (The independent agencies are formally agents of Congress and are exempt from this executive order. A president's influence over these agencies is limited to his authority for appointments and the budget.) A special procedure was established for major rules, defined as those rules for which the expected annual costs are $100 million or more or that have a significant adverse effect on a specific industry. For these major rules the agencies were directed to prepare preliminary and final "regulatory impact analyses," to include an estimate of the benefits and costs of the proposed rule and an explanation of the legal reason why some alternative rule with higher net benefits could not be adopted. OIRA was authorized to review these analyses and all proposed rules prior to their publication in the *Federal Register*. In addition, the agencies were directed to publish semi-annual calendars of proposed regulations and current regulations under review. One irony is that the rather tenuous legislative authority for this executive order, which requires some increase in government paperwork, was the Paperwork Reduction Act of 1980.

The able specialists who drafted this executive order recognized that a numerical estimate of benefits and costs could not be prepared for many rules and that the authorizing legislation for much regulation does not permit the choice of rules by the net benefit criterion. The most realistic objective of the executive order was to ensure that the executive office was informed about major new rules and proposed legislation with sufficient time for review and possible modification. The primary objective of the net benefit standard was to inform the agencies about the criterion by which OIRA would review proposed rules.

These measures were a substantial accomplishment for the first month of the new administration. The difficulty of reducing or reforming federal regulation, however, became apparent very quickly. Of the 172 proposed rules that were suspended, for example, 112 were approved without change, and only eighteen were withdrawn. OIRA's batting average would never again be as high. And in June the Supreme Court's decision in the "cotton dust" case ruled that a regulatory agency must set the tightest "feasible" standard, if that is the criterion established by the enabling legislation, even if the benefits are much less than the costs—a decision that may be good law but is lousy economics.

Economic Regulation

The federal government has regulated the prices, output, means of production, and conditions for entry of some sectors of the economy for many decades. This type of regulation was first applied to the transportation, communications, and financial sectors and is administered by the independent agencies. Some economic regulation—specifically affecting agriculture, energy, and labor—is administered by executive agencies. The Reagan administration was only moderately successful in reducing or reforming the several types of economic regulation.

The web of federal regulations is too complex to summarize briefly. Several thousand new or modified regulations are issued each year by the executive agencies, and many more are issued by the independent agencies. This section and the following two sections thus can only describe a representative sample of the regulatory issues addressed by the Reagan administration.

Agriculture

Several efforts to reduce the extensive regulation of agriculture were largely unsuccessful. In early 1981, for example, the Department of Agriculture initiated a major review of the agricultural marketing orders. These orders in effect are farmer cartels with government authority and cover a variety of fruits, vegetables, and specialty farm products. A few of these orders restricted any new entry, and some others limit how much fresh produce can be released to the market. In January 1982 the Department issued preliminary guidelines that would have eliminated the restrictions on entry and substantially increased the limits on releases to the market. David Stockman forcefully defended these guidelines at a cabinet meeting, displaying pictures of small mountains of rotting California oranges that could not be sold. After a storm of protest from the California growers, the White House weakened these guidelines, and Congress later prohibited OMB from further study of the marketing orders. All that remained when the modified guidelines were released in 1983 was the phaseout of the entry restrictions on two small crops and a slight relaxation of the sales limits on the major crops.

The federal milk orders proved to be even more invulnerable. These orders establish the minimum prices that milk processors pay farmers for Grade A milk, and they eliminate the incentive for the commercial reconstitution of dry milk for human use. The effect of these orders is to protect the dairy farmers in most states from the more efficient dairies in the upper Midwest. In 1979 a consumer group innocently asked the Department of Agriculture to hold a hearing on this issue. In April 1981, however, the department denied this request on the basis of estimates that a more efficient distribution of milk production would increase the budget costs of supporting milk prices. Secretary Jack Block announced this decision to a cheering audience at a major dairy cooperative.

These two examples illustrate both the absurdity of federal farm policy and the somewhat selective focus of the Reagan program of regulatory relief. As consumers, Americans pay more for farm products as a consequence of federal farm programs and regulation. As taxpayers we pay again to reduce the price of farm products to selective groups by food stamps, school lunch and milk programs, foreign aid, and export subsidies. In addition, all too often the administration ruled against a change in regulation that would benefit consumers at the expense of some concentrated business group.

Communications

For more than fifty years the independent Federal Communications Commission (FCC) has allocated rights to use the electronic frequency spectrum by broadcasters in exchange for commitments on program content. In many cases this prevented broadcasters from carrying programming that the audience would prefer. In some cases the FCC used its regulatory powers to restrict competition to maintain the value of the rights used by existing stations. The proliferation of radio and television stations and the development of cable and satellite transmission, however, led many to question the historic rationale for the regulation of broadcasters.

Mark Fowler, appointed as chairman of the FCC by President Reagan, moved quickly to reduce the regulation of broadcasters. In February 1981 the FCC deregulated most commercial radio broadcasting, and in May it introduced a simplified renewal application for radio licenses. In September the FCC proposed legislation to streamline its operations and permit more competition in broadcasting, but this proposal has yet to be approved. In late 1981, however, Congress approved the extension of radio licenses from three to seven years and of TV licenses from three to five years, and it authorized a lottery system for the allocation of new licenses. (The FCC action to implement the AT&T divestiture is discussed later in this chapter.)

Some of the telecommunications decisions, however, restricted potential competition. In 1981 the FCC withdrew its proposal to allow AM stations to broadcast at intervals of 9 kilohertz, the standard in most of the world, rather than the current standard of 10 kilohertz. In 1983 the FCC proposed to relax the "financial interest and syndication rules," which restrict the right of the TV networks to develop original programming and to syndicate reruns. These rules in effect protect Hollywood from competition by the networks. Although this proposal was broadly supported within the administration, the "California mafia" in the White House ruled in favor of Hollywood, and the proposal was withdrawn. On balance, however, the regulation of both broadcast and common-carrier communications was substantially reduced during the Reagan years.

Energy

The Reagan administration wanted to extricate the federal government from the energy business but did not have a clear plan to accomplish this objective. The initial proposal to eliminate the Department of Energy had little support in Congress and was not renewed. The most successful effort to decontrol energy was the immediate termination of oil price controls in January 1981. These controls, which had been established as part of the general price and wage controls in 1971, had previously been scheduled to end in September 1981. After an initial increase, real oil and gasoline prices have generally declined since March 1981. In 1982 oil well completions were nearly 50 percent higher than in 1980, and domestic production (exclusive of Alaska) increased slightly, reversing a ten-year trend, and despite the decline in real prices. A continued decline in energy consumption and the increase in domestic oil production reduced oil imports (net of the increased additions to the strategic petroleum reserve) by 34 percent by 1982. The energy "crisis" of the 1970s was ended by the stroke of a pen, and by 1983 the administration and Congress were already considering several types of oil taxes to maintain the retail price of oil.

One of the missed opportunities of the Reagan program was the failure to achieve a corresponding elimination of the legislative controls on the wellhead price of natural gas. These controls were first established by a court decision in 1954. After a severe gas shortage in the winter of 1977, Congress approved the Natural Gas Policy Act (NGPA) of 1978. This act provided for the phased deregulation of most gas discovered after 1977 but maintained price controls on "old" gas. Another 1978 law authorized the rationing of gas to power plants and industrial users. These acts were intended to encourage gas production while restraining the increase in the price to residential and commercial users. The second oil shock of 1979 and 1980, however, created another artificial shortage of gas because real gas prices were limited to their 1978 levels.

The Reagan administration was slow to address this issue. Secretary of Energy Jim Edwards, a genial dentist and former governor of South Carolina, acted more as a caretaker of the department than a promoter of deregulation. At the initiative of Interior Secretary Jim Watt, however, a series of cabinet council meetings addressed this issue in 1982. Although the cabinet council drafted and approved a simple decontrol proposal, the White House deferred this proposal as part of a general pattern of avoiding any controversial issues prior to the 1982 election. After Secretary Edwards was replaced by Donald Hodel, Watt's deputy at Interior, the Department of Energy assumed responsibility for drafting a gas decontrol bill. This bill, submitted to Congress in the spring of 1983, provided for the eventual decontrol of the wellhead price of all gas by 1986, with a complicated set of transition rules and contract readjustments. This bill satisfied no one and was not approved. At that time, decontrol was incorrectly expected to increase the price of gas to consumers, and the contract readjustments angered the producers.

One legacy of the failure of this bill was a convoluted scheme by the Federal Energy Regulatory Commission (FERC) in 1985 to attempt to replicate the effect of decontrol on wholesale prices without changing the wellhead prices of old gas. Another legacy is that we risk losing old gas reserves that amount to between eighteen and thirty-two months of total consumption. After the partial decontrol authorized by NGPA in 1985, new gas prices declined. It should now be clear that a decontrol of the prices of old gas would also reduce delivered gas prices by increasing the total supply of gas. The administration submitted another proposal to deregulate gas prices in 1986, but Congress has taken no action on this proposal. Following the sharp decline in oil prices in early 1986, however, FERC raised the price ceilings on all old gas to a common level substantially above the then-current price. If this action is not overturned by Congress or the courts, the price of old, gas will be effectively decontrolled until the market price again exceeds the ceiling price. A thirty-two-year period of misguided policy, beginning with a court ruling, may have been ended by this change in regulation.

One remnant of the extensive controls on energy uses established during the 1970s is a requirement that the corporate average fuel economy (CAFE) of new cars and light trucks meet or exceed a phased increase in government standards. These standards, established to increase automotive fuel economy by regulation rather than by decontrol of oil prices, were not binding through 1982 because of the increasing relative demand for small cars. A revival of the demand for larger cars and engines beginning in 1983, however, threatened to lead to conditions that would require the government to impose annual penalties of several hundred million dollars on General Motors and Ford and would limit the opportunity for these and several foreign auto manufacturers to produce those cars for which they are most competitive. In 1984 Christopher DeMuth (who succeeded Miller as head of OIRA in late 1981) and I completed an analysis of these standards and initiated a proposal to reduce or eliminate these standards before they seriously distorted the American automotive market. In the election year, however, the White House again did not want to address any controversial issues. In the winter of 1985, however, the pending termination of the limit on imports of Japanese autos forced a reconsideration of this issue. In March several auto manufacturers petitioned for a reduction of these standards, and in July NHTSA approved a reduction in the standard for new cars from 27.5 miles per gallon to 26 miles per gallon for the model year 1986. This standard was later extended through model year 1988. A change in legislation, however, will ultimately be required to eliminate this set of misguided energy standards.

Financial Institutions

For the most part, changes in financial regulation were forced by major developments in the financial markets. Don Regan, in his prior position as chairman of Merrill Lynch, was probably most responsible for forcing the deregulation of bank deposit interest rates by promoting the money market mutual funds. In 1980 Congress responded to the erosion of deposits in commercial and savings banks by approving a law that phased out interest rate ceilings on time and savings deposits over a period of six years, authorized all depository institutions to offer NOW accounts, authorized the savings bank to make consumer and business loans, and phased in uniform reserve requirements on most types of accounts by 1987.

The special problems of the savings banks, however, only changed in character. These banks, which had previously faced a loss of deposits, now faced higher interest rates on deposits than on many of their older, fixed-rate mortgages. The Reagan administration supported several measures to address these problems. New regulations issued by the Comptroller of the Currency in 1981 and by the Federal Home Loan Bank Board in 1982 authorized depository institutions to offer variable-rate mortgages. The most important of these measures was the Garn-St Germain Act, approved by Congress in late 1982. This act authorized depository institutions to offer a new money market account to small depositors and a new super-NOW account to large depositors. These new types of accounts proved to be very popular and were estimated to increase interest payments to depositors by about $3.6 billion a year. One provision of this act, opposed by the Treasury, provided a temporary infusion of capital by the federal insurance agencies to the savings banks in most distress. Other provisions permitted the acquisition of a failed bank by an out-of-state bank or by banks of a different type.

The administration was less successful in changing other types of bank regulation. In July 1983 the administration sent to Congress a Treasury proposal to broaden the powers of bank holding companies. This proposal would have authorized these holding companies to offer a wider range of financial services involving insurance, real estate, mutual funds, and municipal bonds. Opposition by other types of financial institutions and the May 1984 collapse of the Continental Illinois bank, however, indefinitely deferred approval of this proposal. A task force headed by George Bush worked for two years to draft a proposal to restructure the federal financial regulatory system, but resistance by Paul Volcker to a reduction of the regulatory authority of the Federal Reserve and the replacement of several key officials in 1985 delayed submission of this proposal until 1987.

The combined effects of the 1980 and 1982 laws and the regulatory changes subsequent to these laws have been quite favorable. Small depositors now earn market interest rates for the first time. Savings banks now have broader asset powers, reducing their portfolio risks and increasing their competitiveness with commercial banks. Some interstate banking has been authorized. However, numerous major problems remain. The combination of interest rate deregulation and the current structure of deposit insurance is not viable in the long run because banks now have an opportunity to shift more of their risks to the insurance system; some reregulation is probable unless the deposit insurance premiums or rules are changed. The total net worth of savings banks, by conventional accounting standards, is close to zero, and this system is very vulnerable to an increase in interest rates. Bank failures continue to increase, and the current reserves of the federal insurance agencies may be insufficient. The administration and Congress have not been willing to address the laws, almost unique to the United States, that restrict national banking and prevent banks from owning or underwriting equities in nonfinancial firms. A great deal remains to be done.

Labor

Federal law requires that contractors pay the "prevailing wage" on construction contracts supported by federal funds, and a similar law applies to service contracts. An unfortunate 1980 campaign commitment to the construction unions prevented the administration from proposing a repeal of these laws. In 1982, however, the Department of Labor approved several major changes in the regulations that implement these laws. The effects of these changes are to reduce the minimum wages that must be paid by these contractors and the restrictions on the employment of apprentice workers. The major part of these proposed changes was upheld by a court decision in July 1983. The department was also successful in relaxing some of the restraints on work at home.

The administration was less successful in changing the general minimum wage law. For several years beginning in 1983, the administration proposed a reduction of the minimum wage from $3.35 to $2.50 per hour, specific to young people through age twenty-one for employment from May through September. Although this proposal was broadly supported by the nation's black mayors, Congress has yet to act on this proposal. In 1987, moreover, there was broad congressional support for a bill that would substantially increase the minimum wage for all workers. In the meantime, the teenage unemployment rate continues to be nearly 20 percent.

Transportation

The accumulating experience with the deregulation of aviation, trucking, and railroads since the first initiatives in 1976 has been almost uniformly successful. Service has increased in most markets, and average real rates have declined. Major economies were achieved by increased capital utilization and by more effective discipline of labor costs.

The Reagan administration continued the deregulation of commercial transportation, but at a much slower rate. In July 1982 the administration concluded an agreement with the major European nations to permit greater flexibility in the fares on transatlantic flights. In late 1985, after several years of pressure from OIRA and CEA, the Department of Transportation approved the resale of landing slots at four crowded airports, but this action was later challenged by Congress. Some concern had been expressed that the Interstate Commerce Commission (ICC), under Chairman Reese Taylor, may have slowed the deregulation of trucking. The appointment of Taylor, a Nevada lawyer supported by the Teamsters Union, temporarily stalled the deregulation of trucking and railroads but without lasting effects. For example, the percentage of applications for new operating certificates declined slightly for two years after 1980, but the total number increased sharply. In 1984 OIRA and the Department of Transportation developed a proposal to end all remaining regulations of trucking, review the remaining rail regulation, and terminate the ICC on its one-hundredth anniversary in 1987. This proposal, however, was twice pulled off the cabinet council agenda, reportedly at the request of the Teamsters Union. The first legislative change affecting commercial transportation was the Bus Regulatory Reform Act of 1982. This act substantially deregulated intercity bus transportation, permitting both freer entry and exit and the near-complete deregulation of bus fares in 1985. In 1984, Congress also approved the Shipping Act to enable individual ocean shipping companies to offer lower rates and better services than permitted by the shipping conferences.

At the end of 1985 the prospects for continued deregulation appeared to improve. Heather Gradison, a committed deregulator, was nominated to replace Reese Taylor at the ICC, and the administration proposed to terminate the ICC in the FY 1987 budget. The administration may finally have broken its unseemly relation with the Teamsters Union. In 1986, however, a coalition of electric utilities and coal companies began pressuring Congress to tighten the regulation of rail rates to "captive" shippers, even though average real rates to these shippers have declined, and some reregulation of rail rates may be in prospect.

Social Regulation

Most of the federal regulation of health, safety, and the environment was initiated beginning in the late 1960s. Only the regulation of food and drug safety has a longer history. All this regulation is administered by executive agencies. Although the objectives of this regulation are broadly shared, much of it is seriously flawed, being based on inappropriate criteria or an inadequate data base, and is very costly. Much of this regulation in effect is a web of internal tariffs—protecting old products against new products, declining industries against growing industries, declining regions against growing regions, and, in one case, eastern coal against western coal—and the political support for this regulation clearly reflects both social and protectionist objectives. The Reagan attempt to reform these regulations, however, was a near-complete failure. Some of the major enabling laws have yet to be reauthorized, and the prospect for substantial reform of these laws and regulations is probably worse than in 1980.

The Environment

There was once reason to believe that the administration might propose a major reform of federal environmental policy. In the spring of 1981, Jim Watt initiated a major review of the Clean Air Act by the cabinet council on natural resources and the environment. I took the lead in identifying the major problems of this act and in formulating a proposed reform, with the able support of the holdover CEA staff. At the top of my agenda was a proposal to strengthen the federal commitment to address the problems of air pollution—such as acid rain, which is transported across state and national boundaries—and to increase the research base on these problems. A second proposal was to allow each state to set its own ambient standards on other pollutants. A third proposal would substitute a system of marketable permits for the national technology standards on new stationary sources. The sum of these permits in a given area (in effect, the rights to emit a limited amount of a specific pollutant in a specific time period) would be limited to meet the ambient environmental standard in that area. The opportunity to buy and sell these permits would then permit each polluter to choose the most efficient means to achieve the environmental standard, rather than having EPA prescribe the technology to be used. This proposal also would have eliminated a provision of the 1977 amendments that requires new power plants to reduce their sulphur emissions by the same percentage whether they burn coal with a high or low sulphur content, a provision that now leads to both higher-cost power and dirtier air; this provision was introduced to protect the eastern high-sulphur coal from the western low-sulphur coal. A fourth proposal would allow each state to choose one of two auto emission standards, depending on the relative importance of reducing auto pollution in meeting its own ambient standards. Such proposals had been supported by many environmental analysts for some time.

The cabinet council review of this issue extended into the summer. Anne Gorsuch (now Burford), the new EPA administrator, found herself in an awkward position. Although she distrusted the EPA staff, she was completely dependent on this staff because she and her key aides had almost no substantive understanding of environmental issues. She was also whipsawed by the White House, which gave her no guidance other than to stay out of controversy and to reduce the EPA budget. Her only contribution to this review was to relay the concerns of the EPA staff that my proposals were "too radical." Although my proposals were broadly supported in the cabinet council on substantive grounds, the EPA technocrats won the day. The White House decided against submitting proposed legislation to reform the Clean Air Act. On August 5 Anne Gorsuch went up to Capitol Hill with eleven "guidelines" for reviewing the Clean Air Act and came back with nothing. (Only ten commandments were sufficient for the children of Israel, but Moses presumably had divine guidance.) The Clean Air Act has yet to be reauthorized. Most of the gross inefficiencies resulting from this act remain. And the administration's failure to take the initiative on acid rain was perceived as a callous indifference to the one clear responsibility of the federal government on air pollution issues.

All was not lost, however. In April 1982 the EPA strengthened the emissions trading program on existing stationary sources of air pollution. This program includes a "bubble" policy that treats all sources at an individual plant site as a unit, an "offset" policy that allows states to offset increased pollution from one source by reduced pollution from another source, and a "banking" policy that allows credits to firms for pollution reduction to offset possible future increases. These policies have been broadly implemented by the states. These concepts were also later applied to the program of lead phase-down in gasoline, to auto emissions standards, and to the water pollution regulations affecting the steel industry. Without a change in the law, however, the potential for reform was limited to small regulatory changes to reduce the cost of meeting the standards or criteria established by legislation.

The administration also punted on the renewal of most of the other environmental laws. In early 1983 the administration proposed fourteen minor changes to the Clean Water Act, but within a few months it had backed off from some of these proposals. A proposed renewal of the Superfund (a program to clean up toxic dump sites) was also submitted, but this March 1985 proposal was seriously flawed. This proposal was drafted by the EPA without prior guidance and was approved by the White House without effective review. The basic flaw of this proposal is that it provides 90 percent federal funding to clean up toxic dump sites, although most of the benefits of this program will accrue to the states in which these sites are located. The administration's primary concern was to limit the federal cost of this program, but the structure of the proposal invited Congress to double the proposed spending, a level that was already several times the current level. There was almost no discussion of the merits or the structure of this program; almost all the discussion concerned its size and method of financing. This legislation, which was finally approved at the end of 1986, promises to be a massive pork-barrel program similar in size to the sewer construction grants authorized by the Clean Water Act, with only small local benefits and almost no national benefits. This was a classic case of an agency structuring its proposal to achieve the maximum possible increase in its budget. My own intervention was too late to stop this proposal, primarily because the administration wanted to avoid another environmental controversy. The only constructive change in environmental legislation during the first term was the Coastal Barriers Resources Act of 1982. This act, strongly supported by Jim Watt, eliminated federal development programs and subsidized insurance for new private developments on the fragile barrier islands off the East and Gulf coasts.

The prospect for a substantial reform of the federal environmental laws is now probably worse than in 1980. There is plenty of blame to go around. A part of the problem involved the key appointments. Anne Gorsuch was a feisty lawyer and a former Colorado legislator. She had almost no substantive understanding of environmental issues, however, and she was a poor manager. After scandals involving two key subordinates, she was ungraciously fired in March 1983. William ("Mr. Clean") Ruckelshaus improved the morale of EPA and the relations with Congress, but his one initiative to strengthen the acid rain program was blocked by Stockman. Lee Thomas, who replaced Ruckelshaus in 1985, is a technocrat with no commitment to reform. The most intriguing player in this game was Jim Watt, a more substantial person than was his public image. Watt was well informed and a good manager; he had moderately good relations with Congress, and he had a commitment to reform. He made better use of the cabinet council review process than any member of the first-term cabinet except Don Regan. Watt was also successful in revising some of the surface mining regulations about which he was especially knowledgeable. After a series of crude public comments, however, he was dismissed in October 1983. William Clark, Watt's successor as Secretary of the Interior, proved to be a caretaker with no agenda in his third administration position. (Clark's primary contribution to continued bad resource management was to provide administration endorsement, without any substantive review, of a renewal of the contract on electric power from Hoover Dam at rates much lower than market rates. The California mafia strikes again.)

The White House, however, deserves much of the blame. Stockman's focus on regulatory relief was not a sufficient basis for addressing the reform of regulations for which the objectives were broadly shared. The president has yet to make a major speech on environmental issues. And the Baker strategy of avoiding unnecessary controversy did not allow any key official to make the case for reform. The current debate on environmental policy has unfortu-

nately been polarized by the rhetoric of a holy war, indefinitely deferring the potential for change that could improve both the environment and the economy.

Health and Safety

The primary problem of current federal health and safety regulations is that in many areas, Congress has set a standard of lowest
feasible risk, regardless of the incremental benefits and costs of
meeting this standard. The Reagan administration, without seeking
a change in this legislation, had only modest success in improving
the regulation of health and safety.

In early 1981 the Task Force initiated a major review of federal
auto regulations, building in part on a similar review completed by
the Carter administration in mid-1980. The severe financial condition of the domestic auto industry was the primary motivation for
both of these reviews. On April 6 the administration announced that
thirty-four product standards, involving both safety and emission
standards, would be reconsidered. The most important of these was
a proposal to rescind the pending requirement for air bags or other
automatic restraints. The stated rationale for this change, however,
was seriously flawed, and in June 1983 the Supreme Court ruled
that this proposed change be remanded for additional justification
or that the automatic restraint standard be implemented. In mid-
1984 Transportation Secretary Elizabeth Dole deferred this issue
again by a contrived plan that automatic restraints would be required unless states with two-thirds of the population approved
mandatory seat-belt laws by 1989. Dole had previously replaced Ray-
mond Peck, the administrator of NHTSA who had supported the
repeal of the automatic restraint standard. At no time was the administration willing to make the case that the government has no
business setting standards that affect only one's own safety; it thus
lost the opportunity to establish a principle that would guide other
safety issues. Most of the other changes proposed by this group, such
as the reduction in the standard for dent-proof bumpers that had
no apparent safety effects, were later implemented.

In several cases Reagan appointees made significant improvements in regulatory management. Dr. Alan Hayes, a distinguished
clinical pharmacologist, directed the Food and Drug Administration
through mid-1983. Although his authority was severely restricted by
HHS and OMB, he substantially increased the rate of approval of
new drugs and proposed a greater reliance on foreign test data. Similarly, Thorne Auchter, a former construction company executive
appointed to head the Occupational Health and Safety Administration, substantially reoriented this agency. Federal inspections were

focused on high-hazard work sites and were substantially reduced at low-hazard sites. The rule of the federal inspectors was changed from a police role to a safety monitoring role. Although the OSHA staff was substantially reduced, this approach proved to be effective. For several reasons the workplace injury rate has since declined to the lowest level on record.

This record suggests that the selection of key officials can be important. Hayes and Auchter were both well-informed and effective managers, working with their career staff to reduce the burden of regulation within the constraints of the current legislation. A contrast of their record with that of Anne Gorsuch, for example, should be a lesson to guide future appointments.

State and Local Governments

The administration achieved a substantial reduction in regulations affecting state and local governments, primarily by consolidating a large number of categorical grants into a small number of block grants. As discussed in Chapter 2, however, there is reason to question whether broadening the authority of state and local governments to spend federal money serves any national purpose. Other changes included a substantial reduction in the regulations affecting state education, energy, and transportation programs. In addition, a new executive order issued in July 1982 increased the opportunity of state and local governments to influence federal actions affecting their jurisdictions. These measures have been broadly supported by state and local officials. For those state and local activities which serve a national purpose, however, deregulation may not be appropriate. For those activities which serve no national purpose, the elimination of federal grants would be superior to deregulation. The regulatory dimensions of Reagan's New Federalism primarily involved a deal with state and local officials to give them more authority to spend less money.

A General Assessment

On August 11, 1983, the Task Force on Regulatory Relief published a summary of the *Reagan Administration Regulatory Achievements* and promptly disbanded. This summary concluded that the regulatory actions through mid-1983 led to one-time cost savings of $15 to $17 billion and to annual cost savings of $13 to $14 billion. These estimates, however, have been strongly challenged. In general, for example, these numbers are estimates of the gross, not the net, cost savings; that is, they assume that the current or proposed regulations would have no benefits. In addition, these estimates include the cost savings from rescinding proposed rules that may not have been approved by the prior review process and, as in the case of the automatic restraint standard, changes that were later reversed. These estimates also do not include the costs (or benefits) of the new regulations imposed during this period. A related estimate of saving of 300 million hours per year of the federal paperwork burden is subject to similar qualifications. I am sympathetic with the attempt to quantify the benefits and costs of regulatory changes, but these estimates of the gross savings are not an adequate summary of the effects of the Reagan administration's actions.

Some indirect indicators suggest that the primary effect of the program of regulatory relief was to reduce the rate of growth of new regulations. Compared to the Carter years, for example, the annual number of new rules declined about one-fourth and the pages in the *Federal Register* declined by 39 percent. The growth of real spending by the federal regulatory agencies slowed from 4.5 percent a year from FY 1977 through FY 1981 to 1.4 percent a year from FY 1981 through FY 1985. The total number of lawyers in active practice, an index of all sorts of problems, tells a similar story, increasing by 7.4 percent a year from 1977 through 1981 and by 3 percent a year from 1981 through 1985. The regulatory momentum was clearly slowed, but it was not reversed.

The primary reason why the deregulatory momentum stalled is that the Reagan administration proposed only a few changes in the basis regulatory legislation, some of which were not enacted. The administration's reluctance to propose legislative change derived in part from political commitments to the construction, maritime, and trucking unions, and in part to Jim Baker's general political strategy of (in baseball terms) not going to the plate unless there was the prospect of hitting a home run. The only changes in substantive regulatory legislation approved in the first term were the Garn-St Germain Depository Institutions Act and the Bus Regulatory Reform Act, both approved in 1982, and the Shipping Act of 1984. A 1982 proposal to strengthen the legislative authority for Executive Order 12291 was approved by a Senate vote of 94–0 but was stalled in the House by the EPA scandals and a developing concern about the OIRA review process. The administration's 1983 proposals to reduce the regulation of bank holding companies and of the wellhead prices of natural gas were not approved. The disbanding of the Task Force on Regulatory Relief in August 1983, bracketed by the dismissals of Gorsuch and Watt, permitted George Bush to withdraw from an increasingly controversial activity but marked an indefinite delay of the administration's major deregulation initiatives. The administration did not submit a proposal for change in the major regulatory legislation from that time through 1985.

The able people who led OIRA probably pushed the White House regulatory review process as much as possible, given the limited change in regulatory legislation. Jim Miller, Chris DeMuth, Doug Ginsberg, and Wendy Gramm were each first-rate analysts and aggressive deregulators. (In late 1981 Miller was appointed chairman of the Federal Trade Commission and, in September 1985, director of OMB. In mid-1985 Ginsberg was appointed the assistant attorney general for antitrust.) Their aggressive actions to review, modify, or delay regulatory proposals inititated by the executive agencies, however, were ultimately checked by both Congress and the courts. In 1983 several bills to restrain the authority of the OMB review of regulation were considered in the House. One bill, for example, stated that "the Director [of OMB] may not participate in any way in deciding what regulatory action, if any, the agency will take in any rule making proceeding"—a bill that would have substantially reduced the statutory review authority exercised by each of the past several administrations. Although these bills were not approved, their introduction had a substantial deterrent effect on the activities of OIRA.

A more explicit restraint was the application of a "hard-look" doctrine by the federal court of appeals for the District of Columbia, including application by several key Reagan appointees to this court, to proposals for both regulation and deregulation. This new doctrine of the appeals court most responsible for review of administrative law cases, a doctrine that developed during the 1970s, substantially reduces the discretion of both the regulatory agencies and OIRA in interpreting their legislative authority. Although some officials have complained that the appeals court is substituting its own judgment on the substance of regulations, the primary effect of this doctrine is to require a more explicit rationale, based on the criteria established in the regulatory legislation, for regulatory changes of any kind. This role of the court increases the importance of changing the regulatory legislation if the momentum for deregulation is to be revived.

The maximum net benefit criterion for review of current and proposed regulations will not withstand challenge when this criterion, as is often the case, is inconsistent with the criteria established in the legislation. The basic review procedure established by Executive Order 12291, however, is likely to survive. In 1986 the House tried to eliminate the funding for OIRA on the basis that the review procedure interferes with the agency interpretation of regulatory legislation. At the request of the administration, however, the funding was restored in the final appropriation bill. Although this procedure has been controversial, it has worked reasonably well. On average, regulations were reviewed by OIRA in twenty-five days. About one in nine proposed rules were revised or returned to the agencies for further consideration. The requirement for "regulatory impact analyses" of major rules, however, has been only selectively applied. Of the 142 major rules reviewed in 1981 and 1982, for example, such analyses were prepared for only fifty-nine rules.

In January 1985 the administration initiated a renewed effort to strengthen the regulatory review process. Executive Order 12498 established a regulation review calendar, similar to the budget process, requiring the executive agencies to submit a statement of regulatory objectives and the major regulatory actions planned for the coming year. The objective of this process is to ensure that the actions of each agency are consistent with administration policy and the actions of other agencies. It is too early to evaluate the effects of this new process. The agencies still have little incentive to cooperate with this review process, however, when their interpretation of their legislative mandate differs from the criteria by which their proposed rules are reviewed. Yet this condition is not much different from agency attitudes toward the OMB budget review. Any president will want to maintain an effective review of federal regulation as long as regulations impose a substantial cost on the economy or risk substantial political controversy.

The Reagan administration thus had to rethink its deregulatory strategy if it was to preserve this key element of its initial program. A good team was in place with Miller and Gramm at OMB and Tom Moore at CEA. The key members of the cabinet supported the continued deregulation of energy and transportation. The Bush task force was revived. The primary near-term opportunity was to reduce or eliminate many of the remaining types of economic regulation. The primary long-term challenge was to build the research base and the political case for a substantial reform of the many types of social regulation. One can only hope that the first-term record or an overriding concern about political controversy does not lead to another missed opportunity.

ANTITRUST

The antitrust laws and their implementation should also be recognized as a form of business regulation. The statutory language of U.S. antitrust laws is rather general and somewhat inconsistent. As a

consequence the application of these laws is subject to broad interpretation by the courts, the Justice Department, and the Federal Trade
Commission (FTC).

The initial Program for Economic Recovery did not mention antitrust issues, and there has been no general statement of the antitrust
policy of the Reagan administration. The major changes in antitrust
policy were the consequence of two critical appointments. William
Baxter, a professor of law at Stanford University with strong economic skills, was appointed assistant attorney general for antitrust in
the Justice Department in early 1981. James Miller, after establishing the regulatory review office in OMB, was appointed chairman of
the FTC in the fall of 1981, the first economist to serve in this position. Both Baxter and Miller shared a strong belief that the application of antitrust laws should be focused on collusive activity to fix
prices and should be relaxed in other areas.

Baxter—an intense, sometimes abrupt intellectual—proved to be a
dynamo. By January 1982 Baxter had resolved the two major suits
initiated by the Justice Department. In 1969 Justice had filed a suit
against IBM, under Section II of the Sherman Act, for maintaining
artificially low prices of mainframe computers in an attempt to mo-
nopolize this market. In the intervening years this one suit involved
the expenditure of $1 to $2 million a year by Justice alone and the
accumulation of 104,000 pages of transcript. This suit apparently
led IBM to maintain an artificially high price to avoid prosecution.
One study estimated that the suit increased the price of mainframe
computers by 10 to 20 percent by 1971; another study estimated an
increase of 30 to 35 percent. On January 8, 1982, Baxter dismissed
this suit as "without merit." Resolution of the suit, according to a
1985 study, reduced the price of mainframe computers in 1981
through 1983 by about 20 percent. This proved to be one of the few
Baxter decisions that provoked little subsequent controversy.

A resolution of the AT&T case, an even larger case initiated in
1974, was more complex. A rapid improvement in telecommunications technology increased the potential for competition in telecommunications services, and some partial competition had already been
allowed. A 1968 decision by the FCC permitted compatible equipment from independent manufacturers to be attached to the Bell
system, and soon after, the FCC allowed independent carriers to
compete in some long-distance markets. The new technology of private cable, microwave relay, and satellites permitted some large
telecommunications users to bypass both the local and long-distance
telephone system. A major change in the structure of the telephone
industry and its regulation could not be deferred for very long.
Moreover, Baxter was in a hurry. Bell had long had a somewhat

incestuous relation with the Defense Department, and Weinberger threatened to halt Baxter's proposed plan. Under threat of a court decision imposing a divestiture plan designed by the Justice Department, Baxter and AT&T worked out a plan agreeable to both parties.

This plan, effective on January 1, 1984, allowed AT&T to maintain its long-distance services, unregulated communications services, and manufacturing company but required it to divest the twenty-two local operating companies. The court order codifying this settlement also required the local companies to provide equal-quality access to each long-distance carrier by 1987, and a subsequent FCC ruling required the local companies to charge a flat access charge to each subscriber, increasing to full cost by 1989.

The general effect of these decisions was expected to increase local charges and to reduce long-distance rates. Congress reacted sharply. More than a dozen bills were introduced to prevent or reduce the increase in subscriber charges, and hearings were held in each house. Although no bill was passed, congressional pressure forced the FCC to delay the access charge ruling. The state regulators now face an additional dilemma: any increase in local charges would increase the incentive of large-volume users to bypass the local companies, potentially increasing the average cost of serving low-volume users. The ultimate effects of this process will depend very much on the decisions of state regulators. Although the increase in local rates has been less than expected, few people are very happy about this process. Most analysts, however, believe the initial Baxter decision was right and could not long be deferred, a judgment that I share.

The other major antitrust decision by the Justice Department during the first term involved a proposed merger of LTV Corporation and Republic Steel. Although much of the review of this case was supervised by Baxter, the final decision was made by his successor, Paul McGrath, in early 1984. McGrath rejected this proposed merger, stumbling badly his first time out of the chute, and provoked a sharp response from Commerce Secretary Malcolm Baldrige and a rare critical remark by the president. The primary criticism was the failure to recognize the impact of foreign competition on the effective concentration of the domestic steel market. McGrath quickly approved a slightly revised merger plan. Most of the other antitrust cases addressed by the Justice Department also involved the review of proposed mergers. From my perspective Baxter rejected too many of these proposed mergers, but that may have been the price of protecting his more flexible position on other dimensions of antitrust law.

Baxter also moved quickly to complete a major revision in the merger guidelines by the summer of 1982. These new guidelines incorporated a more sophisticated measure of the degree of industry concentration and provided an opening for considering the potential efficiency effects of mergers and the effects of foreign competition on the effective concentration of the relevant markets. After McGrath's experience with the LTV-Republic case, the second revision of the guidelines in the summer of 1984 strengthened the relative consideration of potential efficiencies and foreign competition.

People do make a difference. In a short period Baxter changed antitrust enforcement from a rather general harassment of American business to more vigorous prosecution of potential monopoly cases under existing law. Working with Baldrige, he also shepherded two minor changes in antitrust law through Congress. One law permits competing firms and banks to form export trading companies. Another law permits competing firms to establish joint ventures for research and development. To no one's surprise, Baxter ultimately pushed the changes in antitrust enforcement further than Congress would accept. In the fall of 1983, after Baxter had prepared a brief arguing for a more relaxed interpretation of the restrictions on resale price maintenance, a position supported by many economists, Congress refused to allow Baxter to appear in court to defend the brief, and he soon returned to academia. Miller was also very effective as chairman of the independent FTC in a less dramatic way. Miller selected a strong cadre of bureau chiefs, terminated the major investigations of the auto, oil, and cereal industries, supported a number of changes in state regulations to increase competition, and reduced the FTC staff. Moreover, his quiet Georgia style protected his congressional relations and smoothed his nomination as Stockman's successor at OMB in the fall of 1985.

At Baldrige's initiative—supported by Miller at OMB and Douglas Ginsberg (McGrath's successor) at Justice—the administration prepared a broader proposal to change the antitrust laws in the fall of 1985. The initial Baldrige proposal was to repeal Section 7 of the Clayton Act, a section that prohibits mergers or acquisitions where "the effect . . . may be substantially to lessen competition or to tend to create a monopoly." This proposal would also require corresponding amendments to the Sherman Act and the Federal Trade Commission Act.

The antitrust working group could not agree on the repeal of Section 7 of the Clayton Act and presented several options to the president. The final resolution of this issue was to propose that mergers or acquisitions would be prohibited only when they "increase the ability to exercise market power," where such power is defined as a "significant probability" of maintaining higher-than-competitive prices for some time. The group, however, reached full agreement on a number of other issues. Treble damage awards would be restricted to plaintiffs, either private parties or the government, who paid higher prices or who, as sellers, received lower prices as a consequence of antitrust violations by the defendant. In all other cases awards would be limited to actual damages, prejudgment interest, costs, and attorneys' fee. A prevailing defendant would receive an award of attorneys' fees where the claims of a private plantiff are ruled to be "frivolous, unreasonable, without foundation, or in bad faith." The joint and several liability standard would be changed to reduce the plaintiff's recovery by the share of damages allocated to any party the plaintiff releases from liability; the current standard, in contrast, makes any remaining plaintiff subject to the full liability of the group. Another measure would relax the absolute prohibition on interlocking directorships. There was also general agreement that private antitrust suits should be dismissed in some cases involving foreign commerce. The most controversial proposal by this group would permit antitrust exemptions for mergers and acquisitions in industries injured by imports, as an alternative remedy to import protection under the trade laws. The general effects of these proposals would focus the antitrust laws on the deterrence of monopolistic behavior, provide more symmetrical treatment of plaintiffs and defendants in both private and government suits, and relax the restrictions in cases involving international trade. An administration proposal based on these recommendations was submitted to Congress in early 1986 but has yet to be addressed.

Overall, the administration achieved a substantial focusing of the antitrust laws while reducing some of the costs of the more peripheral elements of these laws—a tribute to the intellect and energies of the responsible officials.

INTERNATIONAL TRADE

Principles and Pressures

Trade policy in the Reagan administration is best described as a strategic retreat. The consistent goal of the president was free trade, both in the United States and abroad. In response to domestic political pressure, however, the administration imposed more new restraints on trade than any administration since Hoover. A strategic retreat is regarded as the most difficult military maneuver and may be better than the most likely alternative, but it is not a satisfactory outcome.

The initial Reagan program only briefly mentioned international economic policies and conditions, almost as an afterthought. The administration expected that "improving expectations and slowing inflation will enhance the dollar as an international store of value," but the large subsequent increase in the real exchange rate was wholly unanticipated. The administration further expected that "rising U.S. productivity will enhance our ability to compete with other countries in world markets, easing protectionist pressures at home." As it turned out, the growth of productivity increased, but not enough to offset the rapid increase in the real exchange rate, and protectionist pressures increased steadily. Among the major objectives of the initial Reagan program were to increase spending for defense and business investment, but there was little thought about where these resources would come from. Only since 1983, however, was it recognized that much of these resources were indirectly provided by an increase in imports or were diverted from the domestic trade-affected sectors.

The administration later developed a more comprehensive "Statement on U.S. Trade Policy," presented to Congress by Trade Representative William Brock on July 8, 1981. The primary theme of this statement was "free trade, consistent with mutually accepted trading relations." The development of this statement revealed substantial differences within the cabinet on trade policy that were later reflected in the major trade cases. The draft of this statement, prepared by the office of the U.S. Trade Representative (USTR) and the Commerce Department, described the objective as "free and fair trade," providing an opening for a unilateral U.S. interpretation of what constitutes "fair" trade. A last-minute intervention by Treasury, OMB, and the CEA—the core of the free trade coalition in the cabinet—was the origin of the primary theme in the final statement. The statement developed five central policy components:

1. Restoration of strong noninflationary economic growth.
2. Reduction of U.S.-imposed disincentives to exports.
3. Effective enforcement of U.S. trade laws and international agreements.
4. Effective approach to industrial adjustment problems, with a primary emphasis on market forces.
5. Reduction of government barriers to the flow of trade and investment among nations, with strong emphasis upon improvements and extensions of international trade rules.

For the conditions anticipated in mid-1981, these five elements would have been a satisfactory and sufficient statement of trade policy. The combination of some 1980 campaign commitments, controversies with the administration, the long recession of 1981 and 1982, and the rapid increase in the real exchange rate, however, led to numerous breaches of this policy by the administration.

Major Trade Cases

Automobiles

The administration addressed two trade cases in the spring of 1981 before completion of the trade policy statement, which set a pattern for decisions on later cases. The most important of these cases concerned the import of automobiles. I was especially sensitive about this issue. As chief economist for Ford Motor Company, I was fired in July 1980 for my internal opposition to the petition by Ford and the United Auto Workers for "escape-clause" restraints on auto imports. In September the International Trade Commission (ITC) rejected this petition on the basis of a finding, which I had anticipated, that the increase in imports was not the primary cause of the decline in the sales of domestic autos. This ITC decision provoked candidate Reagan, speaking to Chrysler workers in Michigan, to pronounce that "one way or another," Washington must convince the Japanese to reduce their auto sales in the U.S. market.

The position of the new administration on auto imports emerged from the auto industry task force, headed by Transportation Secretary Drew Lewis. This task force reflected a broad agreement on the proposed reduction of auto regulations but divided sharply on import limits. Lewis, Baldrige, Brock, and a few others favored some type of limit, both to meet the campaign commitment and to defer pressure for a quota bill promoted by Sen. John Danforth. Regan, Stockman, and Weidenbaum opposed the auto limits, arguing that the protection of such a visible industry could undermine the whole economic program; at that time they were unaware that Lewis was working with Meese and Baker to develop some sort of import limit. This issue came to a head at a task force meeting with the president on March 19. After the two groups made their points, the president was still reluctant to endorse a specific U.S. position, no vote was taken, and no formal decision was endorsed. The final position developed, without further review, from the initial Meese-Lewis understanding. The proposed reductions in auto regulation were announced on April 6 without any position on import limits. In late April Brock flew to Tokyo to "confer" with the Japanese, and, voila!— on May 1, the Japanese announced a "voluntary restraint agreement" (VRA) to limit their export of cars to the U.S. market. The Japanese agreed to limit their exports to 1.68 million cars during the first year, with some unspecified increase in each of the two following years.

This method of imposing a quota on imports from a specific country represents an envasion of both U.S. trade law and the General Agreement on Tariffs and Trade (GATT) and was used for both autos and the later steel cases specifically for this reason. A VRA, because it is nominally a voluntary action by the exporting country, is not subject to the injury tests of escape-clause cases and does not require compensation of the exporting country. The president was later quite defensive about the auto VRA, stating that this was a unilateral action by the Government of Japan, but this rationalization was disingenuous at best. A few weeks after I joined the CEA, the administration had arranged for a measure for which I had been fired for opposing only nine months previously. My return to Washington proved to be a hard landing.

The auto agreement was later modified several times. In response to the continued weakness in the U.S. auto market through 1982, the Japanese maintained the export limit at 1.68 million cars during the second and third year of the agreement. In early 1984 there was considerable controversy within the cabinet about whether the export limit should be extended for another year. Ambassador Brock argued strongly against extending the export limit, on the basis of the large profits and executive bonuses in the domestic industry and the consequences of extending the agreement during the year in which the GM and Ford labor contracts would be negotiated. We were all reminded, however, that 1984 was also an election year, and the agreement was extended through March 1985 at a limit of 1.85 million cars. A second year of record profits and the reelection of the president finally led the administration not to seek renewal of the VRA in 1985. For its own reasons, however, the Government of Japan set a new limit of 2.3 million cars.

After the fact, it is now clear that the VRA was not binding in 1981 and 1982 because of the weak U.S. demand in these years. In 1983 and 1984, however, the VRA increased the price on Japanese cars sold in the United States and substantially increased the sales, but apparently not the price, of domestic cars. One other effect, common to such quotas, is that it increased the average quality and size of Japanese cars sold in the States and substantially increased the profits of the Japanese auto companies. The annual cost to consumers of the auto VRA was more than $1.1 billion, about $240,000 per job saved in the domestic auto industry. The long-term cost of the VRA may also be substantial, because it increased the cost of the domestic industry labor contracts negotiated in 1984 and 1985, probably preventing the domestic industry from being competitive in the production of small cars.

The auto VRA, moreover, was not sufficient to deter demands for more permanent protection of the domestic industry. In 1982 and 1983 the United Auto Workers pressed for "domestic content" legislation that would require up to 90 percent of the content of cars sold in the United States to be produced here. Strong opposition to this bill by the auto dealers, farm groups, and the administration was sufficient to defeat this proposal. Although this bill was twice approved by the House, it was defeated in the Senate and has not been revived.

Footwear

In the spring of 1981 the ITC recommended an extension of the quotas on imports of footwear from selected countries, but the president rejected this recommendation in June. As with most industries once protected from imports, however, this issue did not go away. The domestic industry again petitioned for protection in 1984. On this occasion the ITC rejected the petition. Congressional pressure forced the ITC to reopen this case in 1985, and, on the basis of much the same information as was available in 1984, the ITC recommended quotas on footwear imports. In September, against the advice of most of the cabinet, the president rejected this recommendation. The Senate later added footwear protection to the textile bill that the House approved in October, but the final bill was vetoed by the president in December. One of the reasons that this industry has not been effective in maintaining protection is that the industry is divided; some of the larger producers are parts of integrated firms that are also major importers and retailers. The footwear coalition also made a tactical mistake in appointing a former Democratic official as its chief lobbyist and Senator Kennedy as its chief congressional spokesman. The footwear industry is the only major industry for which import restraints are now lower than in 1980.

Steel

The U.S. steel industry, like the auto industry, was in serious trouble in the early 1980s, and for much the same reasons. Both of these industries allowed their labor costs to escalate rapidly during the 1970s during the same time that they first faced substantial foreign competition. Following the breakdown of the "target price mechanism" implemented by the Carter administration, the steel industry filed a large number of petitions for "countervailing duties" on imports from the subsidized European steel companies in the spring of 1982. The evidence was clear; most European steel companies, other than those in Germany and the Netherlands, were (and are) receiving small subsidies, and U.S. law provides for an automatic countervailing duty to offset such subsidies. Using the threat of these potential duties,

Commerce Secretary Baldrige gained agreement on a comprehensive quota on steel imports from Europe in September, in the form of VRAs from each country. This action, without effective review by the cabinet-level Trade Policy Committee (TPC), was a major mistake. The European quota covered both subsidized and unsubsidized companies, shifting the focus of the U.S. trade practices from duties based on unfair trade practices to quotas based on the complaints of the domestic industry. The action increased the cartelization of the European steel industry because the governments, as in the case of the auto VRA, allocated these quotas to individual companies. And this action did not much help the U.S. industry because it led to increased imports from other countries such as Brazil and Korea.

A number of other steel trade restraints soon followed. A quietly negotiated "gentlemen's agreement" with Japan in 1983 limited the U.S. market share of imports from Japan. In June 1983, following an ITC recommendation and a divided vote of the TPC, the president approved a combination of tariffs and quotas on imports of specialty steel. The ITC recommendation in this case was based on a new, looser interpretation of the injury test that would increase the probability of an injury finding during a recession. And the Commerce Department continued to process a large number of petitions for countervailing duties on steel imports, primarily those from the developing countries.

The major steel decision, however, was delayed until 1984. In early 1984 Bethlehem Steel Company and the United Steelworkers filed an escape-clause petition for a comprehensive limit on steel imports. This action was carefully timed to require a presidential decision in late September, less than two months before the election. In parallel, the congressional steel caucus submitted a bill that would limit steel imports to 15 percent of the U.S. market. On July 11, following hearings during which there was no significant opposition from steel-using industries, the ITC recommended quotas on several types of steel products that would have limited imports to about 20 percent of the U.S. market.

On Friday, September 21, following two months of intense staff work, the TPC voted to advise the president to reject the ITC recommendation, with only Baldrige and Labor Secretary Donovan supporting some form of steel quota. This outcome, however, was not satisfactory to the White House political officials. Because Brock had a scheduled meeting in Brazil that weekend, Stockman was instructed to develop an administration alternative to the ITC recommendation for presentation to a full cabinet meeting on Tuesday afternoon. This plan was developed with nearly continuous consultation with representatives of the steel industry, who finally signed off on this plan on Tuesday morning. In parallel with Stockman's effort, I was asked to prepare a twenty-minute presentation of the case against additional limits on steel imports. After Brock returned, he prepared the press release on the Stockman plan. On Tuesday morning, I checked with Brock and Stockman for last-minute advice on my cabinet presentation. Brock told me, "As far as I know, Bill, this decision is wired with everyone in the White House, with the possible exception of the president." Stockman's response was similar, advising me not to invest all my capital on this issue. In effect, the decision had already been made to substitute the Stockman plan for the ITC recommendation.

At the cabinet meeting my presentation summarized the very poor productivity and labor cost performance of the steel industry during the prior periods of import restraints and the consumer cost and employment effects of the ITC and Stockman options. Stockman then presented his plan for a series of negotiations leading to country-by-country VRAs that, including the European steel quota negotiated in 1982, might reduce total fabricated steel imports to 18.5 percent of the U.S. market for a five-year period. My case against the proposed steel quotas was supported by Regan, Shultz, Weinberger, and Block. Only Brock and Stockman, reversing their position of the prior Friday, supported the VRA approach. Only Baldrige supported imposing steel quotas under the authority of U.S. trade laws. But the die had already been cast. Shortly after the cabinet meeting, Brock held a press conference on the decision that was a masterpiece of blue smoke and mirrors. The first press reports, with one exception, reported that "Reagan rejects steel import curbs." Only Clyde Farnsworth of the *New York Times* saw through the blue smoke to recognize that the administration had substituted its own system of quotas for those recommended by the ITC, quoting a foreign steel official to the effect that "the administration is either lying to the steel industry or to the importers." In the next few days a more accurate story was reported, but by that time only in the back pages of the business section. As was characteristic of the 1984 campaign, the administration was on both sides of this issue, articulating a policy of free trade and implementing an extensive set of new import quotas.

In retrospect there were two conditions that led to this decision. First, there was no organized opposition to steel import quotas by the major steel-using companies, with the single exception of the Caterpillar Corporation. And, of course, political considerations were dominant in September 1984, when some of the major steel-producing states were still considered uncertain. It is much less clear whether the administration would have made the same decision in 1983 or

1985. The full effects of this decision cannot yet be estimated. It proved to be unusually difficult to gain agreement on a VRA from some countries without the credible threat of a countervailing duty, and the import share of the U.S. steel market declined only to about 22 percent. Full implementation of the quotas was estimated to cost American consumers about $1.1 billion a year, about $114,000 per job saved in the steel industry. These quotas are also likely to reduce employment in the steel-using and export industries. A second effect was to increase the cartelization of the steel industry in all the exporting countries, forcing each government to allocate its share of the U.S. market to individual companies. A third effect, because this decision was not based on either U.S. trade laws or GATT agreements, was to undermine the rule of law in international trade. In summary, the Reagan administration subordinated its own economic policy for a few votes in a landslide election.

Textiles and Apparel

The textile and apparel industry is the most protected major industry in the United States. As of 1980 the average tariff rate was 27 percent, and a complex system of quotas on imports from Third World countries had been in effect for about two decades. This is the only manufacturing industry for which the limits on imports are not based on the criteria, recognized in both U.S. trade law and the GATT, of temporary adjustment assistance, unfair trade practices, or national security. Although the quota system, an outgrowth of the "short-term" cotton agreement of 1961, was initially designed to be temporary, it has become a quasi-permanent feature of the trade environment in the industrial countries. In a private letter to Sen. Strom Thurmond in September 1980, candidate Reagan endorsed the basic features of this system, promising to "relate" the imports of textiles and apparel to the size of the domestic market. That campaign promise set the stage for the major trade measures affecting this industry during the Reagan administration.

The first test of this commitment involved the renewal of the Multi-Fiber Agreement (MFA) in 1981. (The MFA is a multilateral agreement among the industrial countries that establishes the general rules for limiting imports of textiles and apparel from Third World countries.) A small group in the administration attempted to make renewal of the MFA contingent on setting a terminal date for this arrangement. On hearing of this effort, Senator Thurmond arranged for a meeting with the president in the Oval Office. Staring at those of us who were sitting next to the wall, Thurmond said, "You may not be aware, Mr. President, that some members of your staff do not support this agreement," and reminded the president of his prior commitment. The MFA was renewed without a termination date.

In the fall of 1983 the industry filed a large number of petitions for countervailing duties with the Commerce Department. As in the 1982 steel cases, Secretary Baldrige and his trade deputy Lionel Olmer made an agreement with the industry to tighten the quotas in exchange for withdrawal of these petitions. In early December the Trade Policy Committee rejected the Commerce proposal with only Baldrige dissenting. After a six-hour meeting in the White House the next day, Martin Feldstein returned to the CEA office and reported, "I think we have won." A last-minute appeal by Baldrige prevailed, however, so that one word, "and," was changed to "or," thus affecting the conditions under which the quotas would be adjusted. This change was sufficient to tighten the import quotas. The textile and apparel industry won again, at the expense of American consumers, retailers, exporters, and the Third World suppliers. After this episode the position of the White House was quite explicit, and there was no significant opposition to a tightening of the "country-of-origin" tests on the import quotas in 1984.

This industry cannot be satisfied, however, because it probably cannot be competitive in many types of apparel with the low-wage countries. Imports continued to increase, primarily from Europe and from new suppliers such as China. In 1985 the industry turned to Congress for further protection. A bipartisan coalition in the House approved a bill that would have reduced the quotas to the 1980 level of imports, a measure that would especially restrict imports from the new suppliers. The Senate approved a similar bill, adding protection for the copper and footwear industries that had been denied relief by the president. Both of these bills, however, were approved by a lower margin than was sufficient to override the expected veto. On December 17, waiting until the tax bill was approved, the president vetoed the textile bill, braking or at least deferring the strong protectionist momentum that had developed early that fall. Reagan's veto of this bill was sustained by a margin of only eight votes on August 6, 1986. The vote to override the president's veto of this bill was divided on regional rather than partisan lines. Rep. Trent Lott, the Republican whip from Mississippi, voted to override the veto, and Dan Rostenkowski, the chairman of the Ways and Means Committee, voted to sustain the veto.

The quota system involves limits from about two dozen countries on about 140 textile and apparel products. No satisfactory estimate of the total costs of this complex system, or of the increase in costs in recent years, has been made. A 1984 study of the quotas on imports from Hong Kong, the largest foreign supplier, however, provides an insight into the magnitude of these costs. As of 1980 the annual cost to consumers of the quotas on imports from Hong Kong alone, a source that supplied about one-fifth of total textile and apparel imports, was $300 to $400 million, or about $24,000 per job protected in the domestic industry. What explains the continued protection of the U.S. textile and apparel industry? One explanation is the relatively large influence of members of Congress from the South, but this influence has substantially diminished in the past two decades. Another explanation is the relative ineffectiveness of consumers and retailers on trade issues. A more fundamental explanation, however, is that the domestic industry probably cannot be competitive in many apparel products. At some time we need to address how much we are willing to pay to maintain the level of employment in this industry.

Other Trade Cases

There was no general pattern of the other major trade cases. The most egregious of these cases involved sugar. In the summer of 1981 Dave Stockman agreed to a quota system on imported sugar in exchange for a few "boll weevil" votes on the omnibus reconciliation bill. A progressive tightening of these quotas was necessary to maintain the domestic price, in part because of the increasing substitution of high-fructose corn syrup for natural sugar. In turn, sales of corn gluten feed, a byproduct of the corn syrup, led to a minor trade flap with Europe. By 1984 the domestic wholesale price of sugar was about four times the world price, the highest effective tariff on any legal product. The annual cost to consumers of protecting a few thousand cane sugar farmers and the artificial market for corn syrup is now about $700 million. And the lower quotas reduced the export earnings of fragile economies in the Caribbean and the Philippines. What wondrous webs we weave! In 1983 the administration also approved a high temporary tariff on large motorcycles to maintain 2,000 jobs in one company.

In contrast, the administration rejected protection of the copper mining industry in 1984, despite the strong support of Republican senators from Arizona and Utah, because of the strong opposition of the copper products industry. The administration also rejected or deferred two petitions to protect the machine tool industry despite the concerns about the importance of this industry for national security. In May 1986, however, the administration announced that it would seek VRAs on machine tool imports from four countries, a decision that was clearly timed to affect the vote on the omnibus trade legislation being considered in the House. The "white hats," a term used to describe those who opposed the first machine tool petition, had lost again. For those of us who were trying to maintain the administration's commitment to free trade, most of our time was devoted to trying to head off new trade restraints, some of which were developed within the administration. In the absence of any major trade liberalizing measures, however, the new trade restraints increased the average level of protection relative to 1980, the first increase in the average effective trade restraints in many decades.

Trade Legislation

In the face of strong political pressure for import protection, the administration was successful in deterring new protectionist legislation through 1987. In addition to the bills, mentioned in the above section, that would have limited imports of autos, steel, textiles and apparel, footwear, and copper, the administration was also successful in opposing measures that would have established a "reciprocity" standard on imports of telecommunications equipment and wine. Although several hundred protectionist bills were introduced in 1985, the veto of the textile and apparel bill was sufficient to deter other such bills for a while. A cynic might conclude that the administration wanted to maintain control of the distribution of protectionist favors and opposed only those trade restraints proposed by Congress.

The only trade legislation of the first term was the Trade and Tariff Act of 1984. Although the committee version of this bill included many small protectionist provisions, an extraordinary last-minute effort by Bill Brock was sufficient to eliminate most of these provisions. This act renewed the Generalized System of Preferences (GSP) on imports from the developing countries and reduced the tariffs on about one hundred products. Other provisions strengthened the authority to retaliate against unfair trade practices affecting both imports and exports and broadened the criteria for injury on escape-clause cases.

A special feature of the 1984 act provides authority for bilateral negotiations to establish free trade zones, a Brock initiative. An agreement to establish a free trade zone with Israel was completed in 1985. A similar agreement with the Southeast Asian countries was considered but was deferred when the president dropped his scheduled visit to that region after the murder of Benigno Aquino. Negotiations on a free trade agreement with Canada, our largest trading partner, were initiated in May 1986. This approach to expanding free trade on a country-by-country basis may be necessary to break the logjam on the more complex multilateral negotiations that were resisted by the European governments. Bill Brock deserves credit for this creative instrument of U.S. trade policy.

Trade issues continued to be contentious through 1987. Although the dollar had declined about 40 percent since its peak in February 1985, the trade deficit continued to increase. Congressional Democrats believed that the administration was vulnerable on the trade issue, and the Republicans were divided. The administration's position on trade also seemed to shift. In September 1985 the White House speechwriters prepared a draft of a forceful speech for Reagan that would have maintained a strong presidential commitment to free trade. This draft, however, proved to be too strong for the White House political officials, and Regan's "mice" revised the speech to include the first Reagan use of the term "free and fair trade," an opening to all types of mischief. Clayton Yeutter, the new trade representative, also initiated new trade investigations affecting five product groups, with the purported intent of reducing foreign barriers to U.S. exports of these products. This was the environment that led to the House omnibus trade bill of 1986, arguably the worst proposed trade legislation since the Smoot-Hawley tariff of 1930. A major provision of this bill, promoted by Rep. Richard Gephardt of Missouri, would make a substantial bilateral trade surplus with the United States actionable under U.S. trade laws, even in the absence of any specific injury in the States or any specific unfair trade practice by the foreign country; the application of this provision would have required U.S. action to reduce the bilateral trade surplus of Japan, West Germany, and Taiwan by 10 percent a year unless the governments of these countries were to quickly agree to actions consistent with these targets. Other provisions of this bill would have established a reciprocity standard on trade in telecommunications equipment, mandatory retaliation against any countries found to practice "export targeting," optional retaliation against any country that lacks labor or antitrust laws similar to ours, advisory groups to develop industry adjustment plans for industries seeking escape-clause protection against imports, and other measures that would restrict the president's authority on trade issues.

The administration reacted to this bill with a strong veto threat and a flurry of protectionist actions of its own. Baldrige announced that the administration would seek VRAs on imports of machine tools from four countries, overruling the conclusion of a two-year study of a petition to restrict machine tool imports on national security grounds. In the short run this strategy was not successful. The House approved the omnibus trade bill in late May by a sufficient majority to override the threatened veto.

The administration's strategy was to build a five-foot trade wall in order to deter a ten-foot wall established by Congress. In June 1986 a high tariff was established on cedar shakes and shingles, primarily from Canada. The timing of this decision, on the day the first round of negotiations on a free-trade area with Canada was completed, was especially awkward. A strong Canadian reaction led to a quiet apology from both the president and vice-president in an attempt to maintain the momentum for this initiative. A petition for a countervailing duty on semiconductor chips was later resolved by establishing a U.S.-Japan cartel that will substantially increase the price of chips in both countries, even though the study of this issue found that the Japanese sold these chips at a higher price in the States than in Japan in order to avoid a dumping charge. (In March 1987 the administration charged that the Japanese had violated two provisions of the semiconductor arrangement and announced that it would impose 100 percent tariffs on a range of other Japanese products as a sanction for these alleged violations. Brief emergency consultations did not resolve this issue, primarily because the U.S. would not present the evidence on which these charges were based, and the tariff sanctions were implemented in mid-April.) In October 1986 the prospects for a free-trade agreement with Canada were threatened again by a preliminary determination that softwood lumber imports from Canada were subsidized by 15 percent, a determination that was clearly timed to save several Republican Senate seats in the timber-producing states.

Over the summer of 1986 the Senate, led by Sen. John Danforth, developed its own trade bill. This bill included the major provisions of the House bill, further restricting the president's authority on trade issues. During the early fall, however, the press of budget and tax issues and the report of a decline in the trade deficit in August delayed a floor vote on this bill. Many Democrats appeared to want a political issue, not a trade bill. Many Republicans were reluctant to challenge the president. For a time the administration was again successful in braking or deferring the damaging trade proposal of Congress, but only at the substantial cost of additional trade restraints of its own making.

In September 1986 the GATT nations finally convened a new round of trade negotiations at Punte del Este, Uruguay, but the United States did not enter these negotiations with clean hands or the promise of much congressional support for any agreement from these negotiations. As a rule a large congressional delegation participates in such meetings; in this case, only Rep. Bill Frenzel of Wisconsin, the leading Republican supporter of free trade in the House, had the courage to risk his seat by attending this meeting. At the end of the year the administration initiated a trade action against Europe that might have deferred any prospect for a new GATT agreement. In response to a loss of corn sales to Spain and Portugal that resulted from their joining the Common Market, the administration threatened to impose a 200 percent tariff on imports of selected alcoholic beverages and agricultural products from Europe. Although this dispute was resolved, the near-term prospects for trade policy were not encouraging.

In 1987, however, the administration's strategy ran out of steam. In April, after the Gephardt amendment was approved by a close vote, the House approved a trade bill very similar to its 1986 bill by a large bipartisan vote. The timing of this vote, during Prime Minister Nakasone's last state visit to the States, appeared to be a calculated affront to Japan. The Senate later approved a trade bill with other damaging provisions, and a very large conference committee worked to develop a consensus bill for several months. The 1987 trade bills threatened the most substantial reversal of U.S. trade law since the United States took the lead in rebuilding the world trading system in 1934 and may not reflect the end of the resurgent protectionism.

The fundamental misperception of Congress was the attempt to reduce the trade deficit by subsidizing exports or restricting imports. Such actions, however, would strengthen the dollar with no effect on the trade deficit. Congress does not yet recognize that the trade deficit is made in the United States. The trade deficit or, more accurately, the broader current account deficit is the difference between saving by Americans and investment in the United States. The only effective ways to reduce the trade deficit are to increase U.S. saving, reduce the government deficit, or reduce private investment in the States. The administration was not immune to this misperception. In the early fall of 1984, I made a presentation to the cabinet on this relation of U.S. foreign and domestic balances. Although my presentation involved little more than stating the implications of some accounting identities, this relation was not broadly understood. Only the usual courtesies of a cabinet meeting prevented the pragmatists and trade hardliners from commenting that I might understand economics, but I did not understand the real world. I was no more successful in making this point in personal discussions with members of Congress. An alternative explanation of their response may be that they understand this relation perfectly well, but that concern about the trade deficit provided a convenient rationalization for trade measures they believed were important for political reasons. Either explanation is disturbing: our contemporary mercantilists apparently are either dense or deceptive. In any case the measures that will prove most effective in reducing the trade deficit will be Gramm-Rudman and the Tax Reform Act of 1986; one of the effects of the latter, unfortunately, will be to reduce business investment in the United States.

One of the many trade proposals that did not pass was the administration proposal to merge Commerce and USTR into a Department of International Trade and Industry (DITI). This proposal was the result of a private deal between Baldrige and Ed Meese, whose concept of management was to rearrange organization charts. The superficial argument for this proposal was to reduce the diffusion of responsibility for trade policy. The primary problem, however, was of the administration's own making: it diffused responsibility for review of trade policy among four cabinet-level groups. The DITI proposal was broadly recognized as part of the continued battle for turf between Baldrige and Brock. After a 13–1 vote against this proposal in the full cabinet, Meese pulled the issue off the agenda, but the proposal was later submitted to Congress without further review. This proposal failed to gain the support of the Republican leadership either house and died a quiet death. Another administration review of this proposal in the winter of 1985 revealed continued strong opposition within the cabinet, and the proposal was withdrawn. Much of the opposition to this proposal reflected a strong support for Bill Brock, both within the cabinet and in Congress.

The Japan Issue

A rather ugly dimension of U.S. trade policy during these years concerned trade relations with Japan. The administration initiated some new measure affecting Japan every year, and Congress considered much stronger measures. The "Japan issue" developed a political momentum that was almost divorced from the facts. The facts are clear for anyone who cares. Japan has a large trade surplus because it saves more than it invests at home; Japan's surplus on manufactured goods is even larger because it must import most of its energy and raw materials. The dollar appreciated against the European currencies more than against the yen and later declined to a record low against the yen. The largest increases in the U.S. trade deficit involved Latin America and Europe, not Japan. In its market, average Japanese tariffs are lower than in the United States, import quotas cover a smaller range of products, and Japan's domestic subsidies are trivial. In our market, Japanese firms are rarely charged with unfair trade practices. The primary reason that Japan became the primary target of trade actions is that it is such a formidable competitor. A second reason is that both government and business negotiations with Japan are often very frustrating. A third reason is some element of residual racism. In 1985 a senior U.S. trade official was quoted as saying that "the next time we send trade negotiators to Japan, it will be in the nose of a B-52." And Theodore White, the dean of American political journalists, wrote the most blatantly anti-Japanese article to appear in a major publication since World War II.

Within the administration the Commerce Department was the primary proponent of the measures against Japan, led by Baldrige, Olmer, and Clyde Prestowitz. USTR tried to divert this pressure by focusing on measures to open up the Japanese market rather than closing the U.S. market. Many of the issues were trivial. For example, months of negotiation were devoted to seeking a change in the rules of a Japanese softball league to permit the sales of American aluminum softball bats. In response to pressure for some action that would strengthen the yen, a Treasury team headed by Beryl Sprinkel completed a long negotiation in 1984 to open up the Japanese capital market; the CEA, however, estimated that this measure would probably weaken the yen. In preparation for the Reagan-Nakasone meeting in January 1985, a paper prepared by Sprinkel proposed that the United States insist that the Japanese set quantitative targets to increase manufactured imports; this proposal was broadly supported, against my lonely opposition, through four cabinet council meetings until the intervention of Shultz and Weinberger reminded the president of our larger interests with Japan. After Reagan and Nakasone reaffirmed their special relation in a meeting in Los Angeles, U.S. negotiators pressed the Japanese to change various trade and domestic practices to open their market in four product areas. These measures, however, were not sufficient to satisfy Congress; on March 28 the Senate approved a nonbinding resolution by a vote of 92–0 directing the president to reduce U.S. imports from Japan if it did not agree within forty-five days to further open its markets.

Over this period the tone of the U.S. proposals came very close to reasserting our authority during the occupation, and only Nakasone's concern for the U.S. relationship prevented a blow-up within the Japanese cabinet. Although some of these negotiations have been effective, they are not likely to much reduce the U.S. trade deficit with Japan, and they risk pressuring the Japanese into a nationalistic response. During this same time the U.S. government did not relax its own export restrictions, such as the bans on export of Alaskan oil and on logs from the western public forests, products for which there is a substantial Japanese demand. The defense by our trade officials that these measures were necessary to deter stronger action by Congress was not satisfactory. This ugly process of badgering the Japanese for problems largely of our own making will continue unless the president continues to assert our larger interests in our relations with Japan.

Export Policies

The administration's general record on export policy was somewhat inconsistent. In early 1981 Reagan removed the embargo on grain sales to the Soviet Union, promising the farmers that there would be no future selective embargo on farm products. Soon after, however, he embargoed the sale of U.S. equipment and U.S.-licensed equipment made in Europe for the natural gas pipeline from the Soviet Union to Europe. Following a strong protest from the European governments, George Shultz convinced the president to reverse this decision soon after he was confirmed as secretary of state in mid-1982. A continued controversy between Commerce and Defense on the export of defense-related technology delayed the reauthorization of the Export Administration Act until mid-1985, but American businesses still lack clear guidelines on the sale of such technology that are consistent with the rules affecting sales by other Western nations. The administration also imposed selective embargoes on trade with Poland, Libya, Nicaragua, and Syria and, under congressional pressure in 1985 and 1986, with South Africa—measures that are best described as moral posturing rather than as effective instruments of foreign policy. In both 1981 and 1985 Stockman proposed a large reduction of funding for the Export-Import Bank, but Congress maintained most of this funding. The administration decided to renew the tax preferences for Domestic International Sales Corporations in a slightly modified form that is consistent with the GATT. On several occasions, to counter European subsidies on agricultural exports, the administration authorized some targeted export subsidies on American farm products. The administration did not ask Congress to remove the ban on export of Alaskan oil or on logs, or the requirement that 50 percent of government-financed agricultural exports be carried on American ships. For many years the federal government has promoted the exports of some products and restricted the exports of other products, with little apparent rationale. For the most part, that is still the case.

A General Assessment

The president's announced trade policy consistently supported free trade, a position that contrasted sharply with that of Walter Mondale during the 1984 campaign and later with most of Congress. The record was mixed. From my perspective the major adverse legacies involve the steel quotas, the semiconductor cartel, the tightening of the textile and apparel quotas, and the 1987 trade bills. The most risky policy involved the continued badgering of Japan, for the most part over trivial issues. The major achievements were the initiation of free trade agreements with Israel and Canada. The most important missed opportunities were the delay in convening a new GATT trade round and the failure to sort out our confused export policies. Given the strong increase in the dollar and the trade deficit, this may have been the best that could be achieved. The net outcome, however, was unsatisfactory. The percentage of U.S. imports that are duty free declined substantially. For the first time since World War II, the United States added more trade restraints than it removed. The 1987 trade bills threatened to end a half-century of U.S. leadership of the world trading system.

CHAPTER FIVE

Monetary Policy

And, in cooperation with the Federal Reserve Board, a new commitment to a monetary policy that will restore a stable currency and healthy financial markets.

The Reagan administration was the first to endorse the control of the money supply as the primary means of reducing inflation and stabilizing the growth of total demand. Its timing could not have been more awkward. Market developments and financial deregulation changed the nature of money. And, for reasons that are not yet broadly understood, the relation between money and total demand changed substantially.

Substantial changes in monetary policy, rather than the slow, steady reduction of money growth first proposed, characterized this period. A more restrictive monetary policy through mid-1982 was the primary cause of the long 1981–1982 recession. From the fall of 1982 an administration first committed to a slow reduction in money growth tolerated and later endorsed the most rapid sustained peacetime rate of money growth in American history. During the second term, after Jim Baker exchanged positions with Don Regan, the Treasury promoted a policy to reduce interest rates and the exchange rate, replacing both the monetary policies and the key personnel of the first term. Over most of this period, real interest rates were both unusually high and unusually volatile. The failure rate of both financial and nonfinancial firms increased sharply.

For all the turbulence of this period, monetary policy is broadly considered to be one of the more successful elements of the Reagan economic program. As of 1987, monetary policy had contributed to the lowest inflation rate in two decades and had sustained the recovery for five years. This chapter summarizes how an initially doctrinaire administration and a stubbornly independent Federal Reserve worked together, as a rule, to achieve these results.

A BRIEF MONETARY HISTORY

The initial Reagan program correctly described its monetary policy as "a new commitment" rather than a new policy. As with most of the Reagan economic program, there was a strong precedent for the initial monetary policy in the later years of the Carter administration. The major change in monetary policy dated from October 6, 1979, when the Federal Reserve announced a new operating procedure to control the growth of the money supply rather than interest rates. The primary initial contribution of the Reagan administration was a strong presidential endorsement of this general policy. For an understanding of this change, however, it is necessary to understand the conditions that led to the monetarist experiment beginning in October 1979.

The Road to Monetarism

The Constitution grants to Congress the power "to coin Money [and] regulate the Value thereof." Since 1913 Congress has delegated this power to the Federal Reserve System, usually without instruction or (the equivalent) with sufficiently redundant or contradictory instructions to permit "the Fed" to chart its own course. Over its history the Federal Reserve Board, rather like the Supreme Court, has developed an aura, influence, and independence that go far beyond the intentions of its creators. As chairman of the Federal Reserve Board, Paul Volcker was broadly considered to be the second most powerful person in the United States.

One wonders, however, what the Fed has done to earn this esteem. Over its entire history the Fed has demonstrated one consistent bias, at great cost to the nation: the growth of the money supply, in general, has been procylical, increasing during recoveries and declining during recessions. This pattern is illustrated by Figure 5.1. For most of this history, this bias was the result of an operating procedure that attempted to stabilize short-term interest rates. An increased demand for credit would lead to an increase in bank reserves, and vice versa. This led the U.S. economy to be more cyclical than other economies. A failure to be a sufficient lender of last resort, the function for which the Fed was established, was the primary reason for the Great Depression.

In the years since World War II, in addition, U.S. monetary policy has been inflationary. Prior to World War II inflation in the United States was associated only with wars or gold discoveries. The brief periods of inflation were generally followed by long periods of moderate deflation, with no net inflation over even longer periods. The

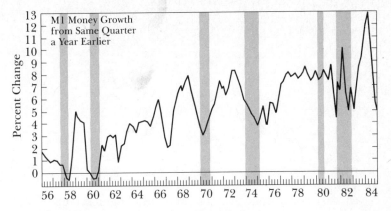

Figure 5.1   Money Growth and the Business Cycle

Note: Shaded areas indicate recessions (peak to trough) as defined by the National Bureau of Economic Research.

price level in 1939, for example, was not much different than in 1800.

Since World War II, however, the general price level has declined in only one year (1949), and the rate of inflation increased from one cycle to the next through 1980. The relation between money growth and inflation is illustrated by Figure 5.2.

The inflation problem developed only slowly, however. Following the accord between the Treasury and the Federal Reserve in April 1951, which relieved the Fed from the obligation to purchase Treasury bills at par, the general inflation rate averaged less than 2 percent a year through 1965. The Fed chairman from 1951 to 1970 was William McChesney Martin, a quiet man whose general success was masked by public obscurity. It became increasingly difficult to maintain the gold backing for the dollar, however, even with this low inflation rate. The gold reserve requirements were removed from bank reserves in 1965 and from Federal Reserve notes (paper currency) in 1968. The inflation rate increased to 6 percent in 1969 and declined only slowly following the 1970 recession. The resulting outflow of gold led President Nixon to close the gold window in August 1971 as part of the larger program that included comprehensive price and wage controls, ending the Bretton Woods agreement on exchange rates and the last formal link of the dollar to gold.

The dollar then became a fiat (paper) currency, and the Fed no longer had any defense against the inflationary bias of politicians. Nixon had named Arthur Burns, a distinguished economist then

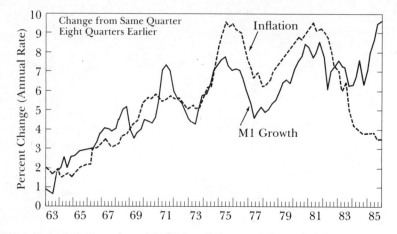

Figure 5.2   M1 Growth and Inflation (M1 growth lagged eight quarters)

Note: Inflation measured by change in GNP implicit price deflator. Based on seasonally adjusted data.

serving as his special assistant, as chairman of the Federal Reserve Board. The first experience with a pure fiat currency was not encouraging. Burns, who had been a pioneer of business cycle research, presided over a monetary policy that led to a 10 percent rate of inflation in 1974, the deepest postwar recession in 1974 and 1975, and the origins of the high inflation in the late 1970s.

After money growth increased sharply again in 1976 and 1977, President Carter appointed William Miller, a leading business executive, as chairman of the Fed in December 1977. Miller fought the Fed establishment but compounded Burns's errors. Money growth continued to increase, inflation increased sharply, and the dollar declined sharply on the foreign exchange markets. "Not since the Depression," in the words of one observer, "has the Federal Reserve seemed so ineffective, so listless, so demoralized." The gloomy prospects were compounded by the confusion in the White House. President Carter apparently believed that Miller had done a good job at the Fed, promoting him to be Treasury secretary in July 1979 before considering any one to replace him. The eight years from Nixon's initiatives in August 1971 to Carter's cabinet shakeup in July 1979 were the worst period of U.S. monetary policy since the 1930s. The stage was set for a major change in monetary policy.

The ideas that shaped this change in monetary policy originated outside the establishment of academic and government economists. In retrospect, the monetary policy errors of this period now seem obvious. At the time, however, most economists paid little attention to these developments, regarding monetary policy as a poor cousin to fiscal policy. The major econometric models (then and now) limited the effects of monetary policy on total demand to those operating through interest rates. The leading government economists in administrations of both parties offered a series of ad hoc explanations of the increasing inflation—at one time or another, budget deficits, oil shocks, or wage push were the leading current explanations—which did not suggest any consistent policy to reduce inflation. A part of the problem is that the prevailing Keynesian theory of demand is expressed in real terms and thus does not provide any explanation of inflation. Keynesian economic models linked real conditions and the general price level by the Phillips curve, a postulated negative relation between the unemployment rate and the inflation rate. A general questioning of the Keynesian perspective developed only after it failed to provide an explanation for the "stagflation" of the 1970s—the combination of slower real growth, rising unemployment, and increasing inflation.

A small community of economists, however, had been developing an alternative "monetarist" explanation of macroeconomic conditions for several decades, led by professors Milton Friedman and Karl Brunner and concentrated at the universities of Chicago, UCLA, and Rochester. The central premise of the monetarist perspective is that a change in the money supply leads directly to a change in total demand, rather than only through a change in interest rates. Friedman first summarized the general analytic framework of monetarism in his presidential address to the American Economic Association in 1967. Early statistical tests by Friedman and David Meiselman suggested that changes in the money supply during the postwar years appeared to have a much stronger effect on total demand than changes in fiscal conditions. A massive study of U.S. monetary history by Friedman and Anna Schwartz interpreted the longer-term experience.

Small monetarist models of the U.S. economy were first developed at the Federal Reserve Bank of St. Louis, at OMB, and at Citibank. (Some of the developers of these models would become more visible in other roles. Jerry Jordan, a coauthor of the St. Louis model, was my colleague as a member of the CEA in 1981 and 1982. Art Laffer, a coauthor of the OMB model, is best known for his conjecture about the relation between tax rates and revenues.) These models revealed a number of general empirical patterns. A change in the money supply leads to a roughly proportionate change in total demand (as measured by current dollar GNP) with an average lag of about six months. A change in the money supply leads to a roughly proportionate change in the general price level with an average lag of about two years, as illustrated by Figure 5.2. Changes in the money supply thus have a substantial effect on real conditions (such as output and employment) in the short run but not in the long run. The ratio of total demand to the money supply (described as the "velocity" of money) increased by about 3 percent a year. Each of these relations was believed to be "trend stationary"; that is, a departure from these trend relations was expected to be reversed in later periods to restore the original trend. (These relations proved to be quite stable through 1981 but, as the figures also indicate, broke down in the later period.)

A later contribution of the Chicago school, called "rational expectations," was developed by Robert Lucas on the basis of some early articles by John Muth. The central premise of this approach is that people base their behavior on current plus expected future conditions, using all the information available to them, rather than on prior conditions. The primary implication of this perspective for monetary policy is that only *unexpected* changes in the money supply should have any effect on real conditions. For example, a 5 percent increase in the money supply would be expansive if people expected money growth to be zero; the same increase would be restrictive if people expected an increase of 10 percent. Another implication is that the lags in the relation between money growth and other conditions are not likely to be stable.

The primary policy implications of the monetarist/rational-expectations perspective were the following:

- The Federal Reserve should attempt to stabilize the money supply, rather than interest rates, around a target path.
- The money supply target should be announced in advance.
- Several changes in operating practices were recommended to improve the control of the money supply.

Almost all these proposals were later adopted. The Federal Reserve first established internal targets for the growth of the money supply in 1970. After a long campaign by congressional staff economist Robert Weintraub, Congress approved a resolution in 1975 requiring the Federal Reserve to announce one-year growth targets for several monetary aggregates. A 1980 law phased in uniform reserve requirements for most types of deposits by 1987.

The announced targets for money growth, however, did not prove to be very valuable information. The growth of the narrow money supply (M1) was well within the target range (more accurately a wedge) in 1976 but was above the upper target band in each of the next three years. The announced target ranges and the actual money stock

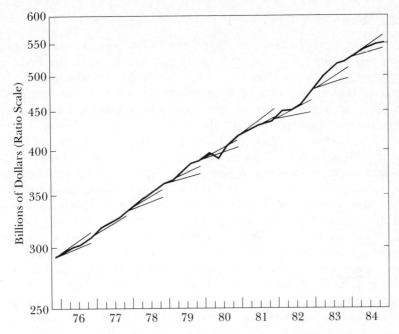

Figure 5.3   M1 Money Stock* and Federal Reserve Target Ranges

*Averages of daily figures; seasonally adjusted.

through 1984 are illustrated by Figure 5.3. Because the base for each new target range was the actual money supply in the fourth quarter of the prior year, money growth outside the range in one year was not reversed in the subsequent year. A part of the problem, which would later be corrected, is that the Fed's operating procedure led to higher money growth in response to an increasing demand for credit. A more important problem, which has not yet been corrected, is that our government may have an inherent inflationary bias. The potential for increasing real growth and reducing the real interest payments on the government debt is dependent on increasing money growth more than the markets expect. For a while the markets may have based their expectations on the announced money growth targets. After excess money growth in 1977 and 1978, however, the money growth targets were no longer credible, and continued high money growth through the summer of 1979 increased the inflation rate without providing any stimulus to real output. The short-term benefits of unexpected monetary stimulus had disappeared. Some action was necessary to restore the credibility of the Federal Reserve.

The Monetarist Experiment

The next step toward the monetarist policy agenda was neither planned by the Carter administration nor welcomed by the Federal Reserve. A few days after Carter appointed William Miller as Treasury secretary, he called Anthony Solomon, the senior monetary official at the Treasury, to ask who should be appointed chairman of the Federal Reserve Board. Solomon had only one name, Paul Volcker. Carter did not know Volcker and questioned why any technical skills were needed for this position. As Solomon and other specialists knew, however, Volcker was superbly qualified for the Fed position. After early experience at the Federal Reserve Bank of New York and the Treasury staff, he had served as the undersecretary of the Treasury for monetary affairs from 1969 to 1974, and he had been president of the New York Fed since 1975. (Solomon would later succeed Volcker as president of the New York Fed.) As a member of the Federal Open Market Committee (FOMC), the primary monetary policy forum, Volcker had twice supported tighter money, in opposition to Chairman Miller, in the spring of 1979. His politics, other than his opposition to inflation and his loyalty to the Fed, were (and are) unclear. Carter, who had no sense about what the Fed ought to do or what Volcker would do, named Volcker to be Fed chairman within one week after nominating Miller to the Treasury.

It was also not clear to others what Volcker would do. He had long been a government employee, not an academic, so there was little written record of his professional views. In his confirmation hearings he described himself as a "pragmatic monetarist," a term that is often used by those who believe that money is important but lack a clear sense of what should be done about it. His first actions were faltering; a proposal to increase the discount rate by one-half percentage point was approved by a bare majority of the board of governors.

The least likely course seemed to be some next step on the monetarist agenda. The board of governors had long regarded monetarists with a view rather like that of the Vatican Council toward the Protestants, as people who take Christianity too seriously without understanding the subtleties of running a state church. Monetarist research and policy positions were tolerated at the smaller regional banks, initially St. Louis and, later, Minneapolis and Richmond. No one with strong monetarist views, however, had ever been appointed to the board of governors or as president of the major regional banks. This should not be surprising. The monetarists propose the substitution of monetary rules for the discretion of the Fed, and few institutions welcome such restraint. It was also not clear that Congress would tolerate a more monetarist policy. The Full Employment and Balanced Growth Act of 1978, a cobweb of Keynesian delusion, charged both the administration and the Federal Reserve to report annually the progress with regard to numerous and often contradictory goals.

The major change in monetary policy was triggered by Volcker's first meeting as Fed chairman with other central bankers. At the end of September Volcker flew to Belgrade for the annual joint meeting of the International Monetary Fund and the World Bank. In the several days before the beginning of the official meeting, Volcker got an earful from the other central bankers about the continued decline in the dollar and the soaring price of gold. On October 2, when the official meetings had just started, Volcker flew back to Washington and called an emergency meeting of the FOMC for October 6. The outcome of that meeting was an increase in the discount rate from 11 percent to 12 percent and, more important, a change in the Fed's basic operating procedure.

The long-established procedure had been for the FOMC to approve a range for the federal funds rate, the overnight interbank interest rate; this range was seldom more than one percentage point. The open-market desk of the New York Fed would then buy or sell government securities, respectively increasing or decreasing bank reserves, to maintain the federal funds rate within this range. The effect of this procedure was to reduce the short-run variability of interest rates but to increase the effect of changes in the demand for credit on bank reserves and the money supply. Under the new procedure the FOMC approved a fixed path for nonborrowed bank reserves consistent with the target growth of the money supply. The relation between this operating target and the money growth target is subject to variation, but some variability was believed to be desirable and self correcting. The target path of nonborrowed reserves was seldom changed between meetings of the FOMC. It was recognized that this procedure would increase the short-run variability of interest rates. The objective of this procedure was to reduce the variability of the level of bank reserves and the money supply. As it turned out, for various reasons the variability of both interest rates and the money supply was unusually high during the period this procedure was used.

The initial effects of this new procedure were quite favorable. For six months through March 1980, the rate of money growth was reduced by half and was quite steady. The Carter administration, however, could not tolerate the resulting increase in interest rates and, in March, asked the Fed to implement credit controls. Volcker had a strong aversion to credit controls but acquiesced to the Carter request. The effects of the credit controls were more drastic than intended. During the spring quarter the money supply contracted and real GNP declined at a 9.1 percent annual rate. The Fed soon reversed course. At meetings in May and August, the FOMC approved higher money growth, the credit controls were ended, and money growth soared through November. Money growth in 1980 was above target for the fourth year in a row and, in addition, was extraordinarily erratic. The primary lesson of the early experience with the new operating procedure was that a change in monetary policy is not likely to be sustainable unless it is supported by the administration.

The Initial Reagan Guidance

In January 1981 financial markets were in close to panic conditions. The consumer price index had increased 11.7 percent in the prior twelve months, the prime rate peaked at 21.5 percent, and the foreign exchange value of the dollar had only slightly recovered from its record low in the summer of 1980. The new administration, however, had a quite clear sense of direction and did not panic. The primary people who shaped the initial administration guidance on monetary policy were Milton Friedman and Beryl Sprinkel. Friedman had long been an informal adviser to Reagan and later served on the President's Economic Policy Advisory Board (PEPAB). Sprinkel, a former student of Friedman and a senior bank economist, was nominated as the Treasury undersecretary for monetary affairs.

The guidance on monetary policy, a part of the Program for Economic Recovery released on February 18, was clear and concise. The administration endorsed the independence of the Federal Reserve. Although the administration cautioned that "better monetary control is not consistent with the management of interest rates in the short run," it withheld endorsement of the specific operating procedure adopted by the Fed in October 1979. The guidance emphasized the importance of steady policies, meeting targets, and a long-term policy orientation. The most specific guidance was the assumption that "the growth rates of money and credit are steadily reduced from the 1980 levels to one-half those levels by 1986." The administration's strategy for reducing inflation was to announce the policy changes, reduce the growth of the money supply to reduce the growth of demand, and reduce tax rates and regulation to increase the growth of output. The potential for reducing inflation without a substantial temporary loss of output was recognized to be dependent on the credibility of the initial policy announcements.

The primary problem with this monetary guidance was that it was strongly inconsistent with the economic assumptions on which the budget projections were based. For the postwar years through 1980, current dollar GNP increased about 3 percent a year plus the percentage increase in the money supply, and a part of this increase in the velocity of money was due to increasing interest rates. The administration's initial economic forecasts, however, assumed that current dollar GNP would increase 5.4 percent a year plus the target increase on the money supply, despite a forecast decline in interest rates. Even if the 3 percent velocity growth rate had continued, either the projected GNP was too high or the money supply targets were too low. Sprinkel pointed out this inconsistency to Stockman, who decided to maintain the GNP forecasts rather than sort out this issue. Inconsistent guidance in turn reduced the credibility of the administration and increased the discretion of the Federal Reserve. As it turned out, money velocity declined after 1981, actual GNP was much lower than the initial forecast, and money growth was much higher than the initial guidance. We will touch on this later.

The Early Record

The initial relations between the administration and the Federal Reserve were proper but not close. There was a lot of conversation but not much communication. Don Regan usually had breakfast with Volcker every week. Sprinkel's staff met with the senior Fed staff every other week. The Council of Economic Advisers usually had lunch with the board of governors every other week, and the chairman had breakfast with Volcker in the intervening weeks. The release of new economic data was often the occasion for a telephone conversation with Volcker about economic conditions and policies. It was extraordinarily difficult, however, to elicit responses from the Fed officials about monetary policy. A frustrated Regan aide was quoted as saying that "trying to question Volcker is like shooting a slingshot at an elephant." My own experience is that members of the board of governors were willing to talk about almost any issue other than monetary policy. The reasons for this institutional reticence were not clear. Maybe the understandable caution about conveying a signal to the public also restricted their openness with professional colleagues in the government. Sprinkel's rigid monetarism, combative style, and influence on Regan particularly irritated the Fed. My CEA colleagues Jerry Jordan and, later, Bill Poole shared Sprinkel's monetarist perspective, but they had better relations with the Fed, largely because they were less tendentious.

The administration and Congress were also concerned about how to institutionalize a commitment to long-run price stability. The first occasion to address these issues were the deliberations of the Gold Commission in the fall of 1981. President Reagan had expressed interest in restoring some relation between the dollar and gold, and the congressionally mandated Gold Commission provided the forum to address these general issues. The staff work for this commission was directed by Anna Schwartz, the coauthor (with Milton Friedman) of the definitive history of U.S. monetary policy. Most of the work of the commission involved a review of the historical experience, in the United States and abroad, under the several types of gold standards. This review concluded that the experience during the gold-standard periods was characterized by lower average inflation and money growth; higher variations in inflation, the money supply, and output; and a higher average unemployment rate than during the period since World War II. (A later study suggests that the higher measured variability of economic conditions prior to World War II was in part an artifact of the available statistical series, but most of the variation remains after the appropriate adjustments.) On the basis of these findings, most of the Gold Commission, including all the members from the administration, concluded that a return to some form of gold standard was not appropriate. A lengthy minority report by businessman Lew Lehrman and Congressman Ron Paul, however, made an effective case that the current fiat currency system, particularly since 1971, also has many problems. My own judgment is that the majority of the Gold Commission was correct in recommending against a return to a gold standard. The Commission, however, failed to reach an agreement on an alternative standard for the conduct of monetary policy, a problem that remains to be addressed.

The tensions between the administration and the Fed developed only slowly. Money growth through the summer of 1982 was lower than the initial guidance, despite a rapid growth of the NOW accounts authorized in 1980, but was initially offset by a high growth of money velocity through the summer of 1981. The beginning of the recession in August 1981 was a cause for neither much surprise nor much concern, and the president was one of the first to acknowledge the recession. The administration expected that renewed money growth and the recent approval of the 1981 tax bill would avoid a deep or extended recession.

At that time the primary concern was that interest rates were still unusually high despite a decline in inflation. The announcement of the new policies, which the administration had hoped would reduce expected inflation, had not yet had their intended effect. The Treasury's first explanation of the high interest rates was the unusual variability of money growth, based on an analysis by Allan Meltzer, a leading monetarist scholar and a Treasury consultant. This explanation did not withstand a preliminary analysis by the CEA staff, and a later study suggested that such variability was more likely to reduce interest rates by reducing the demand for credit more than the supply. In addition, this explanation was not consistent with the observed increase in the value of the dollar on foreign exchange markets. The administration did not yet understand that the 1981 tax law increased real interest rates by increasing the post-tax return on new investment. The Fed and most outside analysts attributed the high interest rates to the increasing deficit, a conjecture that also did not withstand later examination.

A substantial decline in real GNP in the fall of 1981 and the winter of 1982, associated with a sharp decline in money velocity, made it clear that the recession would be longer and deeper than expected. A small increase in real GNP in the spring, however, was cause for believing that the recession was over and delayed any change in policy. In mid-June testimony to Congress, Volcker repeated the usual Fed position that there is "a critical need for judgment in the conduct of monetary policy" but expressed his own judgment that the Fed should not yet ease. In the next several weeks the new data indicated that economic conditions had weakened again, and a consensus developed that some change was probably appropriate. The new consensus was due in part to a change in membership of the FOMC and to pressure from Congress and the Treasury. Congress was threatening legislation that would reduce the independence of the Fed. And the Treasury announced that Sprinkel had started a study of the Fed, a threat that turned out to be a bluff. At the June 30 meeting of the FOMC, an eight-to-four majority approved a slight increase in the money targets and authorized a larger later increase if necessary. After a review of the June economic data first available in late July, Murray Wiedenbaum and I also concluded, without knowledge of the Fed decision, that some easing was appropriate.

A combination of other events locked in the consensus for higher money growth. The Mexican debt crisis broke in late August, threatening the major commercial banks. The new super-NOW accounts that were soon to be authorized by the Garn-St Germain Act and the expiration of the all-savers certificates were expected to lead to a large increase in the money supply. (That expectation proved to be a mistake. In 1981 the rapid increase in NOW accounts was almost completely offset by a reduction in conventional demand deposits. In late 1982 the increase in Super-NOW accounts was substantially offset by a decline in the NOW accounts.) Although interest rates had declined sharply and the stock market had soared in the late summer, the economy was still very weak and the mid-term election was near. The Fed was in a bind. A substantial increase in money growth would substantially exceed the money targets but appeared to be the appropriate response to the current economic conditions. On October 5, almost three years to the day that the monetarist experiment was initiated, the FOMC resolved this conflict by abandoning the target on the narrow money supply (M1). Volcker went out of the way to minimize the significance of this change, describing it as "an operational change" with "zero policy significance." He rejected a proposal for a press conference to announce the change, choosing to explain it as a "small, technical matter" at a speech to the Business Council that weekend. There was little doubt among informed observers, however, about the significance of this change. The three-year experiment with monetarist policies was over, an experiment that started with a bang and ended with a whimper.

The monetarist experiment was widely perceived to be a failure. Monetarists had several valid reasons, however, to claim that it was not a fair experiment. Money growth from the fall of 1980 through the summer of 1982 (at a 5.5 percent annual rate) was lower than the initial Reagan guidance (implying a 6.4 percent annual rate for this period). The composition of the money supply changed substantially as a consequence of the bank deregulation measures authorized in 1980. Most important, money growth was usually variable during this three-year period, reducing the credibility of the monetary targets and other announced policy changes. The credit controls during the spring of 1980, a measure strongly opposed by the monetarists, were a major cause of the variation in money growth during this period. There was ample reason for skepticism about whether the Fed was serious about this experiment. The most important reason for the perceived failure of the experiment, however, was the decline in money velocity beginning in the fall of 1981, a condition that was not anticipated and for which there is not yet a broad understanding. A steady money growth rate is an adequate guide to monetary policy only when changes in money velocity relative to the trend are reversed in subsequent periods, and this condition is not consistent with the accumulating evidence. The monetarists have yet to agree on a money rule that incorporates the observed changes in money velocity.

Another puzzle from this period remains to be explained. Why did the Fed reduce the growth of the money supply somewhat more than the initial Reagan guidance, despite the decline in money velocity beginning in late 1981? One explanation favored by the Fed is that money growth cannot be controlled as precisely as the monetarists believe. My perspective is quite different. My judgment is that Volcker believed that the consensus for monetary restraint was temporary and that the American political system would not tolerate the slow, steady reduction in money growth recommended by the initial

Reagan guidance. He may have wanted to reduce inflation as rapidly as possible, despite the temporary adverse effects on the economy and the destruction of the consensus for sustained restraint. In the same way Weinberger exploited the consensus for a defense buildup to achieve a more rapid increase than, beginning in 1985, Congress was prepared to sustain. Volcker's judgment, according to this interpretation, may have been correct. In any case the costs of this policy, in terms of the loss of output resulting from the 1981–1982 recession, are now behind us, and the inflation rate declined much more than anyone expected. The major enduring cost of this judgment is that we have no consensus for the conduct of monetary policy under current conditions.

Uncharted Waters

The change in monetary policy approved on October 5, 1982, involved three elements—an increase in near-term money growth, the temporary suspension of the M1 target, and another major change in the Fed's basic operating procedure. A more important implicit change was that the Fed no longer followed any obvious rule for the conduct of monetary policy.

Since the summer of 1982 the rate of money growth has been the highest in peacetime history. At the end of 1982 money growth was again higher than the announced target and, for the first time, above the initial Reagan guidance. A new M1 target was set for 1983 and subsequent years, but the targets became increasingly irrelevant. Money growth substantially exceeded the announced targets in 1983, 1985, and 1986. Only in 1984 was money growth within the announced target range, a period during with the Treasury occasionally grumbled that money growth was too low.

An Uneasy Peace

The important issue is whether anyone should care about the high rate of money growth. Since 1983 the leading monetary scholars have expressed concern about the high rate of money growth and predicted that the inflation rate would increase substantially within two years. At least through 1986 the high money growth did not lead to an increase in the inflation rate because money velocity continued to decline. My judgment is that the high money growth during this period was appropriate, but the full effects have not yet been realized, and I must acknowledge that my views on this issue have changed. Continued money growth on the initial Reagan guidance, in light of the decline in money velocity, would have reduced the growth of total demand, output, and employment for several years; the general inflation rate would be about zero, and there would be even greater deflation in some sectors. That seems to be a higher price to reduce the remaining inflation than the American political system would accept. There is still a risk that money velocity will increase at a rate closer to the trend through mid-1981, in which case a lower money growth will be necessary to avoid a substantial increase in inflation. At this time, as I will explain later, I do not believe that will be the case.

The change in operating procedures in the fall of 1982 was not widely understood and was difficult to explain. At first market analysts observed that the daily variation of the federal funds rate was reduced sharply and believed that the Fed had returned to the pre-October 1979 procedure of setting a narrow range for this rate. That was not the case. Under the new procedure the FOMC approves a path of borrowed reserves. The approved level of borrowed reserves is then subtracted from the total reserves necessary to support the target path of the money supply to yield an initial path of nonborrowed reserves. The level of nonborrowed reserves in turn is adjusted weekly in an attempt to maintain the approved level of borrowed reserves.

If the demand for bank borrowing at the discount window were a perfectly stable function of the difference between the federal funds rate and the discount rate, the combined effect of the new borrowed reserves target and the discount rate would be equivalent to setting the federal funds rate. In fact, this relation is not perfectly stable. The new procedure thus permits some variation in both the federal funds rate and the money growth rate, depending on the demand for credit. (The FOMC now also sets a broad range for the federal funds rate, usually about four percentage points. The limits on this range, however, are seldom tested.) Since this new procedure was implemented, the daily variation of the federal funds rate and the quarterly variation in money growth were both reduced relative to the period from October 1979 through September 1982, but both were higher than in the long period prior to October 1979.

In February 1984 the Federal Reserve adopted one more recommendation from the monetarist agenda in order to achieve better control of the money supply. Until that time the level of required bank reserves in each bank was based on the level (and mix) of deposits lagged two weeks. If banks substantially increased their deposits during the intervening two weeks, the Fed was under some pressure to increase reserves in order to avoid a substantial increase in the federal funds rate. After the Fed began to change the nonborrowed reserves on a weekly basis, however, the effective lag was re-

duced from two weeks to one week. The remaining lag was eliminated by a Fed regulation that based the level of required bank
reserves on the contemporaneous level of deposits, further tightening the relation between bank reserves and the money supply. Monetarists have also recommended that the discount rate be set slightly
above short-term market rates to further tighten Fed control of the
money supply. This proposal is most unlikely to be accepted because
it threatens the relations by which the Fed maintains the political
support of the banks. The current control techniques, however, are
probably sufficient to maintain annual money growth within a one-
percentage-point band.

Relations between the administration and the Federal Reserve from
October 1982 through the end of the first term were characterized
by an uneasy peace. As long as the recovery was unusually strong in
1983 and early 1984, the Treasury did not make much of an issue
about money growth substantially above the targets. Some tensions
remained. Treasury comments about monetary policy, although rare,
were often criticized by Congress and the press as interfering with
the independence of the Fed. Volcker's frequent criticisms of the
deficit, in contrast, were regarded as those of an economic states-
man. Don Regan chafed at this asymmetry but learned to live with
it. Dave Stockman, Marty Feldstein, and Jim Baker, for their own
reasons, usually sided with Volcker. The Treasury maintained a general monetarist position but acquiesced to Fed leadership on monetary policy.

The reappointment of Paul Volcker as Fed chairman in July 1983
caused only a minor flap. Regan strongly opposed Volcker's reappointment but had no viable substitute. Walter Wriston, the chairman of Citibank and of the President's Economic Policy Advisory
Board, was the only alternative candidate of sufficient stature, but
Wriston was regarded as too monetarist and potentially compro-
mised by Citibank's portfolio of Latin American debt. Wall Street
and most of Congress strongly supported Volcker's reappointment.
Jim Baker was apparently instrumental in convincing the president
to reappoint Volcker.

A minor issue also arose in the summer of 1984. Money growth
had slowed sharply since the summer of 1983, interest rates backed
up to mid-1982 levels, and there was increasing concern in the administration that this would lead to weak economic conditions during the election season. As in 1981, the Treasury again complained
that money growth was too low, although this time the money supply
was well within the target wedge. On the basis of a prior statistical
study of presidential elections, I forecast that Reagan would win nearly
60 percent of the popular vote and argued against additional mon-

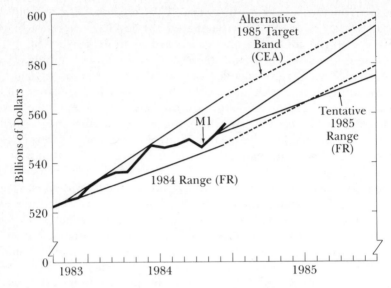

Figure 5.4   Alternative M1 Target Ranges for 1985

etary stimulus. (As a middle-level official in the Nixon administration, I made the same type of calculations and argument in late 1971, with even less effect.) As it turned out, the growth of real GNP slowed sharply during the summer and fall of 1984, but this was too late to weaken Reagan's overwhelming lead in the 1984 campaign.

The last monetarist initiative of the first term involved two proposed changes in the setting of the monetary targets. The combined effect of these two proposals is illustrated by Figure 5.4. In the 1985 *Economic Report* my CEA colleague Bill Poole made the case for expressing the limits on money growth as a band, rather than a wedge, to give the Fed increased flexibility during the early months of each year. The Fed quickly accepted this proposal, stating (correctly) that this had long been its implicit practice. Poole also proposed that the monetary targets for each year be based on the midpoint of the target band, rather than on the actual level of the money supply, in the fourth quarter of the prior year to prevent a "base drift" of the money supply from one year to the next. Although this would have slightly increased the 1985 target band, the Fed rejected this proposal because it would have reduced its future flexibility. I now believe the Fed's rejection of this proposal was correct. A stable path of total demand, I am now convinced, is not consistent with a stable path of the money supply. Steady money growth within announced target limits, the fundamental policy proposal of the monetarists, is probably not the best monetary rule for the U.S. economy. The current problem is that there is not yet a professional or political consensus on a superior rule.

Bakerism

The exchange of positions by Don Regan and Jim Baker in early 1985 caught all of us by surprise. Regan seemed comfortable in his position as Treasury secretary, although he was frustrated in his inability to achieve a dominance over economic policy. It was also not clear that his managerial style was viable in the more collegial environment of the White House. For some time it was rumored that Baker wanted a senior cabinet position, and many of us hoped that he would replace Weinberger. Baker was smooth and had superb political instincts, but he had no apparent substantive credentials for the Treasury position. He had not participated in the cabinet council deliberations on economic policy during the first term, and it was not clear that he had any policy agenda. Most of my experience with Baker was limited to the nine-month period when I served as acting chairman of the CEA. My only clues to his policy views were that he had a Texan's aversion to high interest rates and a politician's indifference to longer-range policy effects. He was also suspicious of economists and, like the president, uncomfortable with complex arguments. More than any Treasury secretary in many years, Baker was flying blind. He was also incredibly lucky.

Baker moved quickly to put his own stamp on the Treasury. Dick Darman, who had been Baker's key aide in the White House, replaced Tim McNamar as deputy secretary. Darman was smart, ambitious, and similarly uncommitted to any policy agenda. He was especially good at summarizing material and formulating options, although he had little substantive experience or technical skills. Baker did not read very much or solicit technical advice, so Darman became his eyes and ears. After Beryl Sprinkel was appointed chairman of the CEA, Baker abolished the office of the undersecretary for monetary affairs, a position that had been filled by distinguished monetary economists for several decades. Sprinkel's move to the CEA served the interests of both Baker and Regan; Baker wanted Sprinkel out of the Treasury and Regan wanted someone as CEA chairman who would operate on a short leash. Neither of these personnel changes were handled with finesse. Both McNamar and I learned of our replacement from reporters, shortly after being told that no decision had been made. Manuel Johnson, the senior remaining Treasury economist, was appointed to the Federal Reserve Board in late 1985, and Johnson's position was not filled for another six months. Baker's first two years would prove to be an interesting test of whether the Treasury could be run effectively without the counsel of senior economists.

Baker's first actions did not indicate any change in policy. In his first round of testimony to Congress, he made a few opening comments and made himself available for questions without staking out any new policy positions. The first test of a possible change in position, interestingly, arose from Don Regan's last meeting with the finance ministers of the Group of Five (G-5) in late January. At that meeting Regan agreed to a slight change of wording concerning the conditions under which the major industrial nations would intervene in the foreign exchange markets. The other countries interpreted this as a significant change in U.S. policy, which, from the beginning of the Reagan administration, had been to intervene only to stabilize "disorderly market conditions" and not to achieve any specific exchange rate target. In February, during Baker's first weeks in office, the dollar reached a record high, and the Fed persistently asked Baker's approval to sell dollars. The British pound was especially weak, and the Thatcher government had substantially increased domestic interest rates to keep the pound from falling below the symbolic threshhold value of one dollar. Baker was surprised to learn that the approval of the secretary of the Treasury was required for each U.S. intervention and was irritated that this issue was taking so much of his time. Although he approved a small amount of intervention at that time, the Treasury maintained the public position that the policy concerning intervention had not changed. The Fed later reported that the United States had purchased $659 million in German marks and Japanese yen, and nine other countries had sold about $10 billion between January 21 and March 1 to curb the dollar's strength at that time. For context, it should be recognized that average daily transactions on the foreign exchange markets around the world are more than $100 billion.

The initial Reagan economic program claimed that "improving expectations and slowing inflation will enhance the dollar as an international store of value and contribute to greater stability in international financial markets," but it did not define any policy concerning intervention in the exchange markets. The intervention policy, developed largely by Beryl Sprinkel, was consistent with conventional wisdom and was not initially controversial. "Sterilized" intervention, offset by changes in domestic bank reserves, was not considered to have much effect on the exchange rate except during the immediate market day. "Unsterilized" intervention, the selling or buying of dollars without an offset to domestic bank reserves, was considered to have the same effect as domestic open market operations. In brief, sterilized intervention was considered ineffective and unsterilized intervention was considered inappropriate, because it would subordinate domestic monetary policy to maintaining some value of the exchange rate. Sprinkel was not convinced that intervention was appropriate even to stabilize disorderly markets, but he acquiesced to this exception. In any case the U.S. government intervened in the exchange market very rarely during the first term.

In the meantime, from the record low in the summer of 1980 to the record high in the winter of 1985, the multilateral trade-weighted value of the dollar increased 74 percent in real terms! The Treasury first misinterpreted the increasing value of the dollar, arguing that it was primarily due to a flow of "safe-haven" capital to the United States. In that case, however, U.S. interest rates would have been lower than those in other countries. The increase in the dollar was directly due to an increase in U.S. real interest rates relative to those in other countries. There was reason to argue whether the reduction in taxes on business investment approved in 1981 on the increase in the federal deficit had the larger effect on U.S. interest rates, but it was clear that the increase in real interest rates was primarily due to U.S. fiscal policy. The increase in the dollar led to enormous benefits, in the form of lower prices on traded goods and services, to the United States and was a major reason for the decline in inflation. The increase in the dollar, however, also led to substantial losses to specific sectors by reducing output and employment in export- and import-competing industries. (There will be more on these issues in Chapters 7 and 8.)

Our political system, as usual, was more responsive to the losers than to the winners. The administration had managed to defer any major protectionist legislation through 1984, but the trade policy environment turned ugly in 1985. Baker wanted to counter the rising demands for trade restraints, and he began the most concerted effort to "talk down the dollar" since Michael Blumenthal's similar effort in late 1977. The Fed cooperated by reducing the discount rate from 8 percent to 7.5 percent in May, and money growth increased rapidly. (The parallels with the Blumenthal initiative were ominous. At that time U.S. money growth also increased, and Blumenthal urged the other major industrial countries to be the "locomotive" of world recovery. The dollar declined 15 percent within one year, and the U.S. inflation rate increased about five percentage points within two years. Blumenthal later acknowledged that "we had no idea of the dangers." In 1985, however, Baker was apparently unaware of the similar Blumenthal initiative in 1977.) During the spring and summer of 1985, the dollar declined 11 percent with no additional intervention. There was still no change in official U.S. policy on exchange rates. The G-10 meeting on June 21 reaffirmed support for the flexible exchange rate system, concluding that "it is questionable whether any less flexible system would have survived the strains of the past decade, while attempting to preserve it would probably have led to increased restrictions on trade and capital flows."

At the same time, however, Baker decided to make a major change in U.S. policy. In secret negotiations during the summer of 1985, Baker won the agreement of the other G-5 governments to devalue the dollar. The formal agreement that "some further orderly appreciation of the main nondollar currencies is desirable" was announced at the meeting of the G-5 finance ministers and central bankers at the Plaza Hotel in New York on September 22. The immediate effect of the Plaza Accord was an appreciation of the Japanese currency, from 240 to 220 yen per dollar, without any intervention. Over the next six weeks the United States and nine other countries sold $10.2 billion on the exchange markets in the second coordinated intervention of 1985. Most of this intervention, except that by the Japanese, was sterilized. The Japanese reported that the G-5 had also agreed to "coordinate their interest rate policies as part of their plan to lower the dollar," but this was quickly denied by a high Fed official. This episode illustrates the futility of trying to affect trade balances by manipulating the exchange rate. The unsterilized intervention by the Bank of Japan was successful in contributing to a relative appreciation of the yen only by reducing the growth of domestic demand. Although the price of U.S. products in Japan declined, the demand for these products also declined. Japan risked a domestic recession to defer protectionist pressure in the United States by an action that did not much change the bilateral trade balance.

Over the next six months Baker periodically expressed that "he would not be displeased" if the dollar declined more. U.S. money growth continued at an unusually high rate, and the dollar continued to decline without any additional coordinated intervention. On February 19, 1986, however, Volcker expressed concern that the dollar "may have fallen enough," and on April 4, Baker agreed that "there might well be a point beyond which we would not want to see the dollar go [down] further," without identifying that level. From the Plaza Accord through May 1986, the dollar declined 30 percent against the yen to a record low, 22 percent against the German mark, and an average of 15 percent against the currencies of the major industrial nations.

The Plaza Accord seems to have been a huge success, and Baker was widely praised in the U.S. business press for rejecting the noninterventionist policies of Regan and Sprinkel. As with the Treasury tax plan, the strongest praise was from liberal critics of the prior

Reagan economic policies. Is it really possible, however, that a small amount of intervention and the public remarks of the Treasury secretary were sufficient to lead to a cumulative 24 percent decline in the dollar from the winter of 1985 through the spring of 1986? Something more fundamental must have occurred during this same period. A more plausible explanation was the high rate of money growth. A corresponding increase in the growth of total demand, however, would be necessary for this explanation to be sufficient; in fact, the growth of current dollar U.S. GNP declined during this period because of a continuing decline in money velocity. Those who attributed the rise of the dollar to the increasing budget deficits suggested that the dollar decline was due to expectations of lower future deficits, reinforced by the Gramm-Rudman legislation. There are any number of problems with this explanation. There has been no consistent relation of budget deficits and exchange rates over time or across nations. The timing is also wrong; the dollar peaked about the time the Senate rejected the president's FY 1986 budget, the Gramm-Rudman legislation was not considered until late 1985, and the federal deficit increased in FY 1986.

My opinion is that the dollar declined because of a reversal of the tax policy that was the primary reason for the substantial increase in the dollar. The 1981 tax legislation increased the post-tax return on domestic business fixed investment and U.S. real interest rates. Each of the major tax reform proposals would have reversed this effect. The timing is also more consistent. The Treasury tax plan was released in late November 1984, the president's proposal was released in May 1985, the major features of the House bill were first revealed in September and approved in December, and the Senate Finance Committee approved its tax bill in May 1986. An expectation of lower future business investment and real interest rates was, I believe, the primary reason for the decline in the dollar. The final tax bill, a compromise between the House and Senate bills, increased the effective tax rate on new business investment and was approved in September 1986. If this explanation is correct, the expected effects of this tax legislation were already reflected in the markets, and no significant additional decline in the dollar should have been expected. There is no evidence that Baker recognized this probable explanation of the decline in the dollar, a process to which he contributed primarily by shaping the president's tax plan.

The other part of the Plaza Accord, less widely publicized, was an agreement by each of the G-5 nations to pursue policies to increase economic growth. This agreement was described as different from the "locomotive" strategy of 1978 because it focused on measures to increase supply rather than to increase demand. The Treasury did not acknowledge and may not have recognized that the two parts of the Plaza Accord were probably inconsistent. A continued decline in the dollar would strengthen the trade sector of the United States only by weakening the trade sectors of other nations more dependent on trade. Moreover, any unsterilized intervention by other nations to weaken the dollar would reduce the growth of the money supply and total demand in the other nations. In any case the commitment to growth policies had little short-term effect. Economic growth continued to be sluggish in 1986 in both the U.S. and the other major nations. The sharp appreciation in the mark and the yen led to a small decline in real GNP in Germany and Japan in the winter of 1986, the first quarterly decline in Japan since 1975.

Baker's own test of the success of his dollar strategy was whether it would defer pressure for restrictive trade legislation. By this standard the strategy was successful. In 1985 Congress approved only the textile bill, and the president vetoed this bill. It was less clear that this strategy would be as successful in 1986. In May an omnibus trade bill passed the House by a large margin over the strong objection of the administration. In August the House attempt to override Reagan's veto of the textile bill was defeated by only eight votes. The Senate developed a trade bill, more restrictive in some ways than the House bill, but a full Senate vote on this bill was deferred by the pressure of other measures during the fall. Baker's policies, combined with several trade restrictions approved by the administration, proved to be sufficient to defer any congressional trade legislation through 1987.

After the perceived success of the Plaza Accord, Baker moved to consolidate an agreement on some change in the international monetary system. A congressional conference on international monetary reform in November 1985, organized by Sen. Bill Bradley and Rep. Jack Kemp, received considerable publicity but led to little agreement about what changes are desirable. The next step, ironically, was the result of the first successful challenge to Volcker's dominance of the Federal Reserve Board. The confirmation of two new Reagan appointees to the Board in January 1986 gave the administration a potential majority of the Board but not of the larger open market committee. In late February the Board voted 4–3 to reduce the discount rate from 7.5 to 7.0 percent, with Volcker opposing. Volcker asked that the vote not be recorded until the end of the day. A few hours later Wayne Angell, one of the new members of the Board, switched his vote, preserving Volcker's official record. The general belief is that Volcker asked Baker to request that Angell switch his vote, promising Baker to reduce the discount rate later if the German and Japanese central banks reduced their rates first. After

Volcker convinced his foreign colleagues to take the lead, the Fed reduced the U.S. discount rate in early March. A similar coordinated reduction in the discount rate was approved in late April. These events convinced Baker that some coordination of economic policy, at least among the central bankers, was possible.

The Treasury first surfaced the outline of a more comprehensive coordination plan at an interim meeting of the IMF in Washington on April 11. The central feature of this plan, promoted primarily by Darman, was a set of unannounced broad target zones for the exchange rate of each major currency. The initial target zones would be rather wide. The zone for the dollar-yen rate, for example, might be from 160 to 200 yen per dollar. In addition, the IMF would develop a set of objective indicators to determine when some policy change is necessary to maintain an exchange rate within the target zone. The target zones would presumably be enforced by peer pressure. According to Treasury assistant secretary David Mulford, "We need a system that signals the need for consultation . . . that increases the peer pressure on countries to comply." In early May the Tokyo economic summit agreed to a system of "enhanced surveillance," and a more detailed plan was expected to be announced at the IMF-World Bank meeting in September. As it turned out, however, the September meeting did not lead to any resolution of this issue. A prior meeting of the European finance ministers at Gleneagles, Scotland, had strongly rejected a general agreement on policy coordination. In private meetings before the IMF-World Bank meetings, the German and Japanese finance minsters rejected Baker's specific proposal for a coordinated reduction of interest rates. Baker later settled for a bilateral agreement with Japan to stop talking down the dollar in exchange for a one-half-percent reduction in the Japanese discount rate.

The most charitable comment on this plan is that the Treasury did not understand what it was doing. The finance ministers of Germany and Japan, the two major nations with the best inflation record during the past decade, strongly opposed the target zone proposal. Neither country wanted to lock in the current high exchange rate of its currency. The Germans, specifically, were not convinced that they wanted to coordinate economic policy with the United States, blaming the high inflation of the late 1970s on the Blumenthal pressure for a coordinated policy during a period of rapid U.S. money growth. Gerhard Stoltenberg, the German finance minister, raised the critical technical issue: "The question is who would decide zones, and even more important, who would enforce them." For example, if the French franc were at the bottom of its target zone relative to the German mark, a frequent condition within the European monetary system, would the French be obligated to raise interest rates or the Germans to lower interest rates? This system would surely fail the first time that Baker was subject to peer pressure to increase U.S. interest rates to prevent a decline in the dollar against the yen.

International economic coordination is often appealing to American officials who expect other nations to coordinate with the United States. It is much less appealing to those governments, necessarily including the U.S., which would be obligated to subordinate domestic economic policy to maintain a target zone system. The United States can best achieve an implicit coordination by being a model of sound economic policy to the rest of the world. The initial Reagan economic program was a good start toward such a model until it was undermined by a continued high growth of federal spending.

A short-term stability of exchange rates, the presumed objective of the current proposals to change the international monetary system, is a false issue. Any person or business can insure itself at low cost against a short-term change in the exchange rate by transactions on the futures market for foreign exchange. It is not possible, however, to buy insurance against the temporary restraints on trade and capital flows and the discrete official changes in exchange rates that are characteristic of fixed exchange rate systems (except by operating on inside information about changes in government policy). A move toward a more stable exchange rate system, as with domestic price or interest rate controls, would reduce uncertainty about exchange rates only by increasing uncertainty about government policy—at best a Faustian bargain.

In any case Baker's primary objective was to devalue the dollar, not to stabilize it. For reasons that he probably did not understand, that had already been achieved. As of early 1987 the dollar had declined enough against the mark and the yen to induce the Germans and Japanese to modify their prior positions. The finance ministers of the summit countries, meeting in the Louvre on February 21 and 22, 1987, indicated that they were prepared to stabilize exchange rates at "about their current levels" and approved a secret "reference range" for these rates. The Germans, reflecting the increased strength of the Free Democrats in the January election, agreed to increase the scheduled tax reductions. The Japanese reduced their discount rate and pledged to propose a new package of fiscal stimulus. The finance minister of Italy left the meeting in a huff after realizing that the basic agreement had been developed without his participation. The United States made no new public commitment; Baker claimed that the federal deficit would decline substantially to meet the Gramm-Rudman targets, apparently without recognizing that a lower deficit would probably weaken the dollar. The "Louvre Accord" reflected more commitment than the Plaza Accord, but a sharp reduction of U.S. money growth was a necessary part of this bargain. Baker's timing, moreover, was again superb. U.S. interest rates started to increase, and the dollar strengthened slightly. For those who focus on the appearance of policy activism, rather than the substance of policy, Baker again looked like a magician.

Some pressure for a change in the international monetary system, however, is likely to continue. For those with little memory or understanding of the technical and political problems, the idea of international economic coordination has a continuing appeal. And Baker, Darman, Bradley, Kemp, and others have a major investment in this general approach. The formal target zone system, however, was opposed within the administration by Shultz, Sprinkel, and Miller. For three years Baker was on a roll. My guess is that when his hand is called on this issue, his string will have run out.

A SUMMARY EVALUATION

Promise and Performance

A comparison of the actual monetary policy during the Reagan years with the initial guidance is complicated by the fact that the initial program provided two targets for monetary policy—a forecast path of current dollar GNP and a target path of the money supply. Moreover, given the historical relation between GNP and the money supply, these two target paths were inconsistent. As indicated in Figure 5.5, the actual growth of current dollar GNP was lower in every year than the initial forecast; by that standard, monetary policy was tighter than the initial guidance throughout the Reagan years. This figure also indicates, however, that the actual growth of the money supply has been higher than the initial target since late 1982; by this standard, monetary policy was too tight only for the period through the summer of 1982 and, in light of the historical relation between money growth and inflation, the subsequent growth of the money supply would have been highly inflationary. (The difference between the growth of GNP and the money supply is roughly equal to the change in money velocity. This figure also shows that the initial Reagan GNP forecast assumed an increase in the growth of velocity, whereas in fact money velocity declined.) Moreover, a comparison of the record of monetary policy during the Carter and Reagan years is somewhat misleading, because the experiment with monetarist policies spanned a roughly equal period at the end of the Carter administration and the beginning of the Reagan administration. These aggregate data

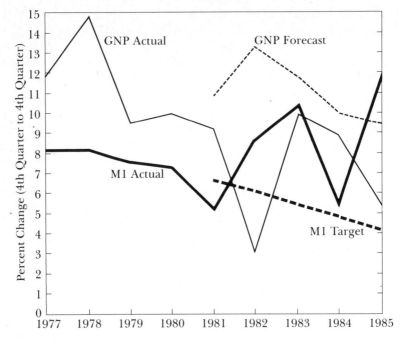

Figure 5.5   GNP and the Money Supply

do not permit a simple evaluation of monetary policy over this period.

A more accurate evaluation should be based on the growth rates and quarterly variation of the primary monetary conditions during the three periods of distinctively different monetary policy. Table 5.1 summarizes these data, including the record during the Carter administration and during the Reagan administration through 1985.

The Carter period through the summer of 1979 was characterized by a high rate of money growth with little variation, a high rate of velocity growth with substantial variation, and a record peacetime growth of current dollar GNP growth with even higher variation. During this period changes in the money supply were independent of changes in velocity, a condition that is more consistent with a constant money growth rule than with the expected effect of the interest rate targeting procedure then in use. This suggests that the Fed had already made some attempt to stabilize money growth relative to the changes in velocity.

The three-year monetarist experiment was characterized by lower rates of growth of money, velocity, and GNP. These changes were the primary reason for the extended recession of 1981 and 1982 and

Table 5.1 Changes in the Money Supply, Velocity, and GNP*

Period	Money Supply	Velocity	GNP
77/I–79/III	8.3	3.9	12.5
	(1.7)	(4.5)	(4.8)
79/IV–82/III	6.0	1.6	7.7
	(5.0)	(6.9)	(6.6)
82/IV–85/IV	9.8	−1.9	7.8
	(4.0)	(5.7)	(3.9)
Carter administration	7.8	3.4	11.6
	(4.2)	(4.6)	(5.4)
Reagan administration (through 1985)	8.3	−0.9	7.3
	(4.1)	(6.7)	(4.9)

*Percentage change, annual rate (quarterly deviation).

for the substantial decline in the inflation rate through 1984. The Fed's new operating procedure, however, was not sufficient to avoid a substantial increase in the quarterly variation of each of these variables. The primary problem of monetary policy during this period was the substantial increase in the variation in money growth, a condition that was directly contrary to the objective of the new operating procedure. Most of the variation in velocity, except for the effect of the credit controls, was probably unavoidable. During this period, however, changes in money growth partly offset the changes in velocity, reducing the variation of GNP relative to the sum of the variation of money and velocity. One step at a time!

The Reagan period since the summer of 1982 has been characterized by a record high rate of money growth, a decline in velocity, and a moderately steady growth of current dollar GNP. The variation of the money supply and velocity declined slightly relative to the prior period but was higher than prior to the monetarist experiment. During this period, however, changes in the money supply substantially offset changes in velocity, leading to the lowest variation in GNP of these three periods. In terms of short-term economic effects, this was an unusually successful period of monetary policy. The general inflation rate was maintained at the lowest rate since 1967. Market interest rates declined to the lowest rate since 1977. The quarterly variation of GNP was unusually low. And the recovery of real GNP was maintained for five years. One major anxiety was whether the deflation in commodity prices would have any substantial adverse effects on the rest of the economy. Another major concern was whether the unusually high rate of money growth would lead to a substantial increase in future inflation. As I will explain

later, I do not now share either of these concerns. Whether by accident or design, the Federal Reserve, with the support of the administration, deserves credit for an unusually successful period in the
history of monetary policy.

Some of my best friends are monetarists. The lessons of this period, however, challenge their most cherished policy recommendations. A low rate of money growth is not necessary to restrain inflation if, for whatever reason, money velocity declines. A low variability
of money growth is not necessary to reduce the variability of GNP if
changes in money growth offset the changes in velocity. Such statements have always been arithmetically correct. A policy of a low,
steady rate of money growth, however, would be appropriate only if
changes in velocity followed a pattern that I now believe is inconsistent with the empirical evidence. For that reason I now consider myself to be a "low church" monetarist. Control of the money supply is
still very important. A low, steady growth of the money supply, however, does not appear to be the best rule for the conduct of monetary policy.

The Velocity Puzzle

From the spring of 1951 through the summer of 1981, money velocity increased at an annual rate of about 3 percent. This pattern
was sufficiently stable to provide a reasonable basis for concluding
that it would continue. Since the summer of 1981, however, velocity
has declined at an annual rate of about 2 percent. What explains the
decline in velocity? What are the implications of the change in velocity for the conduct of monetary policy?

In 1981 there were several reasons to believe that velocity would
continue to increase, maybe at a higher rate. A continued growth in
the use of "plastic money" (credit cards) was expected to increase the
level of transactions that could be financed by a given stock of money.
A consensus of the Keynesians expected that the rapid increase in
the federal deficit would increase total demand even if it did not
increase Fed financing of the deficit. Neither of these expectations
proved to be correct. The subsequent decline in velocity is the primary evidence that the long recovery beginning in the fall of 1982
was not due to a Keynesian effect of the deficit on total demand.

Sorting out the velocity puzzle requires more careful attention to
the 1951–1981 period during which the expected pattern of velocity
growth was developed. It has long been recognized that an increase
in interest rates would increase velocity by increasing the "opportunity cost"—that is, the foregone interest on assets held in the form
of currency and demand deposits. During this period the level of

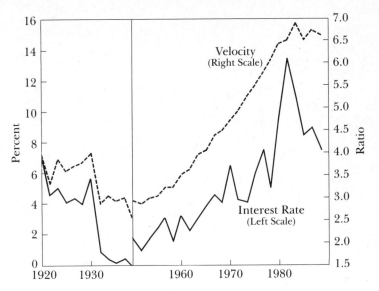

Figure 5.6   Interest Rate and Velocity* (annual average level)

*Estimate for 1985 based on first half results; World War II and immediate aftermath omitted (1941 to 1951).

velocity increased at a moderately steady rate, and interest rates also increased with substantially more variation. Figure 5.6 illustrates these patterns. The relative stability of velocity growth, however, made it difficult to distinguish the effects of a "trend" and interest rates on the level of velocity. The available statistical studies of the "money demand function" have attributed most of the increase in velocity to a trend rather than to the increase in interest rates. An examination of the experience prior to World War II, however, as also shown in Figure 5.6, should have led to questioning as to whether there was any trend growth in velocity independent of the effects of interest rates. In technical terms the money demand functions estimated from a sample of the postwar data overestimated the trend in velocity, which may be zero, and substantially underestimated the "interest elasticity" of the demand for money.

The relation between changes in velocity and interest rates is more clearly illustrated by examining the short-run changes in these variables since 1979. Figure 5.7 illustrates a very close relation between the changes in velocity and the changes in short-term interest rates from 1979 to date. The general decline in velocity since the summer of 1981 appears to be primarily due to the decline in market interest rates. There was also a plausible basis for expecting that bank dere-

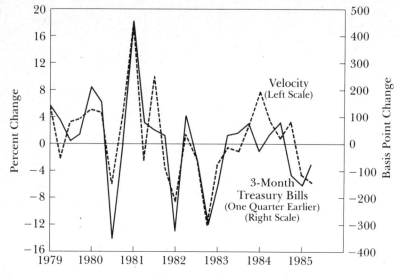

Figure 5.7   Velocity and T-Bills (quarterly change)

gulation also contributed to the decline in velocity, by permitting an increase in the interest rates on personal demand deposits and, in turn, reducing the foregone interest from holding such deposits. The deregulation of bank deposit rates, by extending the authority for NOW accounts in January 1981 and authorizing the Super-NOW accounts in January 1983, however, does not seem to have had much effect on velocity; as indicated in Figure 5.7, there was no unusual change in the relation of velocity to market interest rates around these dates. In fact, a money demand function without a trend term appears to have been quite stable over a long period, despite the considerable changes in the composition of deposits and the nature of the economy. By focusing only on the postwar years, the econometricians had led us to believe that most of the increase in velocity was some inherent trend rather than a response to higher interest rates. The decline in velocity since mid-1981 was due not to a shift in the demand for money but to the normal effects of a decline in market interest rates and an increase in the value of financial assets. In retrospect, there should have been no "velocity puzzle."

The Implications for Monetary Policy

What is the appropriate response by the Federal Reserve to an observed change in velocity in the prior period? The monetarist response to this question is to maintain money growth at a constant rate. This monetary rule, however, would be appropriate only if velocity is "trend stable"; that is, velocity is expected to return to the prior trend in subsequent periods. The accumulating evidence, however, is that velocity is "difference stable"; in other words, changes in velocity growth from one period to the next are not related. This finding was first reported in a 1974 article summarizing the pattern of annual data from 1869 to 1960; unfortunately, this article was not widely read. This finding was first brought to my attention in the fall of 1983 by a senior CEA staff economist, following a preliminary examination of the pattern of quarterly data during the postwar years.

Martin Feldstein and I quickly recognized the important implication of this finding for the conduct of monetary policy, although our monetarist colleague William Poole still had reservations. If the objective of monetary policy is to maintain a stable path of current dollar GNP, this finding implies that the money growth rate should be changed each quarter to offset the difference between the actual and target GNP in the prior quarter. For several years a number of economists had promoted such a nominal GNP rule for monetary policy but without the empirical support to distinguish the effects of this rule from those of a constant money growth rule. In fact, the actual monetary policy of the Fed since the fall of 1982 appears closer to this rule than to any other apparent rule, although the Fed continues to deny that it follows any consistent rule. In July 1986 even Beryl Sprinkel seemed to tentatively endorse this rule.

Subsequent analysis suggests that the rule should be modified in two dimensions. First, domestic final sales (GNP less the change in business inventories less exports plus imports) appears to be a better measure of total domestic demand than is GNP. In other words, the demand for money appears to be more closely related to goods and services sold in the United States than to those produced here. Second, for several reasons the monetary base (currency plus bank reserves) appears to be a better instrumental target of monetary policy. The variation of total demand, measured in terms of either GNP or domestic final sales (DFS), appears to be lower relative to the monetary base than to M1 or the broader monetary aggregates. In addition, the monetary base is more closely controllable by the Federal Reserve, as all components of the base other than coins are directly controlled by the Fed.

A change in institutional responsibilities would be appropriate to implement this new monetary rule. Following a recommendation by the administration, Congress would approve a target path of domestic final sales, preferably over a several-year period. This path would reflect the preferences of Congress for the growth of both real DFS and the general inflation rate. The several monetary targets would be abandoned. Congress should be willing to question the Fed about any persistent divergence of actual DFS from the target path. The Fed in turn would set an instrumental target for the monetary base, consistent with the expected relation between the base and the target path of DFS. Most important, the Fed should change the target for the monetary base as frequently as once a quarter to offset the difference between the actual and target DFS in the prior quarter. There is no reason to monitor the variations in either the monetary base or other monetary aggregates as long as there is no persistent divergence of DFS from the target path.

A necessary condition for this process to be effective is that both the administration and Congress should refrain from pressuring the Fed to achieve any specific rate of inflation, interest, real growth, or unemployment. Stabilizing the path of total demand is probably the most that can be expected of monetary policy. Some variation in other conditions cannot be avoided because of changes in inventory, trade, and supply conditions and other government policies. The effective implementation of a DFS rule, however, is likely to limit the cumulative change in these other conditions.

My primary reservation about this process is that Congress is likely to approve a DFS path that leads to an increase in inflation. One might hope that Congress would resist the temptation of near-term monetary stimulus at the expense of later inflation, but the record is not encouraging. The current system of delegating the conduct of monetary policy, without effective guidance, to the Federal Reserve is not as much of an alternative as may appear. In the short run the Fed is more resistant to inflation than are the politicians, but in the long run monetary policy, for better or for worse, is what the politicians choose. The Fed is independent in the same way that Finland is independent, by accommodating to the strongest external pressures.

The major alternative is to institutionalize some price rule. A target zone system for exchange rates, however, would not be sufficient. A substantial variation in inflation rates is consistent with stable exchange rates, and a convergence of inflation rates among the major countries is not sufficient to stabilize exchange rates—because exchange rates are also affected by other conditions and policies.

A more fundamental alternative, as promoted by Rep. Jack Kemp and his advisers, would be to set a dollar price for some specific commodity, such as gold, or some fixed mix of commodities. The major advantage of a commodity standard is that it insulates monetary policy from short-run political pressure, hence is more likely to lead to long-run price stability. The disadvantages are also clear. The history of the several types of gold standard includes short inflation-

ary periods following major gold discoveries, long periods of deflation, frequent recessions, and the Great Depression. A broader commodity standard may have fewer problems, but there is no empirical
basis for a judgment on this issue. Surely we can do better. Kemp
and others deserve credit for broadening the debate on monetary
rules. My own view however, is that a total demand rule will be the
next stage in the development of U.S. monetary policy.

A Final Note

On June 2, 1987, President Reagan announced that Paul Volcker
had rejected Reagan's belated request to serve a third term as chairman of the Fed and that Alan Greenspan had been named as his
successor. The eight-year Volcker era was the most turbulent period
of monetary policy in the postwar years and, in many ways, the most
successful. The inflation rate was reduced to the lowest rate in two
decades, interest rates were reduced to the lowest rates in a decade,
and the economic recovery was sustained into a fifth year. The most
important lesson of this period is that a successful monetary policy
can be sustained in a world of fiat currencies only with the support
of the administration. Reagan and Volcker deserve shared credit for
this period of successful monetary policy. The most important missed
opportunity was the failure to institutionalize a sustainable monetary
rule that is less vulnerable to political pressure and less dependent
on the wisdom of the Federal Reserve leadership. One might hope
for future leaders as wise as Reagan and Volcker. A better strategy
would be to choose monetary rules and institutional arrangements
that are less dependent on the choice of their successors.

CHAPTER SIX

Crises Resolved, Crises Deferred

An administration reveals its instincts by how it manages a crisis. Similarly, an administration reveals its wisdom by what it learns from a crisis—specifically, whether it initiates measures to reduce the frequency and scope of future crises. The Reagan administration, by these standards, merits good marks for the instincts of its key officials but lower marks for their wisdom.

For this discussion a crisis is defined as an unanticipated change in conditions that will deteriorate, over the politically relevant time horizon, in the absence of a government response. The discussion focuses on the management of the immediate crises, the effects of the government's response on other conditions, and what longer-term changes, if any, were initiated to reduce the frequency and scope of future crises. The major economic crises described in this chapter are the air controllers' strike of 1981, the several types of domestic bank crises beginning in 1981, and the foreign debt crises beginning in 1982.

THE AIR CONTROLLERS' STRIKE

At 7 A.M. on August 3, 1981, the Professional Air Traffic Controllers' Organization (PATCO) initiated a systemwide strike against the Federal Aviation Agency (FAA). All parties recognized that the strike was illegal—under the terms of the individual employment contracts of the controllers; a permanent injunction, to which PATCO had agreed, against a slowdown or strike; and the provisions of several federal laws.

Although the strike was clearly illegal, PATCO had some reason to expect that the strike would be successful or, if not, that the costs of failure would be low. From early 1968, when PATCO was formed, to the 1981 strike, PATCO had organized six serious disruptions of air traffic. At best the governmental response to these prior disruptions had been equivocal. As a rule a small number of controllers were suspended for a short period. For example, following a twenty-day "sickout" by 2,200 controllers in 1970, the FAA discharged sixty-seven controllers; twenty-seven of those discharged were reinstated on appeal, and the remainder were rehired in 1972. Although a slowdown or strike can cost the airlines and air travellers millions of dollars a day, PATCO was subject to a fine of only $25,000 a day for violation of the injunction that settled the 1970 action. In the absence of a firm government response, the bargaining leverage of this small, critical link in the air travel system was substantial. Without any formal agreement on salaries, by 1981 PATCO had used this leverage to achieve for its members an average salary of $33,000, full retirement after twenty years of service at age fifty, and substantial disability benefits.

The stage was set to test the new administration. A thinly disguised strike fund established in 1977 had accumulated $3 million by August 1981. In 1980 Robert Poli, the militant new PATCO president, had begun preparations for a "definitive strike" to convince Congress to establish the FAA as an independent government corporation. After PATCO broke union ranks to endorse Reagan in 1980, Poli presented the new administration with demands for a $10,000-a-year salary increase, a thirty-two-hour work week, higher pension and disability benefits, and a generous number of free airline trips—fully expecting this proposal to be rejected. The initial FAA response was more generous than Poli had reason to expect. Although the FAA had no authority to approve a salary increase, it offered to seek approval for a $3,600 salary increase from a Congress that was significantly reducing the budgets for many domestic programs. Reagan, Congress, and the FAA, however, each warned PATCO that there would be no amnesty for strikers and no negotiations with PATCO during a strike. Poli, however, had a larger agenda, and he triggered the first systemwide strike of the air traffic system.

Although the scope and timing of the strike were not expected, the administration responded quickly. At 11 A.M. the president announced that all controllers who did not return to work within forty-eight hours would be discharged, and he summarized the general plans for restoring the air traffic system. About 5,000 controllers reported to work within the president's deadline, and the other 11,400 stayed on strike and were discharged. Although the number of controllers, including supervisors, dropped suddenly from about 19,000 to about 8,000, 50 percent of flights were restored within a few days and 70 percent within ten days. The remaining civilian controllers were soon augmented by retirees called back and military controllers, and some controllers were reassigned from smaller airports to the more crowded airports. PATCO's initial response to these actions was a claim that air travel was no longer safe, but this claim was rejected by the statements and actions of the airline pilots. PATCO received little support from other unions, the threatened boycott by the Canadian controllers faded away, and the strike fund was sequestered to pay the rapidly accumulating fines. The strike had failed—with only a temporary reduction of air traffic and no apparent effects on air travel safety—leaving over 11,000 skilled controllers out of work.

It soon became clear that the temporary measures to restore air traffic would be sufficient until new controllers could be trained. At the time of the strike, about 7,500 applicants had been approved for training, and the FAA soon received over 120,000 new applications. The existing salary was apparently adequate to attract more than a sufficient supply of qualified applicants, indicating that the PATCO demands were without merit. The system gradually returned to normal. All the military controllers returned to military duty by mid-1983. Although most of the discharged controllers petitioned to be rehired, only a few percent were successful. PATCO is only a bankrupt shell. The average airline accident rate has been lower since 1981 than in most prior years. As of 1986 a level of air traffic 20 percent higher than in 1981 was handled by 10 percent fewer controllers.

Several good lessons were learned from this strike. Most important, President Reagan proved that a political executive can enforce the law against an illegal strike without political damage. Reagan's instinct, in this case, was much superior to that of Nixon, who tolerated an illegal postal strike and responded weakly to the controllers' sickout in 1970, and the many state and local executives who have bowed to illegal job actions by public employees. The strike also demonstrated that large numbers of public employees are replaceable, even in stressful positions that require some training. The problem of handling a strike is that the costs of a strike are immediate but the benefits of avoiding an unreasonable labor demand are deferred. A business or political executive with a short horizon or a weak backbone will often mortgage the future in order to avoid the short-run costs of a strike. President Reagan, Transportation Secretary Drew Lewis, and FAA administrator Lynn Helms deserve high marks for their handling of this strike.

Several wrong lessons were also learned from this strike. Many observers interpreted the administration's response to the controllers' strike as part of a general anti-union policy and attributed the subsequent wage and salary concessions in several industries to a change in federal policy. These observers in turn regarded the breaking of PATCO as an important contribution to the decline in the general inflation rate.

This was an incorrect interpretation of the basis for the administration's response to the controller's strike, the general policy toward organized labor, and the reasons for the slower growth of nominal wage rates and the general price level. Reagan discharged the striking controllers solely because their action was an illegal strike. Reagan is the only president who had also been a union president (of the Screen Actors' Guild), and he was more successful than any recent Republican president in enlisting the support of union members. The administration's general policy toward labor disputes in the private sector and state and local governments was to avoid federal intervention on either side of the dispute. In August 1983, for example, the federal government was scrupulously neutral toward the systemwide strike against AT&T, the largest strike in thirty-seven years.

The administration's policy reflected a change only because prior administrations had occasionally intervened in major private labor disputes to support labor demands, in order to reduce the short-turn economic costs of a strike. The major conditions that led to a restructuring of wages and salaries in selective industries—such as airlines, trucking, communications, autos, and steel—were deregulation or increasing foreign competition, not federal intervention in favor of the employers. The major conditions that led to the substantial decline in inflation were the slower growth of total demand and the rapid appreciation of the dollar until the winter of 1985, not a slower growth of nominal (current-dollar) wages and salaries. Many observers from both the right and the left unfortunately have a cost-based theory of prices and assume that some federal intervention to limit labor costs is necessary to reduce inflation; Nixon's wage and price controls and Carter's "voluntary" wage and price guidelines are the most recent American examples. The empirical evidence is clear: changes in the growth of nominal wages generally follow rather than lead changes in the general inflation rate. Reagan and Volcker achieved a substantial reduction in the general inflation rate by changing macroeconomic conditions, not by intervening in private labor markets. The major lesson of the controllers' strike was that the Reagan administration would not tolerate an illegal strike by federal employees, not that it would intervene in other labor disputes.

Unfortunately, a number of potential lessons from the controllers' strike were not learned. The basic conditions that had led to low morale and labor unrest among the controllers have not been corrected. The FAA maintains a two-grade, nationwide salary structure for controllers, regardless of local wage rates or differences in job demands among air traffic control centers. The growth of air traffic and the slow increase in the number of fully qualified controllers since 1981 have only exacerbated this basic problem. Although these conditions have apparently not increased the air traffic accident rate, they may have contributed to increasing delays at the busiest airports. The slow rebuilding of the controller force may have been a false economy if additional federal spending on controller training would have been lower than the cost of the delays avoided. The one measure that may relieve this problem was the late-1985 approval of the resale of landing slots among commercial carriers at the four most crowded airports. This measure, however, is incomplete in that it does not allow commercial carriers to bid for the slots reserved for private airplanes, and Congress has threatened to reverse this limited measure.

One should not be quick to pass judgment on the continuing controversy about whether some of the discharged controllers should be rehired. The administration firmly resisted a general amnesty for the discharged controllers to reduce the probability of a future illegal strike. Yet the nation has lost the special skills of over 11,000 controllers and may have experienced unnecessary air traffic delays by not rehiring some qualified controllers who were not PATCO officers, perhaps with the loss of seniority. Most current controllers, except at the most crowded centers, apparently oppose any rehiring. This is not an easy call. In any case this problem will gradually decline with a continued increase in the number and average qualification of the controller force.

The administration also passed up the opportunity to "privatize" parts of the air traffic control system—either by turning over airport control centers to local airport authorities or by contracting for air traffic control services. Local authorities or private companies could then have made their own decision whether to rehire the discharged federal controllers and devised a salary schedule and work rules specific to local conditions. The FAA in this case could maintain a certification, monitoring, and coordination role, but there is no compelling case to maintain direct federal provision of air traffic control services. My own investigation of this issue revealed an interesting "Catch-22" condition. The Service Contracting Act requires that any employer providing services under contract (of more than $2,500) to the federal government pay the "prevailing wages" for the required skills in the local community. In the absence of an existing private controller force, however, the prevailing wages are defined as the current wages of the federal controllers. In other words, a private contractor would be allowed to bid to supply air traffic control services only if it paid controllers as much as the current FAA salaries. The air traffic control system is less complicated than, for example, the telephone system. There is reason to expect that a private air traffic control system could provide higher-quality services at a lower cost than under continued federal provision of this service. The FAA, however, has strongly resisted any privatization of this system, and the Reagan administration showed no interest in changing the basic institutional arrangements by which this service is provided.

In this case the Reagan administration earned high marks for its handling of the immediate crisis and low marks for correcting the conditions that led to the crisis. At some time a dramatic accident will be attributed to a failure of the air traffic control system, and some administration will face a new crisis.

FINANCIAL INSTITUTIONS

Conditions Leading to the Financial Crises

Several conditions contributed to severe pressure on U.S. financial institutions and a record postwar rate of bank failures during the early 1980s. The initial problem was caused by the rapid increase in market interest rates from the late 1970s through early 1981, in combination with the regulatory controls on deposit rates. This led to a substantial withdrawal of savings deposits from both commercial and savings banks, to be invested primarily in the unregulated new money market mutual funds provided by securities firms. (Balances in the money market funds increased from $6.4 billion in 1978 to $150.9 billion in 1981, the most rapid development of a new financial instrument in history.) The rapid increase in interest rates also reduced the market value of the fixed-rate loans and mortgages owned by banks. This was a special problem for the savings banks, where most of the assets were older, long-term fixed-rate mortgages with interest rates lower than current market rates. As of 1981, by conventional accounting standards, the combined net worth of the savings and loan industry was about −$110 billion. The balance sheets of these banks, however, did not reflect this bleak condition, because their assets were revalued by special regulatory accounting principles. As a consequence the regulatory actions, which would otherwise have been triggered by bank insolvency, were deferred until individual banks faced a liquidity crisis.

A second set of problems was caused by the change in economic conditions in the early 1980s. The substantial decline in the general inflation rate and the strong increase in the foreign exchange value of the dollar led to a lower price level in some sectors, reducing the ability of many borrowers to repay their loans. This created a special problem for agricultural, energy, and foreign government borrowers, many of which, expecting continued high inflation, substantially increased their borrowing at high interest rates through 1981. The banks, which had previously faced a reduction in the market value of good fixed-rate loans, now faced an increasing proportion of bad loans.

Both the first and second types of problems were a consequence of an unexpected change in economic conditions, in combination with the use of long-term fixed-rate contracts. The first type of problem was the consequence of the unexpected increase in inflation and interest rates in the late 1970s. The second type of problem was the result of the unexpected reduction in inflation (and the price level in some sectors) in the early 1980s. Both types of problems are evidence of the importance of maintaining a steady general price level or, at least, a steady general inflation rate. These types of problems would have been much less severe if the Carter administration and the Federal Reserve had not allowed the inflation rate to increase during the late 1970s, or if the Reagan administration had not allowed its fiscal policy to lead to such a rapid increase in the foreign exchange value of the dollar in the early 1980s.

Several observers incorrectly attributed the bank problems during the 1980s to the deregulation of deposit rates approved in 1980. A more accurate interpretation, as is developed later in this section, is that these problems were magnified by the existing regulation. The ceilings on deposit interest rates led to a substantial outflow of deposits in response to higher market interest rates. Federal laws that have segmented the financial market into specialized institutions providing commercial loans, mortgages, farm credit, life insurance, and securities restrict the opportunity to spread portfolio risks across types of assets. A federal law that restricts interstate banking and state laws that limit branching restrict the opportunity to reduce portfolio risks across regions. The general structure of federal and state regulation of financial institutions thus clearly increases the vulnerability of these institutions to unexpected changes in economic conditions.

The deregulation of deposit rates did create one special problem, however, given the existing system of deposit insurance. For banks with a low or negative net worth, most of the risks of imprudent management are borne by the deposit insurance funds. For example, savings banks that earned less on their existing mortgage portfolio than on the newly unregulated deposit rates had a strong incentive to grow out their problems by offering premium interest rates on deposits to finance new mortgages and loans. This process proved to be successful only for those banks which earned a higher rate on their new investments and maintained effective cost control; in such cases the benefits accrued primarily to the owners of these banks. In other cases, however, banks did not earn enough on their new investments to pay the higher deposit rates and other bank costs, and the costs of this behavior were borne by the deposit insurance funds and, indirectly, by other banks and taxpayers. As expressed by one investor, "It's not your money you're playing with any more—yours is lost. So you take some more [government] guaranteed money and roll the dice once more—you haven't anything of your own to lose."

This general problem has not yet been resolved and, without a change in the deposit insurance system, has already led to some re-regulation. The general effects of the deregulation of financial institutions, as in other industries, has been to reduce the margins of the previously regulated firms, thus increasing the vulnerability of the least well-managed firms. Although this process benefitted both borrowers and depositors, the combined effect of the deregulation of deposit rates and the existing system of deposit insurance increased the risks and costs to other parties.

Savings Banks

The first banking crisis faced by the Reagan administration involved the failure of several mutual savings bank in the fall of 1981. The several hundred (depositor-owned) mutual savings banks, largely in the Northeast, that are not members of the Federal Reserve system are insured by the Federal Deposit Insurance Corporation (FDIC). In this case the FDIC was well prepared. William Isaac and Irving Sprague, the chairman and director of the FDIC, had been reviewing the conditions of the mutual savings banks for nine months and had worked out a rescue plan.

The federal deposit insurance agencies have three alternative means to protect insured deposits. They may simply pay off the insured depositors (now limited to $100,000 per deposit); in this case the bank is closed, and any returns to the noninsured depositors, general creditors, and owners are sorted out in a bankruptcy proceeding. The FDIC may also assume the bad loans and sell the bank to another bank in what is termed a "purchase and assumption transaction"; in this case all depositors are protected. The agency is authorized to choose between a payoff and a sale, depending on which means involves the lowest cost to the insurance fund. In recent years most bank failures are handled by selling the bank, implicitly extending federal deposit insurance to all deposits. Only if an individual bank is judged to be "essential" is the agency authorized to bail out the bank, replacing the management but maintaining the bank in operation, under the temporary ownership of the insurance agency. Such bailouts are very rare.

In the case of the mutual savings banks, the FDIC practice was consistent. Each of the failed mutuals was merged with a stronger mutual or sold to new owners with a substantial FDIC subsidy. There was no case for a bailout because there were numerous other healthy mutuals in the same areas. Three mutual savings banks failed in 1981, eight in 1982, and nine more by the end of 1985. These failures were handled without any significant problems or controversy but at an estimated cost to the FDIC of over $1.5 billion.

The several thousand federally chartered (investor-owned) savings and loan associations (S&Ls) proved to be a more substantial and continuing problem. These banks are regulated by the Federal Home Loan Bank Board (FHLBB) and are insured by its Federal Savings and Loan Insurance Corporation (FSLIC). The first measures were designed to avoid the responsibility of closing the insolvent savings banks. The FHLBB, then headed by Richard Pratt, lowered the capital requirements and redefined capital. For regulatory purposes the accounting principles were redefined to permit a write-up of assets for which the appraised value exceeds the book value; assets that have declined in value, however, are entered at book value. In addition, the savings banks were permitted to amortize losses on assets they sell rather than to record the losses in the year of sale.

In September 1982 Congress contributed to this "funny-money" game by approving two programs to increase the reported capital of the savings banks, the net worth certificate program and the income capital certificate program. These programs represented a paper investment by the deposit insurance agencies and are treated as capital by the savings banks for purposes of meeting their capital requirements. The Treasury grumbled a bit about these programs but without effect.

These several activities by the FHLBB and Congress maintained the pretense that many savings banks were solvent when, by either conventional accounting standards or market value, they were insolvent. In effect they deferred the day of reckoning on the basis of an expectation (that proved to be correct) that a decline in market interest rates would increase the market value of the older fixed-rate mortgages. The only substantive change in FHLBB regulation during this period was its 1982 authorization for savings banks to offer variable rate mortgages; an increased use of these instruments could progressively reduce the vulnerability of mortgage lenders to another increase in interest rates.

Although interest rates continued to decline, many of the basic problems remained. Some savings banks increased their deposits and investments by a multiple of 10 or more in a few years, largely from brokered deposits. Some banks invested heavily in their owners' real estate projects, in effect transforming the banks into real estate investment trusts with federal guarantees, an instrument (without guarantees) that experienced broad failure in the early 1970s. As is so often the case, California and Texas led the way.

The administration's next move was to appoint Ed Gray as chairman of the FHLBB. Gray, a protégé of Ed Meese, had been a public relations officer of a San Diego savings bank and a White House aide prior to his appointment. Gray's general strategy was to reduce the abuses of the deposit insurance system by selective reregulation rather than by changing the conditions that led to these abuses. These changes included a prohibition on the use of brokered deposits (a measure that was later reversed by a court ruling), a regulation to limit the growth of deposits to the growth of net worth, and a prohibition on S&L participation in real estate development and syndication. Gray also tried to maintain the separate and local role of the S&Ls. In general the FSLIC tried to arrange the purchase of an insolvent S&L by another S&L in the same area, then in the same state, and then in the same region. Only in a few cases did it permit the acquisition of an insolvent S&L outside the region or by a commercial bank, a practice that restricted the opportunity to reduce the portfolio risks resulting from a concentration of mortgages in a local area.

In many cases, moreover, the FSLIC could not arrange for the purchase of an insolvent S&L. By late 1986 the FSLIC had acquired the assets of 148 S&Ls with a book value of $54 billion, assets for which the FSLIC was expected to lose about $15 billion. Gray's prior relations with Stockman and Regan, however, were sour, and OMB would not approve additional staffing to manage the disposal of these assets. To liquidate these assets without the staffing and salary constraints of a government agency, the FHLBB established a new quasi-government organization, the Federal Asset Disposition Association.

Some of the abuses by S&L management were curtailed, but the problems continued to accumulate. The FSLIC reserves declined from nearly $7 billion in 1983 to under $3 billion by late 1986. At the end of this period the FSLIC reserves were about 30 cents per $100 of insured deposits; in contrast, the FDIC reserves at the end of 1985 were $1.19 per $100 of insured deposits. As of late 1986 the FSLIC was expected to lose about $8 billion on S&Ls that were expected to be closed within the next twelve months and could lose an additional $10 billion on S&Ls that were then experiencing losses. After the failure of over 800 savings banks since 1980, the remaining FSLIC reserves were grossly inadequate to cover losses that were expected within a few months unless the assets that the FSLIC had already acquired could be liquidated quickly. The vulnerability of the FSLIC was vividly illustrated when a run on a few savings banks in Ohio and Maryland in 1985 led to a collapse of the private deposit insurance systems in these states.

During the summer and early fall of 1986, Congress reviewed a bill that would inject $15 to $30 billion into FSLIC reserves but recessed without approving this bill. In the meantime Gray and a few other FHLBB officials were under investigation for allegations that they had accepted industry reimbursement for travel and lodging expenses. Gray announced that he would retire when his term expired in mid-1987 after having presided over the largest government subsidies to any industry other than agriculture. To his credit, Gray had warned others about the developing problems of the FSLIC over his entire tenure. His own actions, however, contributed little to resolving these problems, and he did not have the skills and credibility of Paul Volcker to convince others to address these problems. (In my final memorandum to the president as acting chairman of the CEA, I also warned about the magnitude of this problem, without apparent effect.) There does not now appear any alternative to a massive contribution of federal funds to the FSLIC to protect the insured deposits.

In the meantime the general health of the savings and loan industry improved substantially, primarily as a consequence of a decline in market interest rates. The total net worth of this industry is now positive, and about 80 percent of the savings and loan banks are profitable. As of late 1986, however, over 400 banks with assets of over $100 billion were insolvent by conventional accounting standards. The capital ratios for the savings banks are still much lower than those for the commercial banks, and the whole industry continues to be unusually vulnerable to an increase in interest rates.

The basic problems of the savings banks developed during the Carter administration as a consequence of the increase of inflation and interest rates. The major contributions of the Reagan administration (and the Federal Reserve) were to reduce inflation and interest rates and to authorize the savings banks to issue variable rate mortgages. The selective reregulation of the savings and loan industry initiated by Ed Gray reduced the abuses of the deposit insurance system but did not address the inherent structural problems of the industry or of the deposit insurance system. The continuing problems of this industry should have led one to question the rationale for separate, subsidized, locally based mortgage lending institutions. The continuing abuse of the deposit insurance system by institutions with a low or negative net worth should have led to a restructuring of the deposit insurance system. The administration and the FHLBB did not resolve either of these issues. In this case the Reagan administration deserves only a passing grade for the management of the immediate crisis, and it failed to address the more fundamental reforms that would avoid a similar future crisis.

Commercial Banks

The nation's 14,000 commercial banks face most of the same problems as the savings banks. The one exception is that most loans by commercial banks are short term or have variable interest rates, so commercial bank portfolios are not as vulnerable to an increase in interest rates. The major commercial banks also face an additional problem, addressed in the next section: the continued weakness of their portfolio of developing-country debt.

The commercial banks face a complex regulatory structure. The Office of the Controller of the Currency (OCC), an agency of the Treasury, regulates the 5,000 commercial banks with national charters. The Federal Reserve regulates the 6,100 bank holding companies and the 1,000 state-chartered banks that are members of the Federal Reserve System. The FDIC provides deposit insurance for all the commercial banks and regulates over 8,000 state-chartered banks. All the state-chartered banks in turn are also regulated by state regulatory commissions. Only the OCC and the state commissions have the authority to close a bank. The Fed and the FDIC have the responsibility for deciding how to handle a failing or failed bank.

Penn Square

The first major bank crisis to be faced by the Reagan administration involved the failure of the Penn Square Bank in Oklahoma City. Penn Square had grown from a bank worth $62 million in 1977 to one worth about $520 million in mid-1982, largely by making loans to the booming market for oil and gas drilling rigs. More important, Penn Square had placed over $2 billion of loan "participations" in small energy companies with five major banks in other sections of the country. Continental Illinois held about $1 billion of the participations, and most of the rest were held by Chase Manhattan Bank, Michigan National Bank, Seattle First National Bank, and the Northern Trust Company.

This network of financial deals began to unravel in 1981. The real price of oil peaked in March, and the price of drilling rigs that were the collateral on these loans collapsed. The magnitude of the Penn Square problem, however, was not apparent to the government until the OCC notified FDIC of these problems on June 29, 1982. A series of meetings over the next several days among officials of the OCC, the Fed, the FDIC, and the bank revealed the nature and extent of the problem. The FDIC officials soon concluded that closing the bank and paying off the insured deposits was the only viable option. The OCC and Fed officials, however, strongly resisted a payoff. Todd Conover, the new controller, had no prior experience with such a crisis and was reluctant to close the bank. Paul Volcker was very concerned about the probable effects on the major banks that had purchased the loan participations. On July 3, Penn Square ran out of cash and resorted to issuing cashier's checks to its worried depositors.

On Sunday morning, July 4, the issue came to a head when Volcker called Don Regan to participate in the deliberations of the regulators. The conditions and options were reviewed. Regan asked several pointed questions that made it clear that he supported the payoff option, but he left the decision to the regulators. Conover continued to gather facts and review the options. Finally, on the evening of July 5, Conover decided to close Penn Square, and FDIC became the receiver of the largest bank to be closed by a payoff. The rest of this story was messy but anticlimatic. Most of the insured deposits were paid out with three months, but a sorting out of the remaining claims involved numerous suits and charges of fraud that are not yet fully resolved.

The closure of Penn Square had several important downstream effects. Volcker proved to be correct in maintaining that it would harm the major banks that had purchased the loan participations. Continental Illinois was later bailed out. Seattle First was sold to avoid failure. The management of Michigan National Bank was replaced, and Chase Manhattan and Northern Trust experienced substantial losses. The Fed blamed the decision not to protect the uninsured depositors of Penn Square for the later run on Continental Illinois. The initial objective of the deposit insurance system, however, was to protect the insured depositors in order to prevent a general flight to cash—to protect the banking system, not individual banks. The officials of Penn Square and the major banks had made a series of very risky loans and had no claim to be insured against their losses. The decision to close Penn Square was strongly supported by the Treasury, for good reasons, I believe. One other effect of the Penn Square experience is that the FDIC developed a modified payoff procedure by which the uninsured depositors and the other general creditors would receive an early partial payoff with only the remainder to be sorted out by the bankruptcy proceedings. The FDIC used this procedure for several smaller bank failures in the winter of 1984.

Continental Illinois

The failure of Continental Illinois in May 1984 led to a substantial change in the relation of the government to the banks—in my judg-ment, a major mistake. At the time that it failed, Continental was a $41 billion bank, about five times as large as the largest prior bank to fail, the First Pennsylvania Bank, in 1980. Although the failure was the result of a run that lasted only a few days, the problems that led to this failure had developed over several years. As of 1978 Con-tinental was regarded as one of the five best-managed companies in the country, and it continued to be a market favorite through 1981. Continental's loan portfolio had increased from about $12 billion in 1976 to $34 billion in 1982, with a substantial amount of these loans to the booming energy industry. As early as late 1981, however, sev-eral financial publications expressed concern about this risky port-folio. There was also evidence of rather casual management by the Continental officials; although Continental had purchased about $1 billion of loan participations from Penn Square, Roger Anderson (the chairman of Continental) was reported as not recognizing the name of Penn Square when he was first informed by the OCC about the failure of Penn Square in June 1982. Continental was also an unusual bank, a $41 billion company that operated out of one build-ing in Chicago because of Illinois' prohibition on branch banking. As a consequence Continental had a very small local deposit base, and most of its deposits were large, uninsured deposits from busi-nesses and other banks around the country and abroad.

Although the outside auditors continued to approve Continental's financial statements through the end of 1983, the Continental board realized that it was in trouble. The portfolio of nonperforming loans increased to $2.4 billion by the first quarter of 1984. The board re-placed President John Perkins in December 1983 and Chairman Roger Anderson in February 1984, in both cases with substantial "golden parachutes," and sold its profitable credit card operation to avoid an accounting loss in the first quarter.

These actions, however, were not sufficient. Rumors of a possible bankruptcy began to circulate soon after release of the first quarterly report. As is often the case, the run was triggered by Continental's vehement denial on May 8 that it was considering bankruptcy, and European and Japanese banks began to withdraw their funds. At about this same time there was also rumors of a serious problem at another major bank, the Manufacturers Hanover Trust in New York City, but a run on this bank was averted without assistance by the FDIC and the Federal Reserve. Although the OCC and the Fed no-tified the FDIC of a probable problem at Continental on May 10, Controller Todd Conover issued a statement on that same day that "the Controller's Office is not aware of any significant changes in the bank's operations, as reflected in its published financial statement, that would serve as a basis for these rumors." On May 11 the key officials of the OCC, the Fed, and the FDIC first met to consider the government's response, and a consortium of private banks led by Morgan Guaranty announced a $4.5 billion line of credit to Continental. These actions were also not sufficient. In the ten days following Continental's May 8 announcement, the bank lost $6 billion of deposits.

The government first began to develop its response on May 15. An assisted merger seemed preferable, but there was not enough time, and no other bank had yet expressed interest. The direct cost of a payoff would have been about $4 billion, as the insured deposits were only about 10 percent of Continental's total assets. The primary problem of a payoff was that over 2,000 correspondent banks were depositors in Continental, including 179 banks whose deposits were more than 50 percent of their capital. Because closing Continental would have threatened a significant part of the banking system, a bailout seemed to be the only option. Don Regan's only comment was to suggest that the other major banks also be included in the rescue plan.

The final package was developed in meetings with the major banks on May 16 and 17. The FDIC offered to make a subordinated loan of $2 billion as their part of the package. The major banks first insisted on a government guarantee of any private assistance but, under pressure from Volcker, finally agreed to pick up $500 million of the subordinated note and to extend their line of credit to $5.5 billion. The Fed agreed to meet "any extraordinary liquidity requirements" but only on a secured basis. This package stopped the run, and the FDIC ended up as the major owner of one of the nation's largest banks.

For the next two months, FDIC tried to find a buyer for Continental, without success. A closer examination of the loan portfolio indicated that it was weaker than first realized. The FDIC developed a plan in which it would own 80 percent of the shares of the bank holding company and replace the top management, hoping to sell these shares later to the public. A review of the developing plan with the Treasury on July 13 led to the most serious controversy between the Reagan administration and the bank regulators. Deputy Secretary Tim McNamar and Assistant Secretary Tom Healey asked the FDIC to reconsider closing the bank or to arrange a merger that would not protect the creditors of the bank holding company. McNamar and Healey argued that it would be a bad precedent for the government to take a subordinate position to the creditors of the holding company and that the FDIC proposal might not be legal. This controversy dragged on for another two weeks. On July 24 the Justice Department found that "the transaction probably would not be held to exceed the FDIC's statutory authority." On that same day, however, a memorandum from Regan to Conover, Isaac, and Volcker concluded that the transaction "is bad public policy, would be seen to be unfair vis-à-vis past FDIC/Federal Reserve bank supervisory policies, and represents an unwarranted and unlegislated expansion of federal guarantees in contravention of Executive Branch policy which lacks explicit congressional authorization." The FDIC argued that the indenture agreements between the holding company and the bank precluded any arrangement that did not also protect the holding company, a position that was strongly supported by the Fed. In the end Conover also supported this position, and the FDIC moved to find new senior managers for both the holding company and the bank. The FDIC has not yet sold its shares in Continental Illinois.

One lesson from this episode is that the government's instruments for rescuing a failed bank are seriously flawed. The FDIC has the correct instrument, the authority to make a subordinated loan, but is subject to finite reserves that may not be sufficient to handle the coincident failure of a number of large banks. The Fed can extend an unlimited loan; however, that loan must be secured by a bank's best collateral, such as Treasury securities. Fed lending thus can cause a secondary run as it dilutes the collateral to other creditors. This problem has not yet been resolved.

A second lesson is that some change in the relations between bank holding companies and their banks is necessary to avoid a future condition, such as with Continental, in which protection of the bank is extended to the general creditors of the holding company. In 1983 the Treasury proposed to broaden the powers of bank holding companies—a worthwhile objective, but one that cannot be achieved unless some procedure is developed to limit the liabilities of the insurance system to exclude the general creditors of the holding company. The procedures used to bail out Continental deferred indefinitely a resolution of this issue.

The third lesson was that the Treasury was correct: the bailout of Continental Illinois set a very bad precedent. The first interpretation was that the government would not allow any major bank to fail. Conover suggested that the largest eleven banks were thus protected, but there was no clear basis for this number. This led to a predictable charge that the government's procedures were unfair to the uninsured depositors and general creditors of smaller banks. William Seidman, who succeeded Isaac as Chairman of the FDIC, compounded Conover's error by announcing an "open bank" policy in March 1986 to avoid the closure of any bank, large or small. Another administration policy was reversed by a Reagan appointee. A policy that had guided the Penn Square closure—to limit the FDIC liabilities to the insured deposits—was changed into a policy that extends the liability to all deposits and the general creditors of a bank or its holding company. There is no longer any significant discipline for large depositors or general creditors so that they will be careful about where they place their assets, and the potential liabilities of the government (and the taxpayers) have been multiplied many times.

The fourth lesson of this episode, as with all recent bank failures, is that the deposit insurance system has far exceeded its original charter. The initial objective of this system was to avoid a general flight from deposits into currency, the condition that led well-managed banks to fail in the early 1930s. At no time in recent years, however, even in the Continental failure, was there a run from the banking system to currency, as distinct from a run from deposits in one bank to deposits in other banks. There was always a possibility that a run on a number of banks that may have been triggered by closing Continental might also have triggered a more general flight to currency. The bank regulators; however, committed billions of dollars to protect the directly affected banks without any evidence of the more general condition the deposit insurance system was designed to avoid.

A final lesson, unfortunately, has not yet been learned. Although the bank regulators have handled most of the bank failures with some skill, the conditions that led to these failures have not been corrected. The number of bank failures continued to increase through 1986 to the highest rate since the early 1930s. At the end of 1986 over 1,450 commercial banks were classified as problem banks, seven times the number so classified in 1980. The overlapping system of bank examinations by both private auditors and government examiners has not been sufficient to detect the conditions that have led to these failures, because no party to this process has the correct incentives. My remarks should not cause anyone to panic, because the financial system is much less vulnerable than individual banks. The substantial recent deregulation of banks, however, is not sustainable without some change in the deposit insurance system. Some amount of reregulation is probable unless these issues are sorted out.

For some years analysts have considered several minor changes to the current system. The changes most broadly considered are to increase the deposit insurance premiums or the required capital ratios as a function of the perceived risk of a bank's loan portfolio and to consolidate the several bank regulatory functions in one agency. My own view is that these measures would not be very effective. It is very difficult for outside examiners to assess the repayment risk of a loan portfolio. A consolidation of the regulators is likely to reduce the information available and the alternative policies considered. The best alternative may be a radical restructuring of banks, allowing bank holding companies to divide the deposit and loan activities among separate institutions. Deposits would be fully secured by Treasury securities and need no longer be independently insured. Loans would be made by other institutions and would be financed by equity and debt, not deposits. A bank holding company would be allowed to own one or more of each type of bank. This type of financial system would require little regulation and no insurance. Such a major restructuring of the banking system, of course, requires further analysis, but a general examination of this issue should not be deferred.

Farm Credit Institutions

Farm credit conditions deteriorated sharply beginning in 1984, a consequence of weak farm income, declining land values, and the special characteristics of the major agricultural lending institutions. For years commercial banks had loaned money to farmers without much concern whether the borrowers had any net cash flow from farming because the value of farm land, the collateral for these loans, was increasing. A decline in the value of farm land beginning in 1981 led commercial banks to restrict their lending to those farmers with some expected net income from farming. Private bank loans to agriculture are now less than 50 percent of total agricultural loans, down from 55.5 percent in 1980.

The conditions of the commercial banks that specialize in farm lending, however, continued to deteriorate. Federal restrictions on interstate banking and state restrictions on branch banking increased the vulnerability of the local banks to a decline in the local agriculture sector. For banks in the Southwest, this condition was compounded by a decline in the energy sector during the same period. The number of farm banks on FDIC's list of problem banks increased from less than one hundred in 1982 to over 300 by the end of 1984 and over 600 by the end of 1986.

In addition to the huge increase in direct agriculture supports (described in Chapter 2), the government's first response to the farm credit problem was in the fall of 1984. Shortly before the election Congress approved a special credit program for agriculture, providing for new federal guarantees on farm loans by private lenders and a deferral of payments on loans by the Farmers House Administration (FmHA). In the winter of 1985 Stockman strongly resisted pressure to expand this program, but direct federal loans and guarantees continued to increase. From FY 1981 through FY 1985, total outstanding federal loans to agriculture increased from $15.1 billion to $43.7 billion, and federal loan guarantees increased from $2.2 billion to $6.5 billion.

The largest lender to the farm and rural sector has become the Farm Credit System (FCS). The local entities of this system are owned by their borrowers, who must buy stock in them in proportion to their borrowing. The FCS in turn is able to borrow at rates only slightly higher than Treasury rates because of an implicit federal guarantee of its debt. As a financial institution with its entire portfolio in farm and rural loans, the FCS is unusually vulnerable to a weak farm economy and is especially vulnerable because of its unusual ownership arrangements. To protect their equity, higher-quality borrowers have an incentive to pay off their FCS loans, leaving the system with the lower-quality loans. Farmers who stay in the FCS experience a decline in the value of their equity at the same time they may be experiencing losses on their farm operations. These problems became serious in 1985, when the FCS first experienced substantial losses, primarily in the Midwest. The FCS experienced continued losses through mid-1987. As of late 1985, however, the total capital of the FCS was about $8.5 billion, and the total system is likely to remain solvent. To avoid the insolvency of some of the regional land banks, legislation was approved in December 1985 to impose assessments on the solvent banks to pool resources across the entire system. Of course, this measure reduced the value of the equity in the solvent banks and will reduce the incentives of the regional banks to avoid unusual risks. The administration and Congress again resolved an immediate crisis by actions that will increase future problems.

Although loans to agriculture have been subsidized for many years, the 1986 *Economic Report* concluded that

> agricultural borrowers are not well served by their credit markets. Commercial banks cannot serve the agricultural borrowers as well as they might because of the barriers to interstate and intrastate branch banking. The FCS makes only agricultural loans, and hence can diversify only across agriculture. By forcing farmers to borrow from it to be its equity holders, the FCS prevents them from transferring equity . . . risk to other parties.

Pension Plans

In 1974 Congress approved the Employment Retirement Income Security Act (ERISA), requiring that private companies with "defined benefit" pension plans insure these benefits with a new government agency, the Pension Benefit Guarantee Corporation (PBGC).

A small flat premium per plan participant was established. Companies were allowed to terminate their plans, at which time PBGC would assume the assets and liabilities of the plan plus as much as 30 percent of the firm's net worth. The PBGC now insures the pension benefits of about 38 million people.

My own experience with this issue was frustrating. Although I had no background on this issue, I was appointed chairman of the interagency pension review group in 1981. The character of the problem was quickly apparent. The premium was too low to cover the expected liabilities of the PBGC. The flat-rate premium, as for deposit insurance, did not provide any incentive for firms to reduce the risks to the PBGC. A firm with substantial underfunding of its pension plan and a low net worth had a strong incentive to terminate its plan at the expense of the PBGC and, indirectly, on other pension plans and possibly the taxpayers. And the Internal Revenue Service had the authority to waive pension contributions by firms in distress without the approval of the PBGC.

On the basis of these prospective problems, I convinced the administration to press for legislation that would increase the premium and tighten the provisions for terminating a pension plan. Such legislation was proposed each year since 1981. Later, studies of a graduated premium and the potential for privatizing some or all of the PBGC were initiated, and an attempt was made to sort out the tension between the PBGC and the IRS. Almost nothing was done. The private pension community resisted change, and Congress would not address a prospective problem as long as the PBGC could meet its current obligations. A substantial premium increase was approved in 1986, but the other problems remained.

In the meantime the magnitude of the problem developed rapidly. By the end of 1986 the PBGC was responsible for managing several thousand terminated plans and had accumulated a deficit of $4 billion, about two-thirds of it in 1986. The largest plans terminated were those of failing steel companies, and more such terminations are in prospect. The PBGC, a small government agency now administered by Kathy Utgoff, an able young woman who was my pension specialist, may end up as the major stockholder in the American steel industry. What an irony! An administration that hoped to privatize some governmental activities ends up nationalizing a major bank and a few steel companies. On the pension issue the administration showed some strategic vision, but in the absence of an immediate crisis it could not convince Congress to address the necessary reforms. All the major sponsors of ERISA had left Congress by 1985, and few other members seemed to care. Congress is not likely to address the major pension issues until it is forced to make a direct appropriation to pay the insured pension benefits. My own efforts were not sufficient to avoid this prospective crisis, but they may help shape the necessary reform when the opportunity arises.

A Retrospective on the Financial Crises

All these problems, unfortunately, are still with us. The segmentation of the financial system among institutions that specialize in home mortgages, commercial loans, or agricultural loans has increased the vulnerability of each type of institution to the weakness of a specific sector. The restrictions on interstate banking and intrastate branching have increased the vulnerability of banks to a weakness in the local economy. The deregulation of deposit rates, although enormously beneficial to depositors, has increased the opportunity for banks to shift the risks to the deposit insurance agencies. The insurance of private pensions and the provisions for terminating pension plans have reduced the incentives for responsible behavior by private firms, at a rapidly increasing cost to other firms and probably to the taxpayer. The general structure of financial regulation, subsidy, and insurance that developed from the 1920s through the 1970s has not served us very well but is still in place. The Reagan administration and the financial regulators handled each crisis as it developed quite well, but they lacked a strategic vision to propose changes in this structure that would reduce the frequency and scope of similar crises in the future.

FOREIGN DEBT

In late August 1982 the government of Mexico announced a moratorium on its foreign debt after an unsuccessful attempt to raise enough new loans to refinance its scheduled debt payments. A few months later Brazil also announced that it could not meet its scheduled debt repayments and threatened to declare itself insolvent if a rescheduling could not soon be arranged. Although there had been some warnings of an increasing debt problem, these announcements hit New York and Washington like a bomb.

After five years during which there was an average of five country debt reschedulings a year, the number of reschedulings increased to thirteen in 1981. At the time, however, this seemed to be someone else's problem. The rescheduling of loans to Turkey in 1979, for example, primarily involved loans by governments and the multilateral institutions, and the rescheduling of loans to Poland in 1981 primarily involved European banks. A more important warning that the maturity of the loans rescheduled in 1979 through 1981 was much shorter than the loans they replaced went unheeded. The general attitude of Western financial officials continued to be that reflected by a March 1980 statement by Paul Volcker that "the recycling process has not yet pushed exposure of other borrowers or leaders to an unsustainable point in the aggregate," and by a fall 1981 statement by Sir Geoffrey Howe, the British chancellor, that "the private markets have also served us well in the continuing success of the recycling process." At the time these statements were correct but were a misleading guide to the future.

In August 1982, when the Mexicans triggered a more general debt crisis, the Reagan administration did not need any more bad news. The United Stated was in the thirteenth month of a severe recession, Congress and many key officials were away from Washington, and the primary focus of political attention was the coming midterm election. Attention to this crisis, however, could not be deferred. At the end of 1982 Mexico's external debt was about $85 billion and Brazil's external debt was about $88 billion. About one-third of this debt was held by American banks, some of which were in trouble for other reasons.

Origins of the Debt Crisis

The origins of the foreign debt crisis were similar to those of the domestic debt crises affecting the agricultural and energy sectors: the conditions that led to a rapid accumulation of debt during the 1970s changed dramatically in the early 1980s. The rapid increase in oil prices in 1973 and 1974, and again in 1979 and 1980, led to a huge current account surplus by the major oil-exporting nations. Most of this surplus was channeled through industrial-country banks to the developing countries, because the return on investment in the developing countries was higher than in the industrial countries during this period. The oil surplus nations ended up with secure investments in the industrial countries, the private banks with higher-yield but more vulnerable loans to the developing countries. The increasing inflation in the industrial countries was associated with a more rapid increase in commodity prices and a decline in the foreign exchange value of the dollar. The increasing inflation also increased the effective tax rate on investment in the industrial countries and reduced the real rate of interest.

All these conditions were reversed in the early 1980s. The real price of oil peaked in early 1981, and the OPEC surplus declined sharply. Commodity prices peaked in 1980 and then declined sharply. The foreign exchange value of the dollar increased sharply from the summer of 1980 to early 1985. The combination of declining inflation and the business provisions of the 1981 U.S. tax law increased the return on investment in the United States and the real interest rate. In addition, the severe recession of 1981 and 1982 and the increasing protectionism in the industrial countries reduced the markets for the exports of the developing countries.

The effects of these changes in general economic conditions, however, differed enormously among the developing countries. A total of fifty-seven countries with about 60 percent of the external debt of the developing countries in 1980 incurred external payments arrears between 1981 and 1983 or rescheduled their external debts between 1981 and mid-1984. Another sixty-six countries with about 40 percent of the external debt of the developing countries in 1980, however, experienced no such debt problems. The major conditions that differed between these two groups of countries is that the problem countries increased their external debt more rapidly in the 1970s and experienced a decline in exports in the 1980s. For the problem countries the ratio of debt service payments to exports increased from 26.9 percent in 1980 to 41.6 percent in 1982. For the other countries, in contrast, this ratio increased from 11 percent in 1980 to only 14.6 percent in 1982.

The problem countries, in turn, presented two quite different types of problems. Many of the countries of sub-Saharan Africa have a high ratio of external debt to exports. Most of this debt, however, was to governments and multilateral insitutions, much of which was on concessional terms; the ratio of debt service to exports was only 20.2 percent in 1982 but has since increased rapidly. Some of these countries are insolvent, in that there is no prospect that they can make their debt service payments, even if the debt is rescheduled on favorable terms. The external debt of these countries (excluding Nigeria and South Africa), however, was only about 7 percent of the total foreign debt of the developing countries in 1982 and did not present a substantial threat to the world financial system.

The major focus of U.S. attention was the foreign debt of the Latin American countries and the Philippines. The Latin American debt was about 44 percent of the total external debt of the developing countries in 1982. Most of this debt was to private lenders at commercial interest rates; about one-third of this debt was held by American banks. For the Latin American countries as a group, the ratio of debt service obligations to exports peaked at 49.6 percent in 1982. For most of these countries, a rescheduling of their external debt plus the prospect of higher exports and lower interest rates was expected to reduce their debt service ratio in future years.

All the major Latin American countries were in trouble by mid-1982. Argentine government spending and borrowing had increased rapidly to finance the unsuccessful war over the Falkland (Malvinas) Islands in the spring of 1982. Brazil's foreign debt had increased rapidly to finance the increased price of oil imports and a rapid growth of the state sector. Mexico, however, was the first to break. Although Mexico had benefitted enormously from the increase in oil prices, the increased oil revenues and foreign debt were used primarily to expand the state sector and to maintain an artificially high exchange rate. The timing of Mexico's problems also suggested a pattern. Mexico had also been forced to request International Monetary Fund (IMF) assistance and devalue the peso in 1976, the last year of the prior six-year presidential election cycle. A rapid development of the recently discovered oil reserves, however, permitted Mexico to repay the IMF in 1978 and free itself from the IMF restraints on the government budget. Government spending and inflation again increased sharply, and by 1982 the peso was enormously overvalued. Government spending, which had been 26 percent of gross domestic product (GDP) in 1970, increased to 35 percent in 1976 and to more than 50 percent in 1982. The number of state-owned firms increased from eighty-six in 1970 to 760 in 1976 and to 1,155 in 1982. In 1982, the last year of the Lopez Portillo administration, the government nationalized the banks and transportation sector, imposed exchange controls, and devalued the peso from 26 pesos per dollar to 148 pesos per dollar. In anticipation of these conditions, Mexico experienced a massive capital flight, more than offsetting the net foreign lending to Mexico. In common with other nations, Mexico experienced a number of problems of external origin. Most of Mexico's problems, however, were of its own making.

The Initial Response

Creditor nations, including the United States, relied primarily on established international institutions to respond to the developing debt crisis. The International Monetary Fund, with Jacques de Larosière as its managing director through 1986, played the lead role. The characteristic IMF response was to organize the rescheduling of external debts through the "Paris Club" and the "London Club," provide some new financing for periods of one to three years from the reserves established by the IMF member governments, and establish targets for the policies of the debtor countries as a condition for the refinancing. The Paris Club is a committee of representatives of the major governmental creditors and guarantors; it was first established in 1956. After reviewing the conditions of the debtor, this committee approves a general plan for debt relief. The debtor must stipulate that no other creditor will be treated more favorably than the creditors represented in the committee. This plan then provides the general framework for bilateral negotiations with each governmental creditor. The London Club provides a similar process for the major private creditors.

This arrangement has sometimes been described as a "creditor cartel." A more accurate description is that this process provides a crude equivalent of Chapter 11 proceedings under U.S. bankruptcy law, with the IMF serving in the role of a court-ordered supervisor of the reorganization. The major difference, of course, is that there is no international bankruptcy law and, in the contemporary world, no "sheriff" with the authority to seize the domestic assets of the debtor. Moreover, the IMF response to the debt crisis that developed in 1982 included one new practice: in addition to rescheduling the existing debt, the private creditors were required to provide some net new financing, a condition that the creditors would not themselves have chosen.

Other institutions had a smaller role. The creditor governments, central banks, and the Bank for International Settlements (a central bank for the central banks) usually provided temporary "bridge" loans until the IMF package was arranged. The World Bank also provided a small amount of "structural adjustment loans" (a new type of loan authorized in 1980) for periods of one to four years.

This international framework for responding to the debt crisis was strongly supported by the Reagan administration because it ensured the contributions of other governments and private creditors in other countries. The administration, however, initially opposed an increase in IMF financing. In September 1982 the IMF governors authorized the first response to the debt crisis but did not approve additional financing. Although the IMF quotas had been increased by 50 percent in late 1980 and special borrowing arrangements were established with Saudi Arabia and some other countries, the available financing did not appear to be sufficient to handle the developing crisis. The U.S. position was modified only when it became clear that substantial additional IMF financing was necessary to induce the debtors to accept the readjustment conditions and the private creditors to make new loans. In testimony before the House Banking Committee in December 1982, Don Regan presented a bleak prospect for the U.S. financial system and economy unless Congress authorized an additional contribution to the IMF. In the meantime the IMF had concluded agreements with Mexico, Argentina, and Brazil with their existing financing.

In the spring of 1983 the administration supported a 50 percent increase in the IMF quota and an expansion of the general borrowing authority but insisted on a reduction of the share that may be loaned to any one country. The next task was to gain approval from

Congress for a quota increase. Congress is generally reluctant to increase funding for international organizations, especially when domestic spending is being curtailed. Moreover, the IMF increase was strongly opposed by leading congressional Republicans and by some of Reagan's outside advisers, such as Milton Friedman. After considerable lobbying of the congressional Republicans by Don Regan, a process that he did not enjoy, Congress finally approved a $8.5 billion contribution to the IMF only after the administration acquiesced to a major expansion of housing credit. The cost was high, but an international response to the debt crisis also served another objective. The "bad cop" role of the IMF permitted the United States to play the role of the "good cop" in nurturing the new democratic governments in Latin America and, later, the Philippines.

There was a good case against an additional contribution to the IMF. In general the IMF approach, like the Continental bailout, reduced the short-term risks by measures that deferred a long-term resolution of the debt-servicing problem. (It is easier, of course, for a policy adviser to recommend a longer-term approach than it is for a political official, whose primary incentive is to minimize the risks of a major crisis on his watch, to do so). For the United States and the other creditor nations, the primary policy problem was that most of the foreign debt was held by banks, and a moratorium on debt service or a default might have caused a more general financial crisis. In the similar debt crisis in the 1930s, in contrast, most of the foreign debt was government bonds held by private investors. A widespread moratorium on debt service by many of the same countries led to severe hardship to the bondholders but created no substantial external problems.

The IMF approach to the 1980s crisis, however, required additional lending by the private banks, most of which was involuntary in response to considerable pressure from Paul Volcker. Of the $30 billion in new loans by private institutions in 1983 and 1984, only $7 billion was outside the IMF framework of agreements to restructure debt. This process increased the total exposure of the banks and deferred measures—such as selling loans on the secondary market, the substitution of bonds for loans, or debt-equity swaps—that would reduce the vulnerability of the banks and reduce the debt service problems of the debtor countries. From the perspective of the banks, adding new loans to a debtor in trouble makes sense only if the debtor's problems are temporary or if there is adequate collateral for these loans. The prospect that the debtors could meet the increased debt service obligations was in turn dependent on an improvement in either external conditions, such as the export market and interest rates, or on a major change in internal conditions in the debtor countries. There is no collateral on loans to foreign governments, and only a small part of these loans are guaranteed by the creditor governments or internal institutions. The fact that most of the additional financing by commercial banks was involuntary suggests that the bankers were skeptical that the problems of most of the debtor nations were only temporary.

Moreover, the IMF, rather like a nagging mother-in-law, imposed some conditions on the debtor countries that, however desirable, were unnecessary to resolve the debt problem. Specifically, IMF insistence that the debtor countries reduce their inflation rate sometimes led to economically and politically damaging price and wage controls that were irrelevant to the necessary actions to reduce the ratio of debt service to exports. Don Regan, however, would not tolerate any criticism of the IMF conditions within the administration because of the U.S. commitment to the IMF strategy.

In any case the IMF strategy seemed to work very well in 1983 and 1984 and led to an increasing sense of optimism. A strong recovery in the United States, a slower recovery in the other industrial countries, and the strengthening dollar increased the exports of the debtor countries. The IMF coordinated rescheduling and the decline in interest rates reduced their debt service ratio. The private banks substantially increased their capital and loan loss reserves, reducing their vulnerability to a debt moratorium or default. A small but growing amount of the debt to banks was sold on secondary markets or was converted to equity. Most of the debtor countries, in response to the IMF conditions, severely contracted their imports, reduced their government deficits, and reduced inflation—at the cost of a severe contraction in their domestic economies. The response of the new de la Madrid administration in Mexico was especially impressive. Real government spending was substantially reduced, the government deficit declined from 17.6 percent of GDP in 1982 to 8.7 percent in 1984, several hundred state firms were sold or closed, and the inflation rate declined from 100 percent to 60 percent despite a huge devaluation of the peso. During this period there was a substantial reverse flow of resources from the debtor countries to the creditor countries. Studies by the IMF and several private institutions projected a slow continuing decline in the debt service ratio for the Latin American countries (although not for the African countries). The case-by-case approach coordinated by the IMF seemed to be sufficient. The worst of the debt crisis seemed to be over.

The "Baker Plan"

Conditions began to unravel again, however, in 1985. U.S. economic growth slowed sharply beginning in late 1984, and an increasing proportion of U.S. imports from the debtor countries was subject to import restraints. The major change, however, was a growing resistance by the debtor countries to the conditions for assistance by the IMF. "No to the IMF" became the organizing slogan of the domestic opposition parties and was increasingly considered by the technocratic elite. In September 1984 the Latin American Economic System proposed that countries "pay no more than they can afford and never more than a quarter of export revenues as debt service," but no immediate action was taken. In July 1985, however, President Alan Garcia Perez of Peru, in his inaugural address, announced that Peru would limit its debt service payments to 10 percent of export earnings and would bypass the IMF. The military leader of Nigeria later announced that debt service would be limited to 30 percent of export earnings, in effect relating debt service to the price of oil. There was more concern that Argentina, a much larger debtor, would choose this route. Argentine inflation had increased to about 1,000 percent in early 1985, real wages had declined sharply, and debt service was six months in arrears. The governments of Brazil and Mexico, after having imposed severe austerity measures in response to the IMF conditions, were concerned that Argentina would break with the IMF and, in an interesting twist, participated in a bridge loan to Argentina until the IMF package was approved. Fidel Castro could not pass up the opportunity to make mischief. At a conference of the debtor countries in Havana in August 1985, Castro urged these countries to consider repudiating their external debt, although Cuba itself has consistently paid its own debt service obligations. Castro's appeal went unheeded, and the debtor countries have yet to form a debtor cartel or agree on any coordinated action.

The leaders of the debtor countries, however, increasingly argued that they should not bear the full burden of adjustment to the debt crisis. This rhetoric served a domestic political purpose but was not consistent with the facts. One study indicates that the market value of American banks in late 1983 was reduced by about 22 percent for each dollar of Latin American debt on their books. A later survey of the secondary market for foreign debt indicated discounts of about twenty-three cents per dollar of loans to Brazil and Venezuela; thirty to forty cents for loans to Argentina, Chile, Ecuador, and Mexico; and discounts of seventy-six cents on loans to Peru and ninety-two cents on loans to Bolivia. The major creditor banks had clearly experienced substantial losses even if the remaining loans were maintained on their books at par.

These conditions set the stage for Secretary Baker to announce "A Program for Sustained Growth" at the annual World Bank/IMF meeting in Seoul, Korea, in October 1985, shortly after the Plaza Accord on exchange rates in September. This program called for the commercial banks to provide $20 billion of additional financing over three years, for the World Bank and the regional development banks to provide an additional $9 billion, and for the debtor nations to undertake structural adjustments to induce higher economic growth. This assistance was to be provided to ten Latin American countries plus the Ivory Coast, Morocco, Nigeria, the Philippines, and Yugoslavia. Costa Rica and Jamaica were later added to this list. The major new provision of this proposal was an increased role for the World Bank and the regional development banks, substituting in part for the unpopular role of the IMF. The major new theme was that the structural adjustments by the debtor countries would be designed to promote growth rather than austerity. The major continuing provision was for additional financing by the commercial banks, a provision that reflects a continued misunderstanding of the primary policy problem of the debt crisis in the creditor countries. One irony is that a major architect of this proposal was Assistant Secretary David Mulford, who had been previously responsible, as a private adviser, for channeling about $100 billion of Saudi Arabian investments through Western banks to the debtor countries.

Some journalist unfortunately described this proposal as the "Baker Plan." A more accurate description would have been the Baker Concept or the Baker Hope. At the time Baker made this proposal, the commercial banks had not agreed to additional lending, and there was no authority for additional financing by the international development banks. The debtor countries were concerned that the additional financing would not be sufficient. The private banks were skeptical that the potential structural adjustments would be sufficient to justify adding new loans to their large portfolio of bad loans.

Mexico, which had triggered the 1982 debt crisis, also proved to be the first major test of the Baker plan. Again, Mexico's problems were a consequence of both external and internal conditions. A major earthquake hit Mexico City in the summer of 1985. More important, the sharp decline in oil prices in early 1986 reduced Mexico's export earnings by about $8 billion, more than offsetting the concurrent decline in interest rates. These conditions reversed the progress of the prior two years. The government deficit increased moderately in 1985 and sharply in 1986; most of the increased deficit was financed by money creation, the inflation rate soared, and the debt service ratio increased sharply. Mexicans continued to invest their own money abroad; according to one estimate, the net additional lending to Mexico during 1983 through 1985 of $10 billion was more than offset by a $17 billion outflow of capital. Commercial banks were not inclined to make additional loans to Mexico under these conditions.

In early June 1986 Paul Volcker made a secretive trip to Mexico, presumably to encourage the government to continue to manage its debt problem through the IMF. And in July Mexico signed a new agreement with the IMF that was designed to provide about $12 billion of new loans by the end of 1987. About $6 billion was expected from the commercial banks, with the rest supplied by the IMF, the World Bank, and other governmental institutions. Consistent with the spirit of the Baker Plan, Mexico was offered a small reduction in interest rates and more flexibility with respect to public finance targets, in exchange for a commitment to implement "supply oriented structural policies" to increase the prospects for medium-term growth. A $1.6 billion bridge loan was made available until the larger financing was approved. Additional financing was promised if the price of oil declined below $9 a barrel or if the expected growth was not realized. Although this package was endorsed at the World Bank/IMF annual meeting in September, intensive negotiations through the end of October were necessary to gain the tentative approval of the commercial banks. In the end a World Bank guarantee of $750 million of the commercial bank loans was necessary to complete the package. Barber Conable (the new president of the World Bank) insisted that the guarantee "should not be regarded as a precedent" but then added that "in a pragmatic world, one can never say never." A week after this package was approved, the Mexican finance ministry announced that it would need a total of $15.9 billion of new loans in 1987, more than twice that provided in that year by the IMF package, so there are likely to be other chapters in this continuing saga.

In early December 1986 the major contributors to the World Bank agreed to provide $12.4 billion to the poorest countries over the next three years, a measure that will be especially important to the countries of sub-Saharan Africa. The U.S. share of this financing was reduced slightly, for a total of $2.9 billion, in exchange for a corresponding reduction in the U.S. voting share in the branch of the World Bank with increasing responsibility for the debt program. In 1987, however, Congress was extraordinarily reluctant to approve this additional U.S. contribution to the World Bank, and a smaller U.S. role in this bank seems probable.

On February 20, 1987, Brazil initiated the most important challenge to the Baker Plan when it announced that it would suspend interest payments on its debt of about $67 billion to commercial banks until such time as the provisions for servicing this debt on terms more favorable to Brazil could be renegotiated. The Brazilian action resulted from the dramatic failure of the "cruzado plan," initiated in February 1986, which led to a consumer spending boom, a sharp reduction in Brazil's trade surplus, and an inflation rate of about 600 percent. During this same period the substantial decline in oil prices, if the cruzado plan had not been implemented, would have led to a large increase in Brazil's trade surplus. Brazil's problems were of its own making. The finance ministers of the major creditor nations, meeting in Paris that weekend to discuss exchange rates, expressed regret about the Brazilian action but dismissed its effects as temporary and limited. The prospective effects, in fact, were quite serious. A delay of more than ninety days in resolving this issue would require the U.S. banks to establish loan loss reserves on the billions of dollars of loans to Brazil as early as the summer of 1987. My prediction is that the Brazilian debt problem will prove to be the most difficult among the major debtors, primarily because of Brazil's erratic domestic economic policies.

The full story of the Baker Plan, of course, is not yet complete. It is not yet clear that the increased role of the World Bank will be any more successful or popular in inducing the debtor countries to make the necessary structural changes. A more important problem, in terms of U.S. interests, is that this approach continues to depend on additional commercial bank lending at a risk to the larger financial system. At his farewell appearance at the World Bank/IMF annual meeting, IMF managing director de Larosière described the major achievements of the IMF during his tenure as the "capacity to respond and react." A similar statement would describe the contributions of Regan, Baker, and Volcker. The debt crisis did not blow up on their watch, but there has been no substantial reduction of the conditions that led to this crisis.

The Continuing Problem

A case-by-case approach to the debt problem may prove to be sufficient. In 1986 the IMF continued to project a slow decline in the debt service ratios of most of the debtor countries, with the exception of those in sub-Saharan Africa, on the basis of moderate growth in the industrial countries, some decline in interest rates, and an avoidance of more severe protectionist measures. Some additional lending by the commercial banks would be consistent with a continued decline in the ratio of their foreign loans to their capital and loan loss reserves.

The case against this moderately optimistic perspective also should be recognized. Economic growth of the industrial countries has been sluggish since 1984, and protectionist measures are increasing. A necessary reduction of the U.S. trade deficit will make it harder for the debtor countries to increase their net exports. The problem of capital flight from the debtor countries has not been resolved. One estimate is that capital flight from the fifteen major developing countries during 1983 through 1985 offset almost half of their increased debt; creditor governments and banks in effect are providing foreign exchange to permit residents of the debtor countries to invest abroad. Some of the adjustment policies implemented by the debtor countries, such as price and wage controls and increased taxes, have been counterproductive. Several studies have estimated that some debtor countries would benefit by a debt service moratorium or default, even at the expense of a seizure of their external assets and a severe contraction of routine trade credits. The political systems in many of the debtor countries are not stable, and foreign bankers provide a useful scapegoat for their domestic problems. One should be reminded that Mexico, Brazil, and Argentina earlier suspended debt service only years after the peak of the debt crisis of the early 1930s.

An increasing number of observers have concluded that "coping is not enough," to borrow the title of a 1986 book by Morris Miller on the foreign debt issue. The several types of "global" alternatives that have been proposed favor either the debtor countries or the commercial banks and range from radical to moderate. Several spokesmen for the debtor countries urge their governments to unilaterally or collectively limit their debt service payments, as Peru and Nigeria have already done—a prospect that sends tremors through the financial community. Some industrial-country spokesmen for parties of the left, primarily out of concern for the economic conditions in the debtor countries, have proposed a large increase in governmental (taxpayer) contributions to the IMF and the World Bank. Congress is not likely to approve such proposals.

Characteristically, the major alternatives proposed by Americans are more moderate. In mid-1986 Sen. Bill Bradley proposed that the official and bank creditors voluntarily reduce their interest rates to the debtor countries by three percentage points and reduce the principal of those loans by 3 percent a year for three years; in addition, the multilateral development banks would increase lending by $3 billion a year. These concessions would be made to any debtor country that makes a commitment to liberalize trade, reduce capital flight, encourage domestic investment, and promote domestic economic growth. The major specific problem of the Bradley proposal is that it would seriously weaken the financial position of the commercial banks. If applied to all Latin American countries, this proposal would reduce the capital of the nine leading banks by 24 percent and the capital of all American banks by 15 percent. There is also little prospect that the banks would participate voluntarily in this arrangement, because an improvement in the debtor-country conditions is a "public good" to all creditors, whether or not they participate. Some compulsion or tax incentive to the commercial banks in all the major creditor countries would be necessary for this proposal to be effective.

A more thoughtful proposal was made earlier by Prof. Peter Kenan of Princeton. Kenan proposed to establish a new international institution that would issue bonds guaranteed by the governments of the creditor countries. This institution would then buy foreign loans from the commercial banks at some discount. This would permit the new institution to reduce the annual payments on the existing loans by lengthening the maturities and reducing the interest rate. The major advantage of the Kenan proposal is that it directly addresses the primary policy problem of the current foreign debt by reducing the amount of this debt held by the commercial banks. For the creditor countries the cost is a government guarantee of the bonds of the new international institution. For the debtor countries this proposal would slightly reduce their debt service payments but would not provide a source of new financing.

The general problem with all these global alternatives is that they do not reflect the very different circumstances among the debtor countries and over time. For example, the large foreign debt of Korea has never been a problem because of the rapid growth of Korea's exports. Conditions in Ecuador improved sufficiently to induce some voluntary new lending before Ecuador suspended interest payments in early 1987. The investment climate in Chile has permitted a growing amount of debt/equity swaps. Similarly, over time an increase in oil prices would help some countries, such as Mexico, and hurt others, such as Brazil. The foreign debt problem is clearly best addressed from a "Chapter 11 workout" perspective involving a different approach to each problem debtor.

The primary problem of the current case-by-case approach is that it has increased rather than reduced the primary policy problem of foreign debt to the creditor countries by increasing the total amount of this debt held by the commercial banks. The central banks, most importantly the Federal Reserve, have exerted considerable pressure on the commercial banks to make additional loans to the problem debt countries, loans that would have been regarded as inappropriate if made to a domestic borrower. The most important change to the current approach would be to *reduce* the total amount of foreign debt held by the commercial banks—by encouraging the increased use of bond financing, sales of the bank loans on the secondary market, and the exchange of debt for equity. A small but growing use of these types of instruments has developed outside the IMF rescheduling process but has not been encouraged by the government authorities. In any case making new loans, either by governmental or private institutions, to countries that do not put their own house in order makes no sense, even on humanitarian grounds. Such loans are likely to be dissipated by a continued expansion of the state sector, an overvalued exchange rate, and continued capital flight.

The next time the finance minister from a debtor country appeals to U.S. officials for special assistance, the best response may be to advise him to make his own deal with the country's creditors. So far, U.S. policy, working through the international institutions, has been successful in limiting the debt crisis primarily by deferring the day of reckoning.

A GENERAL EVALUATION

In each of the crises discussed in this chapter, U.S. government officials responded quickly and proved to be effective crisis managers within the existing institutional arrangements. They deserve credit for these actions, because the alternatives could have been much worse.

All these problems are still with us, however, and the institutions have not been changed. Air traffic delays have increased, and at some time air safety may be threatened. The savings banks continue to be vulnerable to an increase in interest rates and to a weakness in the housing market. Some commercial banks are vulnerable to conditions in the agricultural sector, others to a weakness in energy markets, still others to conditions in the debtor countries, and some to a combination of these conditions. Bank failures continue to increase. The federal deposit and pension insurance funds and the farm credit system may need to be recapitalized or restructured. The incentives of troubled banks and firms to shift risks to these insurance funds have not been reduced. Total lending to the debtor countries, including lending by commercial banks, has increased without any consistent pattern of restructuring of these countries' domestic policies. Some type of reregulation of the airlines and financial institutions is probable unless there is a fundamental change in the current institutions that have allowed these conditions to develop. One should not envy the next generation of officials who will have to address these continuing problems.

In general the Reagan administration proved to be an effective manager of a number of unusual and severe economic crises. Somehow, some day, someone must demonstrate a more strategic vision, however, to avoid such crises in the future. The management of a crisis is newsworthy; the avoidance of such crises is praiseworthy.

CHAPTER SEVEN

The Economy

Taken together, I believe these proposals will put the Nation on a fundamentally different course—a course that will lead to less inflation, more growth, and a brighter future for all of our citizens.

Ronald Reagan, as candidate and president, promised that his economic policies would lead to both lower inflation and higher growth. That was not unusual. Successful politicians seldom acknowledge any trade-offs among desirable economic conditions. A president, however, is correctly judged by his record, not his promises. The Reagan record, like that of most presidents, has been mixed. The inflation rate declined much more than anyone expected, in part because of several unanticipated conditions. The growth record was more complex as will be explained below. The broadest measure of national output, however, increased much less than the initial forecast and at a lower rate, at least through 1987, than during the Carter administration. The Carter record was considered a failure primarily because economic conditions deteriorated during the last two years of Carter's administration. As of 1984 the Reagan record was considered a success primarily because most economic conditions improved substantially during the last two years of Reagan's first term. In politics, as in warfare, timing is apparently the key to victory. Only a longer perspective will indicate whether the decline in inflation has been transient and whether the hope for higher growth is illusory.

INHERITED CONDITIONS

In January 1981 the U.S. economy was in a mess. Although output and employment were recovering from the short, sharp recession of the spring of 1980, total output was only slightly higher and productivity was lower than in the fall of 1978. In both 1979 and 1980, the consumer price index increased by about 12 percent, and real wage

225

rates and earnings declined. The relative tax burden was increasing as inflation pushed many people into higher tax brackets. The foreign exchange value of the dollar had declined for four years to a low in the summer of 1980. Shortly before Reagan's inauguration, the prime interest rate peaked at 21.5 percent. Other conditions contributed to a general sense of concern. The crime rate and the divorce rate continued to increase. Student test scores continued to decline. And the United States seemed to be increasingly impotent in foreign affairs.

Moreover, there was a sense that conditions were out of control and might deteriorate. At the time it was not clear what had led to the poor productivity performance of the U.S. economy since 1973. In retrospect the substantial decline in productivity growth appears to be related to a slower growth of real R&D spending, a declining capital/labor ratio, a slower reallocation of labor among sectors, lower capacity utilization, and increasing regulation—but there remains a considerable dispute about the relative contribution of these conditions. One study estimates that only about one-fourth of the decline in productivity growth was attributable to conditions that were not dependent on government policy. President Carter, however, attributed this decline to a "malaise" of the American spirit (although he did not use this specific word). During this same period, for comparison, productivity growth also slowed in Europe and Japan but was much higher than in the United States.

The rapid increase in inflation and interest rates was more clearly dependent on government policies, but the Carter administration tended to attribute this outcome to inherent conditions in the U.S. economy and to external shocks. The last Carter *Economic Report* reflects this confusion. The primary reasons for the increasing inflation were that the rate of growth of the money supply increased about four percentage points from 1974 through 1978, other policies that contributed to a decline in the dollar, and a small effect of the 1979–1980 oil shock. The Carter economists, however, attributed most of the increased inflation to "the ratchet-like nature of the inflationary process" and to the oil shock. The general increase in the inflation rate during each recovery since the mid-1960s, however, was not an inherent condition in the U.S. economy but a consequence of a general increase in the rate of money growth over this period. The special explanation of the 1979–1980 inflation in terms of the oil shock was especially misleading. The consumer price index, exclusive of energy, increased more than 11 percent in each of these years.

The Carter policies affecting inflation and interest rates were similarly confused. Following two years of rapid money growth, a system of "voluntary" wage and price guidelines was established in late

1978, with the threat of public exposure and loss of government contracts to increase compliance. Although these guidelines may have reduced wage increases, the general inflation rate increased sharply. On leaving office, Carter proposed consideration of a "tax-based incomes policy" (TIP) to provide an incentive for lower wage increases, but he proposed deferring any general reduction of tax rates because of misplaced concern about their presumed inflationary effects. Carter also believed that a reduction in oil imports would reduce the effect of oil prices on U.S. inflation, and he supported several measures to reduce oil consumption. He must not have noticed that the inflation rates in Germany and Japan, nations that import all their oil, were less than half the U.S. rates in 1979 and 1980.

The primary reason for the Carter administration's failure to take effective action against inflation, however, was that the administration grossly overestimated the costs of reducing inflation. It had estimated that reducing inflation by one percentage point would reduce output by about $100 billion (in 1980 dollars). The one important action against inflation was the appointment of Paul Volcker as chairman of the Federal Reserve Board in the summer of 1979. Following implementation of a new Fed operating procedure in October 1979, the rate of money growth dropped sharply. After a rapid rise of interest rates, however, Carter panicked and encouraged Volcker to implement a confused system of general credit controls in the spring of 1980. Although this dangerous policy was abandoned within three months, it was one of the deciding factors that led to the election of Reagan. The deterioration of economic conditions and Carter's confused understanding and inconsistent policies clearly called for "a fundamentally different course."

THE REAGAN RECORD

Output

The Reagan economic program was designed to achieve higher growth by implementing supply-side policies rather than by increasing demand. During the first term, however, real economic growth was much less than expected, primarily because of the extended recession of 1981 and 1982. Figure 7.1 illustrates the level of real GNP during the Carter administration and the forecast and actual levels during the first term of the Reagan administration. This period included two years of rapid growth in 1977 and 1978, four years of no net growth from 1978 through 1982, and two years of rapid growth in 1983 and 1984. This figure also illustrates that real GNP through 1984 was much lower than the early 1981 forecasts.

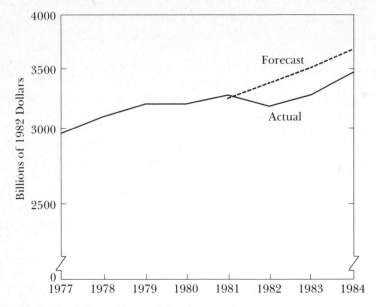

Figure 7.1   Real Gross National Product

The 1981-1982 recession was the first major test of Reagan's economic policies. In early 1981 the Reagan economists (myself included) recognized that the proposed gradual reduction in money growth presented a risk of recession, but we hoped that it would be short and mild. As it turned out, the rate of money growth through mid-1982 was somewhat lower than the initial guidance to the Federal Reserve and was thus the primary reason for the timing and severity of the recession. In February 1982, however, we still expected that the recession would "end early in 1982, followed by a resumption of growth by mid-year." There was some reason for optimism about this forecast when real GNP increased slightly in the spring. On reviewing the June economic data in late July, however, Murray Weidenbaum and I concluded that the recession would continue for some months. A similar conclusion by the Federal Reserve, compounded by the developing Mexican debt problem, ended the period of monetary restraint. For political reasons the timing of the recession was especially awkward—beginning in August 1981, the month after the president's tax proposal was approved, and ending in November 1982, the month of the mid-term elections. One of my few correct judgments during this period was to recognize in November that the recession was over; Martin Feldstein did not share this view for several more months.

As is often the case, the 1982 election produced more heat than light about economic conditions and policies. Democrats and most of the media described the recession as the most severe since the 1930s. Such statements were inaccurate or at least misleading. Real GNP declined more during the 1974–1975 recession than during the 1981–1982 recession. A more accurate perspective would have recognized the 1981–1982 recession as part of the four-year period of stagnant growth from late 1978 through 1982, the longest such period in the postwar years. The administration and Republican candidates were defensive but would not acknowledge that the recession was due to the relative monetary restraint; they variously blamed the recession on the prior inflation or the delay in the tax cuts. For the administration the political costs of the recession were substantial, leading to a loss of twenty-six Republican seats in the House and the end of the coalition that had supported the 1981 legislative program.

Shortly after the election, White House communications director Dave Gergen remarked to me that the initial Reagan program would have been quite different if the administration had recognized the risks of this outcome, a view that implicitly blamed the economists for bad advice and was probably shared by Jim Baker. For those of us who continued to support the program, our primary concern was to avoid a reversal of the program and the legislative mischief that is often initiated toward the end of a recession. For the most part the Reagan program survived the recession, although the prospect for further implementation was reduced. The only major losses were the increase in the federal highway program, the Emergency Jobs Act of 1983, and the one-time "payment-in-kind" (PIK) program for farmers.

The temporary cost to the economy of the recession was substantial, reducing total output by about 3.5 percent from the prior peak and by about 6 percent relative to potential output. The economic recovery of 1983 and 1984 was the strongest in thirty years, a condition that the administration understandably emphasized during the 1984 campaign. An administration, however, should be assessed on the basis of its full-term record, and not on either its promises or its short-term record.

Any one measure of economic growth during the Carter administration and Reagan first term is inadequate. There is no uniquely correct measure of total output. For that reason, Table 7.1 presents the growth rates of four measures of output, in terms of both total output and output per member of the civilian, noninstitutional pop-

Table 7.1 Comparative Growth Rates of Real Output*

	Total		Per Adult	
	Carter Administration	Reagan Administration	Carter Administration	Reagan Administration
Gross national product	2.9	2.5	1.1	1.3
Gross domestic product	2.8	2.6	1.0	1.3
Net national product	2.7	2.4	0.9	1.1
"Command-based" GNP	2.3	2.9	0.5	1.6

*Percentage change, annual rate.

ulation age sixteen and over (the latter term is a measure of the potential labor force). There is also no uniquely correct measure of growth rates. The measure used here is the annual growth rate from the last quarter of 1976 to the last quarter of 1980 and, in turn, from the last quarter of 1980 to the last quarter of 1984. One should recognize, however, that this measure is especially sensitive to unusual conditions specific to these end-point quarters.

As this table indicates, the growth of real GNP during Reagan's first term was lower than during the Carter administration. Similarly, the growth of real gross domestic product (GNP minus the net earnings of American labor and assets in other countries) and of real net national product (GNP minus the depreciation of the private capital stock) was somewhat lower during Reagan's first term than during the Carter administration. These differences, however, were entirely attributable to the much slower growth of the adult population during the Reagan administration. On a per-adult basis the growth of each of these measures of total output was slightly higher during the Reagan administration. A new concept, "command-based" GNP, reflects changes in the international terms of trade and measures how much the United States could purchase from current output. The terms of trade declined sharply during the Carter administration and increased somewhat during the first term of the Reagan administration. As a consequence, the growth of real command-based GNP was somewhat higher during the Reagan first term and substantially higher on a per-adult basis.

These comparisons indicate that the prospects for higher growth have yet to be realized. The growth of total output was somewhat lower during the first term of the Reagan administration than during the Carter administration and was only slightly higher on a per-adult basis. The major difference, of course, is that the Carter growth record was achieved only at the price of a rapid increase in inflation, and the roughly equal Reagan growth record was associated with a rapid decline in inflation. Over the full first term, therefore, there was no permanent loss of annual output as a result of the policies that led to the rapid decline in inflation. For several years the Reagan CEA estimated that potential real GNP through the remainder of the 1980s would increase at an annual rate of nearly 4 percent, on the basis of a more rapid increase in private employment and a high growth of productivity. The experience of the second term, however, was not encouraging. Real GNP increased at an average rate of 2.8 percent from the end of 1984 through 1987, only slightly higher than the annual rate during the first term. In light of the continued decline in the growth of the adult population, further measures to increase employment and productivity would be necessary to achieve the Reagan output targets.

Composition of Real Purchases

The growth of each major component of real purchases during the first term of the Reagan administration was higher than the growth of real GNP. Moreover, the growth of each major component was higher than during the Carter administration, despite a somewhat slower growth of real GNP. How was this possible? The answer is that U.S. imports grew very rapidly, allowing us, for a limited period, to use more goods and services than we produced. One should recall the allocational objectives of the initial Reagan program. These policies were designed to increase real spending for domestic business investment and for defense, but there was no prior understanding as to where the additional resources for investment and defense would come from. Only after the recovery was underway did it become clear that many of these resources were being imported or diverted, within the United States, from the export- and import-competing sectors. From 1985 through 1987, net imports were more than $100 billion. The rapid increase in imports and the trade deficit were the major unanticipated economic effects of the initial Reagan program. As mentioned earlier, the rapid increase in imports permitted consumption, domestic investment, and the government purchases of goods and services to each grow at a higher rate than domestic output.

Table 7.2 summarizes the growth of real purchases during the Carter administration and the first term of the Reagan administration. The top portion of the table illustrates how we were able to use more goods and services than we produced. Gross domestic purchases equal GNP minus exports plus imports. A slight decline in real exports plus the rapid growth of imports permitted gross domestic purchases to grow at a higher rate than domestic output or

Table 7.2 Comparative Growth Rates of Real Expenditures*

	Carter Administration	Reagan Administration
Gross national product	2.9	2.5
Exports	8.1	−0.3
Imports	2.2	9.5
Gross domestic purchases	2.3	3.6
Personal consumption	2.3	3.1
Durables	1.2	7.6
Nondurables	1.3	2.2
Services	3.4	2.7
Gross private domestic fixed investment	3.6	4.3
Producers durables	5.6	5.5
Nonresidential structures	6.7	1.9
Residential structures	−1.7	4.5
Business inventories	2.6	1.7
Government purchases of goods and services	1.6	2.9
Federal	2.0	5.3
Defense	2.1	7.0
Other	1.6	1.0
State and local	1.4	1.3

*Percentage change, annual rate.

during the Carter administration. A review of each component of this table also illustrates the major changes in the composition of real purchases during the Reagan administration.

Exports

Real exports declined only slightly during the first term, despite a rapid increase in the foreign exchange value of the dollar and slow growth abroad. The reduced export share of domestic output thus freed resources for other uses. Moreover, the composition of U.S. exports changed very little during this period. An increase in the U.S. terms of trade, however, increased the amount of foreign goods that could be purchased by U.S. exports. As a consequence, "command-based" real exports increased at a 2.8 percent annual rate during the first term, compared to a 2.4 percent rate during the Carter administration.

Imports

Real imports increased nearly three times as fast as domestic purchases, permitting a higher growth of each major component of real purchases. Imports of capital goods, autos, and consumer goods increased at especially rapid rates, reflecting the increasing domestic demand for these goods. Real imports of petroleum declined despite a decline in real oil prices, reflecting the lagged effects of the 1979–1980 oil price increases on both domestic demand and production. The effects of the rapid increase of U.S. imports on other nations were mixed; their industrial exports increased, but their domestic investment, primarily in Latin America, was reduced. Net imports increased most rapidly from Latin America and Europe and declined from those nations most dependent on exports of oil and other raw materials, thus reversing the pattern of the 1970s. The rapid increase in U.S. imports was most important to the non-oil debtor nations, substantially increasing their ability to finance their foreign debt.

Consumption

The effects of Reagan economic policies on real personal consumption expenditures were mixed. Conventional economic analysis suggests that the phased reduction of individual income tax rates approved in 1981 should have been expected to increase consumer expenditures and "crowd out" investment expenditures. Yet the 1981 reduction in the effective tax rates on the income from new business investment, even as modified in 1982 and 1984, was expected to increase new business investment, displacing some amount of household investment in consumer durables and housing. The first-term record reveals some of each of these effects. Real consumer expenditures increased more rapidly than real GNP but less rapidly than real domestic purchases.

The composition of consumer spending, however, was not consistent with what has been described as "the Feldstein shift." Martin Feldstein had long promoted a reduction in the effective tax rates on new business investment in order to shift investment from consumer durables and housing into domestic business investment. In fact, real spending for consumer durables, housing, and domestic business investment each increased at a rapid rate—at the expense of net U.S. investment abroad. The most rapid growth of consumer spending was for motor vehicles, household appliances, and semi-durables such as clothing and shoes. The most plausible explanations of the rapid growth of real spending for consumer durables are the increase in the quality of motor vehicles, the availability of new products such as video-cassette recorders and personal computers, the increase in real financial wealth, and the higher growth of real disposable income—conditions that apparently overwhelmed the adverse effect of higher real interest rates. Most other components of consumer spending increased at a slower rate than during the

Carter administration, reversing the long-term trend of higher relative spending for services. Although the Reagan administration had no specific objective to increase consumption, the net effect of the Reagan policies and other conditions substantially increased the growth of real consumer spending.

Private Domestic Investment

On the surface the reduction in effective tax rates on business investment appears to have been most effective. Real gross private domestic fixed investment increased at a substantially higher rate during the Reagan first term than during the Carter administration. Moreover, real net investment (excluding the depreciation of the fixed capital stock) increased at an annual rate of 12.3 percent during the first term of the Reagan administration, compared to a rate of 1.3 percent during the Carter administration.

These comparisons, however, are not a sufficient basis for estimating the effects of the reduction in tax rates, in part because investment was severely affected by the 1981–1982 recession and by the increase in real interest rates. Several studies estimate that the reduction in tax rates on investment income reduced the user cost of business equipment and structures by 6 to 8 percent and increased net private domestic fixed investment by about 25 percent during the period 1982 through 1984. In turn, the increase in the business capital stock attributable to the reduction in tax rates was estimated to increase annual net output by 1 to 2 percent by 1990. The change in business taxation approved in the tax legislation of 1986, however, appears likely to reverse the effects of the first-term tax legislation.

An examination of the components of domestic fixed investment during this period, however, suggests that one should be cautious in attributing the entire increase in investment to the reduced tax rates. The sum of investment in producers' durables and nonresidential structures, the two major investment categories most affected by the lower tax rates, increased at a lower rate than during the Carter administration. Moreover, most of the increase in investment in producer durables was for computers and autos, for which there was little change in the effective tax rates. A decline in the real price of computers and autos appears to have been a more important source of stimulus to these investments during this period than was the change in the effective tax rates.

The strong growth of real spending for residential structures, as mentioned earlier, was not expected. After the fact it appears that the increase in new family formation, in financial wealth, and in real disposable income more than offset the increase in real interest rates. The level of real business inventories, in contrast, increased at a slower rate during Reagan's first term than during the Carter administration, as higher real interest rates, the computer revolution, and the deregulation of trucking contributed to better inventory management. The ratio of inventories to sales declined to a record low, reducing the variability of output to a change in demand.

The increase in real private domestic investment during this period is encouraging but should not be a basis for complacency. Gross private investment, including net foreign investment, declined as a share of U.S. output. Moreover, about half of gross private investment in the United States is spent for housing and consumer durables. As a consequence, U.S. domestic business investment is a lower share of output than in any other major nation—less than half the share in Japan. An increase in this share is still dependent on a reduction of the federal deficit, a reduction of the tax bias in favor of housing and consumer durables, and a reduction of the tax bias against private saving.

A review of the overall investment record provides an insight into the unusual "crowding-out" phenomenon during this period. The combined effect of the Reagan policies increased the growth of most components of real private domestic investment. Moreover, the growth of real government investment, primarily for defense, also increased. U.S. saving from current output, however, did not increase by enough to finance the combined increase in private and government domestic investment, and the difference was financed by a huge increase in net foreign investment in the United States. In effect, foreigners financed a substantial part of the increase in U.S. private domestic investment and defense procurement.

This condition, not anticipated in 1981, may have been desirable but is not sustainable. Some reduction in U.S. borrowing abroad is probable without a change in policy. The effect of the reduction in tax rates on domestic business investment probably peaked in 1984 and will gradually decline. The 1986 tax legislation, moreover, will further reduce domestic business investment. Real investment in housing probably peaked in 1986. The growth of real defense procurement was also reduced substantially in 1986 and appears unlikely to be revived. The policy changes to date, however, promise to reduce U.S. borrowing abroad by reducing the growth of domestic investment rather than increasing the growth of U.S. saving. A reduction in government borrowing and a more thorough tax reform are still necessary to increase the unusually low U.S. saving rate.

Government Purchases

Real government spending for goods and services increased at a substantially higher rate during the Reagan first term than during the Carter administration, an interesting record for a conservative president. The increase in defense spending was over 90 percent of the increase in federal purchases, and other federal purchases increased at a somewhat lower rate. Most of the increase in real federal purchases was for investment goods and contract services, with only a small increase in real employee compensation. Real state and local spending increased slowly during the Reagan years—reflecting the combined effects of the tax limitation movement, lower real federal grants, a decline in the school population, and some demonstrable examples of improved management. Most of the increase in real state and local purchases was for contract services, with almost no change in real investment and employee compensation. A slower growth of defense investment and the general pressure on the federal budget promises to reduce the government share of total purchases during the second term.

Employment and Unemployment

Employment

Jobs! All too often, the level of employment has been the dominant index by which federal policies are judged. In fact, the U.S. economy has a remarkable record, especially compared to Europe, of creating jobs under a wide range of policies, some of which are contrary to other objectives. Changes in employment are primarily dependent on changes in the potential labor force, the demand for total output, and the labor costs per unit of output. The first condition is independent of federal policies other than those which affect immigration. The second condition is primarily dependent on monetary policy. And the third condition is a function of several policies that affect real labor costs and productivity.

During the Carter administration, civilian employment increased at a relatively rapid 2.7 percent annual rate, compared to a 1.8 percent annual increase in the adult population. The effect of Carter policies on this record were mixed. Stimulative monetary policy increased the growth of demand through mid-1979, and the resulting increase in inflation reduced real wage rates. Yet the increase in effective tax rates and environmental regulation contributed to the very slow growth of productivity during this period. On balance, the Carter policies contributed to an increase in employment but also led to other conditions that were undesirable or unsustainable.

During the first term of the Reagan administration, civilian employment increased at a 1.6 percent annual rate, compared to a 1.2 percent annual increase in the adult population. About half of the slowdown in the growth of employment thus was attributable to the slower growth of the adult population in the 1980s. The effect of Reagan policies on this record was also mixed. Several Reagan policies contributed to an increase in employment. One study estimates that the selective reduction of transfer payments increased the labor supply by 0.1 to 0.9 percent, primarily affecting low-income workers. This study also estimates that the reduction of individual income tax rates increased the labor supply by 1.2 to 2.9 percent, primarily affecting adult women and both men and women of age sixty-two and over. The rapid increase in the foreign exchange value of the dollar disciplined the growth of wages, primarily in the goods sector. The increase in real wages was more than offset by the increase in productivity, reducing real labor costs per unit of output.

During the Reagan first term, the major policy that contributed to lower employment growth was monetary restraint through mid-1982. Over the full first term, the net effect of these conditions on employment was positive. The civilian employment rate (employment as a percentage of the adult population) increased 1.5 percentage points, with a decline in the employment rates for teenagers and adult males more than offset by a continued rapid increase in the employment rate of adult females. Although the increase in the employment rate was less than during the Carter administration, it was achieved during a period of demand restraint and declining inflation and thus is more likely to be sustainable.

Unemployment

Changes in the unemployment rate primarily reflect cyclical conditions, but there is no longer much political concern when the rate is about 7 percent. Figure 7.2 illustrates the level of the civilian unemployment rate during the Carter administration and the first term of the Reagan administration, as well as the 1981 Reagan forecast of this rate. This figure reflects the opposite pattern, with a short lag, of changes in total demand, as illustrated in Figure 5.1. The unemployment rate declined during 1977 and 1978, increased sharply from 1979 through 1982, and declined sharply during the recovery in 1983 and 1984. From 1981 through 1983 the unemployment rate was substantially higher than the 1981 forecast, primarily because the administration did not anticipate the severity of the 1981–1982 recession. The most striking feature of this pattern, however, is that the unemployment rate was almost identical at the end of the Ford administration, the Carter administration, and the Reagan first term— at a rate of slightly over 7 percent. Neither the policies of the Carter

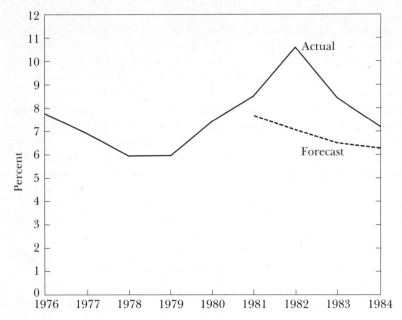

Figure 7.2 Civilian Unemployment Rate (fourth quarter of each year)

administration nor those of the Reagan administration appear to have
had much effect on the base level of unemployment.

In 1978 the Full Employment and Balanced Growth Act (popularly known as the Humphrey-Hawkins Act) established a target unemployment rate of 4 percent and required both the administration
and the Federal Reserve to report progress toward this target on an
annual basis. Soon after passage of this act, however, the unemployment rate began to increase, and the annual explanations of this
condition were not very informative. Why has the unemployment
rate proved to be so difficult to reduce during the past decade except by unexpected increases in money growth, even though the employment rate has continued to increase? The explanation is not clear,
even in retrospect. Conventional explanations are not satisfactory.
The minimum wage clearly increases the unemployment rate, especially for teenagers, but the real minimum wage has declined for
several years. Unemployment insurance also increases unemployment, but the proportion of the unemployed who receive benefits
has declined substantially in recent years, and the ratio of benefits to
earnings has also declined. Moreover, there is no general evidence
that the increase in the unemployment rate is due to a more casual
commitment to employment. In 1984, for example, 52 percent of
the unemployed had lost their jobs, compared with 45 percent in

1977, a cyclically comparable year; job leavers, reentrants, and new entrants were each a smaller percentage of the unemployed in 1984.

One must look to more detailed conditions in the economy for a partial explanation of the higher level of unemployment during the past decade. The rapid increase in the employment of married women has probably contributed to the substantial increase in the unemployment rate of married males and the increased duration of unemployment by reducing the proportionate effect of unemployment on family income. Similarly, an increase in the shift of employment among regions has been compounded by the lower mobility of the two-worker family.

Most of the increase in the unemployment rate since 1973 thus is probably due to changes in the economy rather than to changes in policy. That should not, however, lead one to be complacent about the current unemployment rate. A change in structural policy is probably still desirable to reduce the rate of structural unemployment. The several Reagan proposals—to reduce the minimum wage for teenage summer work, to permit partial unemployment benefits for part-time work, to permit states to use some unemployment funds for retraining and relocation, and to provide an earnings subsidy as an option for extended unemployment benefits—still merit consideration.

Moreover, one should dismiss the concern that higher growth and lower unemployment are by themselves inflationary, a view sometimes expressed by both Martin Feldstein and Paul Volcker. For a given total demand, of course, an increase in output is deflationary. Although there is a weak negative relation between the unemployment rate and the change in the inflation rate in the short run, this relation is not stable over a longer period and is a misleading guide to policy. My CEA colleague Bill Poole and I argued with Marty Feldstein about this issue for two years without convincing him to focus his concern on the increase in total demand rather than the increase in output on reduced unemployment. Similarly, Paul Volcker regularly smothered good news in a cloud of cigar smoke, sometimes leading the stock market to decline in the wake of a decline in the unemployment rate. The responsibility of the Federal Reserve is to maintain a steady path of total demand—a task that it has not performed consistently—rather than to worry about conditions such as a reduction in unemployment, which everyone should welcome.

Productivity

One of the more encouraging developments has been the increase in the growth of productivity. Output per hour in the nonfarm business sector increased at a 1.2 percent annual rate during the first term, compared to a 0.2 percent rate during the Carter administration. Manufacturing productivity increased at a substantially higher rate; output per hour in manufacturing increased at a 3.6 percent rate during the first term compared with a 1 percent rate during the Carter administration. Moreover, because real hourly earnings increased very slowly over the first term, real labor costs per unit of output declined. Farm productivity also increased sharply, but the growth of productivity in the service sector continued to decline. The growth of general business productivity, however, is still low compared to the 2.4 percent annual increase from 1948 through 1973. Moreover, the near-term prospects are not encouraging. Output per hour increased at an average annual rate of only 0.6 percent in 1985 and 1986, compared to the 2.0 percent annual increase on which the administration's forecast was based.

It is not yet clear what led to increased productivity growth during the first term. Among the more plausible explanations are the increased average age of the labor force and the improved allocation of resources as a result of lower tax rates, a slower growth of regulation, and the lower inflation. The higher growth of productivity in manufacturing reflects the cost-saving measures induced by the 1981–1982 recession and the increased competition from imports. In the automobile industry, for example, the break-even output level was reduced about 30 percent since 1979. The combination of these conditions, however, has not been sufficient to date to restore the growth of general business productivity to the average rate of the postwar years. In contrast with popular perceptions, the productivity problem is not in those industries most subject to increased foreign competition, but in the larger service sector. The reasons for the substantial decline in the growth of productivity in the service sector are not yet clear.

Real Wages, Earnings, and Income

The record of real wage rates and income during the first term of the Reagan administration, as indicated in Table 7.3, was mixed. Real wage rates increased very slowly, compared to a slight decline during the Carter administration. (The official series indicates a substantial decline in real wage rates during the Carter administration. This series, however, is based on the consumer price index, which, as will be discussed in the next section, substantially overestimated inflation through 1981.) The very slow growth of real wage rates since 1973 is one of the more disturbing characteristics of the American economy, and it has continued despite the recent increase in productivity growth. Real wage and salary income per adult increased at the same

Table 7.3 Real Personal Income Per Adult*

	Carter Administration	Reagan Administration
Hourly earnings	−0.2	0.3
Employee income	1.0	1.0
Proprietor income	−2.3	−0.9
Investment income	5.8	5.1
Transfer payments	1.9	1.0
Personal income	1.4	1.2
Disposable income	1.1	1.5

*Percentage change, annual rate.

rate as during the Carter administration, despite a slower growth of the employment rate.

Other components of personal income reflect larger differences. Real proprietor income (to the owners of farms and other noncorporate businesses) declined during the first term, but at a slower rate. George Gilder's "age of the entrepreneur" apparently has not yet arrived. Investment income (from rents, dividends, and interest) was the most rapidly growing component of personal income in both periods. This reflected the increase in interest rates, the availability of new financial instruments such as the money market funds, and the deregulation of deposit rates. The increase in real interest rates, about which so much concern has been expressed, was clearly a boon to those Americans who have accumulated some savings. And reflecting the change in budget policy, real transfer payments per adult increased less during the first term than during the Carter administration.

The growth of total real personal income per adult was lower during the first term than during the Carter administration. The net effect of Reagan's policies to reduce both transfer payments and tax rates, however, increased the growth of real disposable income per adult. (The effects of these policies on the distribution of income are discussed in the next chapter.) Over time the growth of disposable income will converge on the growth of total personal income unless conditions permit another reduction in tax rates.

Inflation

The most substantial improvement in U.S. economic conditions during the first term, of course, was the dramatic decline in the rate of inflation. Figure 7.3 illustrates the pattern of inflation during the

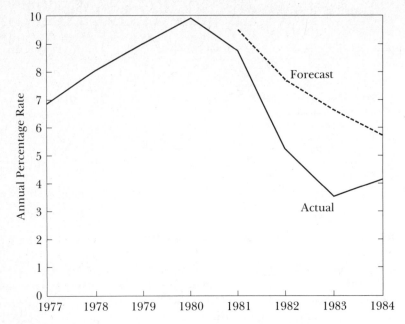

Figure 7.3   General Inflation Rate (percent change during year)

Carter administration, the first term of the Reagan administration, and the 1981 forecasts of the inflation rate. As this figure shows, the broadest measure of inflation (the implicit price deflator for GNP) declined about six percentage points relative to the peak in 1980 and (not shown) to the lowest rate since 1967. Moreover, the actual inflation rate during the first term was substantially lower than the 1981 forecast.

Many readers will observe that the consumer price index increased at a more rapid rate through 1981 than indicated by Figure 7.3. Until this index was revised in 1983, however, the price of housing was measured by the price of new houses and mortgage rates rather than by the "rental equivalence" of existing houses. As shown in Figure 7.4, this led the consumer price index to overstate the rate of inflation on consumer goods and services (relative to the more accurate fixed-weight deflator on consumer expenditures) during the period when new house prices and mortgage rates were increasing rapidly. By 1981 the cumulative overstatement in the price level was about 10 percent. Use of the consumer price index to deflate wage and income estimates unfortunately led to a false impression that real wages were declining rapidly and the continuing impression that the poverty rate was increasing rapidly. (The new consumer price

Figure 7.4 Comparative Inflation Rates (percent change during year)

index is now a more accurate measure of current inflation, but the
historical data for this index, real wage rates, and the poverty rate
have not been revised to correct this bias.) A more important problem is that the major government transfer programs and some important private labor contracts are indexed to the consumer price
index. This technical flaw in the consumer price index prior to 1983
thus contributed to the rapid growth of real transfer payments and
the increase of real wage rates in such industries as autos and steel.

The substantial decline in inflation was the result of four interrelated conditions, none of which were fully anticipated. The most
obvious condition, as discussed in Chapter 5, was the substantial reduction in the growth of the money supply from late 1979 through
mid-1982. As discussed earlier, money growth through mid-1982 was
also somewhat lower than the initial Reagan guidance to the Federal
Reserve. The rapid increase in money growth since mid-1982 did
not increase the inflation rate, at least through 1987, primarily because of the decline of the "velocity" of money, a second condition

that was not anticipated and is not yet broadly understood. The third important condition was the sharp increase in the real foreign exchange value of the dollar from mid-1980 through early 1985, a condition that was primarily the result of the change in U.S. fiscal policy. The increase in the real exchange rate reduced the current price of imports and, through competitive effects, the real price of exports and domestic import-competing goods. The fourth condition was the growing supply of oil, beginning in the spring of 1981— a condition that was partly related to the increase in the real exchange rate.

The general inflation rate in 1984, as already mentioned, was about six percentage points lower than the peak rate in 1980. An exact accounting of the effect of specific conditions on the reduction in inflation is not possible because the several important conditions are somewhat interrelated. A crude accounting, however, would attribute about two percentage points each to the reduction of money growth through mid-1982, the decline of money velocity, and the combined effects of an increase in the real exchange rate and the increased supply of oil. The monetary policy of the Federal Reserve thus was directly responsible for only about one-third of the decline in the inflation rate. The deregulation of bank deposit interest rates beginning in 1980 may have been partly responsible for the decline of money velocity. Federal fiscal policy was primarily responsible for the increase in the real exchange rate, and the deregulation of oil contributed to the decline in oil prices. The substantial decline in the inflation rate during the early 1980s thus was not primarily due to a lower rate of money growth.

Moreover, the continued low inflation rates through 1987 were clearly inconsistent with the sharp increase in money growth beginning in late 1982. As a rule the rate of general inflation had been about equal to the rate of money growth two years earlier. The continued low inflation is therefore wholly attributable to the deadline in money velocity, the increase in the real exchange rate through early 1985, and the decline in oil prices in early 1986. As explained in Chapter 5, monetary policy is still important, but other conditions clearly dominated the changes in the inflation rate through 1987.

Although the popular and political concern about inflation nearly disappeared in the mid-1980s, there is no reason to be complacent about inflation. An inflation rate of 4 percent is only slightly lower than that which led President Nixon to impose price and wage controls in 1971 and is much higher than the longer-term U.S. experience until the 1970s. Moreover, several recent conditions threaten to increase the inflation rate. Money growth has been unusually high since mid-1982, a condition that the September 1985 G-5 agreement reinforced. The foreign exchange value of the dollar has declined substantially since early 1985; this effect was only partly mitigated by the sharp break in oil prices in early 1986. A possible imposition of some form of a value-added tax would lead to a one-time increase in the price level in the year it is levied. And the continued huge federal deficit, although not directly inflationary, presents a strong political incentive to reinflate. President Reagan has continued to support a goal of zero inflation, but the institutional rules that would be necessary to achieve this goal have not yet been implemented. In 1988 Republican candidates may face the awkward task of explaining why the substantial decline in the inflation rate through 1987 was only a temporary condition.

Interest Rates

Market (or nominal) interest rates declined substantially during the first term. Real interest rates (market interest rates minus the anticipated inflation) increased substantially, however. Figure 7.5 illustrates the level of both nominal and real interest rates from 1975 through 1984. As this figure reveals, nominal interest rates increased rapidly through mid-1981 (interrupted only by the short recession in 1980), declined sharply through the 1981–1982 recession, increased somewhat through mid-1984, and (not shown) declined through 1986. Moreover, although the level of nominal interest rates reflects anticipated inflation, most of the variation in nominal interest rates reflects a corresponding variation of real interest rates.

In the short run, interest rates reflect conditions in both financial markets and the real economy. In the long run, however, interest rates are determined by the after-tax rate of return on real assets and the anticipated rate of inflation. The unusual level and variability of real interest rates since mid-1979 reflects a combination of conditions. The sharp increase in interest rates in late 1979 was due to the sharp reduction in money growth associated with the new monetary policy implemented in October. The sharp break in interest rates in the spring of 1980 was clearly due to the credit controls and the associated short, sharp recession. Interest rates increased to record levels in 1981 for two reasons: renewed monetary restraint and the 1981 tax legislation, which reduced the average tax rate on new investment by about four percentage points. A reversal of these conditions led to another sharp break in interest rates in 1982; money growth increased rapidly after mid-1982, and the 1982 tax legislation increased the average tax rates on new investment by about 1.5 percentage points. The increase in interest rates in 1983 and 1984, as in 1977 and 1978, was a normal effect of cyclical recovery.

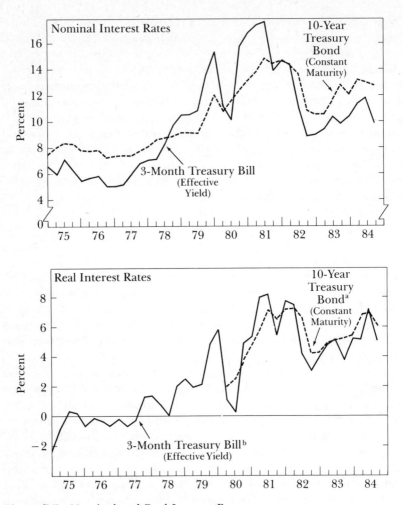

Figure 7.5 Nominal and Real Interest Rates

[a] Nominal yield less anticipated rate of inflation (as measured by change in GNP implicit price deflator) over period to maturity from National Bureau of Economic Research/American Statistical Association *Economic Outlook Survey*.

[b] Nominal yield less anticipated rate of inflation (as measured by change in consumer price index) over period to maturity from *Decision-Makers Poll* by Richard B. Hoey.

Average real interest rates in 1984 were about four percentage points higher than average rates in 1980. About 2.5 percentage points' difference, I believe, was due to the combined effect of the 1981 and 1982 tax legislation on the after-tax return on investment. The additional increase of 1.5 percentage points was, I believe, primarily due to the difference in cyclical conditions between 1980 and 1984, an increase roughly equal to that in prior cyclical recoveries. Real interest rates in 1985 and 1986 (not shown) declined again. The most plausible explanation of this decline was a combination of slower real growth and a decline in the effects of the 1981–1982 tax legislation on new investment. The 1986 tax legislation, which increased the tax rate on new investment, also appeared to reduce the demand for new investment. I do not attribute a substantial effect of the federal deficit to interest rates at any time during this period—a position I will address later in this chapter.

Exchange Rates

The foreign exchange value of the dollar (on a multilateral trade-weighted basis) increased about 72 percent from the summer of 1980 to the fall of 1984 after declining substantially during the Carter administration. The dollar appreciated most against the European currencies and much less against the currencies of our major trading partners. Over this period, for example, the dollar appreciated 96 percent against the British pound, 72 percent against the German mark, 14 percent against the Canadian dollar, and only 12 percent against the Japanese yen. Moreover, most of this increase reflected real conditions rather than a change in relative inflation rates; the real multilateral exchange rate increased about 65 percent over this period. This extraordinary increase in the real exchange rate reduced the dollar price of U.S. imports, increased the foreign price of U.S. exports, and was the mechanism that led to the large increase in net imports.

Most observers attributed the increase in the dollar to the increase in U.S. interest rates and, in turn, to whatever caused the increase in interest rates. In fact, the dollar increased almost steadily over the first term, U.S. interest rates (as shown on Figure 7.5) were highly variable, and there was no significant relation between the changes in the exchange rate and changes in interest rates. The relation between exchange rates and interest rates is more complex. Specifically, the difference between the current and forward exchange rate with a specific foreign currency tends to equal the difference between the U.S. and foreign interest rates. In other words, an increase in the difference in interest rates will increase the current exchange rate by an equal amount only when the forward exchange rate does not change, such as when the increase in the difference in interest rates is expected to be temporary. This relation, called the "covered parity" condition, is strongly consistent with the evidence and was about the same in the late 1970s and the early 1980s. For both periods, changes in the current and forward exchange rates were closely related, which is why there was little relation between changes in the current exchange rate and in U.S. interest rates.

This more complex perspective on the relation of exchange rates and interest rates is also useful in sorting out the reasons for the large increase in the real exchange value of the dollar during the early 1980s. In the guarded language of one scholar, the small effect of changes in the difference of real interest rates "suggests that an increase in the long-run equilibrium value of the dollar, resulting from changes in the taxation of capital, cannot be ruled out as a possible reason for the recent strength of the dollar" and "raise[s] doubts about the magnitude of the decline in the dollar that could be expected from a deficit reduction package that did not affect the tax changes instituted in the early 1980s." The effect of an increased government deficit on the exchange rate is variable, depending on the conditions that lead to the increased deficit. A recession, for example, would increase the deficit but reduce the real exchange rate. Conversely, a reduction in tax rates that increases private domestic investment would increase the long-run real exchange rate.

The effects of the Reagan policies on the real exchange rate were mixed. As described earlier, these policies led to increased real growth of both private consumption and investment. During the first term the net effect of these policies clearly increased the real exchange rate. The dollar peaked in February 1985, however, and declined substantially for the next two years. Most observers attributed this decline to a change in U.S. exchange-rate intervention policy, first suggested by Secretary Regan at the G-5 meeting in January 1985 and reaffirmed by Secretary Baker at the G-5 meeting in September. An increased amount of sterilized intervention (which does not change the domestic money supply), however, would not have had this effect. The more important signal is that the United States appeared willing to increase money growth to reduce domestic interest rates and the dollar. And Japan, in order to defer U.S. protectionist measures, was willing to reduce money growth to increase Japanese interest rates and the yen. These policies may have contributed to the substantial decline in the current exchange rate for the dollar but will have no effect on the longer-term real exchange rate. A more important reason was the proposed change in U.S. tax policy. The Treasury tax plan announced in late November 1984, the president's plan of May 1985, and the Ways and Means bill, the major provisions of which were announced about the time of the G-5 agreement, would each substantially increase the effective tax rate on business investment. The increasing prospect of this tax change reduced the real exchange rate with no change in the difference in interest rates. This effect, however, was again inadvertent. The Treasury's current understanding of the effects of taxes on exchange rates does not appear to have improved since 1981.

The effects of future policies on the real exchange rate will depend importantly on how spending and taxes are changed. An increase in the tax rates on business investment, as approved in 1986, will reduce the real exchange rate (if these changes were not fully anticipated), whether or not the deficit is reduced. Conversely, a reduction of the federal deficit by means that reduce private saving and the state and local surplus by an equal amount would not change the long-run real exchange rate. Again, the details are important. One should not expect changes in the government deficit per se to provide much useful information about expected changes in the exchange rate.

PUZZLES

For some time both the administration and the economics profession were confused about the unusual combination of economic conditions during the first term. The most puzzling conditions during this period were the combination of high real interest rates, the rapid increase in the real exchange rate, the rapid decline of the foreign accounts balance, and the rapid growth of real domestic investment. Many observers tended to attribute most of these economic conditions to the most conspicuous policy outcome during this period—the rapid increase in the federal deficit.

Interest Rates and Exchange Rates

The first of these conditions to become apparent were the high level of real interest rates and the increase in the real exchange rate, conditions that persisted despite the 1981–1982 recession. The administration was understandably defensive in response to the conventional attribution of these conditions to the federal deficit. The Treasury's initial explanations of these conditions, however, were both wrong and inconsistent. The initial explanation of the high real interest rates was suggested by Prof. Allan Meltzer, a leading monetary economist and consultant to Beryl Sprinkel. The Meltzer-Sprinkel explanation was that the high real interest rates were due to the high variability of money growth and interest rates; that is, the higher real rates reflected an increased risk premium to compensate lenders for increased variability. This explanation did not withstand a detailed examination of the longer-term U.S. experience, initially by the CEA and later by academic economists. A later study suggests that average interest rates may decline in response to an increased variability, by reducing the demand for funds more than the supply. Moreover, the Treasury explanation was not consistent with the rise in the dollar, as higher interest rates would not strengthen the dollar if the increase was only a premium for increased risk.

The Treasury's first explanation for the increase in the real exchange rate was that political instability abroad increased the demand for "safe-haven" investments in dollars. This was a plausible explanation, particularly in the summer of 1982 after France and Mexico nationalized their banks and there was some flow of funds to dollars in anticipation of a devaluation. A later study, however, indicates that there was no increase in the political risk premium, at least with respect to the currencies of Europe and Japan, during this period. Moreover, the Treasury's safe-haven explanation was not consistent with the higher U.S. real interest rates. If the dollar had strengthened primarily because of a flow of funds seeking a safe haven, U.S. interest rates would have declined relative to those in other nations.

Martin Feldstein, soon after he was confirmed in late 1982, became the spokesman for the conventional interpretation of several of these conditions. The increase in the federal deficit, according to Feldstein, increases real interest rates, which in turn increases the real exchange rate, which then reduces the foreign account balance. Although this perspective was widely shared among economists and journalists, there are a number of problems with this explanation. First, there was (and is) surprisingly little evidence that government borrowing has a substantial effect on interest rates. Conventional macroeconomic theory suggests that an increase in the deficit would increase interest rates through two processes, by increasing demand and by reducing the net supply of saving. The effect of the deficit on demand, however, is insignificant, and the effect on net saving is very small relative to the total stock of capital. Controlling for other conditions that affect interest rates, economists have found it very difficult to estimate the effects of the deficit using even the most refined statistical techniques.

In response to both Feldstein and outside critics, the Treasury Office of Economic Policy conducted a careful empirical study of these effects. This study, released in May 1984, found no significant effect of deficits on interest rates but did not offer an alternative explanation of the high real interest rates. The Congressional Budget Office reviewed a large number of studies of this relation in a study released in February 1985; most of these studies also found little effect of the deficits on interest rates. The available studies do not provide a basis for rejecting any effect of the deficit on interest rates; they suggest, however, that other conditions affecting interest rates are much larger than the effects of the deficit. Another problem of the Feldstein chain, as explained in the foregoing section, is that there is no simple relation between interest rates and exchange rates. A later study, however, indicated that the federal deficit significantly reduced the foreign accounts balance during the years since the floating of exchange rates. The Feldstein chain thus was a partial explanation of the declining foreign account balance but an inadequate explanation of the increase in real interest rates and the dollar.

A more important problem of the Feldstein chain became apparent as the recovery developed in 1983. If real interest rates were high primarily because of the increased federal deficit, real domestic investment would be unusually weak. In fact, real domestic investment increased at a higher rate in 1983 and 1984 than during the typical recovery. Over this period, Bill Poole and I at CEA and Manuel Johnson at Treasury developed an alternative perspective: the increase in real interest rates was primarily due to an increase in the demand for domestic investment as a result of the business investment incentives of the 1981 tax law. Without a later increase in the tax rates on business investment, moreover, real interest rates, the real exchange rate, and the foreign account deficit should be expected to decline only slowly until the business capital stock increased to the higher desired level. Because the net effect of the 1981 and 1982 tax laws increased the desired stock of business fixed capital by about $200 billion and the 1981–1982 recession temporarily reduced net investment, real interest rates may not return to their prior average level until the end of the decade. A reduction in the federal deficit would accelerate this process only to the extent that it would increase net domestic business investment.

A brief discussion with Feldstein about this issue in January 1984 was not sufficient to change his perspective. As it turned out, this ten-minute discussion was the longest sustained discussion about a professional issue that Bill Poole and I had with Feldstein in the nearly two years he served as CEA chairman. After Feldstein left, the developing consensus on this issue was first expressed in the 1985 *Economic Report:*

It is difficult to sort out the relative magnitudes of the effects on real interest rates of monetary restriction, large budget deficits, and high real rates of return on new business investment. It seems likely, however, that over the 1981–1984 period as a whole, and certainly over the recovery years of 1983 and 1984, the effect flowing from a higher rate of return on new business investment has dominated. The evidence for that proposition is the coexistence of a high real rate of interest and great strength of business investment. If the monetary or budget deficit effects had dominated, then high interest rates for these reasons would have overwhelmed the incentives to invest, making business investment relatively weak rather than relatively strong.

This controversy is not over, however. Economists are still trying to sort out the relative effects of these several conditions on real interest rates. And politicians still choose whatever explanation serves their temporary purpose.

The Foreign Account Balance

A related puzzle is what led to the rapid decline in the U.S. foreign account balance. The simple answer is that imports increased more than exports, but that begs the question of what led to these conditions. For most of the postwar years, net foreign investment by the United States was positive and small, increased during U.S. recessions, and was negative only during some peak recovery years. (Net foreign investment is roughly equal to the current account balance on the trade accounts. The current account balance in turn is equal to the merchandise trade balance plus the balance on services, investment income, and transfers. Since 1971 the merchandise trade balance has been consistently lower than the current account balance.) During the Reagan years through 1986, however, net foreign investment by the United States declined from $13 billion to −$144 billion. This change was the net effect of a huge reduction in U.S. investment abroad and a small increase in foreign investment in the United States.

What led to this dramatic change? An understanding of this condition must be based on a recognition that the U.S. foreign account balance, the difference between exports and broadly defined imports, is also equal to the difference between saving by Americans and investment in the United States. Table 7.4 summarizes the relation of the foreign and domestic balances of the United States from 1975 through 1979 and 1982 through 1986, comparable periods that reflect the recoveries from the recessions of 1974 and 1975 and of 1981 and 1982.

The recovery from the recession of 1974 and 1975 illustrates the

Table 7.4 The Relation of U.S. Foreign and Domestic Balances

Year	NFI	=	X	−	M	=	PS	−	GD	−	PI[a]
1975	1.4		10.1		8.7		19.2		4.1		13.7
1976	0.5		10.0		9.5		18.2		2.2		15.6
1977	−0.4		9.6		10.1		17.8		1.0		17.3
1978	−0.4		10.1		10.6		18.1		0.0		18.5
1979	0.1		11.7		11.6		17.1		−0.5		18.1
1982	−0.0		11.4		11.5		17.6		3.5		14.1
1983	−1.0		10.4		11.3		17.5		3.8		14.7
1984	−2.4		10.2		12.6		18.0		2.8		17.6
1985	−2.9		9.2		12.1		16.4		3.3		16.0
1986	−3.4		8.9		12.3		15.9		3.5		15.8

[a] As a percentage of GNP.
NFI = net foreign investment.
X = exports plus net capital grants received by the United States.
M = imports plus net transfer payments and interest payments by the government to foreigners.
PS = gross private saving plus the statistical discrepancy.
GD = total (federal, state, and local) government deficit.
PI = gross private domestic investment.

usual cyclical pattern. From 1975 through 1979, net foreign investment declined by 1.3 percent of GNP even though the combined government budget changed from a large deficit to a small surplus. The recovery from the 1981–1982 recession, however, illustrates a very different pattern. From 1982 through 1986, net foreign investment declined by 3.4 percent of GNP, even though the government deficit share of GNP was roughly stable. These relations indicate that *annual* changes in net foreign investment have not been closely related to changes in the government deficit.

A comparison of the comparable recovery years 1979 and 1986, however, illustrates a stronger relation of net foreign investment and the government deficit. Net foreign investment was lower by 3.5 percent of GNP in 1986, in combination with an increase in the government deficit of 4.0 percent of GNP. This last comparison indicates that the large recent decline in the U.S. balance of payments was due not to an increase in the government deficit but to the fact that the deficit did not decline as usual during the recovery years. As of 1986 the U.S. balance-of-payments deficit was almost identical to the combined government-sector deficit. In other words, given the current rate of U.S. saving and domestic investment, the United States would have no balance-of-payments deficit if the combined government-sector deficit had been eliminated, as is usually the case, during the recovery years.

This discussion also illustrates the futility of attempts to reduce the foreign account deficit by measures to increase exports or reduce imports—a lesson that the administration and Congress have not yet learned. In the absence of any change in the balance of domestic saving and investment, an increase in exports or a reduction in imports would increase the real exchange rate, in either case without changing the net foreign balance. Trade measures by themselves affect the volume of trade but not the trade balance. My own presentations on this issue to the cabinet and Congress unfortunately fell on deaf ears. The large deficit on our foreign accounts is a proper subject of policy concern, but it must be addressed not by export promotion or import restraints but by measures to increase the balance of domestic saving and investment. The measures by which this balance is increased are also important. An increase in private saving, a reduction in the government deficit, or a reduction in private investment would have the same effect on the net foreign balance but would have very different effects on future U.S. economic growth.

The Saving Rate

A final puzzle became apparent only in the second term. In 1986 the personal saving rate declined to 4.3 percent, the lowest rate since 1949, despite continued high real interest rates. The low average rate of personal saving in the United States is a cause for concern, but the decline in this rate since 1984 should not have been a surprise. Some part of the decline in the saving rate is attributable to changes in the age composition of the population. During the 1980s the population of Americans between twenty-five and forty-four years old and of those sixty-five and older has increased rapidly. Both groups have characteristically low saving rates. The population of Americans between forty-five and sixty-four years old—the group with the highest saving rate—has increased very slowly.

The decline in the measured saving rate in 1986, however, was an artifact of the way we measure saving. An increase in spending for consumer durables, for example, is measured as an increase in personal consumption expenditures, although much of this increase is an increase in household net worth. In light of the continued strong growth of real spending for consumer durables through 1986, the measured saving rate clearly understates the actual rate. In addition, our national income accounts do not include increases in the value of financial assets in measured saving. The boom in stock and bond prices through 1986, however, clearly increased household wealth. A more comprehensive measure of saving that approximates the change in the net worth of Americans would clearly have shown an increase in the effective saving rate during this period.

Our saving rate, however measured, is still the lowest of the major industrial nations. And there is a strong correlation across countries in the growth of productivity and the saving rate. There continues to be a strong case for reducing the remaining biases against saving in our tax system, biases that were not changed much by the 1986 tax legislation.

AN INTERIM EVALUATION

Americans are pragmatic and sometimes impatient about economic policies. Long experience has led them to discount the promises of politicians and the forecasts of economists. As voters they react more to recent economic conditions than to the prospective effects of economic policies. For the most part this is a healthy condition. The promises of politicians are much alike, and most voters should not be expected to understand the relation between policies and conditions. Our political system, however, leads to several types of bias in the choice of economic policies. First, there is a strong bias to choose policies with favorable short-term results at the expense of conditions beyond the term of office. Carter's inflation and Reagan's deficits are the the consequences of this bias. Second, if current conditions are sufficient for reelection, there is little incentive to do even better—a bias that was the source of Reagan's missed opportunities. And third, voters prefer higher government spending for programs they value, but lower taxes. Although this is a rational preference for each voter, our political system seems increasingly unable to resolve the inherent conflict of these preferences. This conflict reflects an erosion of the explicit and implicit constitutional rules that previously constrained the extent of discretion in federal economic policies.

CHAPTER EIGHT

Winners and Losers

President Reagan had reason to hope that his economic program would lead to "a brighter future for all of our citizens." That was a more reasonable hope than most such political rhetoric. The general objectives of the program were higher growth and lower inflation—not a redistribution of income by industry, occupation, income group, race, or region. Only the budget plan, by increasing defense spending and reducing the growth of transfer payments and social services, had clear distributional implications. The tax proposals of both 1981 and 1985 were specifically designed to lead to a roughly proportionate reduction in taxes across income groups. A reduction in inflation would help families at all income levels who were dependent on fixed incomes. At the beginning of this program, there was a reasonable basis for most Americans to expect a brighter future.

Any change in economic policies and conditions, however, will lead to some winners and some losers. This chapter summarizes the combined effects of the changes in economic policies and general economic conditions on the conditions of the major component groups in the American economy. Most Americans are indifferent to the reasons for a change in their economic conditions. A policy analyst, however, does not have this freedom. For this reason I will try to identify the changes in the conditions of specific groups that were most clearly the result of changes in economic policies, although this is not always possible.

CHANGES AFFECTING GAINS AND LOSSES

Some changes in the distribution of economic activity and income were inherent in the initial Reagan program. The rapid growth of defense procurement was expected to change the distribution of manufacturing employment among industries and regions. The reduction of transfer payments to those above the poverty line would reduce the growth of income in the lower-middle class (roughly the second quintile of the income distribution) unless offset by an increase in earnings. The reduction in personal tax rates was expected to increase the relative income of the employed. The reduction in the effective tax rates on new business investment was expected to increase the growth of real business investment and the industries that produce investment goods. The program of regulatory relief had little direct distributional effects, except those operating through an increase in productivity. A reduction of inflation was expected to benefit most those who are dependent on fixed incomes and to reduce market interest rates; there was also reason to expect that a reduction in the general inflation rate would lead to a relative weakness of commodity prices and the incomes of those in commodity-producing industries and regions. The general economic program was expected to increase real corporate profits and stock prices. Most of these expected distributional effects of the initial program were not widely discussed, but they should not have been a surprise. As the record demonstrates, all these expected effects were realized.

The most important changes in the distribution of economic activity and income during the first term, however, were the result of changes in general economic conditions, as summarized in Chapter 7, that were *not* anticipated. Employment, real earnings, and real personal income increased at a lower rate than during the Carter administration. The inflation rate declined more rapidly than was anticipated. Real interest rates increased substantially. And, probably most important, the real foreign exchange value of the dollar increased dramatically. The unanticipated changes in the distribution of economic activity resulting from these conditions were substantial, in some cases reinforcing the effects of the anticipated changes. The major changes in the distribution of economic activity among industries and regions led to substantial tensions in our political system, even though general economic conditions improved.

CHANGES IN EMPLOYMENT AND EARNINGS

Most people earn most of their income by working. A summary of the changes in employment and earnings among groups thus reveals most of the important changes in the distribution of income. This section summarizes the changes in employment and earnings during the first term of the Reagan administration by industry, occupation, race, and sex.

Changes by Industry

Table 8.1 summarizes changes in employment and average real weekly earnings by major industry during the first term. For comparison,

Table 8.1 Employment and Earnings by Industry*

Industry	Employment	Average Real Weekly Earnings
Agriculture	−1.3	N.A.
Mining	−5.2	1.6
Construction	0.0	−0.6
Manufacturing	−4.3	3.6
Transportation and utilities	0.5	−0.2
Wholesale and retail trade	9.0	−2.0
Financial services	10.1	5.9
Other services	16.0	5.1
Government	−0.9	N.A.
Other self-employment	9.5	N.A.

*Percentage change, 1980–1984.

total employment increased 5.7 percent during this period, and average real earnings increased only slightly.

The changes in employment reveal a general pattern of lower employment in the goods-producing industries and higher employment in the service industries (other than government). The largest reductions in employment were in the agriculture, mining, and manufacturing industries most subject to import competition—a direct result of the rapid increase in the real exchange rate and real imports. The most rapid increase in employment was in the broad range of business, travel, and professional services.

To what extent were these changes attributable to the change in economic policies during this period? The problems of several of the weak industries were closely related to the increases in real interest rates and exchange rates, conditions that I attribute primarily to the business investment incentives in the 1981 tax legislation. Some of the problems were related to policies affecting a specific industry.

Agriculture was whipsawed by a combination of conditions affected by both general and specific policies. The combination of a strong dollar, the high loan rates established by the 1981 farm legislation, and increasing farm output abroad reduced total real farm exports by 27 percent and net real farm exports by 38 percent during the first term. As a consequence of the rapid increase in farm supports, however, the total resources used in agriculture declined

only a few percent, and average net real farm income (excluding
capital losses) was about the same as in 1980. A continued increase
in farm output, combined with the decline in exports, reduced the
real price of farm products by 15 percent and the average real price
of farm land by 19 percent during the first term, and the price of
farm land declined sharply again in 1985. The financial problems in
the farm sector, manifested by a wave of foreclosures and agricultural bank failures in 1985, were primarily due to the decline in the
price of farm land and were focused on those farmers who borrowed at the high interest rates through 1981 to buy land. Farmers
who had not increased their debt were less affected. The primary
remaining problems of the farm sector are the high budget costs to
maintain the level of resources in farming and the vulnerability of
the farm credit system.

Mining, other than oil and gas extraction, was affected by the
combination of weak demand by the domestic materials industries
and the strong dollar. The real price of crude materials (other than
farm products and energy) declined 19 percent during the first term
and declined sharply again in 1985. In the face of declining output,
employment in mining was especially affected by the high union wage
rates and benefits. Output of the construction industry declined slightly
during the first term, in part because of the increase in real interest
rates, but there was little change in either employment or real earnings.

Most of the turmoil in output and employment in this period was
within the manufacturing sector, and much of the change was related to the change in economic policies. Defense production and
employment increased in response to the large increase in real defense procurement. Auto employment increased in response to a
higher growth of real disposable income and the four-year quotas
on Japanese imports. The basic materials industries experienced the
largest loss of employment, primarily because of the strong dollar
and the increase in imports. Total manufacturing employment declined, despite an increase in output, primarily because of a strong
growth of productivity and the continued growth of real wages.

The major conditions leading to the strong growth of service employment were the combination of the higher growth rate of real
disposable income and low productivity growth. Although real personal income increased at a lower rate than during the Carter administration, the reduction in individual income taxes approved in
1981 contributed to this temporarily higher growth of real consumer
spending. Conditions in specific sectors were also affected by other
policies. Deregulation contributed to an increase in employment in
airlines, trucking, and financial institutions. A continued growth of

federal health spending contributed to the continued growth of health services. In general, however, those who gained from these changes in economic policy were less visible in the political debate than the losers.

As these changes in employment became apparent in 1983, a chorus of businessmen, union leaders, politicians, journalists, and some academics decried "the deindustrialization of America" and called for an "industrial policy" to revive American industry. During the 1984 campaign Walter Mondale portrayed the future of Reaganomics as one of Americans sweeping up around Japanese computers. This perspective is best characterized as opportunism based on a misreading of the evidence. First, the share of total employment in the goods-producing industries has been declining for more than thirty years, and the rate of decline during the Reagan years was not unusual. Second, the measured decline in this share is somewhat misleading; goods-producing firms have been increasingly contracting for business services that were previously supplied within the firm. Most important, the goods share of the total output increased during the Reagan years to the highest share in more than a decade, with a corresponding decline in the service share of total output. In terms of what we produce, America is not deindustrializing.

The 1983 proposals for some form of industrial policy, promoted primarily by congressional Democrats, proved to be abortive. The general objective of these proposals was to establish a comprehensive federal policy affecting the composition of U.S. output and employment. The specific proposals, in various forms, called for a formal interagency group to coordinate federal policies affecting major industries, government-industry-labor advisory groups for each major industry, and a federal financing bank to provide subsidized loans to specific industries. These proposals floundered for several reasons. Strong general economic growth through mid-1984 diffused the pressure for a change in policy. The advocates of industrial policy never resolved whether they wanted to assist emerging industries or problem industries. The administration was mildly critical of these proposals but characteristically deferred the issue by appointing a presidential commission on international competitiveness and a tripartite steel advisory committee, both groups to report after the 1984 election. The White House, however, approved the publication of a critical review of these issues in the 1984 *Economic Report*. Charles Schultze, the CEA chairman in the Carter administration, deserves substantial credit for his forceful criticism of the intellectual case for the industrial policy proposals.

These issues will not go away, however. Current federal policies affect the composition of industry in many ways, sometimes by design, sometimes by inadvertence, sometimes in contradictory ways. In effect the United States already has a very complex implicit industrial policy. Moreover, any change in economic policies and conditions will create some losers, and these groups will try to use the political process to limit or reverse their losses. And most members of Congress in both parties have a strong preference for interventionist policies that appear to benefit their specific constituencies. The 1986 trade bills, for example, revived the proposals for tripartite industry advisory committees and for a large trade-adjustment assistance fund. The case for relying on the market to organize production, both within countries and across countries, will have to be defended again and again.

The American economy, of course, is more complex than can be adequately summarized by the average changes in ten major industries. There was a considerable change in the composition of employment within many of these major industries. Employment in oil and gas extraction, for example, increased (until the sharp decline in energy prices in 1986), although employment in other mining industries declined. Employment increased in the manufacturing industries producing defense and civilian high-technology goods, although employment declined in most other manufacturing industries; in general, there was a rapid increase in productivity in the manufacturing sector. Deregulation contributed to an increase in employment in airlines and trucking and a rapid increase in productivity in airlines and railroads. Federal defense-related employment increased, and local government employment declined. In general, employment declined in industries with a high proportion of union labor.

Changes in average real earnings by industry during this period were only loosely related to the changes in employment. Real earnings increased most in the rapidly growing private service industries. Real earnings also increased, however, in mining and manufacturing, despite a decline in employment. In general, the effect of unions has been to maintain some growth of average real earnings even in industries subject to a decline in employment.

Changes by Occupation and Sex

Table 8.2 summarizes changes in employment by major occupational group and sex during the first term. For comparison, total employment of men increased 3.3 percent during this period, and total employment of women increased 9.0 percent. (Changes in real earnings by occupation unfortunately cannot be estimated because of a change

Table 8.2   Employment by Occupation and Sex*

Occupation	Men	Women
Managers	7.1	28.0
Professionals	9.5	15.6
Technicians	3.4	22.7
Sales	10.2	23.0
Clerical	−1.0	0.9
Service	8.6	8.1
Skilled production workers	4.0	41.9
Transport operators	−2.1	20.0
Machine operators	−10.7	−8.1
Other production workers	−2.1	−22.0
Farming, forestry, fishing	−0.5	−3.2

*Percentage change, 1980–1984.

in the occupational classification system beginning in 1983.) These changes reflect three general patterns. First, the employment of women increased much more rapidly than the employment of men. Second, there was a general upgrading of the occupational skills of male employees and a dramatic increase in the occupational skills of female employees. And third, employment declined most in occupations with a high proportion of union labor; even in union occupations, however, the number of women employed as skilled production workers and transport operators increased rapidly. The small changes in clerical employment probably reflect the effects of office computerization. These changes in employment by occupation of course also reflect the changes by industry—in particular, the general shift of employment from goods production to service production.

These changes represent a combination of problems, opportunities, and puzzles. The major problem is for workers with low skills; for these workers, employment declined in the goods industries, and average real earnings declined in the service industries. The major opportunity is for women; the number of women employed in higher-skilled occupations in both the goods and service industries increased dramatically. The major puzzle is why the general upgrading of occupational skills was not accompanied by a significant increase in average real earnings. The apparent explanation of this puzzle is that average real earnings declined in some of the higher-skilled occupations. The major losers in this process, which became more visible only during the Reagan years, were those for whom union employment formerly provided wages above their labor market alternatives.

Changes by Race and Sex

Table 8.3 summarizes changes in employment and median real earnings by race and sex during the first term. Again for reference, total employment increased 5.7 percent, and median real earnings increased 1.1 percent. The differences in these changes by race and sex were dramatic, although they are not broadly recognized. For white men, both employment and real earnings increased very slowly. For minority men, employment increased strongly, but median real earnings declined. For women, both employment and median real earnings increased strongly, with the largest gains among minority women. Over this period, therefore, women and minorities increased their share of total employment, and the median earnings of women increased relative to those of men. The ratio of the median earnings of whites and minorities, however, did not change.

The Reagan administration was regularly criticized for opposing policies that were specifically designed to help women and minorities. In general, these criticisms were accurate but misleading. They were accurate in that the administration generally opposed policies that created special preferences by race or sex. They were misleading in that the administration believed that a strong, competitive labor market is the best way to break down employment discrimination. The data summarized above support the administration's case: the employment of women and minorities increased strongly with only a few new policies specifically designed for this objective.

In a few cases the administration supported some preferences by race or sex. Although it opposed racial quotas for employment, it maintained support for some types of affirmative action. Several changes in the tax code and pension legislation were specifically designed to help women. The administration usually sidestepped these issues, however, because of the tension between its general policies and political pressures.

Table 8.3   Employment and Earnings by Race and Sex*

Race and Sex	Employment	Median Real Earnings
White		
Men	2.6	0.4
Women	8.4	4.0
Other		
Men	9.4	−1.1
Women	13.1	5.2

*Percentage change, 1980–1984.

In one case I made the mistake of talking about one of these issues too soon. In early November 1984, in a debate before a group of professional women in Washington, I described the proposals for setting the wages of men and women on the basis of the "comparable worth" of their occupations as "truly crazy." Within hours I was publicly criticized by Walter Mondale and privately chastised by the White House. Jack Svahn, the domestic policy advisor, called to advise me in effect to fall on my sword, commenting that "Bill, you knew the ground rules: there was to be no discussion of issues in this campaign." I acknowledged that I understood the ground rules, and I shut up for a while. Several months after the election, several other administration officials expressed their own views on comparable worth, using similar language.

The administration had a strong case for its general policy on these issues, but it was never quite comfortable about articulating its position. The constitutional standard is "equal protection of the laws," not a proliferation of special preferences for specific groups. There was no reason to be apologetic about this position.

THE DISTRIBUTION OF INCOME AND TAXES

The Reagan administration was often charged with harming the poor, neglecting the middle class, and favoring the rich. What is the evidence?

Money Income of Families by Income Group and Race

Money income from all sources is the best available measure of the purchasing power of different groups in the population. One should recognize, however, that it is not a wholly adequate measure because it excludes noncash benefits, the imputed rental income of owner-occupied homes, increases in unrealized financial wealth, and taxes. In 1984, for example, about 13 percent of white households and 43 percent of black households received some form of federal noncash benefits (other than education and Medicare), which accrue primarily to families with money incomes of less than $15,000. The benefits from higher education subsidies, Medicare, and the imputed rental income from home ownership, however, accrue primarily to middle-income families. And increases in unrealized financial wealth accrue primarily to high-income families which also pay a large proportion of taxes. On balance, the available data on money income understate the relative purchasing power of families with low money income, a result primarily of the income distribution of federal noncash transfers and taxes.

Table 8.4 Distribution of Families by Money Income
and Race

Race and Income[a]	Percentage of Families		
	1976	1980	1984
White			
0–14,999	20.3	21.7	22.2
15,000–49,999	65.4	63.5	60.9
50,000 and over	14.3	14.8	16.9
Other			
0–14,999	42.9	44.3	44.9
15,000–49,999	51.3	48.8	46.9
50,000 and over	5.8	6.9	8.2

[a] In 1984 dollars.

Table 8.4 summarizes the distribution of families by money income and race for 1976, 1980, and 1984. Data for 1976 are included
in this table to permit a comparison of changes in the distribution of
families by money income during the Carter administration and the
first term of the Reagan administration.

These data illustrate several general patterns. The percentage of
families with money incomes of less than $15,000 (in 1984 dollars)
has gradually increased. The increase in the percentage of poor
families, however, was higher during the Carter administration than
during the Reagan first term; other data indicate that real money
transfers per poor recipient declined more during the Carter administration than during the Reagan first term. The percentage of families with money incomes from $15,000 to $49,999 has gradually declined; the decline was roughly equal during both administrations.
The percentage of families with money incomes of $50,000 or more
has gradually increased; the increase has been somewhat higher during the Reagan years. The money income of black and other minority families is substantially lower than for white families, but the
changes in the distribution of families by money income were very
similar for both groups.

There appears to be some basis for the perception that the middle
class is declining. There is more reason for concern, however, about
whether formerly middle-income families are moving down or up
the income distribution. During the Carter years most of the decline
in the percentage of middle-income families was matched by an increase in the percentage of poor families. During the Reagan years
most of the decline in the percentage of middle-income families has
been matched by an increase in the percentage of high-income fam-

ilies. The Reagan administration has had no reason to be defensive about the general effects of its economic policies on the distribution of income. For the most part, however, the general changes in the percentage of families by income class appear to be due to general changes in the economy and are not much affected by the changes in economic policies.

The Special Problem of the Poor

Poverty was first perceived to be a national problem in the mid-1960s, when President Johnson started the Great Society and declared a "war on poverty." Since that time real transfer payments per person (in the total population) have tripled. Although the poverty rate declined for a few years, the official poverty rate is now about the same as in the mid-1960s. Figure 8.1 illustrates these two patterns. The rapid growth of real transfer payments was at least not sufficient to reduce the official poverty rate. Why did this happen? What do we know about the effects of transfer payments on the behavior and status of the poor? What were the effects of the lower growth of transfer payments during the Reagan years? Where do we go from here?

A first step toward answering these questions is to recognize that most transfers go to the elderly and other groups in the population and are independent of their other income. In 1984, for example, the sum of social security, unemployment benefits, veterans' benefits, farm supports, and government pensions was 75 percent of total transfers. Although these programs are not income tested, some of

Figure 8.1   Poverty Rate and Real Transfer Payments

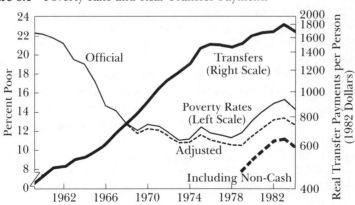

these benefits go to people who would otherwise be poor. Social security, for example, has substantially reduced poverty among the elderly; the poverty rate of elderly families is now lower than for the rest of the population.

A second step is to recognize that most transfers to the poor are in the form of various noncash transfers, which are not reflected in the official poverty rate. In 1984 the basic AFDC program was only 13 percent of total income-tested transfer payments.

A third step is to recognize that the official poverty rate is a quite misleading indicator of the change in the poverty rate over time. One reason for the bias in the official series is that the poverty line ($10,609 for a family of four in 1984) is increased each year by the inflation rate of the consumer price index. As discussed in Chapter 7, however, this index substantially overestimated the consumer inflation rate until it was changed in 1983. As Figure 8.1 shows, the adjusted poverty rate based only on money income has been one or two percentage points lower than the official rate since 1979. A second bias in the official poverty rate is that it does not reflect the rapid increase in noncash benefits to the poor. As also shown in Figure 8.1, the adjusted poverty rate based on both money income and the value of noncash benefits to the poor has been four or five percentage points lower than the official rate since 1979. Either or both of these adjustments indicate that the actual poverty rate declined through 1979, not through 1973 as suggested by the official series. These adjustments do not minimize the effects of poverty on those affected, but they provide a better perspective on the historical changes in the extent of poverty in the United States.

By any measure, however, the poverty rate increased substantially from 1979 through 1983. The primary explanation of this condition is that the U.S. economy experienced no net economic growth from late 1978 through late 1982, the longest such period in the postwar years. As indicated by the experience of the early 1960s, prior to the explosion of transfer payments, strong economic growth is the most effective solution for reducing poverty. In the war on poverty, we may be "losing ground," to borrow the title of the influential 1984 book by Charles Murray, but not primarily for the reasons that he suggests. The rapid increase in real transfer payments does not appear to have increased the poverty rate. The many Great Society programs for the nonelderly, however, do not appear to have reduced the poverty rate. The nonelderly poverty rate is almost completely determined by the ratio of the poverty line to median family income—in other words, by general economic conditions. The primary problem is the much lower rate of economic growth since 1973, not a substantial increase in welfare dependence induced by the increase in transfer payments.

The minor changes in welfare policy by the Reagan administration had no significant effect on the poverty rate during this period. Most of these changes involved a reduction of noncash benefits to those above the poverty line and a generally futile attempt to tighten the work requirements for welfare recipients. The primary effect of these measures was to increase the effective tax rates on the working poor. There is no easy way out of this dilemma. A reduction of these very high marginal tax rates, from 50 to 250 percent for many of the poor, requires either a reduction in benefits to those who don't work or an increase in benefits to those who work. Liberals generally oppose the first option, and conservatives oppose the second option. The currently fashionable moderate option to tighten the work requirements is an illusion. Such measures have not been possible to enforce, do not reduce government spending, and do not increase the incomes of the poor. The option we have chosen is to tolerate a low level of work participation by welfare recipients. The states, which set AFDC benefit levels, were responsible for the primary change in welfare policy during this period. Total real AFDC benefits declined 10.2 percent during the Carter administration and 3.9 percent during the Reagan first term. We should not be surprised by the resulting increase in the poverty rate.

What do we know about the relation of poverty and welfare? A part of the problem is that much of what we "know" about this issue is probably not true. Casual observation, case studies, and the aggregate data have created the perception of a large and growing urban "underclass" that is dependent on welfare from one generation to the next. Statistical studies based on the national or state aggregate data have led Charles Murray and some other scholars to conclude that an increase in welfare benefits may increase poverty. Perhaps; yet Murray recognized that "what we would really like is a longitudinal sample of the disadvantaged." Fortunately, two large samples that track the *same* people over an extended period were started in the late 1960s, and the first studies based on these samples were completed in the early 1980s. These studies present a quite different picture of poverty and the effects of welfare.

For most of those affected, poverty is a temporary condition; although about 25 percent of the population was poor for a year or more during the decade between 1969 and 1979, only about 5 percent was poor for five or more years. At any given time, however, about half of welfare recipients are in an extended period of poverty. Contrary to the perception of an urban underclass, the highest rates of persistent poverty are among those who live outside large urban areas, the disabled, and the single elderly. Most welfare recipients receive most of their income over time from other sources. Changes in family status have a larger effect on changes in welfare status than do changes in other income. More surprising is the conclusion of one study that welfare appears to have little effect on changes in family status, except on the decision of a single mother to live apart from her parents. The earlier negative income tax experiments, however, indicated that higher welfare benefits also contributed to separation and divorce. Most important is that there appears to be little intergenerational transmission of welfare dependence; for example, the percentage of young black women who are highly dependent on welfare does not appear to be related to the welfare status of their parents. Another study, however, indicates that the unemployment rate of black youth is much higher among families dependent on welfare and public housing.

The general patterns that emerge from these new studies are that welfare is an important support system for the small percentage of the persistently poor and an important insurance system for the larger percentage of the temporarily poor. The level of welfare benefits, however, does not appear to have a strong effect on the conditions that lead to either persistent or temporary poverty. Some of these new studies have been strongly criticized, and much more work needs to be done. For the first time, however, we have an adequate data base for addressing one of the more contentious issues of contemporary policy.

Where do we go from here? Many of those who are most knowledgeable about welfare issues are now much more cautious about answering this question than in the past. There is a reasonable case to be made that the current welfare system, however messy and controversial, cannot be much improved. Joseph Califano, Carter's first secretary of Health, Education and Welfare, secured a reputation for understatement by describing welfare reform as "the Middle East of domestic politics." Maybe the federal government should maintain current policies and allow the states to experiment with different approaches to resolving those issues which are primarily of local concern.

Several changes to current federal welfare policy, however, deserve consideration. A good case can be made to cash out programs such as food stamps, special housing assistance, and energy assistance in exchange for either higher cash benefits or an earnings subsidy, at the option of the recipient. This would give recipients more freedom to spend money as they choose, would reduce the administrative overhead, and would improve the accuracy of the official poverty

series. There is a reasonable but more controversial case to be made
for the Reagan administration proposal to deny AFDC benefits to
unmarried minor mothers. A more general option would deny additional benefits to any unmarried mother who bears an additional
child after an announced future date; this option would maintain or
increase the benefits to all families now receiving AFDC and would
probably reduce the number of additional children born out of wed-
lock. A broadly supported change to remove most of the poor from
the federal income tax was approved in the 1986 tax legislation. An
important change to allow the states greater flexibility to address these
issues would involve reversing the several federal court decisions that
prohibit the states from establishing residency requirements for eli-
gibility for state-financed welfare benefits and social services.

The sum of these measures may not much change federal and
state welfare spending or, possibly, the effective poverty rate. These
measures would limit the most adverse effects of the welfare system,
however, and would increase the benefits to those who meet the
changed standards. Only a cautious agenda for welfare reform is
consistent with the current political consensus and our limited current understanding of poverty and the welfare system. My judgment, moreover, is that only an initiative by the Democrats provides
any prospect for significant welfare reform.

Income Taxes and After-Tax Income

A funny thing happened on the way to the tax collector in response
to the individual income tax cuts approved in 1981. In response to
the cuts, as the supply-siders anticipated, taxable income increased
in each income group. Moreover, the total federal income taxes paid
by the highest income group increased, and the share of income
taxes paid by those with incomes of $50,000 or more increased sub-
stantially.

A careful study of the effects of the 1981 tax cuts on taxable income and taxes paid in 1982 indicates the first-year effects of these
cuts. This study, published in 1986, was based on a comprehensive
simulation model of the tax system. The major tax rate changes that
were effective in 1982 were a 5 percent general reduction in tax
rates on October 1, 1981, a 10 percent general reduction on July 1,
1982, and a reduction in the top rate on "unearned" income from
70 percent to 50 percent on January 1, 1982 (a provision introduced
by a House Democrat). The study concludes that 47 percent of the
$33.3 billion estimated cost of the rate reductions effective in 1982
was recaptured by changes in taxpayer behavior in response to these
cuts. Most of the increase in tax revenue apparently was due to a

reduced use of tax shelters rather than an increase in income. Taxes paid by those with adjusted gross incomes of $200,000 or more increased slightly, and the share of total taxes paid by those with incomes of $50,000 or more increased by 1.4 percentage points in response to the change in tax rates. These effects of the tax cuts approved in 1981 are generally consistent with the effects of similar reductions in the top tax rates in the early 1920s and early 1960s. As a guide to future changes in the federal tax code, the most important conclusion of this study is that any tax rate above about 41 percent on income or about 20 percent on capital gains probably reduces tax revenues. In that sense even higher tax rates are regressive in that they reduce the revenues available for transfer payments and other government programs.

Table 8.5 summarizes the combined effects of the changes in economic conditions and the reduction in tax rates on the distribution of federal income taxes and adjusted gross income (AGI) less taxes, by income groups during the first term of the Reagan administration. (For several reasons the distribution of tax returns by AGI is much different than the distribution of families by money income summarized in Table 8.4. Moreover, tax returns also include unrelated individuals, a group for which average money incomes are substantially lower than average family incomes. Some married couples also file as individual taxpayers, thereby reducing the AGI per return. And AGI excludes a substantial amount of money income, such as money transfers to the poor and the interest on tax-free bonds to higher-income groups. *Changes* in the distributions by AGI, however, are a good approximation of changes by total money income.)

For those with adjusted gross incomes of less than $15,000 (in 1984 dollars), the combined effects of these conditions increased their share of federal income taxes by 0.5 percentage points and reduced their share of AGI less taxes by 1.7 percentage points. For this group, federal income taxes increased at a higher rate than AGI because the tax code was not indexed until 1985, thus reducing the real value of personal exemptions and the standard deduction. The 1986 tax legislation has substantially reduced the share of federal income taxes paid by this group in future years.

For those with adjusted gross incomes of from $15,000 to $49,999, the combined effects of these conditions reduced their share of federal income taxes by 2.9 percentage points and reduced their share of AGI less taxes by 1.5 percentage points. For this group the decline in their share of AGI less taxes was primarily due to a decline in their share of AGI, with little distributional effect of the changes in taxes.

For those with adjusted gross incomes of $50,000 or more, the

Table 8.5 Federal Income Taxes by Income Group

Adjusted Gross Income (AGI)[a]	1980	1984
	Percentage of Returns	
0–14,999	46.7	47.9
15,000–49,999	46.0	45.3
50,000 and over	7.3	6.8
	Percentage of AGI	
0–14,999	15.7	14.5
15,000–49,999	60.0	58.4
50,000 and over	24.3	27.1
	Percentage of Taxes	
0–14,999	5.7	6.2
15,000–49,999	52.6	49.7
50,000 and over	41.7	44.1
	Percentage of AGI Less Taxes	
0–14,999	17.6	15.9
15,000–49,999	61.3	59.8
50,000 and over	21.1	24.3

[a] In 1984 dollars.

combined effect of these conditions increased their share of federal income taxes by 2.4 percentage points, substantially more than the first-year effects discussed earlier, and increased their share of AGI less taxes by 3.2 percentage points. The increase in this group's share of AGI less taxes was primarily due to an increase in their share of AGI, with little distributional effect of the changes in taxes.

In summary, the combined effects of changes in economic conditions and taxes reduced the share of after-tax income of the poor and increased the share of after-tax income of higher-income families. Most of these changes, however, were due to changes in the distribution of pre-tax income, changes that were about the same in the Carter administration and the first term of the Reagan administration, and were not much affected by changes in the distribution of taxes.

OTHER DISTRIBUTIONAL EFFECTS

Changes in economic policies and conditions during the Reagan administration also had significantly different effects among investors, across states, across nations, and on future generations. This section summarizes these other distributional effects.

Changes in Investor Returns

Economic policies and conditions during the early 1980s led to a substantial increase of the real equity in most sectors other than agriculture, combined with a record rate of business failures. Table 8.6 summarizes the changes in these conditions during the Carter administration and during the Reagan administration through 1985.

Agriculture was the only major sector to experience a decline in real equity during the Reagan years. The real equity of farm proprietors increased rapidly during the Carter administration, primarily because inflation increased the value of farm land and reduced the real value of outstanding debt. Although net real farm income was slightly higher in 1984 than in 1980, a substantial decline in the real value of farm land reduced the real value of farm equity during the Reagan years. Although the bankruptcy rate among farmers is now about the same as among other businesses of similar size, about one-eighth of all farmers were considered financially distressed at the end of 1984. Subsequent data on farm equity are not yet available, but these conditions probably continued to deteriorate in 1985 and 1986.

The real equity of U.S. corporations increased substantially during the Reagan years, after declining (except in transportation) during the Carter administration. The average real equity of industrial firms increased substantially despite the problems of the trade-dependent industries. The average real equity of transportation, utility, and financial corporations increased substantially, despite the problems of some firms, because of deregulation. Financial corporations experienced the highest growth of real equity despite the weakness of their

Table 8.6 Changes in Real Equity and the Liabilities of Business Failures*

	Carter Administration	Reagan Administration
Equity		
Agriculture	4.9	−10.5
Industry	−1.2	4.0
Transportation	2.9	5.8
Utilities	−7.3	3.2
Finance	−2.9	6.5
Liabilities of business failures		
Less than $100,000	−6.2	24.5
$100,000 or more	3.8	43.4

*Percentage change, annual rate.

agriculture, energy, and foreign loan portfolios. This substantial increase in the real value of corporate equity, an increase in real wealth that is not directly reflected in the national income statistics, was one of the more important effects of Reagan's economic policies. Despite the visible problems of some firms and industries, the real market value of American firms is now the highest in more than a decade.

The improved financial status of American firms, however, was not uniform. From 1980 through 1983 (the latest data available), the failure rate of commercial and industrial firms more than doubled to the highest rate since the 1930s. The rate of net business formation declined slightly after increasing somewhat during the Carter administration. The real liabilities of business failures roughly tripled from 1980 through 1983, with a somewhat higher increase among larger firms. As in agriculture, the failure rate was highest among firms that substantially increased their debt on the basis of expectations of continued high inflation. The failure rate of commercial and industrial firms, however, probably declined in subsequent years. The increase in the average real equity of U.S. corporations indicates that the Reagan policies were, on balance, clearly beneficial to the business sector. The rapid increase in the business failure rate, however, reinforces another lesson of our longer history: an unexpected change in economic policies, even if generally beneficial, increases the variance of economic outcomes among firms and industries. The benefits of a free economy, as observed by Joseph Schumpeter, are the results of a process of destructive change.

Changes in Real Personal Income by State

Figure 8.2 displays the percentage changes in real personal income by state during the first term of the Reagan administration. These changes in real personal income reflect the combined effect of changes in population and changes in real personal income per capita. For comparison, total real personal income increased about 13 percent during this period.

Given the changes in employment and real earnings by industry (summarized in Table 8.1), the changes in real personal income by state are somewhat surprising. The seventeen states with the highest growth of real personal income are especially interesting. Despite the general weakness in agriculture, for example, North Dakota and South Dakota were among the states with the highest growth. Despite the decline in mining employment, the real personal income in Arizona, New Mexico, and Utah also increased rapidly. Despite the general weakness in manufacturing employment, Massachusetts, Connecticut, and New Jersey experienced rapid growth. And de-

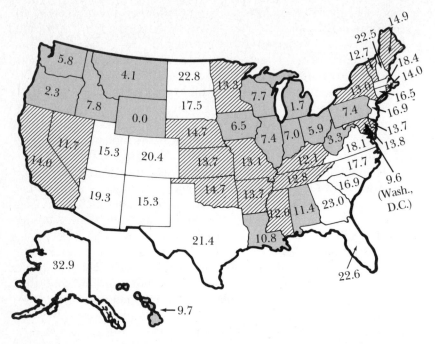

Figure 8.2 Changes in Real Personal Income by State, 1980–1984

spite the decline in the textile and apparel industries, North Carolina and South Carolina were also among the highest-growth states.
As indicated by these examples, states with some problem industry
were able to grow rapidly as long as other conditions were favorable.
In general, with important exceptions, the highest-growth states during
this period were primarily in the East and the South.

In contrast, many of the seventeen states (including the District of
Columbia) with the lowest growth of real personal income were affected by the problems of several industries. For example, Idaho,
Montana, and Wyoming were hurt by the decline in both agriculture
and mining. The growth of real personal income in Pennsylvania
was reduced by the weakness of both local mining and the basic met-
als industries. The upper midwestern states of Wisconsin, Michigan,
Illinois, and Indiana were affected by the weakness of both agriculture and the machinery industries. In general, again with important
exceptions, the central and northwestern states experienced the lowest growth of real personal income.

Changes in the regional distribution of economic growth during
the Reagan first term were very different from those during the 1970s.

The northwestern states and Hawaii, for example, had been among the highest-growth states during the 1970s. The New England states (other than New Hampshire) had been among the lowest-growth states. In general there was no significant relation between the growth of real personal income by state during the early 1980s and the growth during the 1970s. In addition, the growth during the early 1980s was independent of the level of personal income per capita in 1980. During this period, for example, Alaska experienced the highest growth in real personal income and Wyoming had no growth, although both states had among the highest per-capita incomes in 1980. Some of the changes in the regional distribution of economic activity were clearly attributable to Reagan's economic policies, most importantly the indirect effects on specific agriculture, mining, and manufacturing sectors of the increase in the exchange rate. Many of these changes, however, were also due to the differences in economic policies among state governments. The American economy and political system works in wondrous ways.

Effects on Other Nations

U.S. economic policy during the first term of the Reagan administration had two contrary effects on other nations. The major costs to other nations were the increase in real interest rates, the resulting reduction in domestic investment in other nations, and the increase in interest payments on their foreign debts. The major benefit to other nations was the rapid increase in our trade deficit. From 1980 through 1984, U.S. net merchandise imports (excluding military transactions) increased nearly $89 billion. The distribution of this increase in net imports, however, was quite different from popular and political perceptions. Net imports from the developing countries (other than OPEC) increased more than $39 billion, far more than the increase in the interest payments on their foreign debt in 1980. Net imports from Western Europe increased nearly $36 billion. Net imports from Japan increased almost $27 billion, about equal to the reduction in U.S. net imports from the OPEC countries. And net imports from Canada increased nearly $15 billion during this period. The increase in merchandise exports to the United States was one of the major sources of economic growth during this period for all countries other than the oil exporters. On balance, U.S. economic policies and conditions clearly benefitted the rest of the world.

One of the international roles of the United States since World War II has been to serve as an excuse for the problems of other nations, and we heard a good deal of grumbling in international forums about the costs of U.S. policies. As the U.S. recovery developed, however, the benefits of U.S. policies became clearer to other nations. During a period when total employment in Europe was stagnant, the strong growth of U.S. employment was especially impressive. Other nations began considering "positive adjustment policies" such as reductions in tax rates and regulation, with the hope of achieving a similar increase in employment. Reaganomics was not necessarily the only solution to all the economic problems of either the United States or other nations. As of the mid-1980s, however, there was a broader recognition that such policies were the appropriate first step to resolving these problems.

Effects on Future Generations

The primary adverse legacy of Reaganomics, as discussed in Chapter 3, was the huge increase in the federal debt. The annual cost to future taxpayers of the increase in the privately held federal debt from FY 1981 through FY 1985 will be around $60 billion, and continuing deficits of around $200 billion would add about $15 billion a year to these annual costs. The increase in annual interest payments on the accumulated debt would be over $100 billion, even if the annual deficit is (improbably) reduced to zero by FY 1991 according to the Gramm-Rudman schedule. This huge cost is primarily a result of the failure to limit federal spending to the administration's initial targets.

The major favorable legacies of the Reagan economic policies have been the increased rate of productivity growth and the much lower rate of inflation. Productivity growth through 1984 was around one percentage point a year higher than during the Carter administration. For the near future, even if this higher productivity growth is not sustained, this will increase annual output by around $120 billion. The primary benefit of a lower inflation rate, in addition to the effect on productivity growth, is to reduce the risk of another severe recession and the consequent temporary loss of output. In the absence of a substantial increase in inflation, future recessions are more likely to be similar to the brief mild recessions of 1949, 1960, and 1970 rather than the severe recessions of 1974 and 1975 and of 1981 and 1982. The temporary loss of output during the next recession thus is likely to be reduced by more than $100 billion.

The net legacy of Reagan economic policies depends, therefore, on changes in economic policies and conditions that are yet to be realized. A combination of continued high deficits, low productivity growth, and increasing inflation would leave a negative net legacy, the combination of an increased federal debt and the economic conditions of the 1970s. A rapid reduction in the federal deficit, continued moderate growth of productivity, and low inflation, however, would leave a substantial positive net legacy. The history of Reaganomics is not yet complete, but as is often the case, some intermediate outcome is most likely.

POLITICAL RESPONSES TO DISTRIBUTIONAL CHANGES

Our political system is generally most responsive to those who lose from a change in economic conditions and policies. The developing problems in the agricultural sector led to several temporary relief measures and the awful farm legislation of 1985. The problems of specific manufacturing industries, as discussed earlier, led to the industrial policy proposals of 1983 and the increasing demand for import restraints. The special problems of the poor led to the elimination of federal income taxes on most of the poor by the tax legislation of 1986. A considerable divergence of economic conditions among the states led to a strong split among Republicans on budget and trade policies.

On several occasions Democrats made a concerted effort to raise a general "fairness issue" about the Reagan economic policies, although many Democrats had supported the budget and tax legislation of 1981. The administration generally tried to diffuse the issue by selective exceptions to its general policies and by public-relations "stroking" of the leaders of the most vocal groups. Stockman's characteristic response was a blizzard of statistics that denied that there was any fairness issue.

This general issue first came into focus in the spring of 1983 after the Democratic gains in the 1982 congressional election and the beginning of the economic recovery. Congress was considering a repeal of the tax cut scheduled for 1983 and a slower growth of defense spending. The White House prepared a 286-page briefing book for administration officials to use in response to the fairness issue. In testimony before the Joint Economic Committee (JEC) in May, Stockman responded to each of the major charges. Stockman's primary case was that the fairness of recent and proposed changes in policy should be put in context of the actual changes over a longer period. For example, although the administration proposed to reduce real spending for income-tested programs by 7.5 percent relative to the last Carter budget, total real spending for these programs in FY 1984 would be 250 percent of the 1970 level. Similarly, the administration's defense budget and tax policy would only partly offset the major changes in the defense and tax revenue share of GNP during the 1970s. Stockman's "bottom line" was that the administration's program did not reflect a radical shift of priorities. As was often the case, Stockman's testimony was impressive but not wholly convincing to those who consider some groups to have an "entitlement" to the current level of government benefits. (On several occasions I tried to persaude Stockman and other administration officials, without success, not to use the word "entitlement," because it conveys the impression of a right to continued government transfer payments and services.) In any case, strong economic growth deferred this issue for a while. In 1985 and 1986, when Rep. David Obey, the new Democratic chairman of the JEC, tried to revive the general fairness issue, almost no one noticed.

In the calculus of politics there never was a general fairness issue. Our political system responds to the problems of specific groups. The interests of farmers, miners, steelworkers, and welfare mothers, however, are very different and often not consistent. Continued general economic growth at least stalled an effective coalition of the groups that in retrospect turned out to be the losers because of the changes in economic policies and conditions during the Reagan years.

Changes in the distribution of economic activity, however, are likely to lead to some realignment in our political system. For decades Americans have elected Republicans to solve problems of general concern, such as war and inflation, and have elected Democrats to address the problems of specific groups. Strong economic growth in most of the East and South is likely to increase Republican representation in these regions. The special problems in the Midwest and Northwest are likely to increase Democratic representation in these regions. The continued decline in union membership is likely to reduce union influence in both parties. In light of the rapid increase in the employment of minorities and in both the employment and real earnings of women, my view is that neither racial nor women's issues will be very important. Continued general economic growth is likely to increase the concern of both parties about the special problems of the poor.

The major group that is likely to provide the swing votes in future elections comprises the young men and women of the "baby-boom" generation. The polling data suggest that most of this group, with weak party identification, favors laissez-faire economic policies but is anxious about the extended military role of the United States and the social agenda of the "New Right." A candidate of either party who can articulate a vision of international restraint, economic opportunity, and social tolerance, however, would capture most of this new generation. For the Republicans this would require a reevaluation of their recent commitment to an interventionist foreign policy and their developing relations with the social conservatives. For the Democrats this would require a reevaluation of their commitment to an interventionist economic policy and their traditional relations with unions. The prospects are intriguing. Our process of nominating presidential candidates unfortunately reinforces the role of special interests in both parties.

ON THE FAIRNESS OF REAGANOMICS

As is now apparent, the Reagan economic program did not lead to "a brighter future for all of our citizens". As with any process with uncertain outcomes, there were some winners and some losers. Is there any basis for agreement on whether this program was fair or unfair?

The actual outcomes of this program, as affected by other changes in the economy, do not provide any basis for agreement on this issue. The winners are likely to regard these outcomes as fair unless they are also especially concerned about the well-being of the losers. And the losers are likely to regard these outcomes as unfair unless they are also especially concerned about the well-being of the winners. The *expected* outcomes of this program, I suggest, provide a better basis for addressing this issue. In 1981 there was broad support for the key elements of this program, with little concern about the expected distributional consequences. In that sense the program was broadly perceived to be fair.

A more fundamental question is whether the political process that approved these policies is fair. If the process is fair, any outcome of this process, whether expected or unexpected, should also be considered fair. For example, if the increase in transfer payments and taxes was the result of a fair political process, the reduction of some transfer payments and tax rates by the same process during the Reagan administration should also be considered fair. This perspective shifts the focus from the outcomes of government policies to the rules by which these policies are decided. The outcomes of democratic political processes, even within broadly supported constitutional rules, will not benefit everyone, but this may be the best that we can do. A more important problem is that our effective constitutional rules have been subject to continuous change by judicial and legislative decisions—but that is another story for another time.

There are valid reasons for questioning the wisdom of some elements of the Reagan economic program. There is no consensual basis, however, for questioning its fairness. This program was proposed and approved by the same political process that led to the prior policies. As long as the policies of the government are consistent with the Constitution, we are obliged to regard them as fair, whether or not in a specific case they are wise or foolish, and regardless of which of us are winners or losers. There are important fairness issues that are inherent in the powers of government. There were no fairness issues specific to the Reagan economic program.

CHAPTER NINE

People and Processes

PEOPLE

People make history. Or does history make people? A professional observer of government is torn between these two perspectives. As an occasional adviser to governments, I can identify many decisions that would have been different if made by another person who might have served in the same position at the same time. As a public-choice scholar, I have long attempted to explain the general behavior of bureaucrats and politicians in terms of the incentives and constraints specific to these roles—that is, without writing biography. This book will not resolve this enduring tension, in part because I have not sorted out these issues in my own mind.

In any case many readers may be more interested in my personal observations about the key people who formulated and implemented the Reagan economic program than in my professional evaluation of the conditions that shaped this program and its consequences. Although responsive to this interest, I write these observations with some reservations. For some years I worked with these people in a relation of mutual trust. As a rule I enjoyed these relations. I regard some of these people as friends. Some may hold important positions in future administrations. At the same time I recognize that such brief portraits reflect only one perspective on these individuals and that any observer is tempted to settle old scores. In most cases I observed good people trying to do what they believed was best for the nation. In a few cases my observations are more critical. If I have been unfair in either judgment, I apologize in advance.

The President

A French reporter, interviewing François Mitterrand, the president of France, asked Mitterrand to describe Ronald Reagan. Mitterrand replied:

> He is a man of common sense, gracious and pleasant. He communicates through jokes, by telling ultra-California stories, by speaking mainly about

California and the Bible. He has two religions: free enterprise and God—
the Christian God. His time as governor of California remains an important inspiration to him. He is not a man who dwells on concepts, yet
he has ideas and clings to them.

Ronald Reagan has an intuitive approach to things, and he is able to
get the gist of the sophisticated documents his aides place in front of
him.

REPORTER: I think he is the incarnation of a kind of primal, almost
archaic power. He governs less by his intellect than with common sense.
. . . And he doesn't look for anything more than the approval of the
American people.

MITTERRAND: The fit between Ronald Reagan's language and the
American people is indeed a tight one. And I understand what you
meant by describing Reagan's power as "primal": like a rock in the Mor-
van, like plain truth, like the wilderness of Nevada.

Ronald Reagan has been the most transparent person in American
public life. He conveys much the same impression to a television
audience, before large groups, to his cabinet and aides, and to
the socialist president of France. He is at peace with himself, comfortable with his convictions, intuitive rather than analytical,
youthful in spirit, infectiously optimistic, and gracious in his personal relations. The contrast with Richard Nixon could not be more
dramatic.

Although Reagan is extraordinarily friendly, only his wife seems
to be a close confidante. In my experience only a few White House
aides and members of the cabinet had a regular opportunity for a
personal conversation with him. Several minor cabinet members reported to me that they never had a personal meeting with the president. Even when I was acting chairman of the CEA, my interaction
with the president was limited to participation in cabinet meetings
and other small groups. Early in the administration, his key California supporters tried to establish themselves as a "kitchen cabinet,"
but this proved to be abortive. In contrast with every other recent
president, Reagan did not develop an informal parallel channel of
close confidants to discuss issues of either public or private concern.
A perplexing dimension of Ronald Reagan is that this extremely
friendly man seems to have few close friends.

Although Reagan is the first president to have a degree in economics, his economic convictions are based more on his personal
experience than his schooling. From my perspective his convictions
on most economic issues are very good. This made it easier to be an
economic adviser. On most issues, rather than challenging his convictions, the role of his economic advisers was to develop the detailed
policy implications of these convictions.

His strongest economic convictions have concerned the importance of low marginal tax rates and a low inflation rate. As a young actor he faced a marginal tax rate of over 90 percent, and he often generalized from his own experience about the effects of high tax rates. It is probably not a coincidence that Jack Kemp and Bill Bradley, the other two leading advocates of tax reform, also faced very high marginal tax rates as young men, in their case as athletes. Reagan accepted several measures to broaden the tax base, but he consistently resisted any measures, other than the acceleration of the scheduled increases in social security taxes, that would increase tax rates. His sole guidance to the Treasury tax plan in 1984 was to reduce individual tax rates as much as possible without reducing tax revenues. Reagan also attributed all sorts of problems to inflation, emphasizing the unfairness of the resulting distribution of gains and losses, an issue on which his judgment was wiser than that of most economists. On reviewing the economic forecasts by his advisers, he regularly asked why inflation could not be reduced more rapidly. As it turned out, the inflation rate was the only economic condition that was better than the initial forecasts. It is not an accident that the reduction of tax rates and the inflation rate were the two most successful effects of the Reagan economic program.

His convictions on most other major issues are also very good. He was fortunately too old to have been infected by the Keynesian virus as a young man, refusing to believe that an increase in government spending could increase real output. During my tenure he revealed a good sense of the conditions that lead to economic growth. Often, he illustrated his convictions with an anecdote. One of his stories, relayed to a cabinet meeting, illustrated a reason for the difference in the economic growth of India and Japan. In the early postwar years, he had heard, the Indians consumed a shipment of high-yield grain seed. The other half of the story was from his personal experience. After an early trip to Japan, he sent his host a box of high-quality California dates. On his next visit he asked his previous host whether he had enjoyed the dates. The man, looking very sad, responded that he had planted the dates but none of them had produced. Although the large deficits and low saving rates during the Reagan years were contrary to this conviction, he never rationalized these conditions.

In a few cases his convictions changed or were not very strong. In 1981, for example, he proposed a reduction in the effective tax rates on business investment, a position that was reversed by his 1985 tax reform plan. Similarly, he initially supported the flexible exchange rate system but, in 1986, asked Secretary Baker to develop a proposal to stabilize exchange rates. Reagan was an articulate supporter

of free trade, but he learned to rationalize the numerous trade restraints approved by the administration as tactical retreats designed
to deter even more protectionist actions by Congress. Of course,
Reagan is both an ideologue and a politician. His political advisers
were often frustrated by his stubborn convictions on some issues.
Many of his economic advisers were frustrated by his willingness to
make political concessions from his initial program on so many other
issues. Only the president seemed comfortable with both of these
positions.

The primary problem of advising Reagan was his attractive but
incurable optimism. He seemed to believe there was something good
about any condition. Many of us heard his story about the boy looking for a pony in the manure pile several times. He maintained an
optimism that many problems would go away without any change in
policy to reduce these problems. In many cases this is a healthy attitude; all too many politicians overreact to the perceived problems of
the moment or promote solutions in search of a problem. Reagan
would acknowledge some problems but had no compulsion to seek
a federal solution to all problems. One important consequence of
this optimism was the impossibility of preparing realistic economic
and budget forecasts. He resisted trade-offs, where one desirable
condition might have to be reduced to increase another desirable
condition, and prodded us to consider policies that would improve
both conditions. He was clearly uncomfortable with advice that the
monetary restraint necessary to reduce inflation might lead to a
recession, that the reduction in tax rates necessary to increase economic growth might increase the deficit. He wanted all good things
to come in a package and was reluctant to signal priorities when
there was a trade-off among his objectives. In these cases, by neces-
sity, the effective priorities were set by Congress or the Fed, and one
discerned the president's priorities only after he expressed some
concern about the remaining problems. The primary consequence
of this perspective was that the Reagan economic program was more
creative but less coherent than would have otherwise been the case.

Over the years Reagan's relations with economists cooled. As a
governor and presidential candidate, he periodically sought the advice of economists, primarily from the Hoover Institute and the California universities. He claims to have been especially influenced by
the writings of Smith, Mises, Hayek, and the other leading "classical
liberal" advocates of a spontaneous economic order. As president he
appointed a number of economists to high positions in the administration and a distinguished group of outside economists to the President's Economic Policy Advisory Board (PEPAB). Early in the first
term, however, economists were often bearers of bad news, and po-

litical leaders have a long record of blaming the messenger. No administration economist other than Secretary of State George Shultz had private contact with the president, and no economist was close to the president. The president seemed to resent internal pressure, even from those most committed to his initial program. Murray Weidenbaum expressed concern about the rapid growth of defense spending and the escalating deficit. Norman Ture and Craig Roberts were critical of the president's support of the 1982 tax law. Martin Feldstein regularly pressed for a tax increase and embarrassed the administration by his public disputes with Secretary Regan. The PEPAB expressed special concern about the developing trade restraints. Over time the president's speeches and informal remarks included an increasing number of sharp comments about economists. In the fall of 1984, there was serious consideration of eliminating the CEA or restricting its role. The results of this cooling relation were the departures of the senior economists who joined the administration in 1981 and more limited contact with the president for those who remained. This was an unfortunate development for which the president was partly responsible. Our political leaders are not yet comfortable with the role of a loyal internal critic.

There is an inherent tension between politicians and policy analysts. President Reagan, like most politicians, is intuitive rather than analytical. At cabinet meetings he was visibly uncomfortable on being presented with a complex argument. On occasion he would interject some story that was not always apposite. He was impatient to hear conclusions. Although the president would rarely cut off the discussion, Ed Meese or Jim Baker, recognizing Reagan's discomfort with an extended argument, would often defer the issue to a later, often private, meeting. Reagan seemed to judge the conclusion of some presentation not by its internal analysis but by whether it was consistent with his own convictions. If so, he would approve the recommendation. If the issue was not clear, he would usually defer to the judgment of the lead agency. If not consistent with his convictions, the issue would often be deferred. It was never quite clear whether the president used his arsenal of stories to illustrate his perceptions or whether these stories were his perceptions. Reagan is not an intellectual, an observation that should not be regarded as a criticism. Woodrow Wilson, our last intellectual president, was a disaster. A president's reasoning process will affect the relative influence of policy analysts and other advisers, but that is not very important except to the other people involved. A president should be evaluated by the quality of his judgments, not by the process by which he comes to these judgments. On that basis Reagan deserves high marks.

The most perplexing dimension of Ronald Reagan was his endorsement of the social agenda of the New Right. There is every reason to respect his religious beliefs. Reagan, however, seemed to be an unlikely Moses. As president he neither attended church nor arranged for services in the White House. He was the first divorced man to be president. He maintained regular social contact with friends from Hollywood, the contemporary Sodom of my own Baptist upbringing. He tolerated unconventional if all too common behavior by his children. For whatever reason, Reagan was able to maintain the support of the New Right by little more than having Ed Meese toss it an occasional bone. The *New Republic* was probably accurate in describing Reagan as a "closet tolerant." There is more reason to worry about a future candidate whose election may be dependent on a stronger commitment to the New Right agenda.

In most respects Reagan was, in my experience, a good chief executive. He provided general guidance, delegated broad authority to the cabinet and agency heads, inspired the troops and rewarded their loyalty, tolerated innocent mistakes, and avoided an obsession with details. In these respects the contrast with President Carter was substantial. Specialists and journalists often criticize Reagan for factual lapses, but that is a bum rap. An effective president must know the important facts about an extraordinary range of issues. Very few people are knowledgeable about every issue a president must address in a given week. There is more reason to be concerned about a persistent misperception of the facts about an important issue than about temporary lapses or variations in the depth of understanding about specific issues. Few of Reagan's mistakes have been due to a persistent misperception or inadequate understanding of facts. The charge that Reagan does not work very long hours is irrelevant. A tired president is more prone to bad judgments. Carter seemed to age a decade during four years in office; Reagan appeared to have discovered the fountain of youth. A chief executive should not be judged by the standards of a line manager.

Reagan's management style, however, can be faulted on several grounds. He chose to work directly through very few people, and he did not develop adequate parallel sources of information and advice on important issues. For that reason he was more vulnerable to the mistakes of his close aides and was less effective in this regard, for example, than Franklin Roosevelt. He was extraordinarily trusting and not very curious about the behavior of his subordinates, a characteristic that contributed to the "Iranamok" affair that seriously weakened his presidency beginning in late 1986. This condition, moreover, was compounded by his choice of personal advisers who had little substantive understanding or inclination to press an issue to a clear resolution. In an important sense Reagan was also too nice to be a superior manager. Although he occasionally expressed irritation, I never saw him angered. He was very reluctant to discipline or fire subordinates, even for the most egregious embarrassments to the administration. Even Stockman's initial story about being taken to the woodshed turned out to be a fabrication suggested by Jim Baker. Reagan was uncomfortable in making hard choices about many issues, but he could hardly bring himself to make hard choices about people. As a consequence he continued to tolerate casual behavior regarding conflicts of interest, a mediocre White House staff, and poor managers in a number of departments and agencies. Reagan's policy agenda, for this reason, was somewhat undermined by a quality that made him attractive as a person.

Ronald Reagan will probably not be regarded by historians as a great president, primarily because his term of office has not to date involved a great crisis. In any case a valet or economic adviser is too close to make this judgment. He has restored the effectiveness of the presidency. He has articulated an expansive vision of America as a land of opportunity. He deserves credit for resolving some of the major economic issues of the time. He is clearly a good man and has been an important president.

The Vice-President

George Bush is a puzzle. I first met him in August 1979 at his summer home in Kennebunkport as part of a small group that he invited to advise him on economic issues during his bid for the Republican nomination for president. At the time I rejected his invitation because he was not clear about what he wanted to accomplish. After years of observing him in his role as vice-president, I find his views still unclear.

Bush has the best resume in American politics. The son of a Republican senator from Connecticut, he was successively a young war hero, a graduate of Yale, a successful oil industry entrepreneur, a congressman, an ambassador to China and to the U.N., director of the CIA, and chairman of the Republican National Committee. As vice-president he has contributed to a wide range of economic issues. He is chairman of the task force on regulatory relief and of the later task force to address the system of federal financial regulation and deposit insurance. Although he rarely spoke at cabinet meetings, he participated in cabinet council deliberations on a wide range of economic issues. On several occasions he was influential in moderating some of the economic initiatives against Japan. He sought out advice on economic issues and was receptive to requests for consultation. Murray Weidenbaum, Marty Feldstein, and I occasionally met with

him, at his invitation, for a private luncheon to discuss current issues. Although he asked a broad range of questions, he seldom conveyed his own views.

As vice-president his extraordinary loyalty to the president unfortunately masked his own views. A more accurate guide to his own
views must be discerned from his 1980 campaign for the nomination
and his prior political positions. The most relevant event in the primary campaign was Bush's charge that the emerging Reagan economic program was "voodoo economics." (After Reagan's nomination no one wanted to take credit for this term, but it was broadly
attributed to Dave Gergen, then a Bush adviser and later Reagan's
first director of communications.) The basis for this charge was Reagan's endorsement of the Kemp-Roth tax cuts prior to developing
any plan for budget restraint. Bush later explained his endorsement
of the Reagan program by emphasizing the attempt to achieve proportionate reductions in government spending.

His prior record suggests that Bush is best described as a traditional Republican. The record indicates that he favors balanced budgets, responsiveness to business interests, an internationalist perspective on foreign and military policies, and a moderate position on
social issues. (From this perspective the George Bush who later cul-
tivated the support of Rev. Jerry Falwell seems out of character.)
This record suggests that as a president Bush would be more of a
consolidator than an innovator. His caution about being perceived
as questioning any policy of the administration is inherent in the role
of vice-president. However, Bush has yet to articulate any proposals
that would either sustain or develop the Reagan agenda.

Bush is a quite different person than Reagan but very attractive
in his own way. He is earnest, thoughtful rather than quick, well
organized, and very hard working. He lacks the wit of Reagan or
Senator Dole, but he is also very gracious in his personal relations.
He has an attractive extended family. Although he has maintained a
political base in Texas, his roots are clearly in New England. He is
probably the best-informed American politician on international issues. He has the potential of being a good president; someone else,
however, may have to provide the spark.

The Troika

For some years, coordination of economic policy within the administration has been the responsibility of the "troika." As the name suggests, this group initially included three officials—the secretary of
the Treasury, the director of OMB, and the chairman of the CEA.
During the Reagan administration this group also included Com-

merce Secretary Malcolm Baldrige and the White House domestic policy adviser. This group meets each Tuesday morning for breakfast in the personal dining room of the Treasury secretary. During my tenure, on occasion George Shultz and Paul Volcker would also join this breakfast discussion.

Don Regan

The Treasury secretary has long been the senior economic spokesman for the administration. In that position Don Regan also worked aggressively to gain the dominant role within the administration in formulating economic policy—a role that was limited primarily by the independent authority of Dave Stockman and Paul Volcker. As Treasury secretary he was very protective of the department's responsibility for tax policy and debt management. This led to several confrontations with Stockman and Feldstein when they pressed the president to increase taxes. As discussed in Chapter 3, Regan's resistance to sharing a review of these issues also made him vulnerable to the institutional position of his own staff, particularly on the Treasury tax plan of 1984. On small tax issues he performed the characteristic Treasury role of defending the revenue base. For example, he generally opposed White House proposals to create or expand special tax provisions for programmatic objectives, such as expanded IRAs and enterprise zones, although he did not make a strong case for this position. He did not oppose, however, the major reduction in tax rates approved in 1981 or express the characteristic Treasury concern about the increase in the debt.

As chairman of the cabinet council on economic affairs (CCEA) and, later, the senior interdepartmental group on international economic policy (SIG-IEP), Regan made better use of the cabinet council process than any other member of the cabinet. The CCEA usually met twice a week to review both current and longer-term economic policies and conditions. Presentations to this cabinet council were well prepared, the discussion was vigorous, and most minor issues were solved before options and recommendations were forwarded to the cabinet. In this role he was assisted by Roger Porter, the very able secretary of the CCEA. The larger SIG-IEP, a subcommittee of the National Security Council (NSC), was more cumbersome and less effective. Regan used these two councils to exert influence on the broader range of economic policies other than those which are the core responsibility of the Treasury.

As the former chairman of Merrill Lynch, Regan brought a substantial understanding of financial issues to his position. As a former marine officer and a successful executive, he was well organized, strong minded, and self-confident. (Baker, Shultz, and NSC director Robert

McFarlane had also been marine officers, and Baldrige had been an army officer. Shultz and Baldrige had also been chief executives of large business firms.) Although Regan, like his Irish cousin Reagan, was quite charming, he was often prickly. He was uncomfortable dealing with people on a collegial rather than a hierarchical basis. Although he tolerated a forceful argument, one would discern increasing irritation by a reddening of his face and neck when the argument approached an implied criticism. Regan was a man of little guile and less subtlety, although he learned to be a more effective politician. My judgment is that he did a much better job as Treasury secretary than was suggested by his reputation in the press. My major disappointment with Regan is that he did not press his views with the president on important matters such as the defense budget, after the president had signaled a tentative position. My opinion is that his management style would not be effective at the White House; he maintained the chief of staff position about two months longer than I expected, but someone else will have to summarize that record. Regan learned to like Washington and learned enough about its strange customs to be more effective than most business executives in government.

David Stockman

David Stockman was the *wunderkind* of the Reagan administration. Appointed as director of OMB at the age of thirty-four, he organized a comprehensive revision of the FY 1982 budget in the first six weeks of the administration, most of which was approved. Although he continued to make a substantial contribution to budget and regulatory policies, Stockman never regained the momentum and influence of his first year.

Stockman was an extraordinary bundle of ideology, energy, and intellect. An important part of his effectiveness was his ability to select and motivate a group of key associates with these same qualities. Stockman brought to his position a stronger commitment to reducing the size and scope of the federal government than any other senior official in the administration, describing himself as an anti-statist conservative or libertarian. Although he later was portrayed as a scrooge for reducing low-income programs, he was especially offended by the much larger level of spending and credit subsidies to groups who are not poor. The only apparent internal tension of Stockman's ideology was that he was also proud of his political and technocratic skills. In several cases, such as the 1981 sugar program and the 1984 steel import restraints, Stockman had primary responsibility for designing subsidy programs that were strongly inconsistent with his own policy views.

His energy was phenomenal. A bachelor until 1984, Stockman often worked fifteen-hour days or seventy-hour weeks. On several occasions he would reformat a major budget presentation overnight to display material in a way that was more understandable to the president and the cabinet. He had a remarkable grasp of the details of government programs, in some cases greater than that of the cabinet members whose budget was being reviewed.

Stockman was also the brightest but maybe not the wisest member of the cabinet. His natural alliances were with other bright officials, such as Darman, Feldstein, and Volcker. This quality was also the source of some of his problems. He was often visibly intolerant of those who were less bright, and he often ran roughshod over secretaries of the domestic departments. His energy, intellect, and self-confidence also led him to be an imperialist, reaching out for influence on tax, regulation, and management issues. His challenge to Regan over the dominant role on economic policy ultimately led to his resignation after Regan moved to the White House in 1985.

Stockman's grasp of economics was good but not superior. Neither Stockman nor Larry Kudlow, his economic adviser until 1984, had graduate economic training. Stockman had earlier believed that a general reduction in tax rates might increase tax revenues, but he later concluded that this effect was possible only if there is no inflation. This was merely confused. There was no empirical base for expecting that the 1981 reduction in tax rates would increase revenues regardless of the inflation rate. After the fact, it appears that the reduction of the top marginal rate increased tax revenues from the highest income taxpayers in 1982, even though the inflation rate was still over 6 percent. As discussed in Chapter 3, Stockman consistently overestimated the short-term economic effects of the deficit, a position that was more consistent with conventional wisdom than the developing evidence. Stockman's confidence in his own judgment unfortunately confused his important case for reducing the deficit.

As one who shares Stockman's ideology and respected his energy and intellect, I had high regard for Stockman and his contribution to the administration. A similar perspective on the part of the president saved Stockman's job after publication of his interviews with William Greider in November 1981. However, my regard for Stockman, and apparently that of the president, barely survived the publication of Stockman's book in 1986. The effect of this book was to understate the effects of the Reagan economic program and Stockman's own contribution to this program. After failing to reduce the budget as much as he wanted, Stockman concluded that it wasn't worth trying—a sad self-judgment by an extraordinary man.

The CEA Chairmen

The chairman of the CEA is the junior member of the troika. With no program responsibilities, his role is strictly advisory, and his influence is dependent on relations with the president and other senior officials.

Murray Weidenbaum, the CEA chairman through August 1982, was an old-fashioned economist whose judgment was better than his technical skills. A specialist in regulation, industry, and trade issues, he had a macroeconomic perspective that, like that of most of his generation, was vaguely Keynesian. In a new administration staffed by monetarists and supply-side economists, however, he seemed out of place. As an early supporter of John Connally (as was Stockman!), Weidenbaum never developed a personal relationship with the president or effective alliances with other key economic officials. He had a traditional Republican's concern about the deficit but, as the 1982 *Economic Report* suggests, was not very clear about its economic effects. As a group the CEA worked well under his leadership; he had good relations with the other members, and he made effective use of both the holdover and new staff. An increasing concern about the rapid growth of the defense budget and the deficit and exclusion from the "Gang of 17" budget discussions led him to resign, with little notice, in August 1982. Unfortunately, from my perspective, he had little influence on economic policy. Murray Weidenbaum is a friend, and I missed his counsel.

Martin Feldstein, the chairman from the fall of 1982 through July 1984, was probably the best economist ever to serve in this position. A former winner of the prize for the best American economist under age forty, Feldstein was a professor at Harvard and the president of the prestigious National Bureau of Economic Research. In an important sense Feldstein was also the best supply-side economist in the country, having conducted or supervised extensive research on the economic effects of a range of government programs and the tax code. As it turned out, however, his tenure as chairman almost destroyed the CEA.

After Weidenbaum's resignation, the White House sought to recruit a distinguished economist to restore confidence in the Reagan economic program. Although Feldstein's politics were not known, he was a logical candidate. He had supported the 1981 tax legislation, reform of social security, and other elements of the economic program. I was one of those who recommended Feldstein for the position. Feldstein agreed to come on several conditions—that he would have lead responsibility for the economic forecasts and that temporary funding would be made available to add six staff members of his choosing. He also arranged for a special fund for an expensive refurnishing of the chairman's office.

Feldstein quickly fouled his own nest. He rarely sought the counsel of the other members of the CEA, relying primarily on the staff members that he selected. Bill Poole (who had been named to replace Jerry Jordan as the third member before Feldstein's nomination) and I found that Feldstein tolerated little professional discussion of any issue. Poole and I sorted out our own roles and relations. Feldstein missed an early opportunity to make a contribution to the social security issue by failing to gain the confidence of the White House. His major early mistake concerned the economic forecasts for 1983. Against the recommendation of every member of T-2, a subordinate committee of the troika chaired by Bill Poole, Feldstein insisted on a forecast that real GNP would increase only 3 percent in 1983, much lower than the growth during the first year of a typical recovery (the actual increase in real GNP during 1983 was 6.5 percent). In January 1983 Feldstein endorsed the bizarre proposal for a contingent tax increase.

The primary problem that destroyed Feldstein's effectiveness, however, was his public role. Dave Gergen had encouraged him to develop a more public role as part of an effort to restore confidence in the economic program. Feldstein's initial response was cautious; he was not comfortable speaking to lay audiences and had little experience with the press. He chose to focus on the deficit and pressed the case for the contingent tax proposal long after the administration had backed away from it. Feldstein quickly gained a lot of press attention, and a platoon of reporters made a short career of following his pronouncements. He was flattered by this attention and learned to cultivate the press. Before each major speech or testimony, he would have an interview with a small group of reporters and send copies to other reporters with a round yellow stamp to suggest immediate attention. Feldstein's public remarks finally led to a blowup in 1984. Regan and the White House reacted to Feldstein's consistent focus on the deficit as an implied criticism of administration policy. In response to congressional questions about the *Economic Report,* Regan remarked that it "should be thrown in a trashcan." Displaying a rare expression of humor, Feldstein responded that Regan's remark must have been a throwaway line. Apparently on instruction, Larry Speakes ridiculed Feldstein at a press conference in a series of crude remarks.

Feldstein, unlike Stockman, never learned to resolve the external and internal role of a government official. After Stockman got in trouble in November 1981, he saved his job by kissing the ring, doing his job, and shutting up for a while. An economic adviser, especially, must sacrifice any external role that is inconsistent with his internal role. In the absence of any bureaucratic or political base, an adviser can be effective only if his role is accepted in the relevant policy review forums. The Reagan administration tolerated substantial controversy within its policy forums; it would not tolerate an economic adviser who took his case to the public. Feldstein, a man of enormous skill but poor judgment, sacrificed a potentially important internal role because he did not learn this lesson.

After Feldstein resigned in July 1984, shortly before a limit imposed by his Harvard contract, the White House seriously considered eliminating the CEA or reducing its role. As acting chairman, I wrote an extensive memorandum to Baker and Meese making the case to maintain the internal role of the CEA but to severely limit its external role. A *New York Times* survey of former CEA chairmen made the same case. That is what has happened. The reporters who had followed Feldstein for nearly two years misinterpreted the lower public visibility of the CEA as a weakening of its internal role. The major lasting effect of the Feldstein episode was the choice of a new chairman in April 1985 who had no ties to the academic community and was comfortable with a short leash.

The Barons

A number of other officials have an important potential role in economic policy because of the organizations they head. For lack of a better word, I will call them the barons.

Paul Volcker

As chairman of the Federal Reserve Board, formally an agent of Congress, Paul Volcker was the most important of these barons. Occasional tensions between the administration and the Fed, as discussed in Chapter 5, led to a relation between Regan and Volcker like that of two scorpions in a bottle. This relation, however, was not symmetric. Regan was criticized by the press for any suggestion that he was interfering with the Fed; Volcker, however, was free to criticize a wide range of economic policies, regularly expressing concern about the deficit. Volcker's independent authority and his formidable technical and political skills, however, made him too big for the administration to challenge. He clearly knew more about his job than anyone the administration could consider to replace him. Volcker offset the tension with Regan by good relations with Baker, Stockman, and Feldstein. He continued to dominate the board of governors, even after Reagan had appointed a majority, by his control of the staff and the resources available to each member. He maintained control of the larger open market committee by his power over appointments to the regional banks. (In 1986 this authority was challenged by a suit brought by Sen. John Melcher, a Democrat from Montana, on the basis that officials who are not confirmed by the Senate should not participate in a policy body. The Justice Department defended the Fed against this suit, which was resolved in favor of the Fed in September 1986.) The Fed's political influence over the banks derives from its authority to ration access to the discount window and its regulatory powers. With an A&C cigar as his baton, Volcker conducted this system as if it were a fine orchestra, with rarely a false note.

Volcker was especially skilled as a crisis manager, whether handling the complex problems of the debtor countries or the collapse of Continental Illinois. As a product of the Fed, however, he was resistant to reforms that would reduce the prospects for such future crises. He blocked the Bush task force from recommending any substantial reduction of the Fed's regulatory role. The federal deposit insurance system has yet to be reformed to make it consistent with deregulation of deposit interest rates. Although Volcker was the agent for both starting and terminating the monetarist experiment, he resisted any new rule for the conduct of monetary policy. The problems of the debtor countries (and their banks) continue to be papered over by new loans. The Fed has yet to explain why it will not permit the failure of a large bank. In summary, Volcker deserves substantial but not exclusive credit for the rapid decline in inflation and for a successful management of the several financial crises. Someone else, however, will have to be the agent of the necessary reforms.

Alan Greenspan, who succeeded Volcker in the summer of 1987, may be that agent, but I doubt it. Although he is more favorable to financial deregulation, he has few expressed views about monetary policy. Greenspan was the leading candidate to succeed Volcker, who had rejected Reagan's weak request to serve a third term, because he was considered "safe," politically savvy, and responsive to the administration. The White House was apparently not concerned about Greenspan's role in promoting President Ford's absurd "Whip Inflation Now" campaign in late 1974. That campaign, initiated midway through the most severe postwar recession, was designed to reduce inflation by the wearing of WIN buttons, by exhortation, and by example—without recognizing that the monetary restraint that would cut the inflation rate by half within two years had already been implemented. One hopes that Greenspan has learned this important lesson in the meantime. A concern that Greenspan would be unduly responsive to the short-term interests of the administration led to a brief, sharp drop in the bond market and the dollar on the day his appointment was announced.

Malcolm Baldrige

As secretary of commerce and chairman of the cabinet council of commerce and trade, "Mac" Baldrige had an opportunity to play an important role in economic policy. As a White House favorite, he also participated in the troika and the budget review group. As with most prior secretaries of commerce, Baldrige used this position to espouse "mercantilist" policies—the promotion of exports and limits on imports. He served a valuable role in trying to sort out our confused policies on the export of strategic goods, a role that brought him into regular conflict with Weinberger. Aside from the trade bills proposed by Congress, however, he never met an import restraint that he did not like. Baldrige was the primary agent in the administration for the quotas on European steel, the tightening of the textile and apparel quotas, the quotas on machine tools, the semiconductor cartel, and the recurring initiatives against Japan. He made little use of the senior economists in Commerce, leaving them to administer the department's statistical agencies. Baldrige sought to gain the lead role on trade issues by promoting a new department of international trade and industry, but this proposal received no support in either the cabinet or Congress. His contribution was more valuable on other issues. He was primarily responsible for the legislation allowing export trading companies and joint ventures for R&D and for promoting change in the product liability and antitrust laws, and he was a strong supporter of budget restraint. Baldrige was an attractive man—quick, humorous, and gracious in his personal relations. Although I opposed many of his initiatives, we parted with mutual respect. In July 1987 Baldrige died from an accident while engaged in his favorite avocation—steer-roping at a rodeo. The choice of a steel-company executive as his successor was perceived as an endorsement of the role that Baldrige established at Commerce.

William Brock

As U.S. trade representative and the chairman of the statutory Trade Policy Committee during the first term, William Brock was one of the class acts of the administration. As a former senator and chairman of the Republican National Committee, he may have had the best political judgment of any cabinet member. He never gained the trust of the White House, however, because of his role as chairman of the RNC in the 1976 convention, and he did not have an opportunity to contribute to policies other than trade. His most important contributions were initiation of free trade negotiations with Israel and Canada and his extraordinary success in deleting the most damaging provisions of the 1984 trade legislation. It is too early to evaluate his second-term role as secretary of labor, but I was dismayed by his promotion of a substantial increase in the program for assistance of displaced workers. Although Brock's policy views were more moderate than those of the Reaganauts, he would be a credit to any administration.

George Shultz

George Shultz, the secretary of state since mid-1982, was the only professional economist in the cabinet. In the Nixon administration he had served as secretary of labor, director of OMB, and secretary of the treasury. During the Reagan administration, however, he made much less of a contribution to general economic policy than most of us expected. He was first considered as chairman of the SIG-IEP, but Regan moved quickly to capture that position. Shultz provided wise counsel to the troika and the cabinet, but he did not assume a leading economic role. As an economist his primary contribution was to strengthen the quality of economic analysis in the State Department by reinforcing Allen Wallis as undersecretary for economic affairs.

As a rule Shultz is somewhat of a buddha, but he has a strong temper when he is crossed. A development to watch is whether Shultz checks Baker's moves toward a new international monetary system in the remaining years of the second term.

The Courtiers

White House officials, like royal courtiers, had widely varying influences, depending on their skills and personal relationships. During the first term relations among these officials were collegial and somewhat flexible. Someone else will have to evaluate the hierarchical system under Don Regan and Howard Baker in the second term.

James Baker

As chief of staff during the first term, Jim Baker was the most influential of these courtiers. Baker started with a handicap, having been the campaign manager for George Bush. Ed Meese, who had been a long-term aide to Ronald Reagan, was supposed to have lead responsibility for policy issues. Baker earned his influence because he was decisive, well organized, and politically skilled, in particular con-

trast to Meese. According to Meese's initial plan, Baker was supposed to have responsibility for politics and communications, but this
was naive; there is no way to separate policy and politics at this level.

Some conservatives criticized Baker for opposing Reagan's policy
agenda, but this was a bum rap. Baker had no apparent views on
policy, but he was intensely loyal to the president's political interests.
He never attended cabinet council meetings and seldom spoke at
cabinet meetings. His strong influence on policy was the result of his
perception of the political effects of a proposed policy. His political
strategy, although it was perceived to be very successful, seemed to
be quite simple: Do something for every element of your own coalition. Don't alienate any group. Avoid policy proposals that might
lose. Cut losses quickly. Focus on conditions between now and the
next election.

Reagan's overwhelming electoral victory in 1984 and his continuing popularity seem to vindicate this strategy. Maximizing votes,
however, involves a different strategy than maximizing the president's policy agenda. If he were a baseball manager, Baker would
pull a batter if he could not hit a home run. Winning a pennant,
however, also requires bunts, scratch singles, stolen bases, sacrifice
fly balls, and some thought about tomorrow's game. Baker would
not risk the president's personal popularity for straight talk about
the deficit, making the case for reform of social security and environmental legislation, stronger opposition to protectionist measures,
or strengthening the Republicans in the House. Many of Reagan's
policy advisers, however, would have traded 250 electoral votes in
1984 for some combination of these measures.

Baker is an attractive man, straight in his personal relations, and
a favorite of the press. In retrospect, however, I believe that he seriously limited the potential of the Reagan economic program and,
as suggested in Chapter 5, that the exchange of positions with Regan
in 1985 was a mistake for all concerned.

Richard Darman
Dick Darman gained substantial influence as Baker's aide, both in
the White House and the Treasury. He was very sensitive, however,
about being considered only an aide. He chafed at his initial title of
deputy assistant to the president, and the word "deputy" was quickly
removed. At a morning White House staff meeting shortly before
the second inaugural, Mike Deaver presented Darman with a special
inaugural license plate with the designation BAKER AIDE; Darman
was visibly irritated and did not appreciate the general laughter. This
role, however, was his specialty; he had previously served as a special
aide to Elliot Richardson, the prototypical liberal Republican. Some-

what like Stockman, Darman was young, smart, very good at organizing information, and energetic. Unlike Stockman, however, he had
no commitment to the Reagan policy agenda. He was also more manipulative and was widely believed to be the source of press leaks
and rumors about those who checked his ambition. A common sus-
picion was that Machiavelli's *The Prince* was on his bedside table. Darman served Baker very well by gathering and organizing information, by formulating options, and by handling many of the
communications issues. He also became the primary White House
liaison with Jack Kemp, ensuring that the president's public rhetoric
avoided most of the hard choices. One of his most bizarre actions
was his attack on American corporate management in the fall of 1986.
For a government official who had no business experience or special
understanding of business, Darman's attack was a case of the pot
calling the kettle black. The most charitable explanation of this episode is that Darman was trying to revive the progressive tradition in
the Republican party by aligning the administration with the popu-
list sentiment for a more activist economic policy. Whatever his motives, Darman's views were strongly inconsistent with Reaganomics.
Any government probably needs a few ambitious politicrats like Dick
Darman, however, and his manipulative behavior may have led me
to undervalue his contribution.

Michael Deaver

Mike Deaver's role was to stage-manage the first family. The morning staff meeting in the Roosevelt Room was his show, although Baker
was the chairman and Deaver sat next to the bookshelf on the west
wall. My major surprise about the later conflict-of-interest charges
against Deaver was that he was involved in any policy issues. He will
not be missed.

Edwin Meese

As counsellor to the president, Ed Meese was the most conspicuously
mediocre man in American public life. An aide to Reagan for many
years, he had a vague sense of desirable changes in policy, but he
did not have the intellect, convictions, or management and political
skills to contribute to their realization. Although he usually wore an
Adam Smith tie, he confused Reaganomics with the interests of the
last business group to visit his office, particularly if it was from California. Meese had a poor sense of priorities and was a terrible manager. He would often be speaking to some 4-H group at a time an
important issue was being resolved. Memos would pile up in his in-
box for months without being answered. His concept of management was to revise organization charts, issue executive orders, and

arrange for presidential pep talks. He had reason to expect loyalty up the hierarchy, but he was often careless about loyalty down. On one occasion he pulled some testimony of mine minutes before it was to go to Congress, without the good grace to explain his reason. Most of the able young supporters of the Reagan program who were on his staff early in the administration left in frustration after a year or so. After Meese was nominated as attorney general, a former Meese aide argued that he should not be replaced: "Ed Meese's office ought to be put to some other more worthwhile use, such as the National Museum of Lost Memos or Abandoned Briefcases. Or for that matter, Lost Hopes and Abandoned Dreams." Meese was a decent, confused, and mediocre man, a former deputy district attorney for Alameda County who was out of place in the White House, a turtle on a stump.

Meese had every opportunity to make a different record. Among the internal White House troika in the first term, he was nominally the senior official and he was closest to the president. His one substantial contribution was to design a policy review process that was consistent with Reagan's preferred management style. He was supposed to have the lead role on policy issues. For those of us who did not have direct contact with the president, it was very important to have clear policy guidance from someone who could speak for the president. Meese lost this role to Baker and Stockman because he was often not decisive, did not make effective use of his staff, and did not have a clear sense of or strong convictions about many policy issues. After the 1984 election Meese tried to recapture the initiative on policy. He organized a small group to develop a second-term policy agenda, working in parallel with the core group on the budget, but this group produced nothing that was later approved. At the first cabinet meeting after the election, Meese made a case that policy should drive the budget rather than the budget driving policy, whatever that means. Stockman barely suppressed a snicker. At the same time Darman was working with Jack Kemp to develop a communication strategy that would disguise the first serious budget in four years in presidential rhetoric about growth and opportunity. On almost every major issue the other key officials found that they had to work around Meese in order to do their own jobs. He was the wrong man for the White House policy position.

Meese will have a different record as attorney general. After an extensive investigation of his personal finances and a contested confirmation, his spirits and energies were renewed. He chose a first-rate group of young key associates at Justice and energized the department. More than any attorney general in many years, Meese raised important issues about federalism and the role of the courts, but his own interpretation of these issues often seemed confused or wrong-headed. In this position Meese provoked continuing controversy about his concept of jurisprudence and the social policies that he promoted, but there has been less question about his direction and effectiveness.

The Domestic Policy Advisers

One group that could have had a substantial effect on domestic policy was the Office of Policy Development (OPD), an office that reported to Meese. Martin Anderson, the first head of this office, was a Hoover Institute economist and an adviser to Reagan for some years. The office was staffed by able young conservatives and libertarians who had a strong commitment to the Reagan policy agenda. The promise of this office unfortunately was never realized, and it drifted into insignificance.

Anderson wisely focused this office on issues that did not have a substantial budget impact. Early in 1981, for example, he challenged the draft registration system, making a good case that it would not significantly accelerate the rate of mobilization in an emergency and was an unnecessary intrusion into the lives of young people. In the 1980 campaign Reagan had opposed draft registration and, in this case, Meese supported Anderson. Alexander Haig, however, stormed into the White House arguing that draft registration was a necessary symbol to counter a perceived threat of additional Soviet pressure on Poland. And the White House caved—the first reversal of a Reagan campaign promise. The precedent was discouraging. Later, Anderson made a strong case against an administration endorsement of the Simpson-Mazzoli immigration bill being considered in Congress, in part on grounds that the proposed employer sanctions might lead to increased discrimination against Hispanics and other minorities. In this case Meese sided with Attorney General William French Smith, establishing an administration position that was strongly inconsistent with Reagan's vision of a North American "accord."

Anderson was both principled and professional, a rare combination in the White House, and he was a valued ally of those of us who were supporting the Reagan agenda from other positions. His one major mistake, supporting the disastrous social security proposal in May 1981, damaged both his own position and Meese's policy role, however. After Anderson resigned in frustration in 1982, there was no consistent supporter of Reagan economic policies in the White House. Ed Harper, Anderson's successor and a former White House aide under Nixon, was a good manager but had no commitment to

the Reagan policy agenda, and he left to manage a garage-door company. Jack Svahn and Gary Bauer, the later domestic policy advisers,
had no perceptible skills or influence.

In the meantime most of the able young people that Meese and
Anderson had recruited drifted off to other positions or left the government. By the end of the first term, the only core of Reaganauts
in the White House were the speechwriters—a group, ironically, that
reported to Darman. In 1986, after a running controversy with Regan's "mice," the two leading speechwriters also left in frustration.
How sad: in the end, the bland were leading the blind.

PROCESSES

The effectiveness of any large organization is dependent on decen-
tralized management and centralized guidance and review. The federal government is not run very well, in part because Congress and
(occasionally) the White House exercise too much control over detailed management issues and provide inadequate guidance and review of the major policy issues. Reagan was determined to correct
this bias. The policy formulation and review process was specifically
designed to support Reagan's perception of his own role and the
nature of his preferred relations with administration officials and
advisers. For the most part this process served his objectives quite
well when he chose to use it.

The Cabinet Council System

The president was determined to use members of the cabinet in a
consultative role in addition to their responsibilities as department
managers. A system of cabinet councils, subcommittees of the cabinet for each major program area, became the primary policy formulation and review mechanism of the Reagan administration. This
system was initially designed by Meese. The administration inherited
two such councils, the National Security Council and the Trade Policy Committee, both established by law. In February 1981, cabinet
councils were established on economic affairs, commerce and trade,
human resources, natural resources and the environment, and food
and agriculture. In 1982, additional cabinet councils were established on legal policy, international economic policy (a subcommittee
of the NSC), and management. Each of these councils was chaired
by a member of the cabinet or a senior White House official and was
assigned a secretary from OPD. Other members of the councils included members of the cabinet with a related responsibility and (ex-

cept for the NSC) the chairman of the CEA and the White House domestic policy adviser.

The general activities of these councils were to review conditions and proposed policies in each area of responsibility and formulate options and a recommendation for later consideration by the full cabinet and the president. On Reagan's specific instruction, the councils were to address the substance of these issues, not their political implications. As a rule there was little pressure to achieve a consensus at this stage, and the memoranda forwarded to the cabinet summarized the position of each member. The level of activity differed substantially among these councils, depending on the importance of the issues and the energy of the chairman and the secretary of the council. The most active was the cabinet council on economic affairs, with Don Regan as chairman and Roger Porter as secretary; this council, which usually met twice a week, had more meetings than the sum of the meetings of the other councils. In contrast, the councils on human resources and food and agriculture met very rarely. From my experience, which includes participation in faculty meetings and the board meetings of a major industrial company, the quality of the presentations and discussions at these council meetings was quite high. The relations among council members were collegial, every member had an opportunity to make his or her case, and discussions were usually vigorous. As a rule the best-informed people at these meetings were the cabinet member (or his representative) making the major presentation, David Stockman, and the CEA representative.

There were several problems with this initial system. The responsibility for reviewing trade issues was shared by four cabinet councils with overlapping membership. There was no reason for a separate council on food and agriculture, as it primarily involved the activities of one department. These problems were resolved in the second term by concentrating the review in three councils—the NSC, an economic policy council chaired by Baker, and a domestic policy council chaired by Meese. A more enduring problem is that this process did not work well unless issues were first reviewed at the council level without the president. The presence of the president had the effect of suppressing discussion and dissent, not because of Reagan's personal style but because of a shared reservation about arguing in his presence. Several members of the first-term cabinet who were close to the president, such as William French Smith and William Clark, learned to schedule the first discussion of their proposals with the president attending in order to reduce potential criticism of their proposals. In a few important cases, such as the Treasury tax plan,

there was no council or cabinet review before public disclosure of
the proposal. In the second term Baker rarely brought Treasury initiatives to the cabinet council that he chaired.

From my perspective this process worked quite well. After the disastrous May 1981 social security proposal, Baker and Meese ensured that the president was presented with several options. In general the process guaranteed a thorough substantive discussion by
cabinet-level officials before political considerations were introduced.
The process leaked like a sieve, a condition that was sometimes em-
barrassing to the administration but often reduced the probability of
major error. My evaluation of this process, however, may be biased;
the cabinet councils were the primary forums in which the CEA had
an opportunity to make its contribution.

In contrast, a thoughtful early member of OPD described the cabinet council process as "a pernicious system" by which "the policy
agenda is in large measure transferred from the Reagan White House
to the departments. Instead of informing the departments that the
president believes so-and-so, and wants such-and-such done about it
unless there is some overpowering reason not to, the Reagan White
House has instituted itself as an arbitration forum for disagreements
brought up to it by its department heads. The Cabinet Council process creates a mini-legislature, where participants who have no interest in particular issues trade votes to their colleagues in return for
future consideration. . . . Thus, in large measure, was the Reagan
Revolution lost."

In this case I believe that my thoughtful friend was wrong. An
effective review process is designed to frustrate those who are the
strongest advocates of any policy proposal. Many policy proposals,
including those by the White House staff, are ill-conceived. Some
vote trading within the cabinet is desirable as part of the process of
maintaining a diffuse coalition. On many smaller issues Reagan did
not have a clear prior sense of what he wanted to accomplish. The
cabinet council system was a "conservative" process in that it reduced
the frequency of policy errors at the expense of delaying and sometimes moderating those policies which were approved. My judgment
is that a future administration will find something like the cabinet
council system to be very valuable.

The White House Political Review

For most of those who worked on the substantive dimensions of economic policy, the White House political review was a "black hole."
We saw what went into this process and what came out, but we had
no understanding of the considerations and reasoning that led to the

decisions made as a result. The policy advisers were often frustrated
about the number of decisions that seemed to be based on some
unstated political consideration. Any student of government, however, will recognize that a president will make numerous decisions
that are inconsistent with his own preferences. The standard by which
to judge this process is whether the political concessions were the
minimum necessary to further the president's larger agenda. My
judgment is that the political decisions seemed to be designed more
to maximize Reagan's popular support than his policy agenda. The
president's considerable popularity in turn was hoarded like a gold
reserve, rather than invested to serve either his policy agenda or the
interests of the party.

The primary group responsible for the political review was the
legislative strategy group (LSG). This group was the result of a February 1981 memo from Darman to Baker expressing concern about
the absence of any procedure to coordinate legislative strategy and
offering "to call points of conflict, inconsistency, incompleteness, or
opportunity to your attention." Although the group proved to be
very powerful, it had no formal charter and was never displayed on
the White House organization chart. Baker and Meese were nominally co-chairman of the LSG, but this group always met in Baker's
office, usually late each afternoon, and Baker became its effective
head. Darman and Craig Fuller (the cabinet secretary) provided the
staff support. Stockman, communications director Dave Gergen, and
the assistant for legislative affairs were regular participants in this
informal group. (As an outsider, I wondered what qualifies one to
be a political expert, except by self-designation. Baker had been an
unsuccessful candidate for state office in Texas and the manager of
Bush's unsuccessful campaign for the Republican nomination. Stockman, who had once been a divinity student, was the only one to have
served in Congress. In army terms Meese, Gergen, Fuller, and Darman had gained their positions by being "horseholders.") The major
achievements of this first-term group were the 1981 budget and tax
legislation. After 1981 the legislative strategy of the Reagan administration was largely defensive.

The morning staff meetings in the White House provided no more
illumination on this black hole. As chairman of this meeting, Baker
would summarize the major events and news releases scheduled that
day and ask for comments. Most of the discussion was about photo
opportunities for the president and administration "spins" on developing news of any kind. The bottom line for this group was how
well the administration played on the evening television news. One
gained the impression that this group confused the stage managing
of the president with governing the nation. As a clue to its perspec-

tive and effectiveness, the president's popularity continues to be very high, and the federal government is still in a mess of considerable dimension. In contrast to Stockman, I do not pretend to be shocked by "the triumph of politics," only saddened about its effects.

The Economic Summits

The economic summits, an annual meeting of the heads of government of the seven major Western industrial nations plus the European Economic Community, were initiated by Germany and France in 1975. The only apparent value of these summits was that the preparatory work forced a resolution of some issues within each participating government and that the summit meetings provided a convenient opportunity for private bilateral discussions. The summits were carefully orchestrated by the "sherpas," an international committee of second-level officials, who in general prepared the final communiqué prior to the meeting. The summit meetings involved little substance but provided a stage for the politicians to look like statesmen for the press and television. Among those who did not attend these summits were the central bankers and the chief economic advisers, a practice that particularly irritated Paul Volcker. President Mitterrand may not have appreciated the irony of a socialist president of France hosting a summit at the palace of the Sun King at Versailles in the middle of the 1982 recession. Reagan's primary contribution was to maintain a more open agenda at the 1984 summit at Williamsburg. In general, the summits were a waste of time and effort and may have created a false expectation about the potential for increased international economic cooperation. The summits should probably be ended, a conclusion reinforced by the failure to agree on any important issue at the 1987 summit in Venice.

Outside Advisory Groups

As in any administration, Reagan used outside advisory groups not to elicit information but to buy time, identification with some issue, and legitimacy for his own policies. It is more difficult to explain why busy, able people serve on these groups more than once.

The President's Economic Policy Advisory Board, chaired first by George Shultz and then by Walter Wriston, included a dozen or so distinguished Republican businessmen and economists. This group, in meetings about twice a year, offered a wealth of wisdom, but its advice was barely tolerated. The administration was no more eager to hear concerns about increased federal spending, the deficit, and import restraints from friends than from critics. It is difficult to identify a single issue in which this group's generally sound advice contributed to a change in policy.

The only presidential commission that had a significant effect on policy was the Greenspan commission on social security. As discussed in Chapter 2, however, the major contribution of this commission was to resolve a short-term funding problem and a political logjam, largely by increasing taxes at the cost of indefinitely deferring the necessary reform of social security.

A large number of distinguished people served on other commissions on government waste, education, housing, hunger, international competitiveness, and the steel industry. These commissions served their purpose, primarily by permitting the administration to defer any change in policies affecting these issues until after the 1984 election. In retrospect, only the reports of the waste, housing, and hunger commissions merit serious attention.

Such outside advisory bodies are often valuable for different reasons, but they should not be expected to have much effect on government policy. Many people maintain an illusion that the manifest problems of government are due to insufficient information. My impression is that most politicians and government officials have as much information as they want and learn to rationalize new information that conflicts with their preconceptions. Major changes in government policy, rather like changes in a scientific paradigm, are due more to a sea change in perceptions about what government ought to do. Policy advisers, either inside or outside the government, can make a contribution only around the edges of the prevailing perception. The Reagan economic program did not prove to be a revolution primarily because there has not yet been a substantial change in perceptions about what the federal government should do or, more importantly, should not do.

CHAPTER TEN

The Future of Reaganomics

The foundation has been laid for a sustained era of national prosperity. But a major threat to our future prosperity remains: the federal deficit. If this deficit is not brought under control by limiting government spending, we put in jeopardy all we have achieved. Deficits brought on by continued high spending threaten the lower tax rates incorporated in tax reform and inhibit progress in our balance of trade.

We cannot permit this to happen.

Will Reaganomics survive the Reagan administration? The Reagan policies will clearly affect the *levels* of future budgets, the public debt, prices, and so on. Economic history, like biological evolution, is "path dependent." Federal policies and economic conditions in the 1990s will necessarily build on the foundation established during the 1980s. A more important question, for which the answer is less clear, is the direction of future *changes* in economic policy.

The nature of future changes in economic policies and conditions—how much of Reaganomics survives—will depend on the lessons of Reaganomics, the resolution of several unresolved problems, and the outcomes of the 1988 elections. My perspective on these issues is the subject of this chapter.

THE LESSONS OF REAGANOMICS

Spending

The growth of real federal spending proved to be very difficult to reduce—despite the most conservative president since the 1920s, a Republican Senate, and the energies of a remarkable budget director. From FY 1981 through FY 1986, real federal spending increased at a 3.4 percent annual rate, lower than the 5 percent annual increase during the Carter administration but higher than the 2.5 percent annual increase in real GNP. The pattern of total federal spending during the Reagan administration was not significantly different from the pattern of the prior postwar years.

The continued growth of real federal spending was, I believe, the major failure of the Reagan economic program. Moreover, the deficits that were caused primarily by the continued growth of real spending threaten to undermine the two major accomplishments of the program, specifically the reduction in tax rates and inflation. There is plenty of blame to go around.

First, the initial Reagan budget plan severely constrained the potential for budget restraint. A substantial increase was proposed for the defense budget, equal to 25 percent of total outlays in FY 1981. The initial budget also promised to preserve and maintain the core social safety net programs, for which the budget was 35 percent of total outlay in FY 1981. Interest payments on the outstanding debt were another 10 percent of FY 1981 outlays. To reduce the growth of total outlays, therefore, the budget plan required a susbstantial reduction of the *level* of spending for the many domestic programs constituting the other 30 percent of the FY 1981 budget.

A part of the problem is that contemporary campaign politics undermine the potential to govern. At no time during the 1980 and 1984 campaigns, for example, did Reagan acknowledge that a substantial reduction in domestic programs was necessary to permit both a defense buildup and a tax rate cut without an increase in the deficit. The 1980 solution to this budget problem was to reduce "waste, fraud, extravagance, and abuse." The 1984 solution was to increase economic growth. Both solutions to the budget problem proved to be illusory. There is plenty of waste in the federal budget, but most of it is there for the same reason that the programs are there—because someone wants it. An increase in economic growth proved to be difficult to achieve. In the absence of any campaign commitment to reduce domestic spending, therefore, substantial election victories did not provide a sufficient mandate to reduce these programs.

Another part of the problem is that Reagan's agenda included a number of controversial proposals that required congressional approval. The total budget cost of such proposals as the sale of weapons to Saudi Arabia, the MX missile, additional funding of the IMF, and aid to the *contras* was often much higher than the direct budget cost.

A major problem, I now believe, is that the phased tax-rate reductions approved in 1981 were not made contingent on subsequent budget restraint as then proposed by the House Budget Committee. The initial budget proposals were not sufficient to offset the revenue loss of the tax cuts, and not all the initial proposals were approved. The only remaining case for budget restraint centered on the rather vague general benefits of lower deficits—benefits that became increasingly implausible after inflation and interest rates declined and the economy recovered. The political problem of reducing the deficit was due to a developing recognition that the deficit did not lead to substantial economic problems in the short term.

The most important problem, as David Stockman documented, is that there were few consistent advocates of spending restraint in the administration or in either party in Congress. If Reagan had wanted to promote a "revolution," it was important to appoint revolutionaries—not people such as Terrel Bell at Education or Otis Bowen at HHS. Almost every self-styled fiscal conservative strongly supported some part of "the social park barrel." By 1987 the administration also supported substantial increases in spending for displaced workers, catastrophic health coverage, and for space and science programs. I believe Stockman was wrong to conclude that the public also supports these programs, in light of the fact that current taxes finance only about 80 percent of the total budget. There is now no doubt, however, that the contemporary welfare state is broadly supported in Congress. One of the ironic effects of the Reagan administration may be to legitimize the current level and types of transfer payments and social services.

Taxes and the Deficit

The substantial reduction in the federal tax rates on individual income proved to be one of the two most important achievements of Reaganomics but was attained only by shifting some of the tax burden to other groups. The general reduction of tax rates approved in 1981 contributed to the large deficit that, for a given path of total spending, will require a future tax increase. The further reduction of individual rates approved in the Tax Reform Act of 1986 was financed in part by a substantial increase in the taxes on corporate income. A general reduction in tax rates is still dependent on more substantial spending restraint than has been exercised to date.

As the supply-siders anticipated, the reduction in tax rates approved in 1981 induced a substantial increase in taxable income. One study estimated that nearly half the static revenue loss from the tax rate reductions in ERTA was offset by an increase in taxable income. The effect of the tax rate reductions on total income, however, was less than anticipated; most of the increase in taxable income was apparently due to a reduced use of tax shelters. The total taxes paid by those with incomes above $200,000 increased slightly, and the share of federal income taxes paid by those with incomes above $50,000 increased substantially. Contrary to the early promises of outside supply-side polemicists, however, the general reduction of tax rates approved in 1981 reduced total federal revenues. There was never an empirical basis for the assertion that a general reduction in tax rates would increase revenues, and no administration economist or revenue projection ever supported that irresponsible claim.

My judgment (or, maybe, my hope) is that the broad bipartisan support of the Tax Reform Act of 1986 will reduce the prospect of a future increase in individual income tax rates. The early proposal by the new House Speaker Jim Wright to maintain the 1987 transition rates was broadly criticized within his own party. Given the reluctance of Congress to reduce domestic spending, however, some additional revenues are required. My advice to a new administration would be to continue to broaden the individual income tax base before considering any increase in tax rates or a major new type of tax.

The rapid increase in the deficit through FY 1986 was one of the major unanticipated effects of the initial Reagan economic program and will prove to be its most adverse legacy. Most of the increase in the deficit was due to the continued high growth of federal spending, as the total federal revenue share of GNP is now only slightly lower than the initial projections. The major surprise about the effects of the increased deficit, and the primary political problem of reducing the deficit, is that it did not lead to the increase in inflation and interest rates that was broadly expected by outside analysts. Only in the mid-1980s was it broadly recognized that the continued high deficit was a major cause of the decline in the U.S. trade balance. Congress, however, continued to blame the trade deficit on foreign trade practices rather than to acknowledge the one most apparent short-term economic effect of the budget deficit.

Regulation and Trade

On issues such as regulation and trade, a good defense is not enough. All too often, those of us responsible for reviewing regulation and trade proposals faced a no-win situation. On numerous occasions, often with considerable effort, we managed to defeat or defer some new regulation or trade restraint. On other occasions, we lost. The net result of this process is that we ended up with more regulations and more trade restraints than at the beginning of the administration. The reason for this is that most regulations and many trade restraints do not automatically expire, and most of the new proposals are for more such restraints.

An aggressive strategy of deregulation is the only way to avoid a net increase in regulation. The total amount of regulation increased during both the Carter and Reagan administrations, but for different reasons. Under Carter there was a substantial deregulation of prices and entry in the airline, trucking, railroad, and financial industries and a substantial increase in the regulation of health, safety, the environment, and the uses of energy. Under Reagan there was little deregulation and less new regulation; the only deregulatory legislation approved to date involves banks, intercity buses, ocean shipping, and energy use. The major opportunities for the next administration are to continue the reduction of the older forms of economic regulation and to reform those social regulations for which the objectives are broadly shared.

Similarly, an aggressive strategy of reducing existing trade barriers is now necessary to avoid a net increase in protection. Average U.S. tariffs are now less than 5 percent, and the automatic reductions in these tariffs are correspondingly smaller. There is no automatic process, however, to relax most of the nontariff barriers. The Reagan administration successfully opposed the many trade-restriction bills introduced in Congress through 1987, but only at the cost of numerous severe trade restraints implemented by the administration. For the first time in many decades, the new trade restraints exceeded the automatic reductions. The damaging 1987 trade bills are likely to undermine the prospects for the new GATT round initiated in September 1986.

For the most part, Reagan's convictions on these issues were admirable but not strong. My disappointment is that the administration did not demonstrate a political commitment to follow through on these convictions.

Monetary Policy

The reduction in inflation proved to be much less difficult than expected. The last *Economic Report* of the Carter administration estimated that each percentage point reduction in inflation would cost about $100 billion (in 1980 dollars) in lost output. In fact, the inflation rate was reduced by over six percentage points without any reduction in the growth of real GNP per adult. The temporary loss of output relative to this trend proved to be less than half that implied by the Carter estimate. The substantial and continuing decline in inflation was one of the two major achievements of the Reagan economic program and is the one economic condition that is superior to the initial Reagan forecasts.

It is much less clear *why* the inflation rate declined as much as it did. The most obvious reason was the reduction in money growth from late 1979 through mid-1982. The rest of the story is much less clear. Since mid-1982 the narrow money supply has increased at the highest sustained peacetime rate without reigniting inflation, as a result of a corresponding reduction in the velocity of money—a condition that was not anticipated and is not yet broadly understood. The most probable reasons for the reduction in velocity were the increase in financial wealth and the combination of declining market interest rates and the higher rates on bank deposits allowed by deregulation, the latter conditions reducing the cost of holding assets in the form of bank deposits. A third condition was the sharp increase in the real foreign exchange value of the dollar through early 1985, which was primarily attributable to the reduction in the effective tax rates on business investment approved in 1981. A fourth condition was the growing excess supply of oil, in part the result of a stronger dollar. My opinion is that the earlier reduction in money growth contributed only to the initial decline in inflation; it was an important contribution but not the dominant one for which Paul Volcker is credited.

The major continuing contribution of monetary policy since mid-1982 has been to stabilize the path of total demand. This permitted a strong recovery in 1983 and 1984 and a continued recovery, to date, through 1987. This policy involved a termination of the monetarist experiment and abandonment of the monetary targets. Although this policy has been quite successful, the primary threat is that there is not yet any broad consensus for a new monetary rule to sustain these conditions beyond the Volcker era.

The Management of Government

The Reagan administration did not change the basic incentives, constraints, or institutions of government, but there are still some valuable lessons from this experience. Reagan's own management style has been clearly superior to that of, for example, Carter. He has focused on the big issues, provided (in general) good guidance, delegated broad authority, and avoided an obsession with detail. A future president would be wise to follow this example. As discussed in Chapter 9, however, Reagan did not develop effective parallel channels of advice, tolerated a mediocre White House staff, was extraordinarily trusting of and not very curious about the behavior of subordinates, and, in an important sense, was too nice to be a superior manager. The problems attributable to these characteristics also provide a lesson for the selection of a future president.

A number of Reagan review institutions proved valuable and are likely to survive. The cabinet council policy review process worked quite well, at least when the White House forced policy review through this process, and it gave members of the cabinet a sense of participation in the broader agenda of the administration. The OMB regulatory review is also likely to survive, despite occasional attempts by Congress to restrict or terminate it. The extensiveness and costs of federal regulation are now too high to permit unilateral agency interpretation of the often rather general regulatory legislation. The President's Economic Policy Advisory Board was not very valuable; a president is better advised to consult such wise men or women on a private basis.

A continued "war on waste" would be valuable, but one should not expect it to yield much budget savings in the absence of a change in the incentives and constraints of government managers. Departmental reorganization, however, is usually a waste of political capital. The Reagan administration substantially reduced the budgets for education and energy although it failed to eliminate these departments, and it resolved the redundant trade policy review process although the proposed Department of International Trade and Industry was not approved. It is too early to pass judgment on the limited effort to "privatize" the provision of some current federal activities.

My view is that changes in budget concepts and the budget process would also be a waste of political capital, at least without a change in the distribution of political power or an effective constitutional restraint on borrowing and taxation. The major changes in federal fiscal policy from about 1965 appear to be more attributable to a weakening of the political parties and of the congressional committee chairmen as well as to the effective elimination of constitutional restraints on the enumerated powers of the federal government.

In summary, changes in government management and budget processes that are inconsistent with the incentives and constraints of bureaucrats and politicians should not be expected to survive or yield significant improvements in the efficiency of government. The several Reagan management initiatives were valuable but not fundamental.

Economic Growth

The growth of real domestic output proved to be very difficult to increase. Real GNP increased at a 2.7 percent annual rate during the Reagan administration, compared to a 2.9 percent annual rate during the Carter administration. The slower growth of real GNP, however, was entirely attributable to a slower growth of the adult population. On a per-adult basis the growth of real GNP and other measures of domestic output were slightly higher than during the Carter administrations. The growth rates did not change much, despite policies that economists of all persuasions regarded as stimulatory. For the Keynesians the record peacetime deficits should have increased demand. For the monetarists the record rate of money growth since mid-1982 should also have increased demand. For the supply-siders the reduction in tax rates and some deregulation should have increased output. As it turned out, economic growth does not appear to have been much affected by the combination of these policies. There was reason to expect that the growth rate would increase after inflation was stabilized, but the growth rate during the second term to date has been only slightly higher than during the first term. The growth of productivity increased somewhat relative to the dismal record during the Carter administration but is still lower than the prior average. The U.S. economy seems to be on a 2.7 percent real growth path, about the average since 1969 and higher than the average since 1973. A series of higher growth forecasts by the administration unfortunately led to an underestimate of the future deficits and the deferral of hard choices and set the stage for disappointment with the actual record.

The most interesting effect of the Reagan policies is that the growth rate of each major component of real spending—consumption, domestic investment, and government purchases—was higher than during the Carter administration, despite a somewhat slower growth of real GNP. How can this be? The answer is that U.S. imports grew very rapidly, allowing us, for a limited period, to use more goods and services than we produced. The magnitude of the balance-of-payments deficit, about 3.4 percent of GNP in 1986, is not sustainable. As this deficit is reduced, the growth of one or more major components of domestic spending must be reduced below the growth of domestic output. The choice of whether to reduce the growth of private consumption, private investment, or government consumption will be the major economic policy issue for some years.

Lessons for Economists

The experience of the 1980s has been, or should have been, chastening to economists of all persuasions. Only an econometrician could love this period, because it produced such a high variance of the key policy variables. Keynesians, for example, may wish to reflect upon why the record peacetime deficits did not apparently increase total demand, inflation, or interest rates and did not much reduce domestic investment. Monetarists, for their part, need to explain why the record sustained rate of money growth since mid-1982 has not (yet) increased inflation. Supply-siders, not to be left out, should consider why the reduction in tax rates has not (yet) increased economic growth.

No one of those schools has yet offered a coherent explanation of the most unusual and unanticipated economic conditions of this period:

- The combination of strong domestic investment (through 1984) and high real interest rates.
- The strong increase in the real exchange value of the dollar through early 1985 and its subsequent decline.
- The rapid increase in the trade deficit.
- The decline in the velocity of money.

The two major clues for sorting out this puzzle are that the budget aggregates do not provide much useful information, (that is, the details are important), and that the effects of domestic policies in an open world economy are often quite different from those in a closed economy. For economists one of the more important lessons of this period may be that we need to rebuild our understanding of macroeconomic relations on a more precise microeconomic foundation. A little more humility would also be appropriate.

Political Lessons

The major lesson of Reaganomics is that those of us who share the Jeffersonian vision of limited constitutional government have not yet much changed the wondrous ways of Washington. Only one major program has been terminated, and the federal budget share of our national output, until recently, continued to increase. The net amount of regulations and trade restraints increased. Monetary policy still operates without any rules. The basic incentives, constraints, and institutions of government have not changed. One ironic result of Reagan's own effectiveness as president may be to increase the power of a future president with a different agenda. The Reagan administration may prove to be only a temporary pause in the increasing politicization of American life.

The future, however, will be of our own making. We can continue to accept a progressive loss of liberties, usually in the name of some other value such as military or economic security. Or we can restore a constitutional republic that is limited by rules that reflect a broad consensus of the American community. We need a better understanding of the processes of government and the actual effects of government policies. We may need a new Reagan to articulate a vision of an American community of both opportunity and caring, one in which the federal government has an important but limited role. Some one or more constitutional amendments may be necessary to limit the government's authority to borrow and tax and to preserve a viable federal system. Most important, we need to sort out in our own minds the rules by which we expect the government to operate and to hold our political officials accountable to these rules. Reaganomics was a first halting step in this direction. None of us can avoid a responsibility for the direction of the next steps.

UNRESOLVED PROBLEMS

The future of Reaganomics will depend critically on future decisions involving some unresolved problems. Some of these problems increased on Reagan's watch, some were deferred, and some were never addressed. A resolution of these problems by some means would sustain and extend the Reagan agenda; a resolution by other means would reverse this agenda.

The Budget

The federal budget now reflects two unsustainable conditions. Federal spending continued to increase relative to GNP, a pattern that was not much different from that in prior postwar years. The federal debt also increased relative to GNP, a condition that was unique to the Reagan administration. At present the federal budget reflects a fundamentally schizophrenic preference—for federal spending of about 23 percent of GNP and for federal taxes of about 19 percent of GNP. Something must give.

Spending
The case for reducing the growth of federal spending is, I would suggest, overwhelming. A lower growth of federal spending would resolve both of the unsustainable budget conditions. An increase in individual and corporate income tax revenues of about 30 percent would be necessary to balance the budget without lower spending growth, and it is not plausible that American voters would be willing to pay this increased price for the current level of federal services.

An effective strategy for reducing the growth of federal spending will require special attention to those programs for which spending increased most rapidly during the Reagan administration—agriculture, defense, and medical care. Spending for agriculture increased more rapidly than for any major program, and most of the benefits accrued to a minority of the small and declining farm population. A new administration should consider terminating the current agricultural programs and focusing the remaining spending on assistance to adjust to a market-based agriculture over a several-year period.

Our defense program also reflects a schizophrenic preference: we are unwilling to fund our current military commitments or to reduce our commitments to the level of acceptable funding. A new administration should undertake the first major review of our military commitments in nearly forty years, including the continued value of the land-based strategic missiles, the level of troops in Europe and the Pacific, the value of a large force of attack carriers, and the relative use of active and reserve forces.

The medical-care programs must be addressed in any case because the hospital insurance fund is expected to be depleted in the 1990s. A new administration should consider such alternatives as a combined voucher for hospital and physican care or income testing of the Medicare program. Congress unfortunately may be tempted to fund the Medicare and disability funds by borrowing from the accumulating balance in the basic retirement fund, but that would only accelerate the depletion of this fund.

At some time, preferably soon, the government must also address the fundamental flaws in the basic social security retirement program. Although spending for this program is not now growing rapidly, today's young workers will earn low or negative returns from this program, and their children will face much higher tax rates. A new administration should address such alternatives as slowing the growth of real retirement benefits or a gradual increase in the age for full retirement benefits.

Only an administration that is prepared to address these hard choices can claim to have sustained and extended the Reagan economic agenda.

Taxes

An increase in tax rates would address only one of the two unsustainable budget conditions and would directly reverse one of the major achievements of Reaganomics. Some increase in tax revenues, however, is probably necessary. A zero real growth of federal spending for seven years—nearly two full presidential terms—would be necessary to balance the budget without some increase in taxes, and such an extended period of budget restraint is implausible.

The major challenge will be to increase tax revenues without increasing marginal tax rates. Fortunately, such opportunities are still substantial. The Tax Reform Act of 1986, by reducing marginal tax rates and some tax preferences, reduced the value and increased the political vulnerability of the remaining preferences. A new administration, for example, should consider substituting a $300 credit for the $2,000 personal exemption, including fringe benefits other than pension contributions in taxable income, and including one-half of social security benefits in the taxable income of all recipients. There is no substantive reason for maintaining the remaining deductions for state and local income and property taxes. A number of industry-specific tax preferences should also be reviewed. Yet the new capital gains tax rate will probably reduce tax revenues and should be reduced. For other reasons a new administration should also consider indexing both capital gains and depreciation allowances.

An administration and Congress that are unwilling either to reduce the growth of spending or to increase tax revenues are, unfortunately, most likely to reinflate the economy. Such a response should be recognized as a tax on the holders of existing bonds, the act of a desperate government, and the end of responsible economic policy.

Odds and Ends

Several other unresolved problems should also be addressed. These concern regulation, trade, and monetary policy.

Regulation

The deregulation of financial institutions may not be sustainable without a change in the deposit insurance system or a fundamental restructuring of the financial institutions. Similarly, the deregulation of airlines may not be sustainable without a change in the air traffic control system or the methods for allocating congested airspace. The continued deregulation of communications is also probably dependent on changing the methods for allocating the frequency spectrum. In these areas the Reagan administration supported continued deregulation but not the complementary measures that may prove necessary to sustain the deregulation.

The administration would not address several bodies of regulation on the grounds that any proposed change would be too controversial. The newer body of regulations affecting health, safety, and the environment reflects broadly shared concerns, but these regulations have also been used to meet internal "protectionist" pressures, and they impose substantial excess burdens on the economy. At some time we should also review the federal labor legislation, which dates primarily from the 1930s. American unions have maintained a wage premium at the expense of unorganized workers, a premium that is increasingly dependent on limits on imports. One should not be surprised that most of the concern about international competitiveness originates in the unionized industries. One might hope that these issues could be resolved without resort to the rhetoric of a holy war, but the near-term prospects are not encouraging.

Trade

The U.S. balance-of-payments deficit was about 3.4 percent of GNP in 1986, a measure of the difference between the amount of goods and services we are using and the amount we are producing. This condition is not sustainable, primarily because the increase in the trade deficit since 1984 was not matched by an equal increase in private domestic investment. At some time the trade deficit must be reduced by some combination of lower government consumption, lower private consumption, or lower private domestic investment. And the choice among these alternatives will be the central economic policy issue for some years.

The short-run response of our political system to the trade deficit, unfortunately, has been counterproductive or ineffective. The decline in the dollar since early 1985 was probably due to the anticipated effect of the Tax Reform Act of 1986, a measure that will reduce the trade deficit primarily by reducing private domestic investment, although this effect is not yet broadly recognized. The most obvious political response to the trade deficit has been an avalanche of protectionist proposals by Congress and a smaller landslide of protectionist actions by the administration. Trade restraints appear to serve some political purpose, but they will not reduce the trade deficit. In the absence of an increase in domestic saving relative to domestic investment, additional trade restraints would strengthen the dollar and reduce the volume of both imports and exports. The United States has now embarked on a dangerous series of small trade wars, at the expense of both this nation and other countries, for no apparent purpose other than to demonstrate our potential for an irrational international economic machismo. The prospects for a free-trade agreement with Canada and the new GATT round initiated in September 1986, measures that would benefit both the United States and other countries, are not promising.

The first step toward sorting out this mess is to sort out our own thinking. First, a reduction in the trade deficit should *not* be a primary objective of federal policy. The increase in the trade deficit (and the associated capital inflow) has made a major contribution to the reduction in inflation and interest rates and the problems of the debtor countries. In light of current U.S. policies, a reduction in the U.S. trade deficit resulting from an increase in foreign demand would increase U.S. inflation and interest rates. Some changes in U.S. conditions that would reduce the trade deficit, such as a recession or lower domestic investment, are clearly undesirable. A change in the trade deficit by itself is not a sufficient indicator of a desirable change in economic conditions.

Second, a reduction in the budget deficit, preferably by measures that do not reduce domestic investment, is the most desirable way to reduce the trade deficit. Each of the "twin deficits" is unsustainable at their current levels. A reduction in the federal deficit would reduce the trade deficit, but some measures that would reduce the trade deficit would not reduce the federal deficit. The twin deficits in effect represent different dimensions of one problem: the sum of government and private consumption is higher than we can sustain, given current and prospective U.S. output. The trade deficit is the result, not the cause, of this problem.

Third, trade wars damage both the United States and other countries, are likely to undermine relations with our closest allies, and are not likely to be an effective means of reducing their restraints on U.S. exports. Most nations have some restraints that limit the potential for U.S. exports, and in some cases these restraints have recently increased. A reduction in these restraints is a worthy objective of U.S. policy but would not much change the bilateral trade balances and would have no effect on the total trade deficit. Moreover, a unilateral U.S. trade restraint may be reciprocated, leading to a progressive reduction in the level of trade and lower average real incomes in all the affected countries. The more aggressive trade policy initiated by the administration in late 1985 may prove to be a game of Russian roulette. The bilateral and multilateral negotiation of lower trade restraints is often lengthy and frustrating and does not satisfy the political demands for mercantilist machismo. For most of the postwar period, however, such negotiations proved to be the only means to achieve a mutual, balanced, broad, and automatic reduction of trade restraints, which benefitted all the participating countries. This issue should be an important test of the credentials of prospective presidential candidates.

Monetary Policy

Another major opportunity for the new administration would be to clarify the guidance to the Federal Reserve. For some years the Fed has operated without guidance or—the equivalent—with sufficiently redundant or contradictory guidance to permit the Fed to chart its own course. My concern is less about the current performance of the Fed than about its reaction to future political pressures or external shocks. My preferred policy would be for Congress to set a target path for total demand, as measured by nominal domestic final sales. The current targets for the several monetary aggregates would be eliminated. The Fed would then set a tentative target path for the

monetary base consistent with the expected relation between changes
in the monetary base and changes in the target domestic final sales.
Most important, the Fed would then change the target path for the
monetary base as often as once a quarter, depending on the difference between the reported domestic final sales and the target level
in the prior quarter. This policy, I believe, would be superior to
setting a target path for either some monetary aggregate or some
price index and would be much superior to guidance based on interest rates, exchange rates, or any real variable. This is a complicated issue, however, and it deserves further analysis and discussion
before any new monetary rule is implemented.

THE POLITICAL ENVIRONMENT

Changes in the Terms of Debate

The elements of the initial Reagan economic agenda that were most
fully implemented were those for which there was a substantial consensus in both parties in 1980. Similarly, the elements that are most
likely to survive are those for which there is a substantial consensus
in both parties in 1988. Changes in economic policy in general are
more dependent on changes that are broadly supported in both parties than on which party the voters select to implement these changes.
My conviction that ideas are important may be biased, as I am in the
idea business. My judgment on these issues is also subjective, as there
are no adequate objective indicators of the underlying preferences
of American voters or their political representatives. My forecast of
future economic policies, as will be made clear, is also based more
on my professional judgment than on my own apparently idiosyn-
cratic political preferences.

Changes in the terms of debate about economic policies are best
reflected by the two major successes of the Reagan economic program. The substantial reduction in tax rates approved in 1981 and
1986 may prove resistant to a future increase. Some increase in tax
revenues will probably prove necessary to reduce the deficit, but the
next revenue increases are likely to be some continued broadening
of the tax base or new types of taxes. The reader should be warned
that my view on this issue is not shared by some tax experts on both
the right and the left. James Buchanan, the leading public-choice
scholar, believes that a flat-rate tax system, by reducing the economic
costs of a given level of tax revenues, induces higher government
spending. Similarly, Henry Aaron, a Brookings Institution tax expert, concludes that "by improving the fairness and reducing the

distortions without sacrificing revenues, the tax reform act may make it easier for Congress to raise taxes as part of a deficit reduction package." My opinion, however, is that it will prove to be politically difficult to increase tax rates, because low marginal tax rates have become the symbol of a desirable tax system. The prior consensus for a sharply progressive income tax system, which was based primarily on the politics of envy, appears to have been broken.

What is left of supply-side economics? On the one hand, the experience since the tax law of 1981 affirms the basic insight of supply-side economics—that the economic effects of fiscal policy depend importantly on the details of the budget and the tax code. On the other hand, this experience refuted the irresponsible conjectures of some supply-side polemicists that a general reduction in tax rates would substantially increase economic growth and might increase tax revenues. My judgment is that the basic insight of supply-side economics is now more broadly shared but that the term will disappear from popular debate without ever having developed a distinctive theoretical framework.

Similarly, the substantial reduction in inflation since 1980 is not likely to be reversed soon. The experience of the 1980s has demonstrated that inflation is not primarily a consequence of structural conditions in the U.S. economy or of external shocks; it can be reduced substantially by a change in government policy without any long-term effect on the unemployment rate. This experience will make it more difficult for federal officials to claim that inflation is out of their control. Again, the reader should consider that my perception of this issue is not shared by many monetary experts, who continue to forecast a rapid increase in inflation on the basis of the high rate of money growth since mid-1982. My judgment is based on an expectation that the Federal Reserve will continue to restrain the growth of total demand and that the primary near-term source of inflationary pressure will be from the decline in the dollar since early 1985. The long-term prospects for stable low inflation, however, are not yet secure. Political officials still have an incentive to promote monetary stimulus to increase near-term economic growth and to reduce the longer-term real value of both public and private debt.

What is left of monetarism? On the one hand, the experience of the 1980s has confirmed that monetary policy has an important effect on total demand. In addition, the Federal Reserve has implemented most of the monetarist proposals that permit closer control of the money supply. On the other hand, this experience has demonstrated that a stable rate of money growth is not desirable in the presence of unexpected changes in money velocity. In other words, the basic framework of monetary economics has survived, but the primary policy rule of the "high church" monetarists has been rejected. This experience may set the stage for new monetary rule based on maintaining a stable path of total demand.

In contrast, the stability of the political consensus (at least among elected officials) is best reflected by the major failures of the Reagan economic program. Most important, the growth of real federal spending at a rate higher than the growth of the economy indicates continued broad support among political officials for the accumulation of federal domestic programs. Although real spending for many small domestic programs was reduced, only one substantial program was terminated, and real spending for the core social safety net programs and medical care continued to increase. The concern about distributional issues declined in the early 1980s primarily because of a more general concern about a defense buildup, reducing inflation, and increasing economic growth. One ironic effect of the improvement in these general conditions has been a revival of distributional concerns. In 1987, for example, the Reagan administration proposed new programs for displaced workers, catastrophic health insurance, and the homeless. The postwar evidence suggests that spending for existing transfer programs increases during a recession, and spending for new programs increases during a recovery. The Reagan administration had little effect on this strong but ultimately unsustainable trend.

Similarly, the administration's reluctance to address a reform of the regulation of health, safety, the environment, and labor relations also reflects a stability of the political consensus on these issues. The objectives of these types of regulations are broadly shared, but the costs and effects of these regulations are not broadly understood.

In general, most political officials of both parties appear to favor an activist economic policy with complex distributional outcomes. A reduction in intervention in one type of policy is likely to be reflected by increased intervention of another form. Tax reform, for example, may be offset by increased trade restraints. Budget restraint may lead to increased regulation, such as the substitution of mandated pensions, medical insurance, and child care for public programs. If these policies do not reflect the preferences of American voters, something is dreadfully wrong with our system of representation, and one or more constitutional amendments may be necessary. If these policies do reflect the preferences of the voters, under conditions such that they pay their full costs, those of us who share the vision of limited constitutional government have a lot of work to do. We may be winning the war of ideas, but the current political processes continue to generate a larger and more interventionist government.

Table 10.1   Republicans Holding Key Elected Offices

	1979	1987	Change (%)
Senators	41	45	9.8
Representatives	159	176	10.7
Governors	19	24	26.3

Changes in Party Alignment

Changes in party alignment are, I contend, more a reflection than a cause of the conditions that lead to a change in government policy. The change in party alignment associated with the Reagan administration, like the change in the terms of debate, was significant but not overwhelming. Table 10.1 presents the number of Republicans holding key elected offices in 1979 and 1987, both following midterm election years. These changes are important to both parties, but in no case are the Republicans a majority (although Republican governors now serve a bare majority of the total population). The periodic polling data on party identification are more variable but convey much the same story. The major effect of this party realignment concerns which party is likely to govern and who will be selected as key officials and advisers.

The change in party alignment, however, is a very poor guide to future policies. For example, during the postwar years through 1980, real domestic spending increased more rapidly under Republican presidents, and real defense spending increased more rapidly under Democratic presidents. For most of its history, the Republican party opposed foreign interventions and entangling alliances and favored balanced budgets and high tariffs. The Democratic party, in contrast, generally favored a more aggressive foreign policy, fiscal stimulus, and low tariffs. No one of these historical patterns proved to be an adequate guide to the positions of either party during the Reagan administration. There is no reason to expect that future policies, for better or for worse, will be very dependent on the success of either party in future elections. As expressed by Mitch Daniels, a White House political director in Reagan's second term, "Parties give us the means to apply the market system to politics. Republicans and Democrats compete against each other very much the same way rival companies compete in the market place. The parties have no strong ideological base." For those of us with stronger preferences for what government should and should not do, the major lesson of these examples is that we should be prepared to shape the views of and work with the voters, politicians, and officials of both parties.

Who Will Lead?

Ronald Reagan spoiled the policy junkies of all persuasions and set a standard that is not likely to be repeated. He had clear views about many policy issues and told us about most of them before he was elected. The leading candidates for the 1988 presidential nomination will not reveal such a comprehensive agenda, in part because they are less clear about their own policy views. We will be more dependent on an evaluation of their general policy inclinations and skills as revealed by their prior record.

George Bush, as heir apparent, has no alternative but to run on the Reagan record. And his success will depend heavily on how that record is perceived in 1988. As discussed in Chapter 9, however, his extraordinary and commendable loyalty to President Reagan has made it difficult even for insiders to determine his own views. My judgment is that he would be more of a consolidator of the Reagan record than an innovator. Maybe that is what the country needs for a while. The primary economic policy challenge of the next president is to resolve the fiscal stalemate without reversing the two major achievements of Reaganomics, that is, without increasing tax rates or inflation. Bush appears to have a strong commitment to balanced budgets but a weaker commitment to the reduction of federal programs necessary to achieve a balance by spending restraint. For example, he seems unlikely to question the postwar consensus on foreign and military policy that is the rationale for the large defense budget, and he shows no inclination to propose a major pruning of federal domestic programs. This perspective would probably lead to some new type of tax, such as a value-added tax. Bush also appears to have a strong commitment to continued deregulation and a general commitment to free trade and low inflation. His most obvious parochial concern is about low oil prices; this concern may lead him to advocate some protection of the domestic oil industry unless the world market price of oil increases. One of his more attractive characteristics is that he knows what he does not know. Bush would choose a quite different group of officials and advisers, drawn more from the Northeast and Texas, less ideological and more pragmatic, more "establishment," and maybe more competent. For better or for worse, Baldrige and Baker, not Meese or Watt, would be the models for members of his cabinet. A Bush presidency would probably have good relations with Congress, suggesting the prospect of being neither confrontational nor very creative.

Sen. Robert Dole is probably the best politician (other than Reagan) in the Republican Party. He is smart, humorous, attractive, and respected by colleagues in both parties. As the Republican leader in the Senate since 1984, he had the highest voting record in support of the Reagan program. From the beginning of the administration, moreover, he demonstrated a strong commitment to a balanced budget, reflected by such measures as the 1982 tax law and his 1985 proposal to delay the cost-of-living adjustment on social security benefits. As a senator from Kansas, his most parochial concern is the farm programs, including such egregious programs as the ethanol subsidy and the sugar quotas that are important to one of his largest financial supporters. As is characteristic of midwestern politicians, he is also somewhat of a soft-money advocate, regularly encouraging the Federal Reserve to reduce interest rates. These views suggest that he would move toward a balanced budget by some combination of budget restraint, tax increases and, probably, some reinflation. His views on a wide range of other policy issues, reflecting his long service in Congress, are partisan but pragmatic, conservative but not ideological. The most probable explanation of this record is that a congressional leader operates more by seeking consensus than by staking out his own agenda. One of the very few congressional leaders ever to be elected president was Lyndon Johnson, an unhappy precedent. There is not much basis for judging his views on many specific foreign policy, defense, or economic issues, and he has no management record. Although Dole is the second choice for president of most Republicans, they may be buying a pig-in-a-poke.

Representative Jack Kemp has the strongest claim to be the ideological successor to Reagan. He was co-sponsor of the initial tax reduction proposal and one of the early tax reform plans, earning the right to be called "Mr. Supply-Side" in Congress. He has also promoted creative proposals such as vouchers to replace several types of government-provided services, enterprise zones, and privatization. His views on other issues are also quite clear. Kemp seems indifferent to the deficit, and he has undermined the effort to restrain federal spending. He supports a strong defense and the extended Reagan doctrine. His views on monetary policy seem inconsistent; he talks a hard-money game, but he has regularly encouraged the Federal Reserve to increase money growth. To his credit, Kemp has worked hard to broaden the base of the Republican party. He is a forceful advocate and an effective legislator. In personal conversation, however, he does not appear to listen, and he responds as if giving a speech. Although Kemp is strongly supported by the party ideologues, he has not run for office outside his congressional district, and he has a weak base among party officials. As with Dole, Kemp also has no management record. In contrast with both Bush and Dole, Kemp's policy agenda is much more explicit, and a Kemp presidency would be more creative but probably less responsible.

Other Republican candidates seem destined to play specialized roles in the 1988 primary campaign. Pierre S. (Pete) du Pont IV seems too good to be true. As heir to one of America's famous families, he is bright, articulate, and personable, and was a superior governor of Delaware. Du Pont will be the new-idea man in the Republican primary. As the first Republican to announce his candidacy, he early demonstrated some creativity and considerable courage in addressing social security reform in Florida and agricultural policy reform in Iowa. My guess is that du Point and Kemp will compete for some future nomination. Pat Robertson may be the spoiler in the 1988 campaign, playing a role rather like Jesse Jackson's in the 1984 Democratic primary. A TV evangelist and entrepreneur, Robertson represents a narrow but active constituency that is primarily concerned with social issues. Although Robertson has no prospect of winning the nomination, he presents an ominous threat to the party if the successful candidate is induced to make a substantial commitment to his constituency to win the nomination.

The prospective Democratic candidates are a mystery to me. The withdrawal of Governor Mario Cuomo seems to eliminate the only candidate who could unify the traditional Democratic coalition. Former senator Gary Hart proved to be the Icarus of 1987, falling from a high lead in the polls to the collapse of his candidacy within one week. A revival of charges about his personal life destroyed the only Democratic candidate who had written thoughtfully about a range of policy issues and who had taken a courageous position against the protectionists in his party. Former governor Bruce Babbitt, Sen. Bill Bradley, Sen. Sam Nunn, and former governor Charles Robb have attractive policy records, but they seem either unwilling or unlikely to win the nomination. The only Democratic candidates that I have met are Rep. Dick Gephardt and Sen. Al Gore. Gephardt's positions on trade and agriculture suggest that he lacks either the principles or the intelligence to be a serious contender. Gore blindsided me once (see Chapter 2), so I cannot judge him objectively. In any case the Reagan record will be the primary issue in the 1988 campaign. The Democratic candidate is more likely to convey only a general theme than a comprehensive alternative agenda.

A final note on the conditions that will lead to the selection of the next administration: my guess is that the 1988 election will be very similar to the 1960 election. After eight years of a popular Republican president, the Republican candidate will be the vice-president. A younger Democratic candidate will model himself on John Kennedy and run on some vague theme such as "let's get the country moving again." Economic conditions will be moderately satisfactory but weaker than the administration's forecast. The election will be very close.

The economic policies of the new administration, however, are likely to be more dependent on the problems and perceptions of the time than on the outcome of the election.

A SUMMING UP

Ronald Reagan promised us a lower growth of government spending, reduced tax rates, some regulatory relief, and lower inflation. All these objectives were achieved to some extent. That is a substantial accomplishment for which he deserves credit. It seems most unlikely that Carter or whoever else might have been elected in 1984 would have achieved as much.

In the end, however, there was no Reagan revolution. In part Reagan's achievements were limited because he endorsed the major programs of the New Deal and the postwar consensus on foreign policy and defense. In terms of his own objectives, he did not achieve as much as he had proposed. Federal spending continued to grow more rapidly then the economy. Although Reagan achieved a substantial reallocation of the budget from the discretionary domestic programs to defense, most of the Great Society programs are still alive, if not well. A substantial part of the reduction in individual income tax rates was achieved by shifting taxes to the future or to corporations. Some deregulation was offset by increasing trade restraints. Although inflation was substantially reduced, there is still no consensus on a monetary rule to guide future monetary policy. Although the economic recovery was sustained longer than usual, the average economic growth since 1980 was about the same as during the 1970s.

Moreover, the Reagan administration left us with several substantial new problems. The continued growth of federal spending led to a huge budget deficit that has been only slightly reduced since 1986. The budget deficit in turn contributed to the large trade deficit and the resulting pressure for increased trade restraints. The means by which these problems are reduced will determine how much of Reaganomics survives. A policy to reduce the budget deficit by increasing tax rates or by reinflation would reverse the two major achievements of Reaganomics. A futile attempt to reduce the trade deficit by increasing trade restraints would reverse one of the major economic policy achievements of the past half-century.

The core of supply-side economics and monetarism, the two new perspectives of the Reagan economic program, is now more broadly shared, although some of the predictions and policies associated with these perspectives were clearly refuted. The fundamental insight that the economic effects of fiscal policy depend importantly on the details of the budget and the tax code is now broadly accepted. However, the conjecture that a general reduction in tax rates would increase total tax revenues was clearly refuted. The dominant effect of monetary policy on total demand is also more broadly recognized. A steady growth of the money supply, however, no longer appears to be the best policy. These perspectives will continue to affect the economic policies of both parties long after the terms "Reaganomics," "supply-side economics," and "monetarism" disappear from general use.

The primary reason why Reaganomics did not prove to be a revolution, however, is that there has not yet been a fundamental change in the perceptions about what the federal government should and should not do, at least among our elected officials. Ronald Reagan offered a vision for Americans that represents the best of our heritage and may some day shape our future. His reluctance to face hard choices, however, left us with some major new problems and an electorate that is still vulnerable to those who promote the competing vision of an expansive state. The most distinctive characteristic of this century has been the pervasive growth of government. Reaganomics may prove to be only a temporary pause in this progressive loss of liberties. A more general sense of outrage about the contemporary role of government, one or more constitutional amendments, and new leaders who share Reagan's vision are probably necessary to protect and extend history's most noble experiment—the American revolution.

Acknowledgments

My work on this book was supported by the Lynde and Harry Bradley Foundation, the John M. Ohlin Foundation, and the Smith-Richardson Foundation. Their generous support of this work made it possible to devote most of my time to completing this book in time, I hope, to contribute to the shared perceptions that will shape the economic policies of the next administration of either party. The views expressed in this book are, of course, my own and do not necessarily reflect the views of these foundations.

I am grateful to the *American Economic Review* for its approval to publish a selection from Alice Rivlin's article on the federal budget process and to *Harper's Magazine* for its approval to publish a selection from an interview with President Mitterand about President Reagan. Both of these selections contributed to my own understanding and, I hope, to that of readers of this book. I am also indebted to the large number of journalists and scholars who have contributed to documenting and interpreting the history of "Reaganomics." Although I have not followed the academic practice of identifying my references in the text, in order to maintain the flow of the account for an intelligent lay reader, the references for my unique sources are identified in the endnotes for each chapter.

My colleagues at the Cato Institute were understanding and supportive in every way. Ed Crane made it possible for me to avoid most of the burdens of serving as chairman of the institute, for which I owe him a similar opportunity. Several interns were most helpful in amassing references. I am very indebted to Dana Edwards, who typed what seemed like endless drafts with care and good humor. My other colleagues were often helpful sorting out some of the issues of this period. This book also reflects the understanding and special skills of Herbert J. Addison, the economics editor for Oxford University Press.

For various reasons I chose not to have this book reviewed by others prior to publication. This choice preserved the coherence of perspective that can only come from one mind, but I recognize that it risked engendering some errors of fact and interpretation. Thus, I bear the full responsibility for any errors as well as for any misunderstanding of or unfairness to the people mentioned in this account.

My greatest debt is to my fellow Reaganauts, who encouraged me to write this book. We have shared a vision of the importance of limiting government in order to preserve a free society and a healthy economy, the joy of selective victories, and the agony of failures and missed opportunities. They know that we do not agree on every issue, and they will recognize that I have changed my views on a few issues. Although the Reagan era is nearly over, the effort to restore limited constitutional government must continue, and I hope that our remaining differences do not weaken our common effort.

Notes and References

Chapter One

The basic reference for the initial Reagan economic program is *America's New Beginning: A Program for Economic Recovery* (Washington, D.C.: U.S. Government Printing Office, 1981).

The last Carter economic forecasts and budget projections are from *The Budget in Brief,* FY 1982. The initial Reagan economic forecasts and budget projections are from *Budget Revisions,* FY 1982. Off-budget outlays are included in both other outlays and total outlays to make the outlay projections consistent with the budget concept used in later years. All projections of the growth of real outlays are based on the forecast GNP implicit price deflator in the Carter and Reagan budgets for FY 1982, both adjusted from a calendar-year basis to a fiscal-year basis.

My basic source for the early history of supply-side economics and the events of early 1981 is Paul Craig Roberts, *The Supply-Side Revolution* (Cambridge, Mass.: Harvard University Press, 1984). Specifically, my summary of the following events is drawn primarily from Roberts: the development of the initial economic forecasts, the failed attempt to develop a rationale for the initial program, and the several tax proposals from 1977 through 1980. Bruce R. Bartlett, *Reaganomics* (Westport, Conn.: Arlington House, 1981), also provides a valuable history of the early development of supply-side economics.

For Reagan's major early speeches, see *A Time For Choosing* (Chicago: Regnery Gateway, 1983).

The estimate of the average federal tax rate is by Robert Barro and Chaipat Sahasukal, "Average Marginal Federal Tax Rates from Social Security and the Individual Income Tax," Working Paper no. 1214 (Cambridge, Mass.: National Bureau of Economic Research, October 1983).

Chapter Two

The lead quotation is from *A Program of Economic Recovery.*

The major sources of budget proposals and data are the *Budget Revisions* for FY 1982, the *Budget of the United States* for FY 1983 through FY 1986, and the *Historical Tables* published with the FY 1986 budget. Actual real outlays are based on the GNP implicit price deflator, as revised in 1986. Projected real outlays are based on the 1981 Reagan forecast of the GNP implicit price deflator, adjusted to 1982 dollars.

My columns on the Reagan budget arithmetic were published in *The Los Angeles Times* on February 16, 1981, and in the *The Washington Post* on February 19, 1981.

David A. Stockman, *The Triumph of Politics* (New York: Harper and Row, 1986) provides ample documentation of (and Stockman's personal outrage regarding) the role of Republicans in promoting and defending elements of the contemporary welfare state. See also Donald Lambro, "The Republican Pork Barrel," *Policy Review* (Summer 1985).

The data in Table 2.1 are from the *Budget of the United States*, FY 1982 and FY 1986. Other sources for my evaluation of the defense buildup and planning process include "Defense Spending: What Has Been Accomplished" (Congressional Budget Office, Staff Working Paper, April 1985) and "An Interim Report to the President" (President's Blue Ribbon Commission on Defense Management, February 28, 1986). Stockman, *The Triumph of Politics,* and Lawrence I. Barrett, *Gambling with History* (New York: Doubleday, 1983), both provide lively accounts of the politics of the budget process in 1981 and the August–September 1981 attempt to force a review of the defense budget.

The case for adjusting the social security benefits of future retirees on prices rather than wages was made by William Hsiao in "An Optimal Indexing Method for Social Security," in Colin D. Campbell (ed.), *Financing Social Security* (Washington, D.C.: American Enterprise Institute, 1979). For an evaluation of the effects of these two rules, see Robert S. Kaplan, "A Comparison of Rates of Return to Social Security Retirees Under Wage and Price Indexing," also in Campbell, *Financing Social Security*. For the proposals of the Greenspan commission, see *Report of the National Commission on Social Security Reform* (Washington, D.C.: U.S. Government Printing Office, January 1983).

The effects of the welfare and tax systems on the marginal tax rates faced by the working poor are documented in Arthur B. Laffer, "The Tightening of the Poverty Trap," Policy Analysis no. 41 (Washington, D.C.: The Cato Institute, August 1984), and James Gwartney and Thomas S. McCaleb, "Have Antipoverty Programs Increased Poverty?" *The Cato Journal*, vol. 5, no. 1 (1985). The Laffer study is based on welfare programs in California and the Gwartney and McCaleb study on programs in Pennsylvania.

The report of the Emergency Jobs Act of 1983 is from Warren Brookes, *The Washington Times*, February 19, 1987, based on a study by the General Accounting Office.

The estimate of the benefits and costs of the 1981 farm legislation is from a study by the Department of Agriculture, as summarized in the *Economic Report* for 1986, p. 155. The estimate of the costs of the sugar program is from David Tarr and Morris Morkre, *Aggregate Costs to the United States of Tariffs and Quotas on Imports* (Federal Trade Commission, December 1984).

My summary of the activities and effects of the Reagan management program draws from *Management of the Untied States Government*, published with the FY 1986 *Budget*.

The estimates of the effects of federal grants on state and local spending is from the *Economic Report* for 1985, p. 76, based on several academic studies.

The estimates of the effects of the automatic budget cuts under Gramm-Rudman is from Jonathan Rauch, *The National Journal*, January 1, 1984, based on an unofficial House analysis.

The extended quotation about the budget process is from Alice Rivlin, "Reform of the Budget Process," *American Economic Review,* vol. 74, no. 2 (May 1984), used by permission.

Chapter Three

The lead quotation is from *A Program for Economic Recovery.*

The major sources of tax proposals and legislation during the first term are *A Program for Economic Recovery* and the *Budget of the United States,* FY 1983–1986.

My major source for the developments that led to the tax legislation in 1981 and 1982 is Roberts, *The Supply-Side Revolution.* The informed reader will notice, however, that my evaluation of the 1982 legislation is very different from that of Roberts. I am also indebted to Roberts for the estimates of the tax rates on retirement income that are implicit in the social security proposal and 1983 legislation.

The quoted view of the Senate Budget Committee staff about Kemp-Roth is from Rowland Evans and Robert Novak (*The Washington Post,* April 22, 1981).

The estimated effect of TEFRA on the effective tax rate on business equipment is from the *Economic Report* for 1983.

The marginal federal income tax rates reported in Table 3.1 are from the *Economic Report* for 1982, based on estimates by the Office of Tax Analysis.

The marginal tax rates on investment income reported in Table 3.2 are from Don Fullerton and Yolanda Henderson, "Incentive Effects of Taxes on Income from Capital," in Charles Hulten and Isabel Sawhill (eds.), *The Legacy of Reaganomics* (Washington: Urban Institute Press, 1984). (Fullerton later served as the Treasury deputy assistant secretary for tax analysis during the second term.)

An article by David Rosenbaum (*The New York Times,* October 23, 1986) provides a summary chronology of the development of the Tax Reform Act of 1986.

For the Treasury tax plan, see *Tax Reform for Fairness, Simplicity, and Economic Growth* (November 1984). For the effect of IRAs on personal saving, see Steven F. Venti and David A. Wise, "Have IRAs Increased U.S. Saving?: Evidence from Consumer Expenditure Surveys," Working Papers in Economics E-87-13 (Stanford, Calif.: The Hoover Institute, March 1987). For the general effects of the real after-tax rate of return on personal saving, see John H. Makin, "Saving, Pension Contributions, and the Real Interest Rate," Working Paper no. 11 (Washington, D.C.: American Enterprise Institute, April 1987).

For the president's tax proposals, see *The President's Tax Proposals to Congress for Fairness, Growth, and Simplicity* (May 1985). The estimate of the effective tax rate on investment income was made by Don Fullerton, "The Indexation of Interest, Depreciation, and Capital Gains: A Model of Investment Incentives," Working Paper no. 5 (Washington, D.C.: American Enterprise Institute, June 1985).

For the House tax bill, see *Tax Reform Act of 1985,* Report of the Committee on Ways and Means (December 7, 1985). The estimate of the effective marginal rates on family income was made by the author on the basis of material in this report. The estimate of the effective tax rate on investment income was made by Yolanda Henderson, "Investment Incentives Under the Ways and Means Tax Bill," Working Paper no. 6 (Washington, D.C.: American Enterprise Institute, January 1986).

For the Senate tax bill see *Tax Reform Act of 1986*, Report of the Committee on Finance (May 29, 1986). An article by Jeffrey Birnbaum (*The Wall Street Journal*, May 9, 1986) provides a lively account of the development of the Senate bill. The estimate of the effective tax rate on business investment is from Yolanda Henderson, *Tax Notes* (June 2, 1986).

An article by Anne Swardson (*The Washington Post*, August 20, 1986) summarizes the many tax preferences that remained in the conference committee bill.

The effective tax rates presented in Table 3.3 were calculated by the author on the basis of data released by the Joint Committee on Taxation (August 22, 1986). The estimated marginal tax rates on corporate investment presented in Table 3.4 were prepared by Yolanda Henderson, "Lessons from Federal Reform of Business Taxes," *New England Economic Review* (November/December 1986); the estimates for 1980 presented in this table are somewhat different from those presented in Table 3.2, reflecting the use of slightly different assumptions for several parameters. For one study that estimates that the benefits of an improved allocation of investment are higher than the costs because of a lower level of investment from the 1986 law, see Don Fullerton and Yolanda Henderson, "A Disaggregate Equilibrium Model of the Tax Distortions Among Assets, Sectors, and Industries," Working Paper no. 1905 (Cambridge, Mass.: National Bureau of Economic Research, 1986).

For the Buchanan conjecture about the effects of a deficit on government spending, see James Buchanan and Richard Wagner, *Democracy in Deficit* (New York: Academic Press, 1977). My first test of this conjecture was reported in "Deficits, Government Spending, and Inflation: What is the Evidence?" *Journal of Monetary Economics*, vol. 4 (1978). For the 1985 study of the effects of taxes on spending, see George von Furstenberg, R. Jeffrey Green, and Jin-Ho Jeong, "Have Taxes Led Government Expenditures?" *Journal of Public Policy*, vol. 5, no. 3 (1985).

For a summary of the 1986 articles that report results contrary to those by von Furstenberg et al., see Warren Brookes, "Taxes, Spending, and the Tooth Fairy," *The Washington Times*, August 19, 1987.

My own first tests of the effects of deficits on inflation are reported in the article in the *Journal of Monetary Economics*, cited earlier. For more thorough tests, see Gerald P. Dwyer, "Inflation and Government Deficits," *Economic Inquiry* (1982), and Douglas Joines, "Deficits and Money Growth in the United States" (unpublished paper), Department of Finance and Business Economics, University of Southern California, 1983. For studies of the effects of deficits on interest rates, see "Government Deficit Spending and Its Effects on Prices of Financial Assets" (Department of the Treasury, 1984), *The Economic and Budget Outlook: Fiscal Years 1986–1990* (Congressional Budget Office, 1985), and Paul Evans, "Do Large Deficits Produce High Interest Rates?"

American Economic Review, vol. 75, no. 1 (March 1985). For a good study of the "crowding-out" effects of the deficit, see Lawrence Summers, "The Long-Term Effects of Current Macroeconomic Policies," in Charles Hulten and Isabel Sawhill, *The Legacy of Reaganomics.*

Chapter Four

The lead quotation is from *A Program for Economic Recovery.*

For a summary and defense of the Reagan administration's early regulatory record, see *Reagan Administration Regulatory Achievements* (Presidential Task Force on Regulatory Relief, August 11, 1983). For a thorough and moderately critical assessment of this record, see George C. Eads and Michael Fix, *Relief or Reform?: Reagan's Regulatory Dilemma* (Washington, D.C.: Urban Institute Press, 1984). (Eads was a member of the CEA and a key regulatory review official in the Carter administration.) See also Murray Weidenbaum, "Regulatory Reform: A Report Card on the Reagan Administration" (St. Louis, Mo.: Center for the Study of American Business, no. 59, November 1983). A published debate between Christopher DeMuth and Walter Olson in *Regulation* (Washington, D.C.: American Enterprise Institute, March/April 1984) reflects the differences in assessments of the Reagan regulatory record even among those most supportive of its goals.

Estimates of real spending by the federal regulatory agencies are based on data assembled annually by the Center for the Study of American Business at Washington University in St. Louis and are deflated by the GNP implicit price deflator. For the costs of regulation to the economy, see Murray L. Weidenbaum and Robert DeFina, *The Cost of Federal Regulation of Economic Activity* (Washington, D.C.: American Enterprise Institute, 1978). A valuable summary of the effects of increased regulation on the decline in productivity growth during the 1970s is presented in Eads and Fix, *Relief or Reform?*; one of the studies cited estimates that increased regulation may have contributed up to 25 percent of the decline in productivity growth. The estimate of the hours used to fill out federal forms is from the Task Force report cited above.

The "economic Dunkirk" memo is reproduced in William Greider, *The Education of David Stockman and Other Americans* (New York: E.P. Dutton, 1982).

My major sources for the regulatory developments during the Reagan administration are the regulation chapters in the annual *Economic Report.* The estimate of the effects of bank deregulation on the increased interest payments to depositors is from the task force report cited earlier. My general assessment also draws on Eads and Fix, *Relief or Reform?*.

For an assessment of the IBM case, see David Levy and Steve Welzer, "System Error: How the IBM Antitrust Suit Raised Computer Prices," *Regulation* (Washington, D.C.: American Enterprise Institute, September/October 1985). For a general review of the telephone deregulation issues, see the articles by Leland Johnson; Nina W. Cornell, Michael D. Pelcovits, and Steven R. Brenner; and Michael L. Katz and Robert D. Willig, in *Regulation* (Washington, D.C.: American Enterprise Institute, July/August 1983). For a retrospective evaluation of telephone deregulation, see Robert Crandall, "Has the AT&T Breakup Raised Telephone Rates?" *The Brookings Review* (Washington, D.C.: The Brookings Institution, Winter 1987).

For a valuable debate between those who would focus antitrust law and those who would repeal these laws, see Nolan E. Clark, "Antitrust Comes Full Circle: The Return to the Cartelization Standard," *Vanderbilt Law Review*, vol. 38, no. 5 (October 1985) and D. T. Armentano, *Antitrust Policy: The Case for Repeal* (Washington, D.C.: The Cato Institute, 1986).

The initial quotations on trade policy are from *A Program for Economic Recovery*. The statement on trade policy was presented by William Brock before a joint hearing of the Senate Committee on Finance and the Senate Committee on Banking, Housing, and Urban Affairs (July 9, 1981).

For a lively account of the deliberations that led to the auto VRA, see Stockman, *The Triumph of Politics*, pp. 154–158. The estimate of the annual cost of the auto VRA is from Tarr and Morkre, *Aggregate Costs*.

The Farnsworth article on the steel quotas was published in *The New York Times*, September 26, 1984. The estimate of the cost of the steel quotas is from Tarr and Morkre, *Aggregate Costs*.

The estimate of the cost of the textile and apparel quotas is from Tarr and Morkre, *Aggregate Costs*.

The estimate of the cost of the sugar quotas is from Tarr and Morkre, *Aggregate Costs*.

See William A. Niskanen, "Stumbling Toward a U.S.-Canada Free Trade Agreement" (Washington, D.C.: The Cato Institute, June 1987) for a brief summary of these negotiations. For a summary of the relative levels of import restraints in Japan and other countries, see C. Fred Bergsten and William Cline, "The United States-Japan Economic Problem" (Washington, D.C.: Institute for International Economics, July 1985). The quotation about trade negotiations with Japan is from David Gergen, *U.S. News and World Report*, April 1, 1985. The article by Theodore White was published in *The New York Times Magazine*, July 28, 1985.

Chapter Five

The lead quotation is from *A Program for Economic Recovery*.

The quotation about the Fed and the later material about Fed actions through 1982 is from a lively account by Cary Reich, "Inside the Fed," *Institutional Investor* (May 1984).

For the referenced studies by Friedman, see Milton Friedman, "The Role of Monetary Policy," *American Economic Review* (March 1968), Milton Friedman and David Meiselman, "The Relative Stability of Monetary Velocity and the Investment Multiplier in the United States, 1897–1958," Report of the Commission on Money and Credit, in *Stabilization Policies* (Englewood Cliffs, N.J.: Prentice-Hall, 1963) and Milton Friedman and Anna J. Schwarz, *A Monetary History of the United States, 1867–1960* (Princeton, N.J.: Princeton University Press, 1963).

The basic reference on rational expectations theory is Fischer Stanley, ed., *Rational Expectations and Economic Policy* (Chicago: University of Chicago Press, 1980).

The description of Fed operating procedures is based on Henry Wallich, "Recent Techniques of Monetary Policy," presentation to the Midwest Finance Association, April 5, 1984. (Wallich was a long-term member of the board of governors until 1987).

The initial guidance on monetary policy is from *A Program for Economic Recovery*.

For an efficient summary of the views of the majority of the Gold Commission, see ch. 3 of the 1982 *Economic Report*. For the minority report, see Rep. Ron Paul and Lewis Lehrman, *The Case for Gold* (Washington, D.C.: The Cato Institute, 1982).

For the effect of monetary variability on interest rates, see John Makin, "Real Interest, Monetary Surprises, Anticipated Inflation, and Fiscal Deficits," *Review of Economics and Statistics* (February 1983).

The post-October 1982 operating procedure is also described in Wallich, "Recent Techniques."

The report of the April 11, 1986, meeting is from "The Lords of Money," *Business Week*, April 28, 1986.

The Report of the February 21–22, 1987, meeting is from *The Wall Street Journal*, February 23, 1987.

Table 3.1 data are prepared by the author on the basis of 1986 revisions of M1 and GNP.

I am indebted to Michael Keran, chief economist of Prudential Economic Research, for the major insight about the velocity puzzle. Figures 5.6 and 5.7 are reproduced from "Untangling the Velocity Puzzle," *The Prudential Economic Review* (September 1985).

For a good case for a nominal GNP rule, see Bennett T. McCallum, "Monetarist Rules in the Light of Recent Experience," *American Economic Review* 74 (May 1984).

I am indebted to William Haraf, a senior economist on the CEA staff, for clarifing the statistical properties of the time pattern of velocity growth. For the 1974 study, see John Gould and Charles Nelson, "The Stochastic Structure of the Velocity of Money," *American Economic Review* 64 (June 1974). For Haraf's later study, see William Haraf, "Monetary Velocity and Monetary Rules," *The Cato Journal*, vol. 6, no. 2 (Fall 1986). For a good discussion of the velocity puzzle, see also William Poole, "Monetary Policy Lessons of Recent Inflation and Deflation," Working Paper no. 2300 (Cambridge, Mass.: National Bureau of Economic Research, 1987).

Chapter Six

This chapter is based primarily on outside sources, as I was personally involved in only a few of these issues.

My primary source for the air controllers' strike is Morgan O. Reynolds, *Making America Poorer: The Cost of Labor Law* (Washington, D.C.: The Cato Institute, 1987), pp. 126–132. For a carefully developed proposal to privatize the air traffic control system, see Robert Poole, "Privatizing the Air Traffic Control System" (Santa Monica, Calif.: Reason Foundation, November 14, 1986).

The quotation is by Samuel Zell, a Chicago investor and writer, from *Newsweek*, November 10, 1986.

My primary source for the several banking crises handled by the FDIC is a fine book by Irving H. Sprague, *Bailout: An Insider's Account of Bank Failures and Rescues* (New York: Basic Books, 1986). (Sprague had been chairman of the FDIC until 1981 and was a director until 1986.) My brief account of the rescue of the mutual savings banks is from this source.

Unfortunately, a similar book about the more severe crisis of the S&Ls has not yet been written. My primary sources for this account are news columns (see specifically the *Newsweek* article referenced above), ch. 6 of the 1986 *Economic Report*, and Gillian Garcia, "FSLIC Is 'Broke' in More Ways than One," paper prepared for a Cato Institute conference on financial regulation, February 26–27, 1987.

The regulation of the commercial banks and my summary of the Penn Square and Continental Illinois crises are from Sprague, *Bailout*. My evaluation of the controversy between the FDIC and the Treasury about the Continental bailout is, however, more favorable to the Treasury position.

The most creative proposal for restructuring the banking system is in Robert Litan, *What Should Banks Do?* (Washington, D.C.: The Brookings Institution, 1987).

My accounts of the problems of the farm credit institutions and the pension plans are drawn primarily from ch. 6 of the 1986 *Economic Report* as well as from my personal experience with these issues.

My account of the foreign debt crisis is drawn primarily from Harold Lever and Christopher Huhne, *Debt and Danger: The World Financial Crisis* (Boston: Atlantic Monthly Press, 1985), Morris Miller, *Coping Is Not Enough!* (Homewood, Ill.: Dow Jones-Irwin, 1986), and numerous news articles.

The quotations by Volcker and Howe are from Lever and Huhne, *Debt and Danger.*

The summary of the different experience of the debtor countries is from ch. 3 of the 1986 *Economic Report.*

Developments in Mexico from 1976 through 1982 are summarized from Luis Pazos, "The False Austerity Policies of the Mexican Government," *Journal of Economic Growth* (Washington, D.C.: National Chamber Foundation, Winter 1986).

For a description of the operations of the Paris Club and the London Club, see Richard N. Cooper, "The Lingering Problem of LDC Debt," *The Marcus Wallenberg Papers on International Finance* (Washington, D.C.: International Law Institute, 1986).

For a moderately optimistic projection of the debt service problem, see William Cline, *International Debt and the Stability of the World Economy* (Washington, D.C.: Institute for International Economics, September 1983).

For an estimate of the effect of Latin debt on the stock-market value of American banks, see Steven Kyle, unpublished Ph.D. dissertation, Department of Economics, Harvard University, 1985. The discounts on foreign debt in late 1986 are from *The Wall Street Journal*, October 7, 1986.

For a summary and evaluation of the Baker plan, see Patricia Wertman, "Current Debt Service Capacity of the 'Baker Plan' Fifteen" (Washington,

D.C.: Congressional Research Service, March 31, 1986) and "Update" (May 5, 1986).

Estimates of the capital flight from Mexico and other debtor nations are from Rimmer de Vries, "Global Capital Markets: Issues and Implications," *The Marcus Wallenberg Papers on International Finance* (Washington, D.C.: International Law Institute, 1986). For the Brazilian debt action, see *The Wall Street Journal*, February 23, 1987.

The quotations by Conable and de Larosière are from *The Washington Post*, October 4, 1986.

For a defense of the case-by-case approach, see the Cline and Cooper papers cited earlier; the Cooper paper also provides a sound critique of the Bradley plan and a description of the Kenan plan. The books by Lever and Huhne and by Miller, previously cited, make the case for a more global solution.

Chapter Seven

The lead quotation is from *A Program for Economic Recovery*.

The estimate of the contribution of nonpolicy conditions to the productivity slowdown is from John Kendrick, "The Implications of Growth Accounting Models," in Hulten and Sawhill, *The Legacy of Reaganomics*.

For the Carter perspective on inflation, see ch. 1 of the 1981 *Economic Report*.

The quotation is from the 1982 *Economic Report*.

The data in Tables 7.1 and 7.2 are based on the 1987 revisions of the national income accounts by the Department of Commerce.

For the aggregate effects of the tax incentives on domestic business investment, see Michael Boskin, "The Impact of the 1981–1982 Investment Incentives on Business Fixed Investment" (Washington, D.C.: National Chamber Foundation, 1985). For a more skeptical view, see Barry F. Bosworth, "Taxes and the Investment Recovery," *Brookings Papers on Economic Activity*, no. 1 (Washington, D.C.: The Brookings Institution, 1985).

For the effects of the changes in taxes and transfers on the labor supply, see Robert H. Haveman, "How Much Have the Reagan Administration's Tax and Spending Policies Increased Work Effort?" in Hulten and Sawhill, *The Legacy of Reaganomics*.

The data in Table 7.3 are deflated by the fixed-weight deflator for personal consumption expenditures and are based on the 1987 revisions of the national income accounts.

The author is wholly responsible for this crude accounting of the conditions that led to the decline in inflation. I encourage some other economist to develop more precise estimates.

For the relation between exchange rates and interest rates, see Eduardo Somensatto, "Budget Deficits, Exchange Rates, International Capital Flows, and Trade," in Philip Cagan (ed.), *Contemporary Economic Problems* (Washington, D.C.: American Enterprise Institute, 1985). The quotation and the conclusion about the political risk premium are also from this article.

The Treasury and CBO studies are those cited in the notes to Chapter 3.

The effect of the federal deficit on the foreign account balance is from Summers, "Long-Term Effects," in Hulten and Sawhill, *The Legacy of Reaganomics.*

The quotation is from ch. 1 of the 1985 *Economic Report.*

The data in Table 7.4 are based on the 1987 revisions of the national income accounts by the Department of Commerce.

Chapter Eight

The data in Table 8.1 are from the Bureau of Labor Statistics, *Employment and Earnings,* various issues, and are deflated by the fixed-weight deflator for personal consumption expenditures.

For a critical evaluation of the industrial policy proposals, see ch. 3 of the 1984 *Economic Report* and Charles Schultze, "Industrial Policy: A Dissent," *The Brookings Review,* (Washington, D.C.: The Brookings Institution, Fall 1983).

The data in Table 8.2 and Table 8.3 are from the Bureau of Labor Statistics, *Employment and Earnings,* various issues. For Table 8.3, employment data are for blacks and other minority races, earnings are for blacks only, and the changes in earnings are deflated by the fixed-weight deflator for personal consumption expenditures.

The data in Table 8.4 are from the Bureau of the Census, *Current Population Reports,* series P-60, various issues.

For the effect of the overestimation of inflation on the poverty rate, see John C. Weicher, "Mismeasuring Poverty and Progress," *The Cato Journal* (Washington, D.C.: The Cato Institute, Winter 1987).

Charles Murray, *Losing Ground: American Social Policy 1950–1980* (New York: Basic Books, 1984). The later quotation from Murray is also from this book.

For a careful study of the effects of work requirements, see Lawrence M. Mead, *Beyond Entitlement: The Social Obligations of Citizenship* (New York: Free Press, 1986). Mead's own study, however, seems to undermine his endorsement of tighter work requirements.

For an efficient survey of these new studies, see Greg J. Duncan and Saul D. Hoffman, "Welfare Dynamics and the Nature of Need," *The Cato Journal* (Washington, D.C.: The Cato Institute, Spring/Summer 1986).

The quotation by Califano is from Mead, *Beyond Entitlement.*

This study of the effects of the 1981 tax cuts is by Larry Lindsay, *Working Papers 1760 and 1761* (Cambridge, Mass.: National Bureau of Economic Research, 1986). (Lindsay was a senior staff economist at the CEA during the first term.)

The data in Table 8.5 are from the Internal Revenue Service, *Individual Tax Returns.* Incomes in 1980 are adjusted to 1984 dollars by the fixed-weight deflator for personal consumption expenditures.

The data in Table 8.6 are from the 1986 *Economic Report.* Agricultural equity is based on government estimates through 1984. Corporate equity is based on New York Stock Exchange indexes through 1984. Equity values are adjusted to constant dollars using the fixed-weight deflator for personal consumption expenditures. The liabilities of business failures include only commercial and industrial firms and are based on government estimates through 1983.

For the administration response to the fairness issue, see "Statement by David Stockman before the Joint Economic Committee" (May 4, 1983).

For the politics of the "baby boom," see William S. Maddox and Stuart A. Little, *Beyond Liberal and Conservative: Reassessing the Political Spectrum* (Washington, D.C.: The Cato Institute, 1984) and David Boaz (ed.), *Left, Right, and Babyboom* (Washington, D.C.: The Cato Institute, 1986).

Chapter Nine

For obvious reasons this chapter is based primarily on my personal observations. Another observer with a different experience with the same people and processes may come to different judgments, and his or her view should of course be respected.

For the interview with Mitterand, see "Mitterand and Duras on Reagan's America," *Harper's Magazine* (August 1986), Copyright © 1986 by *Harper's Magazine*. All rights reserved. Reprinted from the August issue by special permission. This interview by Marguerite Duras was first published in *L'Autre Journal* (Paris, May 7–13, 1986) and was translated by Jean-Phillipe Antoine.

For a perceptive evaluation of Reagan's management style, see Ann Reilly Dowd, "What Managers Can Learn From Manager Reagan," *Fortune,* September 15, 1986. The revelation of the "Iranamok" affair in November 1986 substantially changed the perception of the effectiveness of Reagan's management style. In retrospect, however, this episode seems more a case of bad judgment (by several officials) than a flawed management style.

For the Greider interviews, see William Greider, "The Education of David Stockman," *The Atlantic* (November 1981).

The quotation about Meese is from John McClaughry, *The Washington Times,* February 28, 1984. (McClaughry, an unreconstructed Vermont Jeffersonian, was a senior member of the Office of Policy Development early in the first term.)

The quotation about the cabinet council system is also from McClaughry.

The quotation from the Darman memorandum is from Barrett, *Gambling with History.*

Chapter Ten

The lead quotation is from the Budget Message of the President (January 5, 1987).

The study of the effects of the 1981 tax legislation on taxable income is by Lindsay, Working Papers 1760 and 1761.

For a thoughtful review of the changes in the terms of debate, see John Palmer (ed.), *Perspectives on the Reagan Years* (Washington, D.C.: The Brookings Institution, Winter 1987).

The quotation by Daniels is in A. James Reichly, "Post-Reagan Politics," *The Brookings Review* (Washington, D.C.: The Brookings Institution, Winter 1987).

Cato Institute

Founded in 1977, the Cato Institute is a public policy research foundation dedicated to broadening the parameters of policy debate to allow consideration of more options that are consistent with the traditional American principles of limited government, individual liberty, and peace. Toward that goal, the Institute strives to achieve a greater involvement of the intelligent, concerned lay public in questions of policy and the proper role of government.

The Institute is named for *Cato's Letters*, pamphlets that were widely read in the American Colonies in the early eighteenth century and played a major role in laying the philosophical foundation for the revolution that followed. Since that revolution, civil and economic liberties have been eroded as the number and complexity of social problems have grown. Today virtually no aspect of human life is free from the domination of a governing class of politico-economic interests. A pervasive intolerance for individual rights is shown by government's arbitrary intrusions into private economic transactions and its disregard for civil liberties.

To counter this trend the Cato Institute undertakes an extensive publications program dealing with the complete spectrum of policy issues. Books, monographs, and shorter studies are commissioned to examine the federal budget, Social Security, regulation, NATO, international trade, and a myriad of other issues. Major policy conferences are held throughout the year, from which papers are published thrice yearly in the *Cato Journal*.

In order to maintain an independent posture, the Cato Institute accepts no government funding. Contributions are received from foundations, corporations, and individuals, and other revenue is generated from the sale of publications. The Institute is a nonprofit, tax-exempt, educational foundation under Section 501(c)3 of the Internal Revenue Code.

CATO INSTITUTE
224 Second St., S.E.
Washington, D.C. 20003

Index

Tax revenue
  future sources of, 321–22, 325–26
  as share of GNP, 71–73
Taylor, Reese, 124–25
Teamsters Union, 125
TEFRA. *See* Tax Equity and Fiscal Responsibility Act of 1982
Textile and apparel industry, 144–46
Thomas, Lee M., 128
Thurmond, Strom, 14, 144–45
TIP. *See* Tax-based incomes policy
TPC. *See* Trade Policy Committee
Trade. *See* International trade
Trade and Tariff Act of 1984, 147
Trade deficit. *See* Balance-of-payments
  deficit
Trade Policy Committee (TPC), 142,
  304
Training services, 43
Transfer payments
  lower-middle class and, 257–58
  poverty rate and, 267–68
  Reagan budget record on, 35–48
  reduction in, 23
  support for, 327
Transportation, 51–52, 124–25, 259
Treasury bills, 186
Treasury tax plan, 91–92, 305–6
Troika, 290–96
Ture, Norman, 5, 79
Turkey, 211

Utgoff, Kathy, 210
Unemployment, 9, 237–39, 270. *See
  also* Employment; Phillips curve
Unions. *See* Labor
United Auto Workers, 141
U.S. economy
  between 1965 and 1980, 15
  and Carter vs. Reagan forecasts, 7–9
  1981 condition of, 225–27
  Reagan record and, 227–49
U.S. Trade Representative (USTR),
  138–39, 151, 152. *See also* Brock
United Steel Workers, 142
Urban underclass, 269–70
User fees, 60–61
USTR. *See* U.S. Trade Representative
Utah, 275
Utilities industry, employment and
  earnings in, 259

Velocity. *See* Money velocity
Venti, Steven F., 339
Volcker, Paul
  appointment of, 21, 171, 227
  financial regulation and, 123
  foreign debt crises and, 212, 216,
    220
  inflation and, 168–69, 239, 316
  monetary policy and, 162–64, 176,
    178–79, 189
  personal observations on, 296–97
Voluntary restraint agreements (VRA),
  139–41, 143, 144, 146–47,
  148
"Voodoo economics," 5, 290

Wages, real, 240–41
Wagner, Richard, 340
Walker, Charls, 12, 73
Wallich, Henry, 343
Wallis, Allen, 299
Wallop, Malcolm, 99
Wanniski, Jude, 19
War on waste, 13, 55–57, 312, 317
Watt, James, 61, 121, 126, 128
Weicher, John C., 346
Weidenbaum, Murray, 5, 12, 110, 115,
  117, 139, 167, 228, 341
  personal observations on, 294
Weinberger, Caspar, 12, 13, 32, 33–
  34, 135, 143, 152
"Welfare economics," 17
Welfare policy. *See also* Transfer payments
  changes in, 270–71
  low-income assistance and, 41–42
  poverty rate and, 269–70
  Reagan budget record on, 42–44
Welzer, Steve, 341
Wertman, Patricia, 344
West Germany, 148
White, Theodore, 152, 342
White House political review, 306–8
Williamson, Rich, 58
Willig, Robert D., 341
Wisconsin, 276
Wise, David A., 339
Women, employment of, 262–63,
  264–65
World Bank, 219–21, 220